DISASTER AT SEA

DISASTER AT SEA

Shipwrecks, Storms, and Collisions on the Atlantic

William Henry Flayhart III

W. W. Norton & Company
New York · London

Printed in the United States of America
First edition
This book was originally published under the title *Perils of the Atlantic: Steamship Disasters, 1850 to the Present.*

Manufacturing by the Haddon Craftsmen, Inc.
Book design by Germaine Clair
Production manager: Amanda Morrison

Library of Congress Cataloging-in-Publication Data

Flayhart, William H., 1944–
[Perils of the Atlantic]
Disaster at sea : shipwrecks, storms, and collisions on the Atlantic / William Henry Flayhart III.
p. cm.
Originally published: Perils of the Atlantic. 1st ed. c2003.
Includes bibliographical references and index.
ISBN 0-393-32651-9 (pbk.)
1. Shipwrecks—Atlantic Ocean. I. Title.
G525.F557 2005
363.12'3'09163--dc22
2004025477

W. W. Norton & Company, Inc., 500 Fifth Avenue, New York, N.Y. 10110
www.wwnorton.com

W. W. Norton & Company Ltd., Castle House, 75/76 Wells Street, London W1T 3QT

1 2 3 4 5 6 7 8 9 0

TABLE OF CONTENTS

To My Wife

ACKNOWLEDGMENTS

Disaster at Sea is a direct outgrowth of *The American Line, 1871–1902* (W. W. Norton, New York, 2000). The latter work consumed more than thirty years and brought me into contact with a wealth of friends, libraries, and organizations around the world. To anyone who ever helped me in any way I offer my sincerest thanks. *The American Line* received the John Lyman Award of the North American Society for Oceanic History as the best American maritime history published in 2000. This encouraged me to continue researching and writing about maritime history in the modern era.

Arguably the greatest single maritime historian of the twentieth century was Noel R. P. Bonsor, of Jersey, Channel Islands, whose five-volume history *North Atlantic Seaway* is unlikely to be superseded. I had the great good fortune to benefit from Noel Bonsor's wisdom as a mentor for a period of nearly thirty years. The several linear feet of correspondence and manuscripts we exchanged over those decades testify to the fact that rarely were we out of touch with each other. The gap in ages between us spanned two generations, and I was very fortunate to have been among the few disciples directly encouraged and influenced by him. I have never met a man in academia with higher or more exacting standards than N. R. P. Bonsor.

I also owe an enormous debt to my parents, William H. Flayhart II and Naomi Laux Flayhart, who made many sacrifices to encourage me in my career. I am delighted that my father will have the pleasure of seeing this book published. My brother, Martin Albert Flayhart, shared many experiences with me and also has been deeply supportive over the years.

I owe a debt of gratitude to my literary agent in New York, Eleanor Wood, who always has been cheerful regardless of what she must have felt upon some occasions. I have had the honor and pleasure of being in Eleanor Wood's stable of authors for more than twenty years. My editor at W. W. Norton & Company, James Mairs, has given me contracts, encouragement, and friendship. I met both Wood and Mairs within twenty-four hours one fine day in 1982. It has been my pleasure to work with Mairs at Norton for over twenty years and through four books. I have said it before, but it warrants reiteration: The superb Norton team causes one to appreciate crafting a book in a publishing house where it is still an art form.

For the past thirty-two years Delaware State University, in Dover, has provided me with a professional home and significant encouragement. I owe a debt of gratitude to Dr. William B. DeLauder, president, and Dr. Johnny Tolliver, provost. The Faculty Development Grants and Academic Excellence Awards at DSU, as well as the Office of Sponsored Research and the MBNA Educational Development Fund, have been of inestimable value in funding research.

Among maritime organizations the warm comradery and encouragement of the members of the North American Society for Oceanic History (NASOH), the Steamship Historical Society of America (SSHSA), the Canadian Nautical Research Society (CNRS), the World Ship Society (WSS), and last, but far from least, the International Maritime Economic History Association (IMEHA) have meant a great deal.

In March 2000 the International Napoleonic Society awarded me the Légion de Mérite for *Counterpoint to Trafalgar: The Anglo-Russian*

Invasion of Naples 1805–1806 (University of South Carolina Press, Columbia, S.C., 1992), a military and naval history in the age of sail. In August 2000 the IMEHA elected me to represent it on the International Commission for Maritime History. These two events and the John Lyman Award remain the high points in my career.

I wish to extend my grateful thanks to the staffs of the following American research centers: Alderman Library, University of Virginia; William C. Jason Library-Learning Center, Delaware State University; University of Delaware Library; Hagley Museum and Library; Van Pelt Library, University of Pennsylvania; Temple University Library, particularly the staff in the Urban Archives Collection; Mariners Museum Library; Lycoming College Library; New York Public Library; Harvard University Library; Library of Congress Prints and Photographs Division; National Archives; Dover Public Library; James V. Brown Public Library, Williamsport, Pennsylvania; Mystic Maritime Museum Library; United States Naval Academy Library; Bermuda Maritime Museum; and Independence Maritime Museum, Philadelphia. Robert Seamens of Oceanview, Delaware, provided a wealth of material from his enormous print collection to illustrate this volume.

Overseas the following libraries and organizations have been of considerable value: Leiden University Library, Leiden, the Netherlands; Mitchell Maritime Library, Glasgow, Scotland; Royal Library, The Hague, the Netherlands; University of Edinburgh Library; University of Liverpool Library; University of Southampton Library; University of Glasgow Library; Public Records Office, London; British Library, London; British Museum, London; Antwerp Maritime Museum, Belgium; Netherlands Maritime Museum, Amsterdam; Prinz Henrik Maritime Museum, Rotterdam, the Netherlands; Musée de Marine, Paris.

Among individuals who must be thanked for their assistance over the years are Professor Jaap Bruijn, the distinguished Dutch maritime historian, who was my mentor for the academic year 1994–1995, when I was privileged to be on the faculty of the University of Leiden, the Netherlands. Drs. Joost Schokkenbroek and Josie Schokkenbroek-Smit, whose friendship continues to be deeply valued. Another friendship that goes back thirty years in the SSHSA is that of my coauthor for *Majesty at Sea,* Jack Shaum, and his multitalented wife, Martha Shaum. Of great assistance in helping with the researching and editing of this volume has been John Samardza, theater director, Delaware State University, whose talents as a researcher and critic I recognized years ago and with whom it always has been a pleasure to work.

Finally, the greatest sustaining influence over the past twenty-five years has been my wife, Debbie, and our children, who often had to indulge their father and his distractions. Debbie and I also are truly rich in terms of a wealth of friends who make life worth living and who are too numerous to acknowledge individually.

The professional debt acknowledged to many individuals and institutions in no way conveys any responsibility for the shortcomings of this work. They are mine, but I fervently hope once again that I will not have led too many readers astray.

William Henry Flayhart III
Delaware State University
Dover, Delaware
March 2002

DISASTER AT SEA

Chapter 1

DISASTER AT SEA:

Shipwrecks, Storms, and Collisions on the Atlantic

The story of the development of transatlantic steam navigation remains one of the most glorious chapters in the history of humankind's application of mechanical power to the solution of transportation problems. Early commentators were thrilled by the success of paddle-wheel steamships thrashing their way across the Atlantic Ocean. Here was an achievement wrought by the hands of man that everyone should be proud of and celebrate. Ships carrying passengers actually could depart at an appointed time and arrive on the other side of a three-thousand-mile-wide ocean within two weeks if all went well.

In their May 1850 issue the editors of the *Illustrated London News* welcomed the maiden arrival of the first Collins liner, *Atlantic,* and the maiden sailing of a new Cunard liner, *Asia,* with paeons of praise. Their comment was: "Scarcely twelve years have elapsed since the great problem of Transatlantic Steam Navigation was solved. . . ."[1] Their optimism soon would be tempered by the tragic sinking of the *Arctic* in 1854, which represents the greatest loss of life on an American-flag liner in history and dramatically emphasized the fallibility of man and his maritime creations. In the future every disaster, or near disaster, was analyzed and reviewed in order to learn what had happened and how it might be prevented in the future.

This work seeks to describe some of the challenges mankind faced trying to cross the vast reaches of the Western Ocean in safety. Some of the stories do not involve the loss of life or vessel and therefore were forgotten as soon as the newspaper was thrown away. Nothing seems to make a story more forgettable than if a ship managed to reach port, but some of these experiences deserve to be remembered. Such a tale is that of the American liner *Pennsylvania* and the great hurricane of 1874. She ultimately arrived at Philadelphia, but under the command of a passenger!

The tragic loss of the White Star liner *Atlantic* (1873) on the rocks near the entrance to Halifax, Nova Scotia, is a gripping tale, and the aftermath, when the owners were accused of having sent the ship to sea without enough coal, threatened to ruin the steamship line. Collisions were part of the history of the North Atlantic ferry. Sometimes, as in the case of the unfortunate liners *Ville du Havre* (1873) and the *Empress of Ireland* (1914), the results were horrendous, but in other cases, such as the *City of Brussels* (1883), the death toll was only a few. A natural phenomenon, a giant iceberg, resulted in the heaviest loss of life ever experienced on the North Atlantic when the *Titanic* (1912) met her doom. She had all the time in the world to launch lifeboats and save every one of her passengers and crew; she simply lacked sufficient boats, and 1,503 persons died. A torpedo in wartime spelled the end of the Cunard liner *Lusitania* (1915) even if she was engaged in a commercial service. Fire at sea always represented a challenge. The *City of Richmond* (1891) managed to survive while the *Morro Castle* (1934) blazed for days and produced a horrifying death toll. The *Andrea Doria* (1956) proved that even in a day and age when radar seemed to make any Atlantic crossing risk-free, this was not necessarily the case. Finally, things still do happen, and the loss of the liner *Seabreeze I* (2000), even if she fortunately had no passengers on board, proves that the sea can still be a harsh taskmaster.

Chapter 2

THE WRECK OF THE *ARCTIC*

September 27, 1854

At the beginning of the nineteenth century the invention of the steam engine and the development of the oceangoing steamship offered hope to contemporaries for dependability with security and speed on the North Atlantic. The paddle steamer *Savannah* made the first transatlantic crossing in 1819 using steam in any form but for only a portion of the trip. Subsequently the British and North American Royal Mail Steam-Packet Company, more famous as the Cunard Line, began operations on July 4, 1840, with the maiden sailing of the PS *Britannia* from Liverpool for Boston via Halifax. The Cunard Line was to enjoy an unsurpassed reputation for safety. Steamships in any form were rare enough, and the ocean was vast enough that fourteen years passed before the first great maritime disaster overwhelmed the public. True, the paddle steamer *President* went missing in 1841 with 136, and the *City of Glasgow* vanished in 1854 with 480, but there were no survivors to provide gripping or lurid details.

On the other hand, the loss of the paddle steamer *Arctic,* a splendid unit of the New York & Liverpool United States' Mail Steamship Company, in September 1854 was one of the first great tragedies on the North Atlantic about which the newspaper-reading public learned a great deal. They were particularly horrified at the loss of life, which included all the women and children on the ship and a very high percentage of the passengers. Other steamships certainly had been lost earlier but often without a trace so that the gruesome possibilities remained a mystery. With the sinking of the *Arctic,* the single greatest disaster for an American-flag liner, a few passengers and crew survived to provide eyewitness tales, which were told and retold to horrify the public consciousness.

The owners of the *Arctic* were much more familiarly known as the Collins Line in honor of the founder Edward Knight Collins (1802–1878). Collins, an American, had founded the Dramatic Line of fast sailing packets between New York and Liverpool in 1836. The Dramatic Line's famous ships were named for great playwrights or actors: *Shakespeare, Garrick, Sheridan, Siddons,* and *Roscius,* and in their day they provided an exceptional service under sail.[1] When the U.S. postmaster general advertised for bids to carry the mail from the United States to Europe on October 4, 1845, Collins submitted a tender. After much deliberation in the halls of Congress, the Collins bid was accepted on March 3, 1847.

The New York & Liverpool United States' Mail Steamship Company was formed with five hundred shares of two thousand dollars each, of which Collins held ninety shares, and James Brown, of Brown Brothers Bank in New York City, one hundred. Besides the income from the sale of shares a substantial loan from Brown Brothers Bank permitted the enterprise to move forward.

Collins was determined that his ships would be the finest in the world and much larger and faster than those of the Cunard Line, his principal British-flag competitor. Plans were drawn and redrawn until the size of the Collins liners was pushed over three thousand tons and their cost of construction substantially exceeded the assets of the firm. To meet this financial challenge, the initial order for five ships was reduced to four, and the U.S. Post Office was persuaded to advance twenty-five thousand dollars on each ship from the time it was launched. The first liner was the *Atlantic* (1850; 2,845 tons, 284 feet, 12 knots), built of wood by the William H. Brown shipyard of New York and propelled by paddle wheels driven by engines from the Novelty Iron Works, New York. The new American liner was over 25 percent larger than the largest Cunarder, *Asia* (1850; 2,226 tons, 266 feet, 12 knots), even if their speed was similar. The *Atlantic* sailed on her maiden voyage on April 27, 1850, with accommodations in great luxury for two hundred first-class passengers. She thrashed her way across the North Atlantic in twelve days, ten hours, five minutes in spite of damage from drift ice and trouble from one condenser.

In Liverpool the luxury of the accommodations on the *Atlantic* was very favorably commented upon. For the first time there was a smoking room for male passengers near the rear of the liner that separated them and their addiction to tobacco from others on the ship. The seven-hundred-thousand-dollar cost of each vessel was reflected in the superior nature of their appointments with a dining room, 60 by 20 feet, and a general saloon, 67 by 20 feet. "Rose, satin and olive woods figured prominently in the decorations; there were rich carpets, marble-topped tables, expensively upholstered chairs and sofas; a profusion of mirrors; all the panels and the saloon windows were ornamented with coats-of-arms and other designs emblematic of American freedom; all of which made, according to an English writer, a 'general effect of chasteness and a certain kind of solidity.'"[2] Among the most revolutionary facilities incorporated in the new Collins liners was a "Men's Barber Shop" complete with a luxuriously padded, reclining barber chair that received very favorable comment in May 1850 on the maiden arrival of the *Atlantic*. Later crossings by the *Atlantic* and her consorts—*Pacific* (1850; 2,707 tons, 281 feet, 12 knots), *Arctic* (1850; 2,856 tons, 285 feet, 12 knots), and *Baltic* (1850; 2,123 tons, 282.5 feet, 12 knots)—averaged about ten days, twelve hours.[3] The *Pacific* even captured the westbound record with a crossing of ten days, four hours, forty-five minutes in September 1850 that resulted in a Liverpool music hall song to the effect that Cunard should hire the Collins ships to pull the Cunarders over. The *Atlantic* and the *Arctic* were products of the Brown shipyard, while the *Pacific* and the *Baltic* came from the yard of Jacob Bell with engines from the Allaire ironworks.

What no one knew was that Collins and Cunard through the Brown Brothers banking interests in New York and Liverpool had struck an agreement almost from the beginning of the Collins Line to split all revenues and sailings. This early shipping trust remained secret from the public and from the respective governments that were paying substantial mail subsidies to the supposed rivals. There may not have been anything illegal in the proceedings, but archcompetition between the premier American- and British-flag steamship lines was noteworthy by its absence because of the agreement.

With only four ships the Collins paddle wheelers were driven very hard. Being wooden, their hulls and paddle wheels required constant attention, and every arrival represented a race against time to have the ship repaired and ready for her next sailing. Sometimes this was not possible. The *Arctic*'s return on her maiden voyage took fourteen days because of bad weather, and three weeks later the *Baltic* came home in nineteen days after running short of coal and having to put into Provincetown for fuel. The greatest fears were raised when the *Atlantic* sailed from Liverpool on December 28, 1850, and no news of her was known in New York for six agonizing weeks until February 15, 1851. Most thought she had been lost with all on board. However, the main shaft of the liner had broken nine hundred miles from Halifax, and it had been necessary to remove all the floats from her paddle wheels so that she could return to Queenstown, Ireland, on January 22 as a sailing ship.[4] The shipping business never was easy for the Collins Line.

In an effort to increase income, accommodations for eighty additional passengers in a second class were added, and the dining rooms were increased in size to reflect this change (1851). As a result, in 1851 the Collins Line carried 50 percent more passengers across the Atlantic on the New York–Liverpool service than the Cunard Line, but it still did not make money. In fact, its losses were so great that the future of the entire enterprise was in jeopardy. Collins prepared figures which showed that its ships had cost the enormous sum of $2,944,142.27 and that it had operated at an average loss of $16,928.79 per voyage over twenty trips for a total operating deficit of $338,574 for the year.[5] Since the U.S. Post Office wanted the Collins Line to increase its sailings to twenty-six throughout the year in order to match what the British Post Office required of Cunard for a much-larger subsidy. Congress was approached and, impressed with the record of the Collins Line, agreed in July 1852 to increase the mail subsidy from $385,000 a year to $858,000. For its part Collins had to agree to maintain a sailing every two weeks all the year round, a quite stringent schedule. Congress also insisted that after December 31, 1854, the government could cancel the contract with six months' notice.[6] This provided a degree of uncertainty to the continued financial well-being of the Collins Line since the subsidy was essential to its survival.

In February 1852 the *Arctic* managed an eastbound crossing from New York to Liverpool in nine days, seventeen hours, four minutes, and this was regarded as remarkable since it was a winter crossing. The liner was dubbed the Clipper of the Seas and became the most celebrated of the Collins Line ships.[7] Her achievements helped the Collins' image. In November 1853 the *Arctic* briefly went ashore in dense fog on the Burbo Bank without suffering serious damage, and her reputation for being solidly built was enhanced. In the spring of 1854 she struck a submerged object off the coast of Ireland and put back to Liverpool for repairs which took eleven days.

On September 13, 1854, the *Arctic* arrived in Liverpool under the command of Captain James C. Luce, forty-nine, who had been at sea since he was sixteen and had earned command of his first ship before he was twenty-one. He had been with the Collins Line since its inception. On this voyage he had brought with him his crippled son, William Robert Luce (eleven years old), in the hope that an ocean voyage might improve his health. Captain Luce and his son enjoyed a close relationship. The *Arctic* lay at her pier in England a week and prepared to sail for New York precisely at 11:00 A.M. on September 20, 1854. The passenger list was so full that not all those wanting to sail on the liner could find accommodations, and some had to wait for the next crossing. Among the passengers were Mrs. Edward K. Collins, wife of the managing owner, and two of their children, Mary Ann (nineteen) and

Henry Coit (fifteen). The owners of the line also were represented by James Brown's daughter Maria Miller; his son William and his French wife; Clara Moulton; and Clara's sister Grace and her husband, George Allen, who was a member of the firm that had built the engines of the *Arctic,* and their infant daughter (two) and son (one). Among the elite names on the passenger list were Robert Christian Godefroy Fernand de Grammont, Duc de Caderousse (twenty), and his manservant Dulaquais, who were en route to the French Embassy in Washington, and Professor Henry Hope Read of the University of Pennsylvania, and Dr. Carter Page Johnson of the Medical College of Virginia. Official dispatches from James Buchanan, American minister to the Court of St. James's, were entrusted to George H. Burns, a special courier. There also was the usual assortment of millionaires who could afford the $125 a first-class ticket cost on a Collins liner. A large contingent from New York society figured in the passenger list. They included Henry Austin Brady, an attorney who was delighted to have bought some rare volumes during his European tour to add to his collection of Americana.

The engines of the *Arctic* kept the massive 25-foot 6-inch paddle wheels churning the Atlantic to push the liner along at the fabulous rate of thirteen knots, covering about three hundred miles a day. Twenty-four brawny firemen and an equal number of coal passers worked in a superheated environment that resembled the popular conception of hell. All went well for the first week of the normal ten-day crossing. On September 27 the *Arctic* was off the Grand Banks, where the cold air from the Arctic meets the warm air of the Gulf Stream and produces ever-changing patterns of fog that cover the sea. Few vessels at this time carried anything like steam whistles, although Lloyd's had exhibited one five years before, and when fog settled or maneuvering room was limited, the Collins Line safety procedure stated a crew member was suppose to stand at the bow and make noise on a tin horn. Musical skill was not noteworthy in hiring the deckhand. In mid-Atlantic at full speed horn tooting was dispensed with and not mandatory.

Captain Luce estimated that his ship was about fifty miles south of Cape Race, Newfoundland, and he had been able to take a noon reading when there was a brief break in the banks of fog. Hence he was fairly sure of himself and his position. Suddenly a cry was heard from a lookout that there was a steamer in their course. The officer in command ordered the helmsman, "Hard a-starboard." Almost immediately a second command was given to stop the paddles and go full speed astern. The officers of the *Arctic* frantically sought to avoid a collision but without success. Captain Luce dropped what he was doing when he heard the engine room signal and raced on deck as disaster struck.

The other vessel was the auxiliary screw schooner *Vesta* (1853; 250 tons, 152 feet, 10 knots) operating a service between the last remnants of the French Empire in North America, the islands of St. Pierre and Miquelon, which lie off the coast of Newfoundland, and Granville, Normandy. The *Vesta* had been built at Nantes for Hernoux et Compagnie, Dieppe, with an iron hull that was divided into three watertight compartments. She was designed to cope with the navigation challenges of northern seas and made two voyages a year to St. Pierre and Miquelon transporting optimistic fisherman and supplies, notably salt, in the spring, and bringing home a cargo of cod-liver oil, fish, and tired fishermen in the fall. The *Vesta,* under the command of Captain Alphonse Duchesne (thirty years old), had sailed from St. Pierre the previous day, September 26, with a crew of 50 men and 147 fishermen and salters who had worked the summer and were anxious to get home.[8]

The *Vesta* was carrying a full set of sails in order to take advantage of a brisk westerly wind and, like the *Arctic,* had been slipping in and out of fogbanks constantly. She was not sounding any fog warning. The lookout of the *Vesta* caught sight of the large paddle-wheeler at the same time as she was seen. The command was given to turn, but it was too late, and the iron prow of the French ship, representing a truly deadly battering ram, slammed into the starboard side of the much larger wooden passenger liner.

The initial shock to those on board the *Arctic* was slight and not taken seriously. Those passengers who rushed on deck saw a horrible sight before them as the bow of the *Vesta* was buckled back for ten feet or more and her hull slashed open to the waterline. The foremast of the schooner had also collapsed and lay in a tangle across the foredeck and over the side as the French ship lay dead in the water. Within a few moments over two hundred people were milling around on the deck of the little *Vesta,* and considerable confusion was evident. Two lifeboats were launched by frantic fishermen, and one immediately capsized, drowning a number of those who could not swim.

Captain Luce on the *Arctic,* without inspecting his vessel, believed his own damage was slight and gave the order for his paddles to start turning in order to get closer to the *Vesta*. One of the *Arctic*'s lifeboats was launched under the command of Chief Officer Robert J. Gourlay, to go the aid of the *Vesta,* and both the paddle-wheeler and her lifeboat slipped through the fogbanks toward the French ship. Those on the *Vesta* thought that rescue was coming when they first saw the much larger *Arctic* approaching through a break in the fog, which soon closed in again. The next time the fog broke the French were horrified to see the passenger liner turning away and abandoning them with its paddle wheels thrashing to carry her away. In the intervening moments Captain Luce had learned that his ship was taking on water rapidly and probably was mortally wounded. The ship's carpenter and engineer had discovered that the *Arctic* had several holes punched through her wooden hull, including at least two below the waterline. In addition, some of the *Vesta*'s anchors, anchor chains, and iron plates were wedged into the holes, making them highly irregular and impossible to close or cover. When a sail was lowered over the side to try to lessen the inward rush of seawater, the result was totally inadequate since no seal was possible. Captain Luce knew that the construction of the *Arctic* was totally open, uninterrupted by a single bulkhead from stem to stern. She had no watertight compartments whatsoever and no hope of salvation. The captain decided that the only hope he had of saving the lives of his passengers and crew was to try to reach shore as quickly as possible. Since he was absolutely sure that the *Vesta* was doomed and that the little vessel offered no hope for anyone, he thought there was no point in staying with her only to increase the ultimate death toll. It seemed to him just possible that the *Arctic*'s pumps could keep pace with the inrushing seawater sufficiently to keep the ship afloat long enough to reach land. Accordingly Luce abruptly abandoned his cautious attempt to approach the injured vessel and also abandoned his highly competent chief officer, a picked lifeboat crew, and one of his precious lifeboats. It would never be seen again. He was to rue the decision.

The *Arctic* barely had begun her race through the fogbanks toward Newfoundland when screams of warning were heard ahead as the big paddle-wheeler suddenly encountered the lifeboat from the *Vesta* that had gotten away and smashed it to smithereens, killing all but one of the fishermen. A single individual, Jasonet François from St. Malo, survived to be thrown a line and pulled on board the *Arctic* by Ferdinand Keyn, a young German passenger. When he recovered, François revealed the name of the *Vesta* and the nature of her voyage. For the first time those on the *Arctic* knew the name of their nemesis.

In the engine room the water began to rise in spite of everything that Chief Engineer J. W. Rogers and his men could do to stop it. The lower fires were flooded, letting loose a huge cloud of sulfurous steam, and finally the upper fires. The huge paddle wheels were so submerged that their ever-slower revolutions were ineffectual, and the *Arctic* slowly drifted to a halt in the quiet vastness of the North Atlantic. It was about one o'clock, and the distance she had covered was less than a fifth of what she had needed for safety. The *Arctic* was sinking fast and had a little more than three hours to live.

One of the largest passenger liners in the world flying the American flag was doomed with virtually no hope of rescue. The *Arctic* had been equipped with six lifeboats, the number required by American law for any vessel over fifteen hundred tons and, in fact, exceeding the number required by Lloyd's of London. The fact that the Collins liners were nearly twice as big had not affected the number of lifeboats. For the first time maritime regulations clearly had not kept up with the size of the vessels being placed in service. The lifeboats of the *Arctic* had

A contemporary impression of the struggle for survival of the passengers and crew of the American liner Arctic *(1850) as the Collins Line paddle wheeler begins her final plunge stern-first to the floor of the Atlantic. Earlier on the same day, September 27, 1854, she had been rammed by the French liner* Vesta *(1853) and the* Arctic's *captain had made a vain attempt to reach shore. The death toll of between 285 and 372 represents the largest from any American-flag disaster on the North Atlantic.*

been built to the design of Joseph Francis, a noted American marine architect, and were of sheet iron riveted together and very strong. Their total capacity was around 180, but there were nearly twice as many persons on the sinking *Arctic.* If the lifeboats had been carefully lowered into the water and gently filled with individuals, they might have held all the passengers on the liner, but that was not to be the case. Discipline broke down, and crew members and some drunken male passengers rushed the lifeboats. Captain Luce could not maintain order. One lifeboat after another, the five remaining boats were launched, filled with sailors and some male passengers, and disappeared into the fog never to be seen again. In spite of the Captain's best efforts, few of the female passengers and none of the children ever made it off the *Arctic* into the potential safety of one of the lifeboats. Second Officer William Baalham, in particular, tried to obey the captain's orders to take on board female passengers, only to be utterly overwhelmed by an avalanche of crew members and male passengers who jumped overboard and had to be pulled from the sea. As Baalham said later, it was impossible for him to differentiate among those who had jumped into the ocean between passengers and sailors. A dying person was a dying person in the grips of the North Atlantic. In the end, as a direct result of mob rule and brute force, Captain Luce was left on deck with his third mate, Francis Dorian, a few crew members, and nearly all the passengers. The evacuation of the *Arctic* ranks as one of the greatest catastrophes in maritime history. Frantic efforts to build rafts came to nothing, and the scenes on the deck of the floundering vessel were heartrending. The French importer George Guynet found that the $150,000 in diamonds he reputedly kept with him at all times could not save the lives of him, his wife, and their three young children. The last view of the Guynets was of the father comforting his tearful twelve-year-old son as the water rose.

Captain Luce on the deck of his foundering ship shook the hands of those around him and with his young son took a place on the starboard paddle box. One young engineer, Stewart Holland, was ordered to fire the signal gun at regular intervals and courageously stood by his task. The last boom from the cannon floated across the North Atlantic as the *Arctic* lurched and began to go down by the stern. Her bow rose out of the water, revealing the mortal wounds she had received, and she slid stern first under the waves with a fearfully magnified shriek from those left on board who were thrown into the cold waters of the Atlantic Ocean. The time was about 4:45 P.M. Some of the men in the lifeboats apparently debated returning to the scene, but the clear majority believed nothing could be gained except their own deaths as the lifeboats would be swamped by the struggles of the dying. Mercifully for them the fog hid the frantic struggles of those who were dying.

When the waves crashed over the *Arctic*'s paddle box, they threw Captain Luce, who had his son in his arms, into the ocean. Seconds later the starboard paddle box ripped loose from the *Arctic* as she plunged to the ocean floor and swept back up to the surface, where it breached amid the struggling swimmers. Captain Luce had his young son, Willie, ripped from his grasp and saw him crushed by the paddle box as it exploded back to the surface of the Atlantic and flipped over like a huge wooden whale. In shock Luce and several others managed to climb onto the paddle box, which then served as a temporary raft, offering some slight hope of salvation. The water was knee deep, and several individuals who had taken refuge on the paddle box raft lost consciousness and slipped overboard. Two days later, on September 29, Captain Luce and two other survivors, George F. Allen and Ferdinand Keyn, were rescued from their precarious perch on the paddle box-raft by Captain John Russell in command of the sailing ship *Cambria* (1846; 397 tons) bound from Greenock, Scotland, to Quebec. (In one of the quirks of the sea Russell himself had been rescued by the *Pacific* two years before, when his ship *Jessie Stevens* had met with disaster in mid-Atlantic.) Russell promptly climbed the mast with his spyglass and succeeded in discovering and rescuing seven others. During the subsequent voyage to Quebec Captain Luce, although physically battered, composed an account of the loss of the *Arctic* for Collins. His letter was mailed from Quebec on October 14, 1854. The portion of the lengthy letter dealing with the actual sinking follows:

> Dear Sir,
>
> It has become my most painful duty to inform you of the loss of the steamship *Arctic* under my command. With many valuable lives, I fear among whom must be included your wife, daughter, and son, with whom I took a last leave the moment the ship was going down, without myself expecting to see the light of another day to give you an account of the heartrending scene.
>
> The *Arctic* sailed from Liverpool, Wednesday, Sept. 20, at 11 A.M., with 233 passengers and about 150 in the crew. Nothing of special note occurred during the passage, until Wednesday, 27th, when at noon we were on the Banks, in lat. 46 45′ [N], and long. 25 00′ W., steering west per compass. The weather had been foggy during the day, and generally a distance of half to three-quarters of a mile could be seen, but at intervals of a

few minutes a very dense fog followed, by being sufficiently clear to see one or two miles.

At noon I left the deck for the purpose of working the position of the ship. In about fifteen minutes I heard a cry of hard starboard from the officer of the deck. I rushed on deck and had just got out when I heard a crash forward. At the same moment saw a steamer under the starboard bow, and the next moment she struck against our guards and passed astern of us. The bows of the strange vessel seemed literally to be cut or crushed off for about ten feet, and seeing that she must instantly sink in a few minutes, and taking a hasty glance of our own ship, and believing we were comparatively uninjured, my first impulse was to endeavour to save the lives of those on board the sinking vessel.

The boats were cleared, and the first officer and six men left with one boat, when it was found our own ship was leaking fearfully. The engines were set to work, bilge injections put on, steam-pumps and the four deck-pumps worked by passengers and crew, and the ship headed for land, which I judged to be about fifty miles distant. Being compelled to leave my boat with the first officer and crew to take care of themselves, several ineffectual attempts were made to check the leak by getting sails over the bow; and, finding the leak gaining on us very fast, notwithstanding all our powerful means of keeping her free, I resolved to get the boats ready, and as many ladies and children placed in them as possible, but no sooner had the attempt been made, than the firemen and others rushed into them in spite of all opposition. Seeing the state of things I ordered the boats to be veered astern by ropes to be kept in readiness until order could be somewhat restored, when, to my dismay, I saw them cut the rope in the boat and disappear astern in the fog.

Another boat was broken down by persons rushing into her while hanging at the davits, and many were precipitated into the sea and drowned. This occurred while I had been engaged in getting the starboard guard-boat ready, and I placed the second officer in charge of her, when the same fearful scene as with the first boat was being enacted, men leaping from the top of the rail down twenty feet, crushing and maiming those who were in the boat. I then gave orders to the second officer to let go and row after the ship keeping under or near the stern to be ready to take on women and children as soon as the fires were out and the engines stopped.

My attention was then directed to the other quarter-boat, which I found broken down, but hanging by one tackle; a rush was made for her also, and some dozen or fifteen got in and cut the tackle, and were soon out of sight. In the meantime I found that not a seaman was left on board, or carpenter, and without any tools to assist in building a raft, as our only hope, and the only officer left was Mr. Doran [*sic*], the third officer, who aided me with the assistance of many passengers, who deserve great praise for their coolness and energy in doing all in their power up to the very moment before the ship sank from under us.

The chief-engineer, with a part of his assistants, had taken our smallest deck-boat, and before the ship went down pulled away, with about fifteen persons. We had succeeded in getting the fore- and main-yards, main-topsail, and two top-gallant yards overboard, and such other small spars and materials as we could collect, when I was fully convinced that the ship must go down in a very short time, and not a moment was to be lost in getting the spars lashed together to form a raft. To do this it became necessary to get the lifeboat, "our only remaining lifeboat," into the water.

This being accomplished, I gave Mr. Doran charge of the boat, taking care to keep the oars on board, to prevent them from leaving the ship, hoping still to get the women and children in this boat at last. They had made considerable progress in securing the spars together, when an alarm was given that the ship was sinking; and the boat shoved off without oars or anything to help themselves with, and when the ship sank the boat had got clear, probably an eighth of a mile to leeward.

In an instant, about a quarter to five P.M., the ship went down, carrying every soul on board with her. I soon found myself on the surface, after a brief struggling with my own helpless child in my arms, when I again found myself impelled downwards to a great depth, and before I reached the surface a second time, had nearly perished and lost the hold of my child. As I struggled to the surface of the water, a most awful and heart-rending scene presented itself to my view; over two hundred men, women and children struggling together amidst pieces of wreck of every kind, calling on each other for help, and imploring almighty God to help them. Such an appalling scene may God preserve me from witnessing again. I was in the act of trying to save my child when a portion of the paddle-box came rushing up edgewise, just grazing my head, and falling it [*sic*] whole weight upon the head of my darling child. In another moment I saw beheld [*sic*] him lying lifeless in the water. I succeeded in getting on to the top of the paddle-box, company with eleven others.[9]

Meanwhile Captain Alphonse Duchesne of the *Vesta* dedicated himself to saving his ship and the lives of all on board. One sailor had died at the moment of the collision. Duchesne specifically had ordered the panicky fishermen not to launch the second lifeboat from the *Vesta*, but in their terror they had ignored him. The lifeboat had capsized in the launching, and most of the fishermen had drowned. The French ship was therefore down two lifeboats with totally inadequate boats remaining. The first task before Duchesne was to restore order, and one of the best means of accomplishing this was to get everyone busy doing something. Among the immediate physical challenges the French Captain faced was to rid the *Vesta* of the foremast, which was lying over the side and acting like a sea anchor as well as holding the ship down by her shattered bow. The mast was chopped away and thrown overboard. Then every bit of cargo, personal possessions, and gear stored in the front of the schooner that could be thrown overboard was jettisoned, raising the bow a bit more out of the sea. Finally, every unnecessary person was ordered aft on the schooner, and that raised her bow a few more precious inches.

Simultaneously the forward iron bulkhead in the *Vesta* was reinforced in the hope that it would hold until the schooner reached safe harbor. Every available piece of bedding and the 150 mattresses on board were placed against the bulkhead and strengthened with boards and planks to hold them in place. A sail was suspended over the bow and pulled in as close as possible over the jagged remains. It never would keep much water out, but at least it provided a cosmetic value in obscuring the grievous damage. These activities occupied everyone on the *Vesta* for the better part of two days. The results were encouraging, and panic was less evident even if everyone remained terribly concerned. After all, the Grand Banks were not known for temperate weather conditions, and a fresh storm could blow up at any time. Duchesne elected to head for St. John's, Newfoundland, the nearest port where repairs could be made to his ship. Any other destination lacked appeal.

Duchesne ordered minimal steam to be gotten up, and the *Vesta* with more than two hundred on board slowly began to make for the Newfoundland capital, over a hundred miles away. The weather began to deteriorate, but the little ship succeeded in rounding Cape Spear and reaching the narrow entrance to St. John's on the evening of Friday, September 29. When the citizens of St. John's woke up on Saturday morning to see their new visitor, they were astonished that the French steamer ever had made port. Captain Duchesne was lauded for his competency as a mariner, his courage in handling so perilous a situation, and his luck in saving his ship and 184 lives. The French fishermen soon were provided for by a generous local innkeeper, M. Toussaint, but after their elation over their safe arrival came their despair over having lost virtually all their hard-won wealth, which had been thrown overboard to lighten the ship. They were alive but financially ruined after a season's work.

A French Navy dispatch boat, *Caméléon*, put into St. John's on October 20 with specific orders to bring the unfortunate French fishermen home before winter set in. Captain Barbet of the *Caméléon* inspected the *Vesta* and expressed his astonishment at her survival. He did more than that, though, for he recommended Captain Duchesne to Emperor Napoleon III for some official recognition. In due course Captain Alphonse Duchesne was made a Chevalier de Légion d'Honneur for his distinguished service. The *Caméléon* sailed from Newfoundland on

October 22 with the passengers from the *Vesta* and those of the *Vesta*'s crew who were not necessary for the reconstruction of the vessel. Duchesne and the remaining crew members had little to do over the winter except combat boredom. Repairs were made to the *Vesta* at St. John's, and she sailed for Liverpool with a new bow on March 20, 1855. Her passengers on this crossing were twenty-six British officers and their families returning home. Her voyage took an agonizing seventeen days, during which she was caught in ice very near the beginning and fought major storms on the Atlantic before finally reaching port.

Captain Duchesne experienced considerable fame in France and became one of the earliest masters hired by the Compagnie Générale Transatlantique (French Line). He was given command of the magnificent new French passenger liner and premier unit of the fleet *Washington* (1864; 3,408 tons, 345 feet, 12 knots) in June 1864 and ultimately of the splendid *Pereire* (1866; 3,150 tons, 345 feet, 13 knots) in 1869. When he died in 1871 at only forty-seven, he had risen to the rank of Officier de Légion d'Honneur, the first high-seas French captain ever to be so honored.

The *Vesta* steamed under the French flag for several years and was sold to Spanish interests in 1863. In her thirty-second year she sank in Santander Harbor at the end of a long career.

Two lifeboats, with fourteen passengers, three officers, and twenty-eight crew members under the command of Second Officer William Baalham, headed toward Newfoundland in a general northwesterly direction. Many of the men already were wet, and the boats periodically were drenched with spray from waves. Furthermore, there was very little available in the way of food and water save for a few biscuits. The threat of starvation as well as hypothermia was very real. Passing ships were sighted, but none saw or took any notice of the two lifeboats from the *Arctic*. Finally, early in the morning of the third day, the sound of breakers was heard, and the men rested on their oars until Baalham could ascertain the best route ashore. As fortune would have it, they were near Cappahayden (Broad Cove), the only place along the rocky shore where a landing might be safely attempted. Around 4:00

A.M. Baalham made the decision to try for the beach, and both lifeboats made it ashore after a forty-two-hour adventure. The company fell on their knees in prayer for their deliverance and then were led by a dog to the cottage of an Irish fisherman, Jack Fleming, who gave them all he could. Fleming's son guided most of the group to the fishing village of Renews. There Second Officer Baalham immediately hired two fishing boats and set off in one of them with two sailors to return to the scene of the disaster in hopes of rescuing others. The other survivors crowded into the second vessel and set out for St. John's, some fifty miles away. Purser Geib sent a message by courier to the American consul informing him that there had been a collision and that both ships probably had been lost. The voyage to St. John's was interrupted by bad weather, which caused them to put into the port of Ferryland, where most rested, but a few set off on foot for a two-day walk to St. John's.

On their arrival at St. John's, October 2, they were astonished to learn that the *Vesta* had made port two days before with all safe who had remained on board. Those who survived the American liner and reached St. John's did not receive a particularly warm reception since it was thought that the much larger *Arctic* had been guilty of a hit-and-run attitude after the collision. The sailors and fishermen on the *Vesta* were sure that the American passenger liner had left them to die. The next day Baalham made St. John's with his chartered schooner, having explored the area of the disaster without discovering any trace of life from the *Arctic.*

Eighteen other survivors from the *Arctic* who reached New York had been rescued by a sailing vessel, *Huron,* bound for Quebec, but had elected to transfer to another sailing ship, *Lebanon,* bound for New York. Their arrival at New York on October 11 represented the first news of the disaster and brought life to a halt as the city mourned its losses. Collins, himself returning to New York City, was greeted by the news that the *Arctic* had sunk with a heavy loss of life, including his wife and two children.

Most of those who had reached St. John's took passage on the coastal steamer *Merlin,* but Purser Geib and one sailor stayed behind to see to the *Arctic*'s two lifeboats and, they hoped, to care for additional survivors. The survivors from the *Arctic* were charged the normal rates for their passage on the *Merlin* and grumbled about that. When they reached Halifax on October 11, they were followed into port by the Cunard liner *Europa* (1848; 1,834 tons, 251 feet, 10 knots), which provided them with accommodations to Boston free of charge. Baalham was presented with a testimonial in recognition of his courage and ability in getting the two lifeboats safely to shore. Those survivors finally reached New York on October 13, two days after the first batch. All the survivors found themselves severely criticized for the fact that every woman and child on the *Arctic* had perished. This was regarded as monstrous.

The final death toll in the sinking of the *Arctic* has been subject to debate because exact figures usually were not known until the vessel cleared customs and immigration in an American port. The death toll certainly was not less than 285 and may have been as high as 372.[10] The best calculation (350–372) appears to indicate that 24 out of 282 passengers were rescued, and 61 out of between 153 and 175 officers and crew, but the precise number of crew members on board the *Arctic* remains unknown. This was the largest American-flag death toll on the North Atlantic. The shock was substantial, but worse was yet to come.

The wooden-hulled *Pacific* left Liverpool on January 23, 1856, with a very substantial winter passenger list of around 145 and an equal number of crew. Three days later the new Cunard iron-hulled paddle-wheeler *Persia* (1856; 3,300 tons, 376 feet, 13.5 knots) sailed from Liverpool for New York. She reached New York after a slow crossing because of very rough weather, but the *Pacific* never was heard from again. It is presumed she must have sunk without a trace after colliding with something such as an iceberg. A rescue vessel was dispatched from New York to crisscross her westbound route but never discovered anything of any nature. Confidence in the Collins Line was shaken substantially by these two tragedies.

Furthermore, the total cost of the subsidy to carry the transatlantic mails was being attacked in Congress. Other offers were made to undertake a similar service or the same service for much less money.[11] Congress therefore gave the required six months' notice in August 1857 of its intention to reduce the Collins subsidy, and the line ceased operation in February 1858. Even the commissioning of a new steamer, *Adriatic* (1857; 4,145 tons, 345 feet, 13 knots), in November 1857 was not enough to rejuvenate the fortunes of the line.

What was learned by future builders and operators of Atlantic liners from the loss of the *Arctic?* First, it was thought that the internal subdivisions of the *Vesta* probably had saved the smaller French ship. The loss of her bow did not doom the auxiliary schooner since she was divided into three sections by two bulkheads. Accordingly internal bulkheads were fitted in the remaining Collins Line ships in an effort to make them safer. However, this improvement apparently did not save the *Pacific.* Secondly, the number of lifeboats (six) on the *Arctic* was deemed inadequate for the number of passengers and crew on board, and the number was revised upward by the addition of another five lifeboats. The view was expressed that there should be enough room in the lifeboats for all those sailing in a vessel. This concept, however, continued to be stated in terms of so many lifeboats per vessel dependent upon the tonnage, which did not keep up with the enormous increase in the dimensions of vessels particularly after 1890. Thirdly, the tooting of a horn by a sailor on the bow of a ship was deemed inadequate, and the proposal was made that steam whistles be fitted and kept blowing whenever lack of visibility warranted. An additional safety measure suggested was that there should be clearly defined westbound and eastbound steamship lanes each three hundred miles wide across the North Atlantic. This would reduce the number of vessels having the potential to meet each other head-on without diminishing the omnipresent need for vigilance by every officer on the bridge of every ship. Lieutenant Matthew Fontaine Maury, famous Virginia naval officer-scientist, specifically recommended this and produced charts in 1855 indicating routes for improved safety on the North Atlantic.[12] The future revealed the strengths and weaknesses of some of these conceptions.

Chapter 3

A HOSTILE SHORE, STORMY WEATHER, AND INATTENTIVE LOOKOUTS MAKE FOR A DEADLY COMBINATION

The White Star Liner *Atlantic* Fails to Make Halifax

April 1, 1873

It was a gloomy night in late March 1873 as one of the premier ships in the world, the gracious and sleek *Atlantic* (1871; 3,707 tons, 420 feet, 14 knots), of the Oceanic Steam Navigation Company Limited (White Star Line), was at sea. She was headed on an unaccustomed course almost due north, bound for the Canadian port of Halifax, Nova Scotia. This was well off her beaten path from Liverpool-Queenstown-New York, and only a desperate situation caused her captain to seek out Halifax. Her chief engineer had informed him that the ship had burned so much coal fighting the seas on this early-spring crossing that she was running short of fuel and might not have enough to reach New York.

The situation was unthinkable since the *Atlantic*, one of the premier vessels in the world, might well find herself in trouble if she ran out of fuel and had to arrive off Sandy Hook under sail. There did not appear to be any solution under steam except to head north for Halifax, where an extra supply of coal could be purchased and loaded.

The history of the White Star Line on the North Atlantic began with the purchase of a line of Australian sailing packets bearing that name by Thomas Henry Ismay in 1867. Shortly thereafter, in consultation with the wealthy Liverpool financier Gustavus C. Schwabe, Ismay was encouraged to switch his primary attentions to the North Atlantic. Schwabe, an astute and accomplished businessman, thought the time was ripe for the expansion of trade between the United States and Great Britain following the end of the American Civil War. He offered to assist in financing the creation of a new steamship line to operate some of the most splendid ships in the world from Liverpool to New York, provided those ships and their maintenance were left in the capable hands of his nephew Gustav Wilhelm Wolff, junior partner in the shipbuilding firm of Harland & Wolff, Belfast, Northern Ireland.

The Oceanic Steam Navigation Company Ltd. (White Star) thus was born on September 6, 1869, with Ismay holding fifty of the four hundred shares, worth about five thousand dollars each, in the new company. Over the next half century it was said that White Star and Harland & Wolff never signed a formal contract for any ship. The line simply indicated what it needed, and the shipbuilder in due course delivered a suitable vessel. The White Star liners became famous for their long, sleek proportions, their gorgeous accommodations, the spaciousness of their public rooms, and their classic, clean-cut external appearance.

The *Atlantic* was the second ship of the White Star Line's North Atlantic fleet. She was a 420-foot, iron-hulled, single-screw steamer with a ratio of beam to length of ten to one (420 feet × 40.9 feet), which made her a long, slim vessel. Some criticized the length of the White Star ships and expressed the view that this compromised the structural

The beautiful and graceful Atlantic *(1871) of the White Star Line glides through the North Atlantic with all sails set on her four masts. The long, slim lines of the first White Star quartet of ships built by Harland & Wolff are shown to perfection. A liner with sails was regarded as a safe ship since she had an alternative to her single propeller. On April 1, 1873, this would not hold true.*

integrity of the vessel and that the more traditional eight to one ratio made for a stronger vessel. However, other lines (Bibby and Inman) had built long, slim vessels before, and there is no particular reason to give credence to this view.[1]

The first White Star liner, *Oceanic,* captured public attention on her maiden voyage in February 1871, when she was described as far superior to all the competition. The *Atlantic,* the second splendid unit of a fleet that was being described as more like transatlantic yachts, began her maiden voyage from Liverpool to New York via Queenstown three months after the *Oceanic* on June 8, 1871. The single funnel and four masts made for an attractive ship as well as one which could really sail if anything happened to the single screw. Her machinery was built by George Forrester & Company, Liverpool, and consisted of four compound engines with forty-one- and seventy-eight-inch cylinders, sixty-inch strokes, and a nominal horsepower of six hundred. Her ten boilers operated at sixty pounds pressure per square inch (psi), and the engines could drive her single screw at up to fifty-eight revolutions per minute, providing a service speed of fourteen knots. For safety she was fitted with five watertight bulkheads running from keelson to main deck with three iron decks from bow to stern. Each of the original quartet cost approximately six hundred thousand dollars to build and outfit.

The managements of the Cunard Line and the Inman Line in particular were stunned by the luxurious nature of the new White Star ships. The first-class accommodations were moved to the center of the ship, where there was much greater stability and much less noise. Prior to the introduction of the new White Star ships the expensive accommodations, by tradition, largely had remained at the stern, where they had been placed in the days of the paddle-wheel steamers. Virtually every cabin on a White Star liner had a porthole that was much larger than those in vogue before. An iron promenade deck with open railings made for an appearance of strength and openness that allowed passengers to stroll the open area. The saloon on the new White Star liners extended to the sides of the ships, making this important public room much more spacious.

The *Atlantic* was followed by two virtually identical sisters, the *Baltic* (MV September 14, 1871) and the *Republic* (MV February 1, 1872). The decision was made, even before the initial quartet was completed, to order two additional vessels, the *Adriatic* (MV April 11, 1872; 3,888 tons, 14 knots) and the *Celtic* (MV October 24, 1872; 3,867 tons, 14 knots), which were about 17 feet longer and 200 tons larger than the original quartet. All were outfitted with the new compound engines and, as a result, burned one-third less coal—60 tons instead of 110—than their slightly earlier rivals, such as the *City of Brussels* (1869; 3081 tons, 390 feet, 14 knots), built for the Inman Line. With the commissioning of the new White Star liners all the competition was going to have to consult with their builders.

On her maiden voyage the *Atlantic* sailed from Liverpool on June 8, 1871, and crossed to New York in a little short of eleven days, arriving there on June 23, 1871. After public inspection the *Atlantic* began her first eastbound crossing on July 1, 1871, with a celebrated passenger list and romped home in eight days, nineteen hours, when she arrived off Crookhaven, Ireland.

The White Star Line needed to prove itself and did not immediately garner a tremendous share of the transatlantic trade. Yet its ships were far superior in their accommodations to the competition's, and it seemed as though nothing could compromise the good fortune of the line. This was the situation when Captain James Agnew Williams sailed from Liverpool on Thursday, March 20, 1873, with a very good winter passenger list of 35 in first class, 776 in steerage class, a crew of 141, and a general cargo of 1,836 tons. Williams was a forty-five-year-old Welshman who had been at sea most of his adult life. His father had been a master of transatlantic passenger liners before him, and he had risen to be master of Guion Line ships in the 1860s before White Star lured him away. He was married with three children, and he joked that his wife always was fearful of his going to sea but that it was his life. The *Atlantic* turned to port after crossing the Mersey Bar and made for Queenstown, Ireland, her first port of call. There on March 21 she picked up the Royal Mails, which were rushed to the ship by Royal Mail train, Irish Sea ferry, and Irish Mail train in order to make possible the latest possible posting in London. In the 1870s the several hours gained in a later closing of the Royal Mail in London were deemed significant, well worth the enormous effort required to get the precious sacks to Queenstown for a transatlantic mail ship to put in and pick them up. After departure from Queenstown 14 stowaways were discovered and apparently either permitted to work their passage or locked up.

The *Atlantic* had 967 tons of coal in her bunkers, which, at 65 tons a day, should have provided her fuel needs for between fifteen and eighteen days, more than a 20 percent margin of safety. The average fuel consumption during the previous eighteen voyages had been only

744 tons, and the highest amount used during a winter crossing had been 896 tons. The margin should have been adequate, but the quality of the coal for this crossing was a combination of good Welsh and fair English, resulting in the need to burn more. The crossing was relatively uneventful until March 25, when a gale set in which produced mountainous seas and slowed the *Atlantic* from her normal fourteen knots to around five knots.[2] As time passed, more and more of the coal in the bunkers was consumed without getting the liner appreciably nearer her destination of New York. At fourteen knots the White Star ships normally covered the roughly 3,000 miles of the crossing in nine to ten days, but by March 31 the *Atlantic* had been at sea for eleven days and was still another two to three days' steaming from New York. Chief Engineer John Foxley came to Captain Williams on the morning of March 31 and regretfully informed him that by his calculations they had only 127 tons of coal left in the bunkers. The gale force winds and the heavy seas were slowing the liner to about seven to eight knots. New York was 450 to 500 miles away. At their present speed and coal consumption they had sufficient coal to cover about 350 miles. Thereafter they would have to depend upon their sails. Captain Williams did not think he had any choice in the matter because the barometer was dropping, indicating more bad weather. He promptly gave the orders to turn the bow of the *Atlantic* almost due north and head for Halifax, about 200 miles away. Putting into Halifax for coal was a common experience on the North Atlantic although among the White Star officers only the young third officer, Cornelius Brady, had ever entered the Canadian port. Dinner that evening in the first-class saloon was a festive occasion for a number of reasons. The *Atlantic* would be in port the next day even if it was Halifax instead of New York. The weather seemed to be abating a bit, and many more passengers seemed to have gotten their sea legs after ten days of rough weather, turtle soup, and biscuits.

Captain Williams stayed on the bridge until midnight, and with a sore leg, he was exhausted. Earlier, while serving as second officer of the

Republic in 1872, he had been crushed between a loose lifeboat and the wheelhouse by a rogue hurricane wave.[3] As a result, Captain Williams's leg was very painful at times, and he had to use a cane upon occasions. At midnight he retired to a bunk in the chart room thirty feet from the bridge, and Third Officer Brady also went to his cabin for a brief rest before dealing with the possibly difficult approach to Halifax. It was thought that the Sambro Light along the Canadian coast was between forty and fifty miles away.[4] Captain Williams left his second officer, H. J. Metcalfe, in command with orders to awaken him in about three hours at 2:40 A.M., when the *Atlantic* would be nearing the treacherous coast.

At 2:00 A.M. Quartermaster Robert Thomas came on duty in order to take the helm. Thomas, an exceedingly outspoken young man, apparently had little respect for Second Officer Metcalfe, who had command of the ship. Immediately he felt very uneasy and began to make some very pointed comments. He told Metcalfe in no uncertain terms that because of his calculations he believed the *Atlantic* was too far inshore and they should have seen Sambro Light by that time. Metcalfe told Thomas that he was neither captain nor mate. Thomas was so concerned that he did not take no for an answer and went to Fourth Officer Brown, who also was on duty, and asked permission to go to the main yard, where he would be able to see ahead better. Thomas told Brown that he never would be able to see the shore from the bridge until he hit it. Brown refused permission and told Thomas to take the wheel. Thomas's warnings went unheeded.

At 2:30 A.M. Second Officer Metcalfe told Captain Williams, still resting in the chart room, that the weather was getting thick. Apparently the captain's leg had been hurting a great deal. What medication for pain he may have been taking remains unknown. When the captain's steward went to awake him fifteen minutes later, at the appointed time, Fourth Officer Brown stopped him and said that there was no need to call him yet. This act of kindness directly disobeyed the captain's explicit orders. Complicating the situation was the fact that the winds had turned favorable and the *Atlantic* had picked up a great deal of speed. The possibility was that the liner was no longer doing anywhere near as little as seven knots and instead may have been making as much as fourteen knots. The distance to the Canadian coast was narrowing dramatically. Quartermaster Charles Raylance at about 3:20 A.M. hove the log, which said the *Atlantic* was making better than twelve knots. He went into the aft wheelhouse and was looking through one of the windows when he thought he saw breakers on the starboard side. He dashed from the aft wheelhouse to the bridge and asked the lookout if he had seen the breakers. Seconds later the lookout screamed, "Ice dead ahead!" Second Officer Metcalfe frantically rang full speed astern on the engine telegraph, and Quartermaster Thomas tried to turn to starboard, but all this was futile. Captain Williams was jolted awake thirty-five minutes later than he had ordered as the *Atlantic* crashed into the rocks at full speed. The White Star liner had run ashore on Meagher's Rock at Mars Head on the tip of Prospect Cape about twenty-two miles from the entrance to Halifax Harbor.[5]

Prospect Cape, a rocky, peninsular cape, seventy feet high, forms the western limit of Pennant Bay, the entrance to which is three miles wide and two miles deep. This little bay is strewn with rocky shoals and irregularly shaped islands that can provide shelter to local vessels with knowledgeable captains but never should be attempted by anyone else. The land at the head of the bay is moderately high; the highest point, Hospital Hill, rises fully 250 feet above the ocean.

According to witnesses, the White Star liner pounded herself on the rocks at least five times, utterly destroying her hull and dooming the vessel. Captain Williams, now fully awake, rushed to the deck and took command. All of the lifeboats on the port side of the liner were swept away immediately by the violent seas. Third Officer Brady arrived on deck, grabbed an ax, and began clearing away a lifeboat. Williams and the other officers were engaged in doing the same thing. Brady got his lifeboat out with two women in it who were joined by about a dozen frantic men. The lifeboat was launched, and Brady had

The White Star liner Atlantic *(1871) writhes in agony on the rugged Nova Scotian Coast during a desperate attempt to reach Halifax for additional fuel. The catastrophic loss of the liner on the stormy night of April 1, 1873, cost at least 585 persons their lives and nearly ruined the White Star Line.*

joined the fourteen passengers when it sank. Only the third officer managed to scramble back on board. The *Atlantic* suddenly was shifted onto her beam ends by the violence of the waves, and the lifeboats were shattered, killing all in them. The stern half of the liner swiftly filled with water, and many of the nearly eight hundred steerage passengers were drowned in their berths even before the stern suddenly broke away from the forward section of the liner and sank beneath the waves. No other lifeboats could be launched, but the bow and some of the rigging remained above the stormy seas and the freezing winds. A few rockets lighted up the night sky before the liner rolled over but did not appear to have attracted any attention.

The only possible salvation appeared to be a large rock halfway between the wrecked liner and the shore. Third Officer Brady and Quartermasters Edward Owen, George Speakman, and Robert Thomas not only were physically fit young men but also knew how to swim. This was not necessarily common in the nineteenth century. Brady, Owen, and Speakman made a valiant effort to get a rope to the nearby rock. They tied the signal halyards around their waists and managed to swim the forty yards through the freezing water to the rock. Thus a rope was rigged between the wreck and the rock. By this means survivors could pass over the breaking waves between the wreck and the large rock. The trip was full of peril, however, since if the buoy was rigged incorrectly, the person became upended and suspended in the water long enough to drown before he reached the rock.

The next stage was placed in the capable hands of Quartermaster Thomas, who later stated:

> I swam on shore and landed on a rock. I traversed from rock to rock, falling sometimes from exhaustion, with this man with me, until I found the signal-post, a place where fisherman have to look out and signalize [*sic*] to the boats, and then I called out for help. Two old men and a boy came to our assistance. I went to the house with them, and procured a line and retraced my steps to the beach, where I saw a lot of passengers and crew upon the rock. Speakman, the Quartermaster, swam toward me with a line from the rock, and I hove my line and caught him and pulled him ashore. As soon as I had done this we hauled in the line, which he had from the rock, and made fast my end of the line to it, so as to make it stronger. As soon as I got the line made fast I told those that were on the rock to come on shore, one by one as I would save them. The first man saved in this way, I don't know, but the second one was Mr. Brady, third officer. I saved in this manner about seventy, as near as I can remember. In some instances, as the line was some distance overhead, and the person too exhausted, I had to reach down and pull them up. Some I had to go into the water for–it being out of me depth–with a line fastened around my waist. In this manner the two old men would drag me, and the man I rescued ashore. I remained there from 4 o'clock till 8, when I fell down through exhaustion.[6]

After five hours of strenuous labor Thomas was relieved and carried away to a nearby house, where he was given dry clothes and food and collapsed into a bed.

Over the next few hours two hundred men made it over the rope to the frigid, uncertain safety of the rock and then, in some instances, to shore. Looking back, they could see those left on board the *Atlantic* slowly succumb to the freezing temperatures, the spray, and the waves. One after another people fell into the sea and were swept away to their deaths.

"Patrick Leachy, a young Irishman, had a good view from where he hung in the rigging: 'Then I saw the first and awful sight. It was just gleaming day; a large mass of something drifted past the ship on the top of the waves, and then was lost to view in the trough of the sea. As it passed by, a moan—it must have been a shriek, but the tempest dulled the sound—seemed to surge up from the mass, which extended over fifty yards of water; it was the women. The sea swept them out of the steerage, and with their children, to the number of 200 or 300, they drifted thus to eternity.'"[7]

Those on the rock found the night long and bitter. Some awaiting rescue actually went mad. In the first light of the morning local fishermen launched their boats and succeeded in saving some of those clinging to the rock and the rest of those clinging to the rigging. Captain Williams told the fishermen that the people clinging to the rigging of the ship were in greater danger than those on the rock. He offered a five-hundred-dollar reward for every full boat of survivors brought from the ship.[8] Some of the fishermen took their vessels to the wreck and managed to remove most of those who had survived the night. In this manner Quartermaster Raylance was rescued. Some bodies were frozen stiff to the rigging, and not a single woman was saved.

Miraculously among the survivors was Captain Williams, who survived in spite of his bad leg. Third Officer Brady on Williams's orders took word of the disaster to Halifax. Local authorities sent the Dominion Government steamer *Lady Head* to the scene, and Cunard, which represented White Star in Halifax, dispatched its steamer *Delta* to see if any additional lives could be saved. The *Delta* brought back to Halifax most of the survivors (about three hundred), while the *Lady Head* brought the rest (about seventy-seven). Asked by a reporter for his explanation of the disaster, a stunned Captain Williams said: "I can hardly say, unless it was because we had overrun our distances. I thought we were going about eleven knots, but the speed must have been much greater, or we could never have got so far off course."[9]

Williams was particularly despondent over the loss of all the women on board the *Atlantic*. He told a reporter: "To think that while hundreds of men were saved, every women should have perished. It is horrible. If I had been able to save even one woman I could bear the disaster; but to lose all! It's terrible! terrible!"[10] One boy, John Hendley, age about twelve, was the only child saved. He had climbed out a porthole, held on to a rail at first, and then with First Officer John W. Firth, scrambled into the rigging of the doomed ship from which he had been rescued. His entire family, mother, father, and brother, from Ashton, Lancashire, were drowned when the *Atlantic* went down. When he reached shore in one of the courageous fishermen's boats, he had no one and there was slight chance of any member of his family having survived. A kindly local lady with two children of her own, Sarah Riely, took him to her cabin, gave him warm clothes, and put him into her own bed.[11] All he had left were two older sisters living in New York, to whom he was sent in due course.[12]

Chief Officer Firth was the last soul left on board, and he remained high in the rigging of the *Atlantic* screaming to be rescued, but the wind and the seas were so violent that Brady onshore could get no one to attempt a return to the wreck. Ultimately Firth was saved through the heroic exertions of the Reverend William Johnson Ancient, the resident Anglican priest at the small fishing village of Terence Bay. Ancient had served in the Royal Navy and then accepted a call to a life of religious service in 1867. Having done well as a missionary-deacon, he was ordained a priest in 1872, and he proved an inspiring figure as he served his flock by rowing across stormy inlets and climbing rugged terrain to minister to them. He and his wife, Mary, had three young daughters. At 7:00 A.M. he was awakened by the shouts of young Joseph Slaunwhite, whose wedding service was to be the next week, that there was a large ship on the rocks. Reverend Ancient pulled on his reefer jacket and cap and joined the local fishermen for the hike to Lower Prospect since it was too rough for them to launch their boats at Terence Bay. When they got to the scene, the seas were still violent, and the rescue of the survivors was very difficult indeed. Still, slowly but surely all the men were gotten off the rock and away from the wreck until only Chief Officer Firth remained. It looked as if no additional effort would be made when Joseph Slaunwhite and a few of the Terence Bay fishermen came forward and said that they would make the effort to take another boat out if Reverend Ancient would take charge of it. Ancient wasted not a minute, and a courageous team of priest and parishioners soon were rowing toward the *Atlantic.* As they neared the wreck, the seas had moderated a bit but still were terrifying, particularly to First Officer Firth, who could not swim. In the rowboat Ancient wrapped a rope about himself, said a prayer, and, seizing the precise moment, jumped from it to the wreck. Luck was with him, and he was able to grab a section of railing before the next big wave broke over him and passed. Then he inched his way along the deck until he reached the mast. A young woman clothed only in a nightgown but obviously dead was with Firth in the rigging. Firth himself was close to death. Ancient fastened the rope around the middle of the portly Firth and then tried to pry his hands loose from the rigging. The struggle seemed futile until a large wave ripped the man away from his perch and flung him over Ancient's head into the sea. The rope held, and Ancient played Firth along the side of the wreck like a fish until they reached the rowboat and the first officer could be "landed."[13] The fishermen and their minister were acclaimed as heroes when they reached shore with the last survivor from the *Atlantic.*

It fell to Captain Williams to cable Thomas Ismay the news of the disaster to his passenger liner with a tremendous loss of life. Ismay took the news very hard. Two months earlier he had given every one of his captains a personal letter ordering them to take no risks because the worst thing that could happen to the White Star Line was to lose a ship.[14] That nightmare had occurred.

Williams almost immediately found himself subject to considerable personal criticism. His act in leaving the bridge when approaching a dangerous shore was severely commented upon. The belief was that the *Atlantic* was at least twenty miles off course and that given the horrendous weather conditions, Williams had absolutely no reason for feeling secure in his position. One old sea captain commented: "The position of the vessel on that fatal night demanded the utmost care and attention. Any prudent man would have doubled his lookouts, sent a man to the mast-head to keep a bright lookout for land or lights, and slowed his ship down until he saw something from which to take a sure departure; and he should have taken the further precaution of taking an occasional toss of the lead, and even stopped the ship 'dead' to do it. None of these precautions seem to have been taken, and the *Atlantic* went along at a 'happy-go-lucky' gait until she brought up all standing, pounded on the bottom two or three times, and then rolled over."[15] Captain Williams's actions on the fateful night were described as criminal. The publicity was horrendous, the end result being the dispatching of a schooner loaded with coffins from Halifax to Prospect.

More damaging for the White Star Line was that almost immediately critical questions were raised about why the *Atlantic* had had to make for Halifax if she had been provided with enough coal at the beginning of the voyage. The managing concern, Ismay, Imrie & Company, at once cabled New York that it had paid for placing in the liner 967 tons of coal, which should have been enough for eighteen days' steaming. It stated that the average coal consumption on the previous eighteen crossings of the North Atlantic had been only 741 tons. The New York agent for White Star, Mr. Gartner, said that the *Atlantic* rarely needed more than 42 tons a day. He thought either that the chief engineer had made a mistake on how much coal was left or that the weighing-in operation in Liverpool had been inaccurate.[16] Accusations flew fast and furious.

Those who had been rescued were cared for by generous-hearted Nova Scotians as much as possible. The Legislature voted a special grant to cover the needs of the rescued passengers. They were given food, dry clothes, and accommodations until they could continue their travels. Some 250 were to leave for Portland, Maine, on Thursday morning, April 3, on the steamers *Chase* and *Falmouth*. Wreckers and divers were on the scene with apparatus and vessels, and attempts to save the cargo would be made as soon as possible.[17] One of the more difficult assignments for the divers would be removal of the bodies of passengers who had drowned in their cabins. Captain Sheridan, a leader of the divers, asked for fifty-nine dollars per body for recovering cabin passengers from the wreck, and twenty dollars a head for steerage, which White Star apparently accepted. Over the next two weeks until April 17 Sheridan and his men recovered 42 bodies, mostly women and children. When the seas died down and the holds were opened, many bodies were found floating among the cargo since the bulkheads had given way. A substantial force of local men immediately was engaged in retrieving bodies which had washed up onshore. By April 6 over 225 corpses, mostly women, were said to have come ashore. These bodies were being searched under the supervision of a magistrate who cataloged whatever valuables were found and authorized their burials as quickly as possible.

The White Star Line management was to have a rough time of it for several months. When the Canadian inquiry into the disaster opened in Halifax on April 5, public feeling was critical of the line for not having ensured that the liner had enough coal to reach New York. Captain Williams was forthright in testifying that he never had taken a ship into Halifax before and had misjudged both the speed of his vessel and the local current. The primary fault was his. The loss of 585 lives made for the second-largest loss of life in the history of the Atlantic, according to some sources. Only the loss of 800 on Admiral Sir Cloudesley Shovell's flagship *Association* in 1707, when she went aground on the Isles of Scilly, surpassed the death toll on the *Atlantic.* At the conclusion of the Canadian inquiry the court rendered judgment that the White Star Line management was at fault for failing to provide enough coal so that its liner could make New York. The inquiry noted that the *Atlantic* had been provided a mixture of high-grade Welsh and low-grade English coal and had burned over 70 tons a day of it at full speed, so that she had used more than 80 tons from her bunkers before she even cleared Liverpool. The result was that the *Atlantic* because of the quality of her fuel did not have sufficient on board, and the management should have realized this. Ismay and his associates in Liverpool were thunderstruck. The loss of the *Atlantic* was horrible enough without the line's being blamed for incompetence. Commissioner E. M. McDonald also ruled that Captain Williams had been "glaringly defective" in resting while his command approached an unknown and dangerous shore.[18] The only mitigating circumstance was that Fourth Officer Brown had violated the captain's explicit orders to wake him. Captain Williams's certificate was suspended for two years, and Brown's for three months.[19] Williams also received a testimonial from the survivors for his courage and resourcefulness in saving them. The Canadian inquiry recorded a death toll of 535 lives out of 957 souls on board, but this was not regarded as final, and other sources state 565 and 585 lives were lost.[20] Ultimately 428 bodies were recovered, and 277 were buried in a mass grave overlooking Sandy Cove, Nova Scotia.

In Liverpool Thomas Ismay, horrified by the findings of the Canadian inquiry, promptly sought redress through a new hearing. It was unthinkable that the White Star Line should have its reputation ruined by a finding that it had sent a ship to sea without enough coal to reach her destination. A new hearing was granted, and on May 10, 1873, the Board of Trade in London opened hearings on the loss of the *Atlantic,* which lasted four days. Ismay thought everything was going to be all right when the board elected to hear additional testimony on May 28. The final ruling of the Board of Trade was handed down in June. Once again it was unfavorable to the White Star Line. Ismay did not give up. This time the Board of Trade was persuaded to refer the whole matter to the principal technical authorities, the chief surveyor and the London surveyor, for a professional assessment. After additional testimony and voluminous paper work, which dragged the proceedings out for six months, the White Star Line in January 1874 finally was exonerated for any responsibility by virtue of insufficient fuel for the loss of the *Atlantic.* The surveyors found that the ship had sailed with sufficient coal and wrote: "The question of fuel supply cannot, therefore, have had anything whatever to do with the loss of the *Atlantic* on her voyage to Halifax."[21] Ismay and his associates were enormously relieved at being freed of this albatross since the very future of their line was at stake only three years after its founding. The published comment of the surveyors is correct in that the *Atlantic,* by all contemporary standards, should have had enough coal. At the same time, if there had not been a perception of a problem on the part of her engineer and her captain, the bow of the liner never would have been turned toward Halifax and she never would have hit those dreaded rocks so far off her normal course. The circumstances of the tragedy remain horrifying even after the passage of well over a century.

Chapter 4

THE *VILLE DU HAVRE* AND THE *LOCH EARN*

The Sudden Loss of the Second-Largest Ship in the World

November 22, 1873

The second major industrial revolution in the modern world customarily is credited to France. If the British industrial revolution was a product of the 1780s, the beginning of the French transformation occurred in the 1840s. In 1840 there were approximately 600 steam engines of all types in France. By 1847 the figure had soared to 4,853. Certainly one area of economic life most dramatically affected was transportation. The possibility of dependable steamship services replacing the uncertainties of wind and sail lured interested entrepreneurs. Attempts were made to establish a French-flag steamship service on the North Atlantic in 1847 with the Compagnie Générale des Paquebots Transatlantiques[1] and in 1856 with the Compagnie Franco-Américaine.[2] The brothers Émile and Isaac Pereire had watched these developments, and on October 24, 1854, they made their move by founding the Compagnie Générale Maritime (CGM), which was registered in February 1855 with the substantial capital of thirty million francs. One of the principal objectives of the CGM was the establishment of a first-class transatlantic steamship line flying the tricolor. The first step in its expansion involved the purchase of the Société Terreneuvienne of Granville, Normandy, a two-year-old firm with a fleet of twenty-seven sailing ships and two small iron screw steamships, the *Diane* and *Vesta* of 280 tons. The two steamers were engaged in carrying supplies and passengers to St. Pierre and Miquelon, the last vestiges of the French North American empire off the coast of Newfoundland. Tragically the *Vesta* was notorious for having rammed and sunk the much-larger Collins passenger liner *Arctic* (1850; 2,856 tons) off Cape Race on September 27, 1854, with a horrendous loss of life.[3] The *Vesta* was homeward bound with 147 passengers and manned by 50 crew members when the accident occurred. She barely made St. John's with a death toll of 13 in what ranks as one of the earliest steamship disasters on the North Atlantic.

The Pereire brothers rapidly expanded the CGM and within two years (May 1856) possessed a fleet of seventy-six sailing ships that were sailing from Le Havre and Bordeaux to destinations all over the world, including Australia, the West Indies, Mexico, Latin America, and California. Steamship services were opened up and down the European coast with ships sailing to Spanish and Portuguese ports and ultimately into the Mediterranean to Algiers and Marseilles. Two new steamships, the *Paris* and the *Hambourg* (1856; 427 tons), were assigned to open a regular service between Le Havre and Hamburg.

In 1857 a transatlantic service proved elusive even if the Pereire brothers certainly were ambitious. Their rivals included Michel Victor Marziou of Havre, whose ambitions for a North Atlantic line were backed by the imposing Rothschild family. In 1858 L'Union Maritime was formed with a capital of fifty million francs and the avowed purpose of opening services to both New York and the West Indies. The government of the Second Empire under Napoleon III (1852–1870) was susceptible to ideas of international expansion, whether political or economic, and a substantial mail subsidy of 9.3 million francs was arranged. The economic challenges of establishing two major services with a fleet of at least ten large passenger liners proved too much for Marziou, and the franchise was transferred on October 20, 1860, to the Pereire brothers. With the approval and encouragement of His Imperial Majesty Napoleon III the formal name of their company was changed by Imperial Decree on August 25, 1861, from Compagnie Générale Maritime to Compagnie Générale Transatlantique (CGT), and the most famous name in French maritime history was born.[4]

The concessions offered by the government were enormous, but so were its demands. It was recognized that the financial risk involved in creating a North Atlantic service was substantial. The preliminary terms of the government mail contract called for five 11.5-knot ships for the North Atlantic service and six 10.5-knot ships for the Caribbean service, supported by a minimum of three smaller vessels to maintain a feeder service within the Caribbean. Financial security was assisted by the signing of a mail contract on July 27, 1861, which encouraged public confidence.[5] A loan was raised on the market for 13.6 million francs, and the French government advanced a sum of 18.6 million francs, equal to no less than two years' subsidy, and sweetened the deal by making the advance a loan repayable in twenty years at no interest. The Pereire brothers thus had the imposing sum of 72 million francs available to create the North Atlantic services. Part of the unofficial agreement involved an understanding on the part of the Pereires to concentrate exclusively on the first-class service. They therefore disposed of their sailing ship and minor steamship interests by 1873.

Extensive surveys of the principal ships of the British-flag British and North American Royal Mail Steam Packet Company (Cunard Line), which had maintained a service between Liverpool and Boston since 1840 and which had been extended to New York in 1847, were undertaken by the Pereire brothers.[6] The result was their decision to increase substantially the size and power of their first units if they were to face the North Atlantic on a regular basis. The initial desire for all the ships to be built in France proved impossible. The state of the French industrial revolution in the early 1860s was not capable of meeting the challenge of building eleven large passenger ships in three years. Therefore, bids were solicited from shipyards all over Europe for the initial units of the fleet. John Scott & Company of Greenock, Scotland, won the bid for six ships at £78,000 ($390,000) for each hull and £25,000 ($125,000) for the machinery. Since these units were built outside France, the import duties on each liner added another £18,000 ($90,000) to the cost (18 percent), yet the total bill of £121,000 ($605,000) per unit still was £27,000 ($135,000) cheaper than the prices yards in France and the Netherlands had quoted. The Pereire brothers were particularly infuriated by the bids from their countrymen and immediately sought their own solution. They bought a substantial strip of land near the mouth of the Loire at Penhoet, St. Nazaire, and contracted with John Scott to send a dozen Scottish craftsmen to supervise and teach five hundred to six hundred local French workers how to build transatlantic liners. The Penhoet facility was to grow into Chantiers de l'Atlantique, one of the foremost of all French industrial concerns with an international reputation of the first magnitude, and most of the principal units of the CGT, as well as many other vessels, were built there. Machinery to construct the first French-built units, as well as many fittings, was imported from Scotland, but nearly all the raw materials were obtainable in France by 1864. Furthermore, the contracts for the engines for the five French-built paddle wheelers were ordered from Schneider of Creuzot, an area already famous for its cast-iron cookware.

John Scott rushed the construction of the first units, and the paddle-wheeler *Washington* (1864; 3,408 tons, 346.5 feet, 12 knots) was launched on June 17, 1863, and sailed on her maiden voyage from Le Havre to New York on June 15, 1864. The fact that the CGT and the French government had pushed through the creation of the new transatlantic line in spite of the American Civil War resulted in a very favorable reception in New York. Sailings occurred every four weeks as the other new units came on line: *Lafayette* (1864; 3,375 tons, 346.5 feet, 12 knots) on August 24, 1864, and *Europa* (1865; 3,400 tons, 346.5 feet, 12 knots) on May 3, 1865. The first of the French-built units, whose construction paralleled the creation of the shipyard itself, was laid down on October 15, 1862, and launched eighteen months later, on April 23, 1864. The original name designated for this ship was Atlantique, but she was launched with appropriate fanfare as *Impératrice Eugénie* (1865; 3,200 tons, 346.5 feet, 12 knots) and took her maiden sailing from St. Nazaire to Veracruz on February 16, 1865, in order to reinforce the Mexican service. The final French-built units were named *Nouveau Monde* (1866; 3,200 tons, 346.5 feet, 12 knots), *Panama* (1866; 3,400 tons, 355.5 feet, 12 knots), *Saint Laurent* (1866; 3,413 tons, 355 feet, 12 knots), and *France [I]* (1866; 3,200 tons, 346.5 feet, 12 knots). Most of these units were employed in the run to Mexico. The *Saint Laurent* represented a major advance in terms of marine propulsion in that although she was laid down as a paddle steamer, she was outfitted with a single screw, which gave her both a half-knot increase in speed and a significantly reduced cost in operation.

The final three first-class units were ordered from British yards in 1863 and were named *Pereire* (1866; 3,150 tons, 13 knots), *Ville de Paris* (1866; 3,014 tons, 13 knots), and *Napoleon III* (1866; 3,376 tons, 13 knots). The French engineering firm of Clapeyron and Eugène Flachat was responsible for their design, and it apparently had few qualms in copying the plans of the successful Cunard paddle steamer *Scotia* (1862; 3,871 tons). The *Pereire* and the *Ville de Paris* were ordered from Robert Napier of Glasgow, the Cunard builder, and during construction the decision was made to outfit them with clipper bows and single screws. The days of the paddle-wheel steamer definitely were numbered. The maiden voyage of the *Pereire* on March 29, 1866, from Le Havre to New York gave the CGT enough ships to institute a biweekly service. The *Napoleon III* was completed as a paddle steamer and proved a great disappointment in terms of speed and operating costs. She was kept in reserve as the relief ship for the fleet.

Passenger accommodations on the *Washington* and the other New York–bound boats were provided for 128 first-class, 54 second-class, and 29 third-class passengers. No provision was made for the transportation of steerage passengers, and the average passenger loads for the first year numbered only about 80 passengers per voyage. On the other hand, the units employed in the Mexican service were outfitted to carry steerage passengers as part of the desire for French colonization. Subsequently a number of the Mexican units were assigned to the New York service. The *Vera Cruz* sailed for the United States with a total of 473 passengers, most in steerage, on June 30, 1866, taking advantage of an increased demand in the summer season. Additional services were opened in 1867 to Colombia–Panama–Martinique and to Havana–Veracruz–Puerto Rico.

The substantial economies in operating expenses of the screw steamers over the paddle wheelers brought significant changes almost immediately. The *Washington* was sent to Britain in 1867 for conversion to twin screws, and the *Lafayette* (1864) was rebuilt in 1868 at St. Nazaire in the same manner. They were the first examples of this type of conversion for transatlantic steamers.

In 1870, the Franco-Prussian War had repercussions on the North Atlantic. At the start of the war the CGT headquarters were transferred from Paris to St. Nazaire, and for the duration of the hostilities the French Line ships terminated their transatlantic crossings at Southampton. The ships from New York were loaded with patriots returning to the colors and with military supplies for the Imperial Army. With the defeat of France and the fall of Napoleon III the passenger liner *Napoleon III* was converted to compound engines and screw propulsion in 1871–1873. The work was undertaken at the British yard of A. Leslie & Company, Hebburn-on-Tyne, and also involved lengthening the hull from approximately 366 to 422 feet. For political reasons, with the advent of the Third Republic (1870) the *Napoleon III* was renamed *Ville du Havre*. The *Impératrice Eugénie* underwent a similar transformation at the same time and was renamed *Amérique*. "Imperialism" in ships' names had gone out of style. The last transatlantic crossing by a French paddle-wheel steamer occurred in August 1872, and it was believed that the transformation of the fleet represented a major advance in marine technology. Some individuals expressed the reservation that the hulls of these liners had been weakened by the process of lengthening them and the reconstruction necessary to transform them from paddle wheel to screw propulsion. These views seemed overly pessimistic.

The *Ville du Havre* left the Leslie yard virtually as a new vessel in the spring of 1873. Her maiden arrival in New York occurred on April 9, 1873, and she received a warm reception in the American port, as most French Line ships usually did. With the exception of the *Great Eastern* (1860; 18,915 tons, 680 feet, 12 knots) she was the largest vessel ever to enter the port of New York with a length of 422 feet. The *Ville du Havre* was described as having a gross tonnage of 3,950, making her the largest ship in service on the North Atlantic in 1873.[7] This was about 40 percent larger than any American Line vessel.[8] Her new compound engines were rated at twelve hundred horsepower but were capable of working up to the incredible power of thirty-nine hundred horsepower. The engines had four cylinders, two eighty inches, and two thirty-eight inches in diameter, with a stroke of four feet six inches. The steam was provided by six boilers, heated by thirty-two furnaces, and the average consumption of coal was fifty-five tons a day. She was bark-rigged with two funnels, eight lifeboats, and four winches for hoisting cargo and sails. In all she had five decks, three for cargo and two for passengers.

The passenger accommodations of the *Ville du Havre* were divided between 190 first class, 120 second class, and 500 steerage. The first-class saloon was amidships and extended from side to side, creating a compartment 52 by 46 feet. Marble was much used in the wall paneling, with oil paintings to enrich the room, and a piano for entertainment. The ship also carried a small library, and the main saloon was heated by a double stove while steam pipes ran throughout the ship to provide additional heat. The ladies' boudoir, or public room, adjoined the saloon and was decorated with paintings and lounges covered with blue velvet. The first-class and second-class staterooms were described as large and airy. The second-class public room was about 150 feet forward of the first-class lounge and was 40 by 25 feet. The second-class cabins were on the deck below. The upper deck provided a magnificent promenade for the passengers which stretched nearly 130 yards and was regarded as extraordinary for its spaciousness. In short, the *Ville du Havre* was one of the most beautiful and comfortable vessels of her day and well warranted the confidence of those who booked passage on her.

Her master was Captain Marius Surmont, a product of the French Navy and one of the most trusted officers in the French merchant marine. He was about fifty years old in 1873, with an earnest appearance and was clean-shaven save for a small tuft of beard under his chin. He had a high reputation for seamanship and had received the command of the *Ville du Havre* as a special mark of the confidence of the CGT in his character and skill. He was ably assisted by Second Captain Eugène de Garny, Second Officer Gaillard, Third Officer Durbée, Fourth Officer Meillour, Chief Purser Vie, and Chief Engineer Parent, who had seven special assistants in his engine room staff.

The *Ville du Havre* backed away from her New York pier on November 15 for a wintry transatlantic crossing. Conditions on the Atlantic Ocean had been severe for more than a year with violent storms and harsh weather conditions taking a heavy toll on ships and travelers. The *Ville du Havre,* at 422 feet and 3,950 tons, was the largest passenger liner in active service and the second-largest ship in the world. As the flagship of the French Line she carried with her a celebrated list of passengers when she left New York. From Chicago Mrs. H. G. Spafford, wife of the senior partner in the prestigious Chicago law firm of Spafford, McDaid & Wilson, boarded with four little girls, ages two, five, seven, and eleven, to begin a two-year tour of Europe in hopes of regaining their health. Only a little earlier Mrs. Spafford with great resourcefulness and courage had saved herself and her daughters from the Great Chicago Fire. The experience of fleeing the conflagration caused by Mrs. O'Leary's cow had shattered the health of Mrs. Spafford and that of her daughters, and her husband had agreed to send them overseas for a prolonged rest and vacation. From Boston a party of eleven from socially prominent families also boarded the *Ville du Havre.* In upstate New York Judge and Mrs. Rufus Peckham left Albany, where the judge was a member of the appeals court, for the French liner and a trip to Europe. In the mid-nineteenth century a trip abroad for an American traveler often was calculated to restore health and was taken for that reason.

Every Atlantic liner carried a generous amount of cargo in addition to her passengers. Cargo shipped on a passenger liner often involved luxury goods, which could stand a higher freight and still remain profitable, but this does not seem to hold true for a November crossing. The general cargo shipped on the *Ville du Havre* provides an interesting view of what was involved in the trade between the United States and France in 1873. The French ship was carrying 1,615 bales of cotton, 800 cases of bacon, a large quantity of wheat in bulk, 17 bags of shinbones, 15 tierces of rice, 30 barrels of potash, 1,333 bundles of hides, 6 sacks of seeds, 51 casks of jewelers' ashes, 9 casks of crockery, 1 case of books, 1 case of silverware, 250 tierces of lard, 21 logs of cedarwood, 7 barrels of pork, 7 bales of leather, 8 casks of copper, 52 cans of canned goods, 1 case of ribbons, 5 cases of peppermint, 1 case of silk, 114 cases of assorted merchandise, 1 barrel of apples, and 2 barrels of oysters.[9]

The crossing involved substantial fog during the first five days until the ship cleared the Grand Banks. By the evening of November 21 the fog had cleared, and visibility was good, although the French Line flagship was fighting her way through heavy seas. All her lamps were lit, and a full lookout was being kept. At about 2:00 A.M., Captain Surmont had just retired for the night, and Second Officer Gaillard was in charge of the bridge.

Suddenly out of the thick darkness loomed a very large sailing ship, the *Loch Earn* (1869; 1,200 tons) of Glasgow, Scotland, bound for New York. The collision was wholly unsuspected as the *Loch Earn* struck the

The French liner Ville du Havre *(1873) was the second-largest liner in the world. During the night of November 21, 1873, she was rammed in mid-Atlantic by the British sailing vessel* Loch Earn *(1869), whose bow sliced a large hole directly into the engine room. The* Ville du Havre *sank in minutes with the loss of a minimum of 226 lives.*

Ville du Havre amidships, slicing a huge hole into the engine room, the most vulnerable section of the ship. The wedge in the side of the French liner was described as twelve feet deep and from twenty-five to thirty-five feet wide. It was a mortal wound. Passengers were tumbled out of their beds, and those who fled to the open deck immediately had a chance, but only a chance, of surviving. Two lifeboats rapidly were filled with passengers and preparing to launch when the huge main- and mizzenmasts of the liner with their full load of spars, booms, and riggings came crashing down on the deck and across the lifeboats, smashing them to smithereens. The screams and howls multiplied the atmosphere of panic as the *Ville du Havre* lurched and began to go down within minutes of the collision. The frantic crew managed to launch successfully only a whaleboat and the captain's gig before the liner slid under the waves less than twelve minutes after being hit. Captain Surmont and his officers were praised by the few survivors for their efforts, but there was precious little anyone could do when the second-largest passenger liner in the world sinks in twelve minutes in the wee hours of a winter night in the middle of the Atlantic Ocean. The best estimate of her last position was latitude 47° 21′ west, longitude 35° 31′ north.[10]

The *Loch Earn* had been launched at Glasgow, Scotland, in November 1869 and had an iron hull. She was 236 feet long, with a beam of 35 feet and a depth of hold of 21 feet. Described as a "medium model" sailing ship, she had visited New York in 1871 and attracted some attention for her size and the cleanness of her lines. She was under the command of Captain Robertson and had sailed from London on November 12 bound for New York with a call at Deal, England, on November 14. After striking the larger passenger liner, the *Loch Earn* continued to sail for about a mile before drifting to a stop. In spite of the severe damage to his bow Captain Robertson immediately launched a lifeboat to go to the aid of those on the stricken liner. Meanwhile the French whaleboat under the command of Second Officer Gaillard reached the sailing ship with one load of survivors and transferred them. Gaillard turned around and rowed the mile back to the scene of the disaster as quickly as possible in order to attempt to rescue anyone still surviving among the wreckage in the freezing water. Many of those rescued were almost lifeless from hypothermia, and they included Captain Surmont, who had swum away from his command as it went under and been in the ocean for over forty-five minutes. The cold was intense, and the decision was made that it was fruitless to search for any other survivors in the prevailing conditions. On the *Loch Earn* everything possible was done to care for the unfortunate survivors who had lost everything and been pulled from the sea bereaved and destitute.

Later, on November 22, the *Loch Earn* encountered the American ship *Trimountain* (1850; 1,307 tons), a full-rigged ship of New York, bound for Britain with a large general cargo.[11] The two sailing ships hailed each other, and Captain Robertson informed Captain Urquhart of the tragic loss of the *Ville du Havre.* Since his vessel apparently was badly damaged, Captain Robertson had turned about and intended to make for Queenstown, Ireland, as the nearest major port of refuge. Captain Urquhart of the *Trimountain,* in view of the damage to the *Loch Earn,* offered to take on board his ship any survivors who wanted to complete their crossing with him. Of the eighty-seven survivors (fifty-three crew, twenty-four male passengers, and ten female passengers), three were too injured to be moved and elected to remain on the *Loch Earn.* The larger number accepted Captain Urquhart's offer to transfer to the *Trimountain* in order to complete their eastbound crossing of the Atlantic on an undamaged vessel. The *Trimountain* made Cardiff, Wales, on December 1, bringing the earliest news of the disaster, and landed the survivors at Bristol, her British port of call. In addition to the official list of officers, crew, and passengers on the *Ville du Havre* there were six stowaways who presumably were locked belowdeck when the liner took her final plunge.

On December 1, eight days after the sinking of the *Ville du Havre,* the first news of the disaster reached London, New York, and Paris. Newspapers in the affected metropolitan areas immediately posted copies of the telegrams announcing the disaster. The French authorities in Le Havre, home port of the Compagnie Générale Transatlantique, lost no time in ordering an investigation into the loss of the ship. Commentators wondered at how one of the most modern and safest vessels in the world could have been involved in such a terrible collision on a clear night. "The lost steamer was one of the best vessels afloat. She had been fitted with all the latest improvements in marine engineering, both for speed and safety; in construction and equipment, everything had been done for her which ingenuity could suggest; her accommodations for the comfort of her passengers were of the most complete and costly character; and an able and experienced navigator commanded the vessel with a crew of picked men under him. Notwithstanding this, an ordinary sailing vessel, coming down in the dead of the night, strikes the ponderous steamer amidships, and sends her almost instantly to the bottom, with four-fifths of her living freight."[12] Of the Spafford family only Mrs. Spafford survived, all four of her young daughters, who had survived the Great Chicago Fire, succumbing to the cold waters of the Atlantic. An anguished person inquiring about the Spafford children to the French Line offices responded to the news of their deaths with a cry "My God, all lost, all lost!" Judge and Mrs. Peckham also died when the *Ville du Havre* sank. It seems as though those passengers with cabins closest to the stairways had the best chance of survival. The chances of surviving the sinking diminished the farther away from the stairs one's cabin was, particularly since the liner took her final plunge within twelve minutes of being rammed. In the final analysis at least 226 lives were lost and only 87 saved. No indication was given of whether the unfortunate stowaways counted.

Why did the *Ville du Havre* sink? The hole made by the *Loch Earn* was sufficiently large for enough of the Atlantic to flood into the stricken passenger liner that she could no longer remain afloat. The French liner also was struck at her most vulnerable point where the great engine room represented a cavernous space and the adjacent boiler room also was compromised. No Atlantic liner in 1873 probably could have survived such a wound. Only much greater advances in the internal subdivision of hulls and improvements in watertight bulkheads would have provided a chance for survival. Once again the human factor looms large since it would have helped if either ship had seen the other in time to avoid so violent a mid-Atlantic meeting.

Chapter 5

THE SS *PENNSYLVANIA* OF THE AMERICAN LINE AND THE GREAT HURRICANE OF 1874

February 23, 1874

Mother Nature was not to be kind to any steamship braving the North Atlantic during the fierce winter of 1873–1874. It was one of the worst seasons the transatlantic trade ever experienced. The American Line vessels did not escape unscathed, yet none was lost, and this in itself was a major accomplishment. One crossing in particular deserves a place in the annals of American maritime lore.

The *Pennsylvania,* premier unit of the American Line, lay at Liverpool on February 21, 1874, preparing to sail. The liner had loaded all the freight available, and it was worth the substantial sum of approximately $250,000. The Liverpool ticket agents sold passage on such vessels until the gangplank was pulled away. About an hour before the departure one last passenger, an individual with a definite air of the sea about him, bought a ticket for the sailing and went on board. He gave his name as C. L. Brady. The anchor was raised about 2:30 P.M., and the *Pennsylvania* steamed down the Mersey bound for Delaware Bay. She was under the command of the experienced and reliable Captain Lewis P. Bradburn, who had sailed the North Atlantic for twenty-five of his forty-two years and, as first officer and then master, had been with the ship since her commissioning. He was on his last voyage. He had just been promoted to port captain at Liverpool in order to be near his wife, who lived in Britain. While the American liner was carrying a substantial general cargo, she had only two saloon passengers and twelve steerage passengers for this dead-of-the-winter crossing.

The *Pennsylvania* was a rarity on the North Atlantic because she flew the Stars and Stripes. There were not many American-flag steamships in 1874. The *Pennsylvania* and the American Line, her owners, were the result of the desire of the Pennsylvania Railroad Company (PRR), as the largest and most prosperous American corporation, to expand the trade of the port of Philadelphia. The PRR's challenge to local merchants after the conclusion of the American Civil War was that if they took the initiative to establish a steamship line, it would invest $400,000 in the stock of the concern and guarantee a bond issue of $1.5 million.[1] Local merchants did seek to raise funds to set up a steamship company for transatlantic service. The Commonwealth of Pennsylvania through the General Assembly granted a charter for a new shipping venture, the American Steamship Company, on April 18, 1871. The charter was issued "for the purpose of establishing a line of first class steamships to run between Philadelphia and Liverpool; the steamers to be constructed in American ship building yards, and as entirely as possible of American Materials."[2] The best bid of $400,000 per ship came from the Cramp shipyard and was for vessels of approximately 3,016 tons, with a length of 336 feet, a beam of 43 feet, and a hold of 32 feet, 2 inches. The board of directors of the American Steamship Company promptly awarded the contract to William Cramp & Sons, which began planning immediately.[3] The ships were given the names of the states to the west along the main line of the Pennsylvania Railroad: *Pennsylvania, Ohio, Indiana, and Illinois.*[4]

Each liner was to be outfitted to carry 76 first-class and 854 steerage passengers, and the total price for the four vessels was $2,080,000. The ships were designed by the marine architect Barnabas H. Bartol,

The Pennsylvania *(1873) of the American Steamship Company was the premier vessel of a new service from Philadelphia to Liverpool begun with the financial backing of the Pennsylvania Railroad Company. In February 1874 the liner would encounter a horrendous North Atlantic storm, which at one point ripped the bridge off the ship and swept away to their deaths the captain, first mate, and several seamen. Ultimately the* Pennsylvania *arrived safely at Philadelphia under the command of a passenger.*

one of the directors of the line, and the engines by Charles H. Cramp of the Cramp shipyard.[5] There were many delays, but the majestic *Pennsylvania* finally backed out into the Delaware River on May 22, 1873, for her maiden sailing.

With her single towering funnel and two graceful masts the *Pennsylvania* was a beautiful sight under way. Her masts were outfitted to carry full-brig rigging, and the sails she carried were always kept ready for service. This proved fortunate even on her maiden voyage, when some of the blades were knocked off her propeller in mid-Atlantic, and she arrived under sail at Liverpool. The first six months of service proved the *Pennsylvania* and her sisters to be staunch ships capable of meeting most of the challenges of the North Atlantic at any time of the year.

The *Pennsylvania* passed down the Mersey without incident on February 21 and steamed down the Irish Sea in good time. The first two days were unexceptional, but as the liner rounded the coast of Ireland and headed into the open Atlantic, she encountered stormy weather. The direction of the wind shifted to the northwest, and a violent hurricane began to slam the liner about. The crew was forced to exert the utmost effort to keep the vessel under control. The scene was horrifying as mountainous waves and highly confused seas washed over the ship and carried away everything movable from the decks. The ship labored and strained very hard without making much progress because of the pounding she was receiving and the heavy seas that swept the decks. During the night of February 27 the *Pennsylvania* shipped the first of several colossal waves that broke over her bow with such force that it fractured and stove in the forward end of the "Social Hall" and sent seawater sweeping down the length of the ship. When this happened, most of the passengers and some of the crew apparently believed that the ship was doomed and that her end was near. The ship's carpenter, assisted by other crew members and desperate male passengers, proceeded to repair and reinforce the forward part of the deckhouse in an effort to prevent further seas from flooding the saloon.

The *Pennsylvania* received a reprieve around midnight, when she entered the eye of the storm. However, even if the winds temporarily abated, very severe cross seas were running from the southwest to northwest, and the liner was still straining hard to maintain any forward movement. The worst was yet to come.

Suddenly, while the crew was changing watches at midnight, the *Pennsylvania* encountered an extraordinarily huge wave that loomed out of the darkness on the starboard bow and broke with a thunderous crash over her superstructure. The mountainous sea carried away a portion of the bridge, the wheelhouse, the mates' house, four of the lifeboats, and all the life rafts, unshipped the ventilators, ripped off the railings, broke the stanchions, and stove in all four forward hatches. The force of the wave was so great that it broke the foreboom and flooded both the steerage and saloon areas of the ship until they were about one-fourth full.[6]

The *Pennsylvania* appeared bound for a watery grave. The liner was completely disabled and placed in a very critical and dangerous position. For a time she lay in the trough of the seas, rolling heavily and losing all headway or direction. Those belowdecks were stunned by the concussion of the monster wave, cold and wet from the insurge of seawater, and dizzy from the wild rolls of the ship. As they wondered what had happened, additional information brought the magnitude of the disaster home.

The mammoth wave which struck the *Pennsylvania* swept away to their deaths Captain Bradburn, First Mate Sweetman, Second Mate James Ross, and two seamen who had been at the wheel. None of these five men was ever seen again. This was a tragedy of staggering proportions. Drownings at sea were a common factor on the North Atlantic, but the loss of the three senior officers of the *Pennsylvania* and two experienced sailors by the action of one gigantic wave certainly was unsurpassed as a disaster.[7] The perilous position of the vessel was not helped when the third officer, Charles Rivers, upon whom the command of the liner devolved, took one look abovedeck at the rampaging seas and refused to take command!

Cornelius L. Brady, the last person to pay six guineas ($31.50) to purchase a ticket for the February 21 sailing of the *Pennsylvania*, shared the saloon accommodations with only one other gentleman, Charles Walton of London. Brady had no intention of going to a watery grave. Technically a passenger, he held a master's certificate in steam and was determined to do everything conceivable to save the ship and the lives of those still on board. He already had worked alongside the ship's carpenter to shore up and reinforce the forward end of the deckhouse when it had been ruptured by waves earlier in the evening. Now the situation was infinitely more perilous for the ship and all on her.

Brady had narrowly survived one shipwreck less than a year before, when he had been third officer on the ill-fated *Atlantic* (1870; 3,707 tons) of the White Star Line, which had been wrecked near Halifax with a loss of 585 lives (April 1, 1873). The *Atlantic* was the worst disaster in the period 1873–1874, but eleven other liners were lost between January 1873 and November 1874 on the North Atlantic, and collision had figured in only a single case.

Brady had no desire to repeat his narrow brush with death on the *Atlantic.* He struggled forward to see the damage and found the majority of the crew and passengers standing around Third Officer Rivers, who was leaning up against a pump well with a lamp in his hand and saying nothing. The lamp may have given some comfort but no salvation. The chief engineer, Mr. Eddons, said to Rivers: "Why don't you take your men on deck?"

He replied: "I can't find a man to go on deck."

The purser then said, "Go on deck yourself and set your men an example," but instead of so doing, he continued walking up and down."[8] He seemed paralyzed by the magnitude of their imminent peril and refused to take action.

Brady took one look at the scene belowdecks and asserted himself. Conditions could not have been worse. The *Pennsylvania,* her hatches stove in, was lying in the trough of the sea in the midst of a hurricane. The most critical problem was to stop the flow of water into the ship. Brady issued orders for all those present to divide into three gangs in order to strip the lower decks of their hatches and pass them up to the upper decks so that the stove-in hatches could be resecured and keep the ship from filling any further.

Immediately after issuing those orders, Brady saw Captain Bradburn's steward, Edwin Coleman, standing nearby. Coleman, a twelve-year veteran of the North Atlantic, was a respected individual. Brady sent him on deck to tell Bradburn what had been done and to obtain the captain's sanction for the emergency measures. Coleman stumbled back to Brady with the horrifying news that the ship was steaming along with a quartermaster at the helm but minus all the officers who had been on deck. In Brady's words, "This knowledge greatly increased the excitement, confusion and consternation among all on board."[9] Those passengers and crew members within hearing clearly were at the limits of their endurance. Brady did not hesitate. He thought the preservation of the lives on board and the cargo and the ship required that he assume command immediately. On his own authority and by his own judgment he decided to do so. His decision was upheld by those on board. As Brady headed for the open deck, he was met by a delegation of the ship's surgeon, purser, first assistant engineer, quartermaster, carpenter, and others who implored him to take command for the sake of saving the ship and the lives and property of all on board. By this vote of confidence, or desperation, his decision to take command of the liner was confirmed.

Brady struggled through the gale to the midships wheelhouse, where he found Michael Murphy, quartermaster, at the wheel. Murphy informed Brady that the captain had gone forward to the bridge sometime before and had not been heard from since. Brady told Murphy what had happened and that he was assuming command for the time being. The quartermaster appeared greatly relieved. The steps that had to be taken immediately were to slow the liner and heave her to so that she could regain some stability and seaworthiness. This might make it possible for the deckhands to secure the hatches. Brady rang down to the engine room to slow the *Pennsylvania*'s engines to dead slow. Simultaneously the helm was put hard aport and the ship's head brought from the southwest to west northwest. Hove to in this manner, the bow was turned into the wind, and just sufficient revolutions were maintained to keep the ship under control. Murphy later testified: "Without Captain Brady I believe we would never have reached port."[10] Brady left the quartermaster and with great effort made his way to a point where he could inspect the forward section of the ship. He saw the portion of the bridge that remained twisted and mangled. The bridge house itself was completely torn away and missing. No trace of it existed anywhere on the *Pennsylvania*. Brady clawed his way back to the midships wheelhouse and told the quartermaster what he had or, more correctly, had not seen. The storm continued to rage around the stricken liner. All able-bodied crew members not needed in the engine room worked frantically against the seas to resecure the hatches and, after three hours, managed to replace one. This information was brought to Brady by Rivers, who acknowledged Brady's command by reporting to him and taking orders from him.

During the rest of the night the exhausted crew managed to secure the remaining hatches, and the liner was given a chance to survive. As the immediate crisis lessened somewhat, Brady let his mind move ahead to the challenge of reaching Philadelphia. He soon discovered that the location of the *Pennsylvania* on the broad North Atlantic was virtually unknown since the dead officers had been able to make only one observation after leaving Liverpool a week before. On the morning of February 28 the storm broke after five days, and Brady mustered the crew on deck. He informed them that he had assumed command at the request of a majority of the officers and asked them if they were satisfied with his command. All were. The third officer acquiesced in the proceedings, standing behind Brady and accepting the temporary position of first officer under Brady. Rivers told Brady that this was his first trip on a steamship, that he had previously served all his time in sail, "and that he did not understand handling them."[11] Brady received reports of the fuel and provisions remaining on board, and since they were adequate for proceeding to the United States, he gave orders for the *Pennsylvania* slowly to steam south toward smoother seas.

As fate would have it, the *Pennsylvania* was not yet finished with foul weather. Gales were encountered on March 3–4. Ultimately on March 9 the ship under the command of Captain Cornelius L. Brady passed the capes of Delaware Bay and picked up the pilot off Lewes, Delaware. The next morning, March 10, the *Pennsylvania* was secured alongside the American Line pier at Philadelphia, and the exhausted survivors staggered ashore. The liner was seventeen days out from Liverpool on what was normally a ten- to eleven-day voyage.

The tributes to Brady's courage and seamanship by passengers and crew were of the first magnitude. He was hailed as a hero, while Rivers was placed on the "retired list." Local journalists commented upon the fact that for all he had gone through, Captain Brady was a man of few words.

The nearly bankrupt American Line was faced with a big problem. What was a suitable reward for someone like Captain Brady, who had saved one of their four passenger liners, the lives of all on board, and a considerable cargo under these conditions? The board of directors of the American Steamship Company erred on the side of conservatism by voting him the munificent sum of $1,000 for saving a $600,000 vessel and cargo worth another $250,000, not to mention the passengers' lives. Brady indignantly returned the company's check, and Philadelphia set back to watch one of the more interesting legal tussles of the 1874 season.

Brady filed a libel suit against the American Line for salvage in connection with services rendered. The documents submitted to the U.S. district court requested he be awarded compensation on the basis of the value of the passenger liner *Pennsylvania,* the cargo she was carrying, and the cost and expenses that he was sustaining in pursuing the matter. A four-month court case was held before Judge John Cadwalader. The testimony of those involved in the struggle to save the *Pennsylvania* weighed heavily in Brady's favor during the trial. Depositions taken from such individuals as Joseph Pullius, quartermaster and later second officer of the liner, substantiated all of Brady's recounting of the story. Pullius stated: "If Captain Brady had not taken command when he did, and stopped the speed of the ship, the next sea that boarded her would have filled her, and sunk her, as no vessel could stand taking so much water in board in the condition she was in."[12] In this a number of other American Steamship Company employees heartedly concurred. The dead captain's steward, Edwin Coleman, testified "that only Captain Brady's prompt and efficient actions saved the ship and all lives on board."[13] He also testified that Brady after he assumed command of the *Pennsylvania* never left the deck day or night until he was sure the ship was safe. Peter McCarroll, another quartermaster, who had been a seaman for sixteen years, swore under oath: "My opinion is Captain Brady was the only man on board capable of bringing the ship safely into port. If there had been nobody on board who understood handling the ship as Captain Brady did, she could not have lived through the night."[14] Frank Reedstone, seaman for nine years, stated: "What I give Captain Brady credit for is for doing what he did at the time, slowing the vessel and putting her head to the sea; without that I don't believe she would have lived through the night."[15] George Keabea, a sailor for twenty years and one of the most experienced hands on board, summed up the reactions of all who had been there: "I am satisfied the steamer would never have lived through the night if Captain Brady had not taken command when he did."[16] Brady's lawyer laid claim to a more substantial compensation based on the extraordinary character of the services that he had rendered and that were testified to my numerous members of the crew of the *Pennsylvania*.

At the end of the trial Judge Cadwalader reviewed the testimony and handed down a ruling that increased the award to Captain Brady by 420 percent but fell short of any judgment based upon pure salvage. Brady received the substantially increased sum of $4,000, plus $200 for expenses. This hardly represented clear profit, however, since from it he had to deduct legal fees of $1,650, ending up with $2,550 as his compensation for saving nearly $850,000 in private property from the North Atlantic. The buying power of $2,550 in 1874 represented a significant legacy, and Brady appears to have been content with the outcome even if he had hoped for more.

During the annual meeting of the American Steamship Company on Monday, April 6, 1874, the horrendous weather conditions in February on the North Atlantic were mentioned with considerable relief that all the units of the fleet had survived and proved themselves seaworthy. The loss of the commander, two officers, and two seamen from the *Pennsylvania* was acknowledged with deep regret.

Chapter 6

GROUNDING OF THE STEAMSHIP *RUSLAND* OF THE RED STAR LINE OFF LONG BRANCH, NEW JERSEY

March 17, 1877

Often the sheer number of vessels at sea in the latter part of the nineteenth century seems incredible. In an average year (1894) the port of New York saw the arrival of 4,761 vessels, 2,984 of which were steamships, while the sailing vessels comprised 185 ships, 450 barks, 144 brigs, and 998 schooners.[1] New York Harbor is bordered by two strips of land, forming a natural guideline into Lower New York Bay. To the north, running almost from east to west, lies the peninsula of Long Island, marked by the Fire Island Light, approximately thirty-five miles east from the entrance to the bay. To the south, stretching almost due north-south from the Sandy Hook entrance to the bay and guarded by the Sandy Hook Lightship, is the New Jersey coast. Some ten miles south of Sandy Hook, near the seaside resort of Long Branch and overlooking the beach, stood the West End Hotel.

On the very windy and cold morning of Sunday, March 18, 1877, the panoramic view from the hotel presented a spectacular sight. About five hundred yards to the south there was the huge form of a ship, lying with her starboard side toward the beach. It was the steamship *Rusland*, which had run aground the previous night. A southeastern gale had been blowing in combination with a heavy sea. The captain had lost his way, his ship had headed straight for the beach and had keeled over on her starboard side. Immediately afterward she had filled with water, and it was supposed from the volume of water that had rushed in she had struck a rock, making a hole in her hull.

The International Navigation Company (Red Star Line) was the new owner of the *Rusland* although it had operated her on charter for a number of years. The INC was representative of those American shipping interests in the post–Civil War period who wanted to establish transatlantic steamship lines but did not believe that such a business could be run successfully under the American flag. These financial interests therefore, though having their headquarters in the United States, built their fleets in foreign yards, operated the vessels under foreign flags, and manned their ships with foreign crews. Such was the case with the International Navigation Company that originated in Philadelphia but whose foreign-flag operations became exactly the opposite of the American Steamship Company's American-flag organization.

The chief American backer of the INC was the mighty Pennsylvania Railroad Company, which had guaranteed the bonds of the shipping company, provided virtually free wharfage at Philadelphia, and whose management were significant stockholders in the shipping concern. The general agent for the shipping company was the Quaker ship-brokering firm of Peter Wright & Sons, one of Philadelphia's oldest and most successful import-export houses. Its ship brokerage and management operations largely were in the hands of Clement Acton Griscom (1841–1912), who had one of the most successful careers of any American Quaker.

The history of the *Rusland*, formerly named the *Kenilworth*, was closely linked with the history of both the American Line and the Red Star Line.[2] Within less than one month, between April 18 and May 5, 1871, these two steamship companies received their charters from the state of Pennsylvania. Officially they were the American Steamship

Company, better known as the American Line, and the International Navigation Company, or Red Star Line, named for the red star on the white house flag. In both instances there was considerable financial involvement on the part of the Pennsylvania Railroad Company. Officially there was no indication of a common interest between the American Line and the Red Star Line although from January 1874 both fleets were managed by Peter Wright & Sons. The latter had founded a Belgium-based subsidiary, the Société Anonyme de Navigation Belge-Américaine, on September 5, 1872, because of the opportunity to foster a very beneficial Belgian government connection and to obtain a mail subsidy for a service from Antwerp to New York and Antwerp to Philadelphia.

Peter Wright & Sons needed ships in 1873 and sought to charter tonnage immediately. The Gourlay Shipyard, Dundee, Scotland, recently had built two sister ships, the *Kenilworth,* launched in August 1872, and the *Abbotsford,* launched in March 1873, for Williamson, Milligan & Company of Liverpool, which were intended for the South American trade. Both ships actually were needed to start the American Line's Liverpool–Philadelphia service. At the same time the American Line was endeavoring to obtain a U.S. government mail subsidy by claiming that it was a company founded with American capital and operating American-built ships flying the "Stars and Stripes." It was unwise to introduce into the American Line service chartered ships flying the British flag. It was "logical" to arrange through Peter Wright & Sons for the Red Star Line to operate the chartered ships temporarily. Hence, it was stated in Philadelphia on May 27, 1873, that the *Abbotsford,* "pioneer steamer of the Red Star Line's Liverpool service, arrived yesterday from Liverpool and Queenstown on her first voyage, bringing 294 passengers."[3] Soon afterward advertisements stated that the Red Star Line fleet consisted of the *Abbotsford, Kenilworth,* and two other steamers. Although this Red Star Line service seemed to be trespassing on the American Line service, proof of the logical arrangement can be found in the Twenty-Fifth Annual Report of the Pennsylvania Railroad, issued on February 20,

1872, which stated "that arrangements had been reached between the American Line and the International Navigation Company for certain interchanges, of which this was undoubtedly one."[4] Two other observations support this proof: The first is that the sailing schedules of the Red Star Line and the American Line never clashed, and the second is that Thomas C. Scott, senior vice-president of the Pennsylvania Railroad, sat on the board of the Belgian subsidiary of the Red Star Line, an unthinkable conflict of interest had the two companies been real competitors. The *Abbotsford* and the *Kenilworth* continued to sail in the Liverpool–Philadelphia service of the Red Star Line until the spring of 1874, when the management of the two lines were combined and the two ships finally could join the fleet of the American Line. The reason for this was that the American Line's endeavor to obtain a U.S. mail subsidy had failed. Instead it had secured a mail contract that did not stipulate the nationality of the chartered ships. The *Abbotsford* and the *Kenilworth* were active on the American Line service until 1875, when the former was wrecked on Anglesey (July) and the latter transferred to the Red Star Line (December).

On March 11, 1874, Red Star was awarded a subsidy from the Belgian government consisting of one hundred thousand dollars a year for ten years with certain privileges worth an additional thirty thousand dollars, in return for a new line of steamers between Antwerp and New York.[5] In the spring of 1876, after having run the service with several ships, the Red Star Line chartered the *Kenilworth* at short notice and entered her on the Antwerp–New York run. She made seven round trips during the following year and proved highly successful. At the beginning of March 1877 she was bought by Red Star, and renamed *Rusland.* Flying the Belgian flag, she sailed from Antwerp on March 3.[6]

The *Rusland* of the Red Star Line was carrying 5 cabin passengers, 111 steerage passengers, and a cargo consisting mainly of wines, glass, and iron. She was due in New York on Friday, March 16, but there would be no St. Patrick's Day celebration for her crew. Her former chief officer, Jesse de Horsey, had been promoted to captain and was bring-

The Rusland *(1877) of the Red Star Line went ashore at Long Branch, New Jersey, on March 17, 1877. Hopes that she could be refloated were dashed when it was realized that her hull lay on top of another wreck. Instead of soft sand the* Rusland *was balanced on a hard surface, which meant that in the next storm she broke her back and became a total loss.*

ing her to New York for the first time under her new name. The crossing of the Atlantic, according to passengers' reports, had been pleasant and uneventful until the *Rusland* reached the Newfoundland banks, where she ran into a thick fog and snow squalls.

The statement Captain de Horsey, the ship's master, made to a correspondent of the *New York Times* a few days after the grounding, described the sequence of events from that moment in more detail:

> After passing the Banks we ran into a fog, which continued with clear intervals until Sunday night. On Thursday morning we took pilot Benjamin Simonson of the pilot-boat . . . *Webb* when we were 276 miles from Sandy Hook Lightship. At noon on Friday I took an observation and ascertained our precise position. Immediately afterward the fog,

> which had lifted for a brief time settled down again. The weather was thick on Saturday, with occasional snow squalls, the wind blowing from the east. No canvas was carried. To allow for the effect of the tide and the wind the vessel was steered half a point to windward. I thought she would thus be kept on her true course. At 6 o'clock we sounded and found 28 fathoms and from the appearance of the soil brought up by the lead, I concluded that my previous observation was correct.[7]

The information acquired by Captain de Horsey played a paramount roll in his decisions during the following hours. The sounding was done using a weight of lead attached to a rope. The rope was marked at regular intervals with strands of colored cloth, each color depicting a length of fathom. The lower end of the piece of lead contained a hole for the special purpose of taking a sample from the ocean floor. The ship's officer doing the sounding mounted a little platform protruding from the ship's gunwale and was secured by a sounding breech so that he would not fall overboard. A couple of sailors brought the lead to the foredeck outside the rigging. On a signal from the officer they dropped the lead away from the ship, and he immediately started hauling in the slack in the rope, keeping the lead on the bottom of the sea. When the rope was in the perpendicular position, the officer read the water depth from the marking on the rope and called this reading to the ship's bridge. This could be repeated a couple of times as a check, and that was the case on the *Rusland.* The hole in the bottom end of the lead was filled with grease, which, upon the lead's hitting the seabed, collected some soil and other material to be brought up for inspection. The sample from the ocean floor can be looked at, it can be felt, it can be smelled, it can even be tasted, and an experienced captain who knows his sea bottoms can, from all these readings, establish the ship's position. That was what Captain de Horsey relied on. He said:

> At 6 o'clock we sounded and found 28 fathoms and from the appearance of the soil brought up by the lead, I concluded that my previous

observation was correct. At 8 o'clock another sounding was taken, and 20 fathoms were found, the nature of the bottom again confirming my belief that we were on the right course. Again at 9 o'clock 20 fathoms were found, and sea cakes were brought up. As these cakes have never, as to my knowledge, been found west of Mare Island, I concluded that the vessel was off the Long Island Coast and kept a strict watch for the Mare Island and Highland lights. At 10:10 16 fathoms were found and the bottom was satisfactory. The pilot and engineer were on the bridge with me, and there was nothing to make me fear disaster. Twenty-five minutes later, at 10:30, the lookout cried "Light on the port bow!" I thought that a mistake had been made by the sailor, as there should have been a light on our starboard bow, but I made out the land and I telegraphed for the vessel to be put about. Before that could be done, however, she struck. Then she slid up the beach. The blow when she struck was so slight that I did not feel it, and turning to the pilot said: "that was a close shave." A second after we found the vessel was hard aground. The cabin passengers were not aroused, but some of the steerage passengers felt the shock, and became excited. As soon as I found there was no immediate danger, I ordered the steerage to be locked, to prevent the people from coming on deck and making trouble. I thought that we had struck on Fire Island and was surprised to learn from the Life Service crew next morning that we were at Long Branch. The pilot and myself conferred as to our position from the time Simonson came on board. The vessel is full of water but I do not anticipate any trouble in getting her off. I do not know how the water entered but I believe that in trying to back the vessel off one of her thrust bearings of the propeller may have broken and made a hole through which the water entered.[8]

At the time the *Rusland* ran onto the beach many of the passengers had not retired, and the sudden shock created commotion among them. The captain and the other officers did all in their power to calm the cabin-class passengers, while enforcing discipline among the steerage passengers, and their efforts were successful. To attract attention, rockets were discharged, and indeed the crews of nearby Life-Saving Stations came to the assistance of the stranded steamer. After many fruitless efforts they succeeded in getting a line over her bow at four o'clock in the morning. Equipment used for propelling a lifesaving car was attached to the ship, connecting it with the beach, and the laborious work of landing the passengers started. Only two at a time could be transferred in the car, and it was six hours later at ten o'clock before the last passenger reached the shore. The crew in the meantime labored at transferring the baggage from the lower to the main deck, and following the passengers, their baggage was brought safely to the beach. The passengers were received at the East End Hotel, where everything possible was done to make them comfortable. The crew landed at four-thirty in the afternoon after having done all it could do during the prevailing heavy weather.

The cold weather did not prevent a repetition of the scene on the beach at Seabright, just north from Long Branch, when early in January the French steamship *Amerique* also was stranded in the midst of the storm of wind and rain. Almost everybody in Long Branch turned out to look at the *Rusland* lying off the shore at the East End, and wagonloads of visitors from outlying villages were brought to the scene. They thronged the beach and watched the vessel until the icy wind drove them to shelter. With the gale still blowing and the heavy sea running, the ship was filling with water and gradually settling into the sandy beach.

The Coast Wrecking Company's steamship *Relief*, on her way to New York from the steamer *Amerique* at Seabright, passed the wreck on Sunday morning. Captain Dale, who was in charge, made an effort to come alongside the wrecked steamer, but the heavy weather at the time prevented him from doing so. There was about fifteen feet of water in the hold of the *Rusland* at that time, and the *Relief* went to New York to take on board a boiler, pumps, cables, and other necessary equipment for the purpose of assisting her. Unfortunately the spot at which the *Rusland* had struck was precisely the same position where twenty years earlier another ship, loaded with grindstones, had gone down. Those familiar with the coast said the *Rusland* was resting on the hulk of that vessel.[9]

During the following days the weather deteriorated, and it was not possible for the rescue boats to unload the cargo of the *Rusland.* Some of her passengers were sent to New York on the morning of Monday, March 19, when it was obvious that their ship would not be freed quickly. The steamer *Jesse Hoyt,* of the New Jersey Southern Railroad Company, arrived at her pier, No. 8 North River, at ten o'clock with the cabin and steerage passengers. The cabin passengers were received with joy by their friends. For the steerage passengers there were only curious sightseers. A steam tug soon came alongside the *Jesse Hoyt* and took the steerage passengers off to Castle Garden and the immigrant-processing facility. About half of them were Italians, and the remainder were German and French. Very few of them could speak English, and those who could were still too excited to be able to tell anything about what had happened to them. The brief time that many of them spent in Castle Garden was needed to get ready for their westward journey since many were bound for interior destinations. They were glad to have survived and, finally, to have arrived safely in the United States.

Mrs. Ferdinand Duysters of 342 Lexington Avenue, New York, was a saloon passenger and was accompanied by her two children. She had the following story to tell:

> I was awakened about 2 o'clock on Sunday morning by Capt. De Horsey, who told me to rise and dress myself and children, as the vessel had struck. He told me, however, not to be alarmed, as there was no further danger to be apprehended, and I would have ample time to dress myself and children comfortably. This was the first intimation I had received of the accident. I dressed myself and my children, and wrapped them up warmly, after which we sat down in our state-room at the captains [*sic*] request to await further directions. I cannot say that I was greatly frightened although I had considerable apprehension. The hours dragged

along wearily until about 4 o'clock when Capt. De Horsey reappeared and told me to come on deck as, if the vessel would break, it would probably part in the vicinity of my room. I followed his directions and the children behaved nobly and gave me no trouble. The little girl was somewhat frightened, but my little boy seemed to enjoy the excitement immensely. It was very cold on deck and the air was full of snow. The officers, and all connected with the ship, treated me with the greatest kindness and did all they could to make me comfortable. I watched the movements of the life car with some alarm, and as I saw its occupants became more or less drenched from contact with the surf I decided to go ashore in the life boat. I watched its passage five times successfully and it appeared to be manned by a good crew and to be perfectly safe. Capt. [Frank W.] Call and myself entered the boat and the children were tied in an arm-chair and lowered to the boat. We crossed the surf safely and reached the shore in a dry condition. We were taken in a wagon to the life-saving station where we were kindly cared for, and, after becoming thoroughly warm, we were conveyed to the East End Hotel.[10]

Captain Frank W. Call, one of the saloon passengers, made the following eyewitness statement to a *New York Times* reporter:

We left Antwerp on Saturday March 3, and from that time until we reached the Banks of Newfoundland the weather was very fine, and we proceeded at a good rate of speed. As we left the Banks the weather became thick, the air was filled with snow and the sun was only visible at intervals. I went to bed at about 10 o'clock on Saturday night, and was asleep at the time the steamer ran aground. The stoppage of the steamer roused me, and, hastily dressing, I went on deck. It was snowing hard, and a cold raw wind was blowing. I made my way to the bridge where I found the captain and pilot in consultation. I do not think the pilot had taken formal charge of the steamer at that time. The sailors were shouting wildly "Light, ho!," being apparently under the impression that the lights on shore were the lights of sailing vessels in the vicinity of our boat. The passengers were not excited, although they looked considerably frightened, and the ship's officers were cool and collected, and assured them that there was no immediate danger. I don't know who was to blame for the accident. The engineer, Mr. Clark, told me last night that the cause of the vessels filling with water so rapidly was that the tube through which the propeller shaft rode was split by the concussion which resulted from running aground. As soon as it was light enough, the work of landing the passengers commenced. The life saving crew got a line over the bow of the boat and attached the life car to the ship, and about 7 o'clock on Sunday morning commenced hauling the passengers ashore. Only two could go in the car at a time. I crossed in a life-boat. All passengers were landed by 10 o'clock. We were taken in wagons to the nearest life-saving station, where we got dry and warm, and were then conveyed to the East End Hotel at Long Branch. Everybody did all in their power to make us comfortable, and all the baggage of the passengers as well as their lives were saved. I hail from Maine and am a seafaring man. I formerly commanded the bark *Union,* running from this port to Boston.[11]

The names of the ship's officers, as reported by the *New York Times,* were as follows: captain, Jesse de Horsey; chief officer, Ernst Wiesman; second officer, Thomas Dobann; third officer, George Maxwell; and fourth officer, Ernst Gehl.

The rest of the Sunday until late afternoon the *Rusland* was exposed to breaking seas from stem to stern, which broke over the hull in a cloud of spray. Fortunately both wind and sea calmed down during Sunday night. The next day the water was comparatively smooth with the surf breaking along the shores. The vessel remained on the sand in the position she struck on Saturday night, and at that time there was no fear that she would break. Even the wrecking company expressed hope of getting her off, but of course its success in doing so would depend greatly upon the weather. A northeaster would greatly complicate matters.

The *Rusland* was lying diagonally to the beach, keeled to starboard with her bow pointing slightly northwest and elevated high in the air, while her stern was not more than three feet above the water. The starboard rail was missing, having been carried away by the sea, and the bridge was partly collapsed. The water that broke over the side of the vessel was freezing, and the ice-covered wreck was glistening brightly in the sun. The hull settled down and filled with water, so that the furniture of the saloon was floating about, while the engine room was flooded to the base of the cylinders. The *Relief* returned to the wreck at eight on Monday evening. The officers of the Coast Wrecking Company were of the opinion that if the weather was good, the greater part of the valuable cargo might be saved but that the steamer would probably prove a total loss.[12] The next morning the *Relief* came down to the *Rusland* but made no attempt to get the vessel off. She arranged cables on the wreck and made preparations to lighten her of some of her cargo.

Over the following days nothing much changed, and on Thursday the *Rusland* was lying about the same as the day before, although the surf was high and the wind south to southeast all the time. The weather was so thick at times that day that the vessel could hardly be seen from the shore. The lighters that came down on Wednesday had to leave at three o'clock on Thursday morning. Nothing was done toward discharging the cargo that day because it was too rough to work the surfboats. The *Relief*, waiting for orders, had been anchored off the shore about half a mile. The prospect of getting the steamer off were considered bad. There was now more anxiety about the cargo and fear of the weather's growing worse. The auxiliary pumping equipment of the *Relief* was put to work for a short time, discharging a barrel of water each second but to no effect. It was decided to resume pumping the next morning at low tide in the hope the water would lower and the leak could be reached. Meanwhile the movement of the *Rusland* crushed the timbers of the old ship, and the shore was strewn with debris for miles. The *Rusland* bow rested on the wreck, preventing it from going down, but the stern was settling fast. It was feared that she would break, and chances of getting her off were marginal. The longshoremen said the steamer showed signs of weakness. Old seamen said that should a strong easterly wind arise that night, the *Rusland* surely would break her back. This is what happened, and in the end the ship could not withstand the forces of wind and sea. Her hull broke beyond salvaging.

The *New York Times* reported on Tuesday, March 20, 1877, that the cargo was valued at about two hundred thousand dollars. It included window and plate glass, cloth, 506 bales of old paper, 19 packages of tiles, 1 case of oil paintings, 25 miscellaneous cases, 50 packages of dyestuff, 12 cases of zinc, 1,000 packages of iron wire, a case of chasubles, besides bags, wine casks, and church ornaments for Savannah. Messrs. Johnson & Figgins were appointed adjusters for the wreck.

On May 3, 1877, it was reported that a sale had taken place at Robinson's Stores, Brooklyn, of a large quantity of material recovered from the wreck of the Red Star steamship *Rusland* together with the hull of the vessel, which was lying off West End, Long Branch. About five hundred people had assembled at the sale. The property to be disposed of had consisted of sixty thousand pounds of chain, boats, sails, cordage, and miscellaneous stuff. The broken hull, including everything except the cargo remaining in it, had been sold for nine thousand dollars to George W. Townsend, of Boston. The boats had been sold at forty-five dollars each, and the life raft, *Nonpareil*, had brought fifty dollars. John H. Draper & Company, the auctioneers, considered the sale altogether a very good one.

It would appear that everything which could have been done to bring the *Rusland* safely across the North Atlantic and to her pier in New York had been done. The procedures of her captain could not be faulted, and all her passengers and their baggage had been saved. Even the ship might not have been lost if the *Rusland* had not had the misfortune to strand on top of another, earlier wreck instead of the soft sands which lay everywhere about her.

Chapter 7

THE GRACEFUL *CITY OF BRUSSELS* AND THE DEADLY FOG OF THE IRISH SEA

January 7, 1883

In the 1860s and 1870s the Liverpool, New York & Philadelphia Steam Ship Company, universally known by its nickname the Inman Line, was one of the major maritime enterprises on the North Atlantic. It remains one of the most famous and celebrated of all the great nineteenth-century steamship lines carrying on the trade between Europe and America. While the primary route served was from Liverpool to Philadelphia and New York, feeder services from the Continent, such as the port of Antwerp, resulted in a wider casting of the net for cargo and passengers.

The origin of the line lies with William Inman of Leicester, England, who was born on April 6, 1825,[1] and was the fourth son of Charles Inman, a partner in the freight distribution firm of Pickford and Company, and his wife, Jane Clay Inman. The elder Inman retired from Pickford and moved to Liverpool, where William Inman grew up and was educated. He attended the Collegiate Institute at Liverpool and the Liverpool Royal Institution. Upon leaving school, William

Inman served as a clerk to Nathan Cairns, then moved on to Cater & Company and, finally, to one of the leading Liverpool ship-brokering firms, Richardson Brothers & Company. Richardson Brothers (Liverpool) was a joint owner, with Richardson, Watson & Company of Philadelphia and New York, of a regular line of sailing packets trading between Philadelphia and Liverpool.[2]

In 1850 Inman was the driving force behind the formation of the Liverpool & Philadelphia Steam Ship Company, which always was known as the Inman Line in his honor. The company bought the new passenger liner *City of Glasgow* (1850; 1,609 tons, 227 feet, nine knots), which made her maiden voyage from Liverpool to Philadelphia on December 11, 1850. The original accommodations for 52 first- and 85 second-class passengers were increased to 130 first with the combining of the private cabin rooms, supplemented by the addition of 400 third-class or steerage berths. Prior to this it had been said that first-class passengers would never travel on a ship carrying steerage class, but Inman thought differently and proved the naysayers wrong. Unfortunately the *City of Glasgow* sailed from Liverpool with 480 passengers and crew on March 1, 1854, and was never heard from again.

The Inman Line continued operations with a fleet of liners, many bearing "City of" as part of their names. In 1853 with the outbreak of the Crimean War between the Ottoman Empire, Britain, and France versus Russia, virtually every passenger liner on the North Atlantic could command a high figure on the charter market. Inman's Quaker partners wanted nothing to do with a wartime charter and sold out their interest in the company, permitting him to make several very advantageous charters to the French government. The Inman flag was removed from the North Atlantic for sixteen months until the war was over in 1856. The American terminal of the Inman Line was switched to New York from Philadelphia in 1857, and the name of the line changed to the Liverpool, New York, & Philadelphia Steam Ship Company.

As the result of obtaining a subsidy from the British government to carry the mails in 1868, the Inman Line ordered from Tod &

McGregor, Glasgow, a new liner that was launched as the *City of Brussels* on August 10, 1869. She was one of the largest in the world at 3,081 tons with a length of 390 feet and a speed of fourteen knots. The *City of Brussels* had accommodations for two hundred cabin-class passengers and six hundred steerage passengers, later (1872) increased to one thousand. She was the first passenger liner in the world to have steam steering gear and ultimately gained the Blue Riband of the Atlantic for the fastest crossing in December 1869 at a speed of 14.70 knots over a 2,771-mile course (Sandy Hook–Queenstown).

The Blue Riband of the Atlantic customarily was held by the liner completing the fastest transatlantic crossing in terms of speed, and the earliest use of the term appears to date to 1892.[3] In the second half of the nineteenth century the passage time often was reduced by minutes, rather than hours. The fact that the *City of Brussels* bested by nine hours the record of the Cunard paddle-wheeler *Scotia* (1862; 3,871 tons, 379 feet, 14 knots), which in December 1863 had thrashed her way across from New York to Queenstown in eight days, five hours, forty-two minutes, was regarded as truly remarkable. Never again would the Blue Riband be held by a paddle-wheel vessel since propeller-driven ships proved so much faster and more reliable. The *City of Brussels,* with the record crossing of seven days, twenty hours, thirty minutes, became the first ship to cross the North Atlantic in under eight days. This greatly redounded to the fame of the Inman Line and enhanced the popularity of the *City of Brussels.* When the *Baltic* of White Star beat the record in November 1873, it was with a speed of 15.09 knots, which equaled a faster crossing of only twenty-four minutes.

The accommodations of the *City of Brussels* were improved in 1872 by the addition of an iron promenade deck in order to keep pace with the newer White Star ships; it also increased her tonnage to 3,747 tons. In 1876 she again was sent back to her builders to have her machinery replaced with the much cheaper and more efficient compound engines. A compound engine permitted more than one utilization of the steam power generated in the boilers and made it possible for the ship to travel

The City of Brussels *(1869) was the first passenger liner to cross the North Atlantic in less than eight days, in December 1869. On January 7, 1883, the* City of Brussels *was waiting off the entrance of the Mersey River, England, for the fog to lift, when she was rammed by the* Kirby Hall *(1883) and sank with a loss of ten lives.*

either faster or a much greater distance on the same amount of fuel. In many ways the invention and popularization of the compound engine after 1859 made possible steamship routes spanning the world.

The *City of Brussels* remained one of the most popular vessels on the North Atlantic throughout her fourteen-year career. On December 28, 1882, she sailed from New York for Liverpool, England, via Queenstown, Ireland, to drop the transatlantic mails. This was her normal homeward voyage. She was under the command of Captain Frank S. Land, who had been with the Inman Line for many years. He had risen through the Inman ranks and earned his first command in 1876. The chief engineer was James Tod, who had been with the Inman Line for more than sixteen years and was regarded as an exceedingly competent individual. His brother, David Tod, was the principal partner in the British shipbuilding firm of the Tod & McGregor Company, Glasgow, which had built the *City of Brussels.*

Captain Land brought his command safely into Queenstown on January 6 at 8:00 P.M. and landed the bulk of the transatlantic mails and a few of her passengers bound for Irish destinations. The mails would be transferred by fast Irish trains and Irish Sea ferries to English trains, which would deliver the precious letters to their British destinations while the *City of Brussels* was still attempting to reach her dock in Liverpool. As the Inman liner steamed up the Irish Sea toward the Mersey estuary and her destination, Liverpool, a thick fog set in, reducing visibility to zero. When the liner neared the vicinity of the Northwest Lightship around 6:00 A.M. on Saturday, Captain Land decided to lay to and wait for conditions to improve. Steam was kept up in order to take advantage of the first favorable development, and a careful lookout was kept on the bridge consisting of Captain Land and his second and fourth officers. The pilot was also on board, and extra men were stationed around the open decks of the liner. According to Inman regulations and usual navigation procedure, bells were kept ringing and the foghorns were frequently sounded.

For some time the *City of Brussels* lay safely in the thick fogbank. Suddenly the ominous low gurgling sound of water passing down the side of an approaching vessel was heard. She was very near and still under way in the thick fog. To the horror of Captain Land, his officers and crew, a large steamer loomed out of the fog and without any opportunity for evasive action slammed into the *City of Brussels* forward of the bridge. The bow of the *Kirby Hall* sank into the Inman liner so far that she almost cut off the bow. The point of impact could not have been worse because it crushed the bulkhead between two large forward compartments and doomed the *City of Brussels.* The *Kirby Hall* backed off and disappeared into the fog almost immediately. Even if she had stayed, she would have been of little assistance because she was on her maiden voyage from her builders to Liverpool and had an absolutely minimum skeletal crew on board. The balance of her crew was due to join her at Liverpool with her cargo of coal and passengers for a voyage to the Far East. The captain of the *Kirby Hall* said that he did not even have enough sailors on board even to lower his own lifeboats.

Captain Land marshaled his officers and crew and exercised great presence of mind and coolness in seeing to his passengers. Even after the collision some of the passengers seemed unconscious of the gravity of the situation and the terrible gap in the forward part of the vessel. It was realized that the *City of Brussels* was taking on water rapidly as she began to settle in the water. Passengers and crew were mustered to their lifeboat stations without hurry or confusion. Lifeboats were provided, the boats were swung out, and every preparation was smoothly made in connection with the emergency. Some of the passengers even returned to their beds after the collision, thinking that nothing was wrong. Cabin stewards rousted them out with cries of "Man the boats." The passengers were helped into the boats with some of the crew assigned to man each boat. "As one of the seamen said to a correspondent, 'It was the coolest thing you ever saw in this world.' "[4] Supposedly Captain Land reacted with fury when one individual jumped into a lifeboat ahead of time and had him yanked out of the boat to await his turn. The captain and the remainder of the men stayed on board until the safety of all the passengers was assured. Those of the crew who had no place in the lifeboats climbed into the rigging to await the end.

A number of the lifeboats from the *City of Brussels* pulled back near their ship in order to be available to save as many more lives as possible. However, it was thought that they should not get too close to the sinking liner lest they be sucked under when she went down. When the bow sank so low that the waters reached the bridge, Captain Land hollered out for every man to save himself and jumped into the water. Shortly thereafter, only about twenty minutes after the collision, the *City of Brussels* gave a tremendous lurch, flinging off those in the rigging, as she plunged into the depths with a fearful swirl. The scene in the cold waters of the Irish Sea was desperate. People were struggling in the water, and the darkness of the winter night had not lifted, making the situation even more horrifying. The boats of the *City of Brussels* picked up all they could. One of those individuals was Captain Land, who was found clinging to a spar from his ship. As the fog lifted around 5:00

P.M., the lifeboats made for the *Kirby Hall,* which emerged from the mist a short distance away. As the first lifeboats neared the freighter, the purser shouted that they should send some boats at once. The captain of the *Kirby Hall* responded that he only had five or six seamen on board, his bow was stove in, and he could part with no one even if he could find a means of lowering a lifeboat. Slowly and carefully the passengers and crew reached the deck of the freighter. When all were mustered on the deck of the *Kirby Hall,* it was learned that two Italian immigrant passengers were missing, and eight members of the crew, including Second Officer Young and Carpenter Woods, whose bodies later were recovered. It was said that the missing passengers may have leaped overboard from the liner before they could be rescued. The missing crew members may have been struck by spars and rigging when the ship went down and lost their lives as a result. The *Kirby Hall* searched the area for several hours without success and then proceeded on to Liverpool, where she arrived at ten o'clock in the evening and landed the survivors. It was reported that the *Kirby Hall* lay at the Morpeth Dock with her damage all above the waterline. Her owners lodged a claim for thirty thousand dollars in damages against the insurers. The Inman Line claimed at least eight hundred thousand dollars for the *City of Brussels* from its insurers exclusive of cargo or passenger losses.

The passengers drew up a memorial. "We, who have just been rescued from a watery grave, wish to express our sincere gratitude, and admiration of the courage, promptitude, and coolness in danger exemplified by the Captain, purser, and other officers of the ill-fated vessel, which has just gone down so near the termination of her voyage."[5]

The ill-fated *City of Brussels* lay at the bottom of the channel in the approach to the port of Liverpool with her masts and funnel top sticking out of the water. Officers of the Mersey Dock Board and of the Liverpool Salvage Association immediately visited the scene. To them it was obvious that there was no hope of raising the hull, but if they were lucky, it might be possible to save a portion of the cargo. Salvage would be dependent on the weather. Meanwhile divers were at work removing the masts and funnel, which were regarded as first-class obstacles to navigation in the Mersey estuary. The cargo list revealed the *City of Brussels* was carrying 783 bales of cotton, 146 bales of hops, 4,027 boxes of bacon, 2,448 boxes of cheese, 55 cases of beef, 26 tierces of pork, 70 barrels of pork, 250 barrels of apples, 32 barrels of oysters, 173 bags of flour, 70 tubs of butter, 254 bags of clover seed, 83 casks of salted sealskins, 122 cases of tobacco, and about 100 miscellaneous packages.[6] The cargo was said to be worth $350,000, and the insurance on the cargo was reported to be between $75,000 to $100,000 held by various Boston insurance firms.

The *Times* of London was scathing in its assessment of the disaster. "If vessels manned and equipped as the *Kirby Hall* was are sent on trial trips, it is no wonder collisions and wrecks occur."[7] The captain of the *Kirby Hall* claimed he had stopped all engines upon hearing the foghorns of another vessel and that the force of the tide carried his vessel on at a rate sufficient to cut the *City of Brussels* nearly in two. Not everyone accepted his explanation. There also was a general outcry for the creation and enforcement of watertight compartment regulations. As the *New York Times* editorialized, "The company which first takes this means of protecting its ships will be abundantly repaid by the confidence with which it will inspire the travelling public."[8] The British courts were going to have a busy time. The *Kirby Hall* ultimately was found at fault, and her captain censored for proceeding at excessive speed in dense fog. There also was considerable adverse comment about owners' permitting a vessel to leave a shipyard on her maiden voyage with nothing more than a skeleton crew on board.

Chapter 8

THE LOSS OF THE CUNARD LINER *OREGON*

March 14, 1886

The Cunard Line normally ordered its own ships for the important first-class service of the line from Liverpool to New York, but in 1884 a vessel that simply was too magnificent to ignore came on the market. She was the brand-new *Oregon* of the Guion Line, and she was to be both a transatlantic record breaker and a part of the first-class service of the Cunard Line for a brief two years.

The Liverpool & Great Western Steamship Company Ltd. was better known as the Guion Line in honor of its American founder, Stephen Barker Guion (1819–1885). At an early age Guion was a partner in the New York firm of Williams & Guion, which managed the old Black Star Line of fast sailing packets between New York and Liverpool. Guion had many associates and friends in Liverpool, and in 1851 he moved to England, where he soon established a major passenger agency, Guion & Company, which for a while even handled all the Cunard business. At times in the 1850s, in the aftermath of the Irish Famine, Guion's ships carried a thousand emigrants a week from Liverpool to America during the summer season.

Starting in 1866, Guion built some very fine ships, and he was expert in the mass movement of passengers in the immigrant trade. His line experienced hard times adapting to the trade depressions of the 1870s and 1880s. His death in 1885 removed a strong figure from the management of the Guion Line. Attempting to strengthen its position in 1883, the Guion Line ordered from the John Elder yard on the Clyde a record breaker to join its earlier successes, *Arizona* (1879; 5,147 tons, 450 feet, 15 knots) and *Alaska* (1881; 6,932 tons, 500 feet, 16 knots). The new liner was launched as the *Oregon* (1883; 7,375 tons, 501 feet, 18 knots) with a capacity for 340 in first, 92 interchangeable, 110 in third, and 1,000 in steerage. She was a four-masted steamer with two enormous smokestacks, and her main deck sloped very gradually from stem to stern. Somewhat incredibly, after the Inman fiasco with the *City of Rome* (1881; 8,415 tons, 560 feet, 16 knots) two years before, it was agreed that the new liner could be constructed of iron instead of the much lighter steel. The *City of Rome* originally was to have been of steel construction and designed to be fast enough to take back the Blue Riband for the Inman Line. In the end, owing to a shortage of steel, she had been built of iron, which greatly reduced her carrying power, and she had plowed across the North Atlantic at a much slower speed than the rivals she had been built to beat. The Inman Line management threw up its hands over the *City of Rome* after six months and returned the largest ship in the world to her builders for failing to meet the contract specifications.

When the Guion Line agreed to a new liner with an iron hull, it looked as though no one had learned anything, but a superior hull design would make the difference. The *Oregon* was one of the largest ships in the world when commissioned and took her maiden voyage from Liverpool, via Queenstown, to New York on October 6, 1883. She appeared to be an instant success and, after settling down, produced a record-breaking crossing in April 1884 as she steamed from Sandy Hook to Queenstown at an average speed of 18.09 knots, besting the record times of the *Arizona* and *Alaska.*

No expense had been spared by the Guion Line in the appointments of the new liner. Her Grand Saloon in particular was magnificent. Forward of the engines it ran for a length of sixty-five feet and stretched the width of the ship (fifty-four feet). "It was laid with a parqueterie floor, and its fittings were luxurious. The ceiling decorations were in white and gold; the panels were of polished satinwood, and the pilasters were of walnut, with gilt capitals. A cupola, 25 feet long and 15 feet wide, rose 20 feet from the centre of the saloon ceiling, and this was topped with a skylight which could be kept open for ventilation in the stormiest weather."[1] Her staterooms were large and well lighted, and she was provided with Edison incandescent electric lights throughout the ship, a relatively new feature. The wood used in the finishing of the Ladies' Drawing Room had been especially selected in the state of Oregon, for which the ship was named, and shipped to Scotland for incorporation into the liner. The Gentlemen's Smoking Room was finished in Spanish mahogany and had a mosaic floor.

However, the handwriting was on the wall because of the economic depression which had depressed passenger and freight traffic. The Guion Line found it impossible to make the huge payments to her builders that its contract required. The Cunard Line stepped in and bought the *Oregon* at an advantageous price. This removed a major financial liability from the ledgers of the Guion Line in a time of economic adversity but also lost it its transatlantic record breaker one month after her triumphant crossing. This must have been a bitter pill to swallow.

The *Oregon* sailed under the Cunard flag for the first time on June 7, 1884, in the same service for which she had been built (Liverpool–Queenstown–New York). Shortly thereafter she produced another record crossing in August 1884, giving Cunard the Blue Riband of the Atlantic as the result of its Guion purchase.

In 1885, when war clouds loomed with Russia over the control of Afghanistan and the passes through the Himalayan mountains to India, the British government chartered a number of major transatlantic liners, including the *Oregon,* for service as armed merchant cruisers. Only the *Oregon* actually was fitted out and commissioned as a cruiser and joined Royal Navy units in Bantry Bay, Ireland, during July 1885. Officially she was described as a dispatch boat with the responsibility for carrying messages in a day and an age before wireless communication. As such she was a rather large dispatch boat, being one of the largest liners in the world, but her speed at over eighteen knots was the critical factor here. Knowledge was power particularly with regard to the character, nature, and position of an imperial Russian fleet if it should enter the North Atlantic to prey on British merchant shipping. When a peaceful settlement of the Afghan troubles was achieved by diplomatic means, the armed merchant cruiser was returned to the Cunard Line in the fall of 1885. She was refitted for commercial use and took her first postwar sailing on November 14, 1885, in the normal first-class service from Liverpool to New York. Rumors had it that she was scheduled to be transferred to a greatly enhanced Boston–Liverpool service of the Cunard Line in May 1886.

The *Oregon* pulled away from the Liverpool Landing Stage promptly at ten o'clock on Saturday morning, March 6, 1886. She was carrying a heavy complement of passengers for a late-winter crossing in that she had 186 first-class, 66 intermediate, and 395 steerage passengers on board. Her crew numbered 205 for this crossing, for a total of 852 persons on board. She also was carrying approximately 575 bags of mail as the official Royal Mail vessel taking the prestigious Saturday sailing. The *Oregon* was under the command of Captain Philip Cottler, one of the younger masters of a Cunard ship at the age of forty-five. He had been at sea most of his life and a captain for twenty years, although he had been with Cunard for only seven years. He was highly respected to hold the position he did.

Captain Cottler later reported that the *Oregon* had enjoyed fine weather all the way across in a very pleasurable crossing. The last night out considerable baggage had been brought up to the deck in order to expedite unloading in New York. Everything was peaceful, and the 12,000-horsepower engines were driving the *Oregon* at full speed for New

York. Chief Officer William George Matthews was in charge of the bridge. Matthews, forty years old, had been at sea for twenty-five years and with Cunard for eleven. This was his fourth voyage on the *Oregon.* He had come on duty at 4:00 A.M. and was on the starboard side while the fourth officer was on the port side. Three men were on lookout, two on the turtleback, and one on the forepart of the promenade deck. Suddenly at about 4:30 A.M. the majestic, but horrifying, sails of a schooner were seen bearing down on the *Oregon* at a distance of only about thirty to forty yards away. The lookouts screamed a warning to the bridge, but there was little time to take any action as the sailing ship sank her bow into the *Oregon* for the first time a few feet forward of the bridge. Captain Cottler was in his cabin sleeping when the schooner loomed out of the darkness and rammed the liner with a tremendous bang. Subsequently at least one additional hole was made in the side of the *Oregon* before the vessels parted. Matthews described the ramming as a "glancing blow," but Captain Cottler later commented, "There was not much glancing about it."[2] Matthews, who already had ordered a turn to port, immediately ordered the engines stopped, but the single huge propeller continued to turn for a while. The combination of the turn to port and the ramming caused the *Oregon* to turn around in a full circle so that she ended up with her bow facing toward the east away from New York. The identity of the sailing vessel remains unknown to the present day, but it is suspected that she was the *Charles Morse,* which went missing about that time. It is also thought that the schooner herself was mortally wounded by the ramming, which probably split her bow and caused her subsequently to sink without a trace.

The damage to the *Oregon* amidships was described as large enough to drive a horse and carriage through. Captain Cottler heard the engine room telegraph and rushed on deck. Finding some confusion, he restored order, took command of the bridge, and immediately began preparations to get the passengers safely away in the lifeboats. In the confusion some said that all the passengers were awakened by the shock of the collision and rushed on deck, while others said that many slept through the ramming and had to be awakened by stewards. At the

The Cunard liner Oregon *(1884), the fastest ship on the North Atlantic with a speed of eighteen knots, wallows dead in the water on March 14, 1886, and is slowly sinking after being rammed in the dead of the night by an unknown schooner off Long Island. The pilot boat* Fantome *laboriously makes sail with a full load of rescued passengers toward the approaching North German Lloyd liner* Fulda *(1883).*

beginning Captain Cottler did not think she would sink, but she was taking on an enormous amount of water. The hull of the *Oregon* was divided into watertight compartments, but nothing designed to preserve her from so tremendous a gash in her side. Her pumps were manned, but in no way could keep abreast of the inrushing Atlantic. Captain Cottler also made the observation that since there was no sign anywhere of the vessel that had rammed them, she must have gone to the bottom immediately.

The *Oregon*'s position was about fifteen miles from New York and northwest of Watch Hill, Long Island. In the early hours of the morning off Long Island it soon became apparent to Cottler that the *Oregon* would not survive the collision. The only question was how much time they had before she sank. In his dramatic recounting of the events he said: "When I found that the vessel was sinking I took the necessary steps to save our passengers. We first sent up rockets as signals of distress. Then the boats were lowered, but before 8 o'clock Pilot Boat No. 11 hove in sight. She came up to us between 7 and 8 o'clock, and two hours later the schooner *Fannie A. Gorham,* of Belfast, Me., Captain Mahoney, hove to."[3]

The passengers commented: "We were somewhat anxious on board, not withstanding the assurance given us by the officers that we were in the path of vessels which would surely pick us up before nightfall."[4] The shivering crowd on the deck was greatly relieved to see the two sailing vessels even if they were quite small for the job at hand. Captain Cottler went on the bridge, where he could be heard and seen better, and told the passengers: "Here's a pilot boat, and there will be other boats here soon. I think the *Oregon* is safe, but I want to be sure of the safety of everybody. I want you to go on board the pilot boat or into the lifeboats for about half an hour until we can assure ourselves of the situation."[5] The temperature was thirty-two degrees, and only the absence of a breeze saved the ill-dressed group from much greater distress. Nonetheless, no one must have been thrilled about transferring to the relatively small lifeboats from the broad deck of the *Oregon.* Yet all did obey Captain Cottler and follow his direction.

One group that obeyed their captain with a shade too much enthusiasm was a group of firemen from the *Oregon* who had narrowly escaped death in the blinding steam immediately after the collision. They seized the initiative and clambered into the first lifeboat to leave ahead of any passengers. A sailor tried to beat them off with a belaying pin but failed. Then one elderly gentleman from Chicago reportedly drew his pistol and shouted at the firemen that if they did not return at once, he would shoot them. According to him, they obeyed, and an additional sixteen passengers were put into the lifeboat. The undisciplined action of the firemen did not receive favorable comment, but it was brief-lived and did not represent the beginning of a general crew panic. Captain Cottler soon reasserted control, and the rest of the abandon ship procedure went off smoothly. One first-class passenger commented that if he had come as close to sudden death as the firemen had, he might have reacted in the same manner.

A heroic effort was made to stem the flow of water into the *Oregon.* A sailor by the name of John Huston went with the Second Officer Peter Hood and the ship's carpenter to try to close the huge holes that the schooner had punched into the ship's side. Mattresses, pillows, and huge spreads of canvas were let down over the side of the *Oregon* in an effort to block the inward flow of the Atlantic. The idea was to hold the canvas in place by chains and toggles, but this proved very difficult. The seawater in early March was close to freezing, and the risk of hypothermia acute. Nevertheless, Seaman Huston stripped off his clothes and dived into the icy dark sea in an effort to secure the canvas over the hole. The danger to him was not just from the freezing water but also from the risk of being sucked into the sinking ship. Three times Huston dived beneath the surface and wrestled with the heavy chains and canvas but to no avail. His courage was remarkable, and only the direct orders of Second Officer Hood to the half-frozen sailor not to do it again stopped him from a fourth attempt.

The delicate process of transferring the passengers and crew was made even more difficult by the pronounced list to the starboard that the liner had taken. The first lifeboats made for the pilot boat *Fantome* and transferred their passengers to her until she was totally full. The ten empty lifeboats of the liner returned to the *Oregon* and took off additional passengers and crew. In addition, four rafts were launched with some difficulty from the sinking ship and provided supplemental lifesaving capacity, which was not intolerable since the seas were so calm. One passenger commented:

> I was among the passengers who were taken off before the pilot boat came alongside and furnished temporary shelter for part of us. From there we saw other passengers taken from the sinking vessel, and our hearts sank

when we saw that over half the passengers and crew were left behind, and it seemed that no possibility of succor remained. The suspense was simply horrible, while minutes seemed to grow into hours and hours into years before Providence sent to the rescue of those remaining behind the schooner *Fannie A. Gorham.* She, too, was loaded until there was no room to squeeze another person on her deck. Then the officers and crew and a few of the brave passengers who remained to the last filled the boats and the life raft, and we all drifted about waiting to see the beautiful steamer go to the bottom as we knew she must. Her gorgeous cabins were not half so inviting to us as the homely vessels whose decks now stood between us and death. The Pilot Boat No.11 is now in my eyes the handsomest craft in the world.[6]

As Captain Cottler said, "The passengers and crew of the *Oregon* were transferred to the pilot boat and the schooner in our own boats. Four hundred were placed on the pilot boat and the balance, about 500, on board the schooner."[7] All the passengers had been transferred by eleven o'clock, and the two rescue vessels indeed were crammed full of humanity and very low in the sea, which happily remained placid.

Seaman Huston's heroism was not over for the day. As he sat shivering in one of the lifeboats with a dry coat over him, several passengers hurrying to get into other lifeboats slipped and fell into the Atlantic. Two of those plunged into the sea were the young son and daughter of an emigrant, Andrew McNab. The boy and girl drifted some distance from the *Oregon* as passengers screamed, and the children's lives seemed lost. Huston, seeing the situation, threw off his coat and, although still half frozen from his earlier efforts, dived into the sea, and swam to the two children. He managed to grab them and tow them back to one of the waiting lifeboats, where they were pulled to safety. Subsequently Huston also pulled from the sea an elderly man who had fallen overboard while trying to board another lifeboat. Huston's record that day was well above the call of duty, particularly given the icy nature of the water. He was the outstanding hero of the *Oregon* disaster.

The passengers showed their gratitude to the captain and crew of the two rescue vessels. A subscription of one hundred pounds (five hundred dollars) was presented to Captain Mahoney of the Maine schooner *Fannie A. Gorham,* who was described as a "down East Yankee." A sum of about sixty pounds (three hundred dollars) was presented to the captain of the pilot boat *Fantome* for him and his crew.

The distress rockets which were fired from the deck of the *Oregon* brilliantly lighted the heavens and were clearly seen against the starry sky since there was no fog. Nevertheless, a large outward-bound steamer ignored the rockets and the guns and continued eastward without stopping. Captain Cottler later made the observation that he thought it was a National Line ship, but he could not be positive. Distress signals did not always bring the desired response from passing ships intent upon their schedules.

Distress flags were run up the mast as soon as sunrise made it possible for passing ships to see them. At this point, to the relief of all concerned, the first-class North German Lloyd liner *Fulda* (1883; 4,816 tons, 430 feet, 16 knots) under the command of Captain Ringk and inward-bound to New York appeared on the scene. The captain brought his liner as close to the two sailing vessels and the lifeboats as possible, while they maneuvered as close to the *Fulda* as they could, and the delicate job of retransferring the survivors to the big German ship began immediately. The Atlantic Ocean remained as flat as a ballroom floor according to observers, incalculably adding to the smoothness of the effort. As the transfer to the *Fulda* was under way, the *Oregon* finally took on so much water that she went down, bow first, in twenty-two fathoms of water. A passenger later said:

> She lay there seemingly in a struggle for life against the waters trying to engulf her. Five minutes before she sank the great vessel rocked backward and forward and rolled from side to side, a great helpless mass. Then, as her bow dipped, the great waves rolled over her, and the slender foremast gave way and swayed to one side. Then the prow rose for the

last time. It stood well up in the air for an instant and then, with a sort of spring from her keel as if preparing for a dive, the bow cut its way down into the waves she could not longer ride. There was a swirl of waters. Her dive was continued and the heavy stern swung well up, so that we almost could see her keel. Down she went head first, and the blades of the great propeller were thrown high and clear of the water. They, too, went down in the great gulf and the water boiled and bubbled and gurgled and lashed itself into a great mass of foam. We had seen the last of the *Oregon*.[8]

When she sank, she touched bottom so gently that some of her masts remained upright, soaring out of the Atlantic Ocean to mark the site until a couple of changes of the tide took them down.

The Fire Island Signal Station early in the day notified the Cunard agent in New York City, Vernon H. Brown, that the *Oregon* apparently was in distress fairly near to shore. When he received the telegram, Brown, noted for his competency, immediately went down to the Cunard Line piers and chartered three tugs to head for Sandy Hook in order to do whatever was necessary. The Cunard liner *Aurania* (1883; 7,269 tons, 470 feet, 16 knots) was still lying at her pier because of fog in the harbor, and Brown sailed on her at 2:00 P.M. Off Sandy Hook Brown ordered one of the tugs to be signaled for, and he transferred to her. The captain of the *Aurania* was ordered to cruise within twenty-five miles southeast of Fire Island to see if he could discover anything of the *Oregon* or any of the people who might have taken to the boats. Her orders were to take the *Oregon* in tow if she was found afloat and bring her back to New York. After a prescribed time the *Aurania* was to feel free to continue on her crossing to Liverpool.

Late in the afternoon Brown returned to his office in New York, where he could be at the center of any developments. Meanwhile Mr. Taylor, third officer of the *Oregon*, came onshore at Moriches, Long Island, and sent Brown a telegram officially informing him of the loss of the liner. He told Brown that the *Oregon* had been rammed by an unknown vessel between Shinnecock and Fire Island and that all passengers and crew had been rescued. Of course Brown wanted to know more details, but by the time his reply reached Moriches, Taylor had gone back down to the beach, and there was no way to reach him.

The crew members who had rowed Third Officer Taylor to shore had quite an adventure. Jack O'Brien, Jack Fowler, and Tom Lacy were three sailors from the *Oregon* assigned to Taylor's lifeboat. Pilot William Parker of Pilot Boat No. 11 volunteered to accompany them as a guide, and they set off with orders to land Taylor at the nearest point from which he could send a telegram to Agent Brown. As they neared the Long Island shore, the surf was so bad that when one of the Life-Saving Service patrols saw them, it launched a surfboat, which met the lifeboat offshore and brought Third Officer Taylor ashore. When he returned to the beach after sending the telegram, the surf was worse, and he could not be returned to the lifeboat. The three sailors and the pilot then set sail for New York on their own. There was a high wind, and they were not able to make much headway for much of the day. As they drifted along, they were encountered by a Philadelphia-bound collier, which picked them up and turned around to take them to the Sandy Hook Lightship. There they rested a bit and then set out in the lifeboat for New York Harbor again. At 2:00 A.M. they were overhauled by the Swedish bark *Herold,* which was being piloted in by Captain Russell of Pilot Boat No. 2, and they finally came up the harbor about 8:00 A.M. The trio of Cunard sailors reached the Cunard pier in midmorning, signed in, and were sent over to the Sailors' Home, where they received a joyous welcome from some of their colleagues who had thought them lost. A square meal was particularly welcome because they only "had two jolly meals off a barrel of crackers and a keg of water that were in the ship's boat."[9]

Intending to spend the night awaiting additional information, Brown went to the Cunard Line pier at the foot of Clarkson Street. There he received a dispatch from Sandy Hook saying that the lifesaving crew had boarded the *Fulda,* which had anchored outside the bar, and that the German liner had approximately eight hundred passengers and crew on board. Everyone had been rescued from the *Oregon* even if they had lost virtually everything except their lives. Captain Cottler was the last person to leave the stricken liner and joined Surgeon McMaster and the ship's carpenter in the last lifeboat to get away before the liner sank.

Captain Mahoney of the *Fannie A. Gorham,* a no-nonsense man, continued on his way as soon as his unexpected passengers had been transferred to the *Fulda.* He had sailed from Jacksonville and was bound for Boston. On the *Fulda,* which was carrying 56 cabin-class passengers but had capacity for 250, 851 additional passengers and crew were accommodated wherever possible. Women and children were placed in any available cabin and in every square inch of the public rooms. Nonetheless, many male passengers and crew members had to remain on the open deck and seek refuge from the cold wherever they could. Passengers on the *Fulda* broke out what clothing they could from their luggage to meet the needs of those who had been rescued with scant attire.

Reporters from the *New York Times* hitched a ride on the mail boat *William Fletcher,* which went out to meet the *Fulda,* and achieved a newspaper reporting coup with firsthand interviews and commentary. The postal officials on the *William Fletcher* said that everyone on the *Fulda* seemed in relatively good spirits. The loss of between 500 and 600 bags of mail when the *Oregon* went down represented nearly half of all the mail from Great Britain to the United States in any given week. The registered mail was considered the most valuable, and of 2,400 pieces dispatched on the *Oregon,* only 94 reached the New York Post Office, and it had originated in France, Italy, Sweden, and Russia. All the British registered mail was lost as well as that from South Africa, Germany, Denmark, Switzerland, Belgium, and Portugal. The total number of mailbags on board involved approximately 260 bags of letter mail for the United States and Canada and 470 bags of newspaper mail. When evaluating mail losses, it is always important to realize that a substantial proportion of virtually every mail represented newspapers and journals so that not all mail losses by any means meant letters. Nevertheless the mail losses on the *Oregon* were substantial, and the communication gap took months to resolve as private citizens and businesses realized that their letters were at the bottom of the Atlantic.

The *Oregon* herself was valued at $1,250,000, and her cargo at an additional $700,000, while passenger baggage losses were placed at $216,000. One of the largest items lost was an estimated $1,000,000 in bank bills and coupons, bringing the total to $3,166,000. The losses also involved two magpies belonging to a man from Chicago, but three dogs—a terrier, a bulldog, and a Skye terrier—were saved.

Through the courage and foresight of the *Oregon*'s purser, a very large shipment of diamonds bound for New York jewelers had been rescued from the ship's safe. It was said that there were some frantic individuals in the diamond district of Lower Broadway when it was thought the Cunard liner had gone down with one of the major spring shipments of precious stones. The *Oregon* was estimated to have several hundred thousand dollars in diamonds on board when she left Liverpool. Since the diamonds usually were consigned directly to the purser and were in small packages, the New York dealers devoutly hoped the purser had done his duty and saved the gems inasmuch as the *Oregon* had taken nearly eight hours to sink. They were not reassured until they heard from him on the *Fulda* that he had their shipments in his care. The fact that they could not claim the jewels from American customs until new paper work arrived from Europe was a relatively small concern.[10]

In the smoking room on the *Fulda* Captain Cottler held an impromptu news conference during which he gave unstinting praise to Captain Ringk and the crew of the German liner who had taken all survivors on board over a period of less than two hours with such dispatch and smoothness. The women passengers rescued from the *Oregon* were given three cheers in their absence by the assembled men for their courage and fortitude. No one had fainted or become hysterical, and until the end all had kept their courage up splendidly. A reporter asked:

"The passengers lost all their baggage, I suppose?" The question brought a roar of laughter from the men. "Captain Cottler pointed to several of those who sat around him. They were in wonderful attire and to a man could not boast of a full suit of clothes. 'Tell the Custom House officers when you return to New York,' said one of variegated attire, 'that it will be entirely unnecessary to examine our baggage when we land.'"[11] Everything was at the bottom of the sea.

The *Fulda* dropped the 395 steerage passengers from the *Oregon* at Castle Garden, where they arrived in America penniless and destitute. A representative of the Cunard Line visited Castle Garden and instructed the officials there to feed the immigrants at the expense of the line. This was noted in the newspapers as an act of magnanimity on the part of the Cunard Line. The majority of the immigrants were from England, Ireland, and Scandinavia. If the immigrants had lost their railroad tickets to the West when their luggage went down with the *Oregon,* these were reissued to them. However, to their sorrow they were informed that the Cunard Line bore no responsibility for their luggage, and they would not be reimbursed for those losses. In many instances this meant everything they possessed in the world. Within twenty-four hours most were cleared through immigration and, thankful to be alive, proceeded on to their destinations.

When the *Fulda* made her way to the North German Lloyd docks at Hoboken, New Jersey, shortly after 7:00 A.M. on Monday, March 15, 1886, the rescue ship was greeted by a crowd of well-wishers. As a reporter noted, "It was in the matter of dress, however, that the motley procession represented its most curious phase. At first glance it seemed as if not more than one-third of the shipwrecked persons were clad in their previous garments. Some of the men and women were scantily attired, and others were bundled up in wraps much too large for them. Some of the men wore coats that were too small and trousers that were too short, and some of the women appeared to have left the greater portion of a woman's usual wearing apparel on the sunken steamer. These conspicuous indications of haste and carelessness in dress conveyed to the minds of the on-lookers a quick sense of the dangers to which the *Oregon*'s passengers and crew had been exposed."[12]

Disembarkation was relatively swift because as one observer noted, "Why, there isn't a silk hat or a gripsack in the party."[13] Every one of the first-class and second-class passengers had lost nearly everything when the *Oregon* sank. None had been permitted to return to their cabin to rescue anything once they were on deck after the accident. Captain Cottler had been too concerned about when the *Oregon* might go down to let anyone belowdecks again. They soon organized a committee to approach the Cunard Line for redress but were informed that unless the *Oregon* was found at fault, there was little possibility that the line would reimburse them for anything. The amount in question was substantial; one gentleman claimed a loss of $4,000, and another of $2,000. The average loss suffered by each of the 251 first- and second-class passengers was estimated to be $750, and of the 395 steerage passengers, about $50 each. The officer's uniforms that went down with the ship were valued at $100 per man and the seaman's kit at $20 per man. The total of $216,000 was thought to be rather low.

The surviving passengers from the *Oregon* were not slow to assess blame for the collision as soon as they recovered from the shock of the disaster and their subsequent rescue. Since the night was clear, and visibility excellent, outspoken passengers failed to see any reason except "gross carelessness" for the loss of the *Oregon*.[14] First Officer Matthews, who had been in command on the bridge, initially was not available to anyone for a statement or cross-examination, although Agent Brown later let him meet the press after careful coaching on what to say.

Captain Cottler, who had been asleep at the time of the collision, stated that the schooner had shown no lights when first sighted and then had shown a white light just before the collision. This view was contradicted by several passengers, including Mrs. Hurst in Cabin 54, who claimed that just before the collision she saw a red light on the sailing vessel. She was a very good witness and described a shadow passing her stateroom window seconds before the ramming, followed by the grinding and crashing of timbers as the schooner lost her foremast. It appears as if the sailing vessel that rammed the *Oregon* stayed afloat for only a short time owing to a stove-in bow which left her open to the sea. Certainly when others on the *Oregon* looked for her shortly after the ramming, they could find no sign of her or her lifeboats anywhere, and the consensus was that she had gone straight to the bottom.

The initial story of how the accident occurred was provided by Captain Cottler. He said that there was a fresh breeze from the west, and the *Oregon* was running under full steam at eighteen to twenty miles per hour for New York. The importance of their being a fresh wind from the west is that the *Oregon* was running west and she was struck by the schooner on her port side. This was provided as a partial explanation for why the sailing vessel was not seen. The schooner apparently was on the port tack—that is, with the wind blowing over her port side and with her sails billowing out to starboard, covering her green starboard light. As she approached the liner at an oblique angle, her sails covered her lights until suddenly Officer Matthews on the bridge of the *Oregon* saw her white binnacle light appear as a flash through her sails at the last moment. The Cunard officers at first contended that the schooner had shown no lights when she was first seen, but Mrs. Hurst's testimony about seeing a red light outside her cabin just before the crash indicates that it may have been obscured. When Matthews saw the light, he thought it was one of the pilotboats, and he had given an order to turn to port because he knew Captain Cottler did not want a pilot until they were much nearer the entrance to New York Harbor. The *Oregon* had not had sufficient time to begin to respond when the schooner rammed her on the port side. Some passengers and crew were very critical of Chief Officer Matthews, even to the point of claiming that it was by his negligence that the liner was lost. Some said he had left the bridge to get a cup of coffee, an accusation he vehemently denied, stating that he did not even drink coffee.

Questions also were raised in 1886 as to how a modern passenger liner divided into watertight compartments could sink after such a collision. Brown responded that the *Oregon* could have stayed afloat with several of her forward, or stern, compartments flooded, but not with the huge engine room compartment in the center of the ship. He said: "Had the *Oregon* been cut into anywhere else than in her engine space, she would probably have remained on the surface. You see the steamship was struck amidships and the water was let into the largest open space in her, a compartment 127 feet long, with 3000 tons of water into a vessel, of course the vessel must go down."[15] Others were less certain and expressed surprise that the ship had sunk. During her construction some attempt had been made to build a longitudinal bulkhead through the engine room to divide it, but this had proved impossible and had not been part of the finished liner. Naval architects were to take heed of this problem in the future.

Although an incredible degree of good luck was evident, from rescue vessels on the scene to smooth seas throughout, the loss of the *Oregon* remains one of the most remarkable accidents at sea in the history of the North Atlantic because no lives were lost. Today her still-majestic ruins beneath the Atlantic lie so close to shore that she is a popular diving site.[16]

Chapter 9

AN INCONCEIVABLE HORROR

Two White Star Liners Collide off New York—The Collision of the *Celtic* and the *Britannic*

May 19, 1887

A little girl on the White Star flagship *Britannic* (1874; 5,004 tons, 455 feet, 15 knots) cried: "Mamma, look at Mother Carey's chickens. I guess we are going to have an accident."[1] While this may represent literary license, "Mother Carey's chickens" were petrels, seabirds which spend virtually all their lives at sea and were regarded as harbingers of bad luck. Shortly thereafter on May 19, 1887, the prophecy came true as the fog parted some four hundred miles off Sandy Hook and the officers on the bridge of the *Britannic* saw the bow of another large ship bearing down on them. The other passenger liner was the *Celtic* (1872; 3,867 tons, 437 feet, 14 knots), another substantial unit of the White Star Line. No greater horror could be imagined by the two captains than for two large liners of the first-class service of their own steamship line to be involved in a collision, but it was about to occur.

The *Celtic* had sailed from Liverpool nearly a week before on May

The White Star liner Britannic *(1874, 5,004 tons, 455 feet, 15 knots) was a strikingly beautiful product of the Harland & Wolff Shipyard, Belfast, with three towering masts and two evenly spaced funnels. She achieved a record passage of the North Atlantic in November 1876 with a crossing at 15.43 knots. On May 19, 1887, the* Britannic *would be rammed by the* Celtic *off New York in a spectacular accident.*

13, taking the usual Saturday-morning sailing of the White Star Line in the Liverpool–New York service. She had a good passenger list of 869 (104 cabin, 765 steerage) out of the 166 first-class and 1,000 steerage berths she had available. On the premier North Atlantic run the White Star Line always sent a ship westbound from Liverpool each Saturday and one eastbound from New York every Wednesday. The *Celtic* had been built by Harland & Wolff, Belfast, Ireland. Her compound engines were by George Forrester, Liverpool, and could provide sufficient power to drive the single screw at fourteen knots. She was a slightly enlarged version of the first White Star quartet and had been delivered in 1872. She took her maiden voyage from Liverpool to New York on October 24, 1872, and soon proved to be a popular ship with accommodations that were superior to many of her competitors. Her career had proved uneventful.

The *Britannic,* under the command of Captain Hamilton Perry, had backed out into the North River the day before, Wednesday, May 18, bound for Queenstown and Liverpool. The White Star liner had 469 passengers on board (176 cabin, 293 steerage) out of a maximum total of 240 first and 1,500 steerage, which also was a good eastbound load for the time of the year.[2] Captain Perry was a very popular master, and the *Britannic* was the ship chosen by many knowledgeable travelers.

Thursday, May 19, was a pleasant day with mixed sun and fog as the *Britannic* steamed eastward along the North American coast. She was regarded as an exceptionally beautiful vessel with two funnels and four masts gracing a long, slim hull. She also was one of the most luxurious creations of the Harland & Wolff Shipyard, Belfast, Ireland, in terms of her interior accommodations. Her saloon and staterooms were in the center of the ship where the least motion was felt. The Saloon, or Dining Room, was reached by a broad, well-lighted staircase that swept upward from the principal cabin deck. In the Dining Room every passenger had an assigned seat for the voyage, and every effort was made to make the passengers think they were in a grand hotel instead of at sea. "The floor is inlaid with polished oak, ebony and walnut. Into the panelling of the walls is introduced polished maple, pleasantly relieved with white and gold enamel. Close by is the ladies' boudoir, as cozy as it is pretty, beautifully upholstered in red velvet, and having the advantage of being situated on the promenade deck. The smoking room is on the main deck, opening to sky and sea, or closed to both, as the smokers may desire, and is quite a narcotic paradise."[3] Staterooms ranged along the deck fore and aft of the principal saloon. The Hurricane Deck in good weather provided a comfortable promenade that cabin passengers could enjoy, and this was the case as the travelers enjoyed their first full day at sea.

Captain P. J. Irving of the *Celtic*, westbound, awoke to rather dense fog and, when he took the bridge, could not see the bow of his liner as she continued to plow along at half speed (7 knots) with her whistles blowing.[4] The eastbound *Britannic* had intermittent periods of sunshine, and Captain Perry felt no compelling need to reduce speed, although the foghorns were sounded occasionally. The big liner was romping along through the fogbanks at close to 14.5 knots. After all, there was a schedule to be kept and Liverpool lay some three thousand miles and nine days of steaming ahead. Late in the afternoon a white fog descended over the sea, substantially obscuring everything. Both captains were on their bridges when the fog signals of each were heard. Captain Irving thought he heard a whistle three points off his starboard bow. He ordered a course change a point and a half to starboard and engines slowed. During the course change Irving ordered the whistle sounded twice (I am turning to starboard) and two minutes later ordered the engines dead slow. Neither knew the identity of the other ship. Passengers thronged the railing in order to see the thrilling sight of two liners passing in mid-ocean. The white fog was playing tricks with the ear and bouncing sound. "Crowds of *Britannic*'s passengers ran from side to side as the sound of the *Celtic*'s hoarse warning came weirdly, now from one direction and now from another through the damp, thick vapor. Both vessels slackened speed as they came nearer and nearer."[5] At 5:25 P.M. this was regarded as a special treat before passengers returned to their cabins and began dressing for supper.

To their horror the instant the other ship appeared out of the fog both White Star captains realized that they were not going to pass each other. The *Celtic* was only an eighth of a mile away and on a collision course to ram the *Britannic*. Some passengers thought they might miss, but the equation of time, speed, and distance was against them. At an eighth of a mile with their combined speed seconds, not minutes, were involved.

One passenger on the *Britannic* commented: "She'll give us a devil of a dig, but I don't know just where."[6] There was just enough time to realize that an accident was going to happen before the bow of the *Celtic* knifed some ten feet into the stern steerage compartment of the *Britannic* on the port side. Because of the speed of the two ships, the *Celtic* rebounded from the *Britannic* and then struck again, but with less power as Captain Irving had rung for full speed astern on his engines

The bow of the White Star liner Celtic *(1872) knifes into the side of the* Britannic *(1874) on May 19, 1887, in dense fog off the East Coast of the United States a day from New York Harbor. The* Celtic *was eastbound to Queenstown and Liverpool while the* Britannic *was westbound approaching New York when they collided.*

and had turned his wheel so that the angle was more oblique. Thus the second blow was more a glancing blow than a puncture. Yet a third blow, involving a prolonged scrape down the side of the *Britannic,* occurred before the two liners finally parted. A few seconds earlier, and the *Celtic*'s bow would have sliced into the huge engine room of the *Britannic,* and she would have gone to the bottom like a stone. The accident was bad, but fortune had smiled.

On the *Britannic* full speed ahead had been ordered by Captain Perry on the bridge in an effort to get away from the *Celtic,* but this had proved futile. Nonetheless it was believed that everything possible had been done to avoid the collision. As it was, the *Celtic* hit the *Britannic* a terrible blow. The *Celtic* lost something like twelve feet of her bow, which was crumpled back, but the thick collision bulkhead held, and she was not in danger of sinking if the weather held. As a result of the *Celtic*'s ramming her, the *Britannic* had a hole extending below the waterline that a man could walk through. Eighteen of her iron plates were smashed, twenty frames were broken, and nine beams damaged. On deck there was an awesome amount of damage. From Hold No. 4 aft for a distance of 180 feet the *Celtic* had stripped and swept away everything on the deck of the *Britannic.* No. 4 Hold, which was open to the sea, was loaded with seventeen thousand bushels of grain and some light merchandise. It filled rapidly with seawater, and the *Britannic* began to settle into the ocean. "The bulwarks curled like cardboard, and davits of wrought-iron four inches through bent like reeds in the wind. Worse than all, dismembered bodies lay about, the wounded shrieked, the sailors busied themselves about the boats, and the terrified passengers put on life preservers."[7] The Reverend Mr. Deputy as a result of his personal inquiries on the *Britannic* was sure that twelve were killed in steerage, and twenty wounded, but other sources took little or no note of passenger losses.[8] Reportedly the little girl who had first seen the seabirds, "Mother Carey's chickens," and had a premonition of disaster had been decapitated, but this also might be nineteenth-century romantic writing, a journalist wringing every last bit of pathos out of the scene.

On the *Britannic* there was some confusion and dismay, but little panic. Three of her lifeboats and some of her life rafts had been destroyed and swept away. Everyone was aware of the destruction of the lifesaving equipment. The passengers in some instances behaved better than the crew. Since danger of sinking seemed imminent, a group of fifteen to twenty firemen reached the deck, scrambled into a lifeboat, and started rowing toward the *Celtic.* Reportedly Captain Perry grabbed a pistol and restored order. Most of the passengers retained control of themselves and awaited their turn to take a place in the remaining undamaged lifeboats. Thereafter five lifeboats were loaded with woman and children and sent to the *Celtic.*

Captain Perry and Captain Irving consulted and reached the reasonable conclusion that since both vessels were seriously damaged, but neither was in danger of sinking immediately, they should keep company. By midnight on Thursday the carpenters on the *Britannic* had been able to stop the inrush of water through some temporary repairs to the gash that extended four feet below the waterline. The liner stopped settling in the water, giving hope that her bulkheads would hold and she could be saved. If the two White Star liners stayed together and anything unfortunate happened, they would be able to help each other. Shortly thereafter they began to make their way toward New York at very slow speeds. As they steamed westbound along the Long Island Shore, they were overtaken by two other liners, the *Marengo* and the *British Queen,* which stayed with them until they reached New York. At around 1:00 A.M. on Sunday—two days later—the damaged ships reached safety. It must have been a remarkable sight as the four liners came into port together.

The *Britannic* was met outside the harbor by the *J G Merritt,* the Merritt Wrecking Company's steamer, which had powerful pumps as part of her salvage equipment. By this time the *Britannic* was drawing thirty feet (normal was twenty-five feet) and had a pronounced list to starboard. The tug *Fletcher* came down the bay and through the Narrows to take off the mail from the *Celtic* and the *Britannic.* The Royal Mail from the *Celtic* would be three days late reaching their American destinations. The U.S. mail on the *Britannic* would be forwarded by the next express steamer on Wednesday and would be about a week late reaching their European destinations. The *Britannic* was towed to the Brooklyn dry dock for surveying and emergency repairs. Remarkably this was accomplished in three weeks, and the White Star liner took her next normal crossing on June 15. The *Celtic* also was towed to the White Star Line pier at West Tenth Street, where she could be unloaded at leisure and frantic repairs made so that she could take her next scheduled sailing.

The passengers on both liners united in giving Captain Irving and Captain Perry testimonials of thanks for their deliverance. The authorities were not so pleased. A hearing was held at the Office of the British Consul in New York on June 7, 1887. William R. Hoare, the vice consul, presided over the inquiry and was advised by three masters of Atlantic steamships. Things moved fast in 1887. A full day of testimony, followed by a day of deliberation, brought a decision on June 9. Both White Star captains were censured for not observing regulations and for making unwarranted speed during foggy conditions. Captain Perry was "very severely censured" for failing to blow the steam whistles of the *Britannic* in fog as long and as often as he should have and for the speed of his vessel. Captain Irving was "severely censured" for failing to reduce his speed adequately when in fog. Hoare's decision went to the Board of Trade in London and was not questioned by the White Star Line. The captains concerned probably felt that they had gotten off relatively unscathed since both could have lost their tickets (professional certification papers) for such an accident.

Chapter 10

AN ATLANTIC DISASTER NARROWLY MISSED

The Explosion of the Engines on the *City of Paris*

March 25, 1890

Technological innovation sometimes can exceed the boundaries of industrial design and durability. This was vividly shown in the construction and operation of the American-owned *City of Paris* (1889; 10,499 tons, 528 feet, 20 knots). She and her sister, the *City of New York* (1888; 10,499 tons, 528 feet, 20 knots), were the largest and fastest ships in the world when commissioned. The two liners were the premier units of the Inman & International Line of Liverpool trading between Great Britain and the United States.

The background of the two Atlantic greyhounds involves one of the earliest attempts at an international corporate expansion by American commercial interests through the acquisition of a significant foreign business enterprise. Clement Acton Griscom (1841–1912), an important Quaker shipping magnate of Philadelphia and the principal owner of the American-controlled International Navigation Company

(Red Star Line), pulled off the international business coup of 1886 when he bought the famous Inman Line of Liverpool, England. Inman shared with Cunard and White Star the honor of carrying the Royal Mails as one of the premier British-flag steamship lines on the North Atlantic and in the world. The Inman Line had fallen on hard times because of the economic depression of the mid-1880s, the death of its founder, William Inman, and an unsuccessful building project. The British competition was prepared to bury their colleague when Griscom, backed by the Pennsylvania Railroad Company, intervened by buying control of the debt of the firm, which made possible the purchase of the Inman Line itself.[1]

The new concern combined American, British, and Belgian assets and was christened the Inman and International Navigation Company. Griscom, who already controlled the American Line (U.S.) and the Red Star Line (Belgian), now also owned the Inman Line (British) The next move was to resuscitate the Inman fleet of aging steamers. Griscom caught the earliest steamer for Liverpool to discuss the future plans of the Inman Line with his British associates, James Spence and Edmund Taylor of Richardson, Spence & Company. Before he returned, negotiations had been completed with James R. Thomson of J. & G. Thomson Shipbuilding Yard, Clydebank, Scotland, for the building of the two largest, fastest, and finest commercial vessels in the world, calculated to surpass any existing competitors.[2] The order was placed for these two exceptional vessels in the spring of 1887.

Griscom was determined to make the greatest possible impression upon the steamer trade with his new liners. The keel of the *City of New York* was laid in June 1887, and the hull was formed of steel plates supplied by the Steel Company of Scotland and the Mossend Steel Company's works. The order was one of the largest ever for steel plates since it involved some thirty thousand separate pieces for each ship, weighing more than seven thousand tons. The plates were specially treated to prevent corrosion.

Griscom was knowledgeable about naval architecture and a

fanatic about safety. The vessels were to be as nearly unsinkable as possible. Thus each was constructed with fifteen transverse bulkheads that ran from the keel all the way up to the saloon deck with no breaks in the partitions below this level. The two liners were the most perfectly subdivided transatlantic vessels ever built and put many contemporary warships to shame with their built-in safety measures. The chief surveyor of Lloyd's, B. Martel, was credited with having supervised every part of the design and construction of the new liners. Thomson moved fast, and during some months when the ships were under construction, an average of over one hundred tons of steel a day went into them. The industrial revolution as applied to shipbuilding had come a long way.

The first of this famous pair was ready for launching by March 1888. A contemporary observer described the scene: "The *City of New York* stands on the ways ready to be launched, while the other steamer, the *City of Paris,* is in an advanced state. The former, as she now stands in the yard, presents a fine appearance. Her great length of 560 ft., her beam 63 ft., and her height, 44 feet, might well attract the attention of passengers on the river steamers. With the buildings on deck, she measures close to 10,500 tons, making her the largest passenger steam in the world."[3]

Each vessel was outfitted with two completely separate engine rooms. The engines were of the three-crank triple-expansion type, having piston valves throughout, and each engine was capable of driving the ship at four-fifths the maximum speed in the event that either set of engines should have to be stopped for any reason. The largest of the steel castings for the engines from the Steel Company of Scotland weighed fifty tons. The construction of the engines was overseen by Mr. Parker, chief engineering surveyor of Lloyd's, and Mr. Doran, superintending engineer of Inman and International. The safety measures taken with the propulsion plant were a matter of considerable pride to Griscom, who maintained his deep interest in naval architecture.

> In the ship the engines will be placed in two compartments, the division being effected by a watertight bulkhead running longitudinally

and separating the port from the starboard engines, while transverse bulkheads on either side isolate them from other parts of the interior of the vessel. The boilers which supply the steam are in three separate compartments. The whole moving power of the ship is therefore divided between five compartments, so that if a collision did occur and a fracture in the ship's hull were at the bulkhead, resulting in two spaces being flooded, there would still be at least one set of engines and one set of boilers to allow the vessel to steam along at about four-fifths her MAXIMUM speed.[4]

With the exception of the air pump all thirty-seven auxiliary engines in each liner were set up to work independently of the main machinery just in case anything might open her interior to the sea.

Finally, each liner was constructed with a double hull so that if the ship should strike anything that might open her up, the second skin would be there to keep the vessel safe.

In each vessel there are two bottoms, and the interior of the ship is divided by transverse partitions into 15 separate watertight compartments. This principle of complete subdivisions has been more fully developed in this than in any other passenger vessel. Attempts have been made in many first-class ships to minutely subdivide them, but this has always been rendered useless by doors being fitted at the bottom of the bulkheads to admit of passage from one compartment to another. These were supposed to be always shut, and in some cases were fitted with patent apparatus for closing them almost instantaneously; but even with these safety cannot be insured, as it has often occurred at the critical moment either no one had the presence of mind to close the door when the collision occurred or the way was blocked. In the case of the Inman steamers there are no doorways, and, therefore, there is no need of patent or other doors. Passage can only be obtained by going to the upper deck, which is above the waterline. The compartments are each 35 feet long, and will hold to load-line 1,250 tons of water, so that even should two be filled the flotation of the vessel will not be seriously affected. Thus the vessels are provided against a collision.[5]

The space between the two hulls was available for carrying ballast, to the extent of sixteen hundred tons, that could be pumped fore and aft.

The value of the many safety features incorporated in the two Inman record breakers was soon demonstrated. At three-thirty on the afternoon of March 19, 1890, the graceful *City of Paris* backed away from her North River pier, slipped down the bay, and headed for The Narrows. Six days later, on March 25, 1890, she was in the Atlantic Ocean two hundred miles from Ireland when in a sudden series of catastrophes her starboard propeller shaft broke loose, and the broken shaft rose up in the engine room. This caused the ten-thousand-horsepower

Steamer Day *by J. O. Davidson shows the majestic* City of Paris *(1889) picking up speed as she threads her way down the busy North River. The Inman & International queen is outward bound to Queenstown and Liverpool while a large White Star liner, either* Teutonic *(1889) or* Majestic *(1890), is in pursuit.*

starboard engine, which was running at full power, to disintegrate suddenly because there no longer was any connection to the propeller to utilize the power. Pieces and chunks of twisted metal flew everywhere, and the starboard engine room was utterly destroyed. The disaster was compounded by shrapnel that knifed through the longitudinal bulkhead into the port compartment, destroying the watertight integrity of the liner's other engine room and flooding the remaining engine. The largest and fastest ship in the world drifted to a halt in the North Atlantic and almost instantly became a waterlogged barge minus power two hundred miles from land. While it never was funny for a liner to have engine failure in mid-Atlantic, in 1890, prior to radio communication, the situation was acutely perilous.

Nine days later a brief newspaper article at the top of the front page of the *New York Times* conveyed the information to an anxious public that the largest and fastest liner in the world had not yet reached Liverpool. The *City of Paris,* which normally slammed across in six days, was missing without a trace. There were no great storms reported on the Atlantic, and the *Britannic* of White Star, which had sailed on the same day as the *City of Paris,* had long since dropped the mails at Queenstown and proceeded on to her home port of Liverpool. There was an air of acute uneasiness at the Liverpool, New York, and Philadelphia offices of the Inman & International Steamship Company. The hopeful explanation was given that Captain Francis Watkins of the *City of Paris* was taking a longer, more southerly route to avoid icebergs. They were believed to be the only menace on the North Atlantic capable of giving serious damage to so strongly built a vessel. In London the Associated Press reported dense fog off the Irish coast. The report offered the opinion that for reasons unknown the Inman record breaker was heading directly for Liverpool without putting into Queenstown on this crossing.[6] The only sure thing was that no one knew anything.

Profound relief was experienced the next day when cables carried the news:

THE CITY OF PARIS SAFE

FOUND NEAR LIVERPOOL, IN TOW WITH HER MACHINERY DISABLED

> The Inman Line steamer *City of Paris,* Capt. Watkins, which sailed from New York March 19 for Liverpool, and for whose safety some fears were entertained, she being some days overdue, was spoken twenty-five miles west of Crookhaven this morning with her machinery disabled. She was being towed by another steamer. The *City of Paris* signaled that all was well.[7]

She had experienced one of the narrowest escapes from disaster in the history of the North Atlantic. At half past five in afternoon of Tuesday, March 25, the liner was running at full speed about 216 miles off the coast of Ireland. Her triple-expansion engines, capable of approximately eighteen thousand horsepower, were at full ahead. These engines were among the largest in the world, with cylinders 45 inches, 74 inches, and 113 inches × 5 feet. Boiler pressure was 150 pounds, with the engines making about eighty-five revolutions per minute. Each engine drove one of the twin screws, which were supported by steel struts extending from the sides of the ship. The propeller shaft was held in place by a brass collar as it passed through the strut and was secured to the screw.

The weather had been gorgeous, and many passengers were still on deck enjoying the late-afternoon sunshine. The first-class dinner gong had just sounded, and some people were moving toward the dining saloon when the accident occurred. A passenger on deck noted: "Suddenly there was a long, low rumbling, then a grating and tearing sound, as if the vessel was on the rocks, followed by a dull report which reverberated through the body of the steamer."[8] Others noted a series of loud thumps and tearing noises, while still others felt the *City of Paris* tremble from stem to stern, after which she began to drift to a stop and the lights flickered before going out. Panic brought people swiftly to the open deck, but Captain Watkins soon appeared after checking the engine room, asserted control, and immediately averted any hysteria. W. O. Hitchcock, a merchant from New York, described the captain as

The City of Paris *was steaming at full speed some two hundred miles off the coast of Ireland on March 25, 1890, when the manganese collar supporting the starboard shaft wore away, the shaft wrenched loose, and the engine room self-destructed as huge chunks of metal flew in all directions. The wreckage in the engine room was photographed in Liverpool after the liner reached port.*

being as cool as a June cucumber. Hitchcock also noted later that Watkins did not inform his passengers of the full extent of the damage to the propulsion machinery or they might not have been so confident of the future.[9]

The crew at once turned to a variety of assignments. Almost immediately the lifeboats were swung out, and provisions were brought up from the pantries for each unit. No one on the *City of Paris* went to bed that night. All stayed on the upper decks, and it was fortunate that the weather was very moderate. Rockets were fired every half hour in the hope of drawing the attention of a passing steamer. None appeared, and no sleep was had.

The near disaster had occurred when the brass collar of the propeller shaft began to wear away while the engines were being driven at full speed. The starboard screw revolving at eighty-five revolutions per minute dropped downward slightly, causing the shaft to wrench loose and rise up in the engine room. This tremendous force shattered the gears and caused the starboard engine suddenly to race wildly, disintegrating in all directions. Within seconds the smoothly pulsating triple-expansion engines of the fastest liner in the world had ceased to be functional. The sea cocks and valves were buried under tons of debris, and water poured into the ship through pipes that had been wrenched apart by the colossal force of the accident. The puncturing of the bulkhead into the Port Engine Room by flying shrapnel destroyed the integrity of that portion of the power plant also, and only the swift action of engineers in turning off the flow of steam from the boiler rooms saved the liner from an enormous explosion. Miraculously only one engineer, who courageously had remained at his station to turn off the steam, was injured, and while partially scalded, he would live.

Morning came with the seas still calm and the weather moderate. By this time the *City of Paris* had taken on several thousand tons of water and was lying deep in the water. Hitchcock, having occasion to go to the cabin forward of the engine room, saw a number of stewards up to their waists in water, which they were bailing with buckets. He could not believe his eyes because of the futility of the exercise and asked them what they were doing. They replied: "We don't know, Sir. We simply got orders to bail it out." One of the problems faced by Watkins and his engineering staff was that all the pumping equipment was underwater in the flooded engine rooms, and nothing else was available to them. The unthinkable had eliminated access to all the pumps at the same time that the accident occurred. Initially some thought that the double bottom had been punctured, so quickly had the ship settled in the water, but this was not true.

Since no steamer had been sighted, about one o'clock in the afternoon of Wednesday, March 26, Captain Watkins had a lifeboat lowered away with six oarsmen under the command of Chief Officer Passow. They rowed away from the stricken liner in order to broaden the chances of attracting attention during daylight. They knew of course that there were a number of other liners at sea, such as the *City of Chester* and the *Adriatic,* on the run from New York to Liverpool, and they hoped to meet with one of them.

No vessel was sighted throughout the long day as the lifeboat from the *City of Paris* bobbed about on the open ocean. Should fog or inclement weather have arisen the situation of the seven men in the lifeboat might have turned even more critical than that of their anxious compatriots on the liner. Their vigil was not to be brief. Those in both the lifeboat and the liner saw no other vessel on Wednesday, March 26, or Thursday, March 27. By late afternoon on Thursday the liner had been without power for forty-eight hours and the courage of all concerned was being strained to the utmost.

At about 1:30 A.M. on March 28 the lights of an approaching steamer were seen by First Officer Passow and his men in the lifeboat. They fired rockets from the lifeboat that attracted the attention of Captain Roberts and others on the bridge of the White Star liner *Adriatic* (1872; 3,888 tons, 437 feet, 14 knots), and course was altered toward the distress signal. Nearly an hour later, when the lifeboat was sighted the engines of the *Adriatic* were stopped, alarming some of her passengers who were afraid their vessel was in trouble. George W. Stearns, a passenger on the White Star liner, left his cabin and came on deck just as Chief Officer Passow boarded the *Adriatic.* He learned that the *City of Paris* was totally disabled and at the mercy of the sea. Passow told Roberts that Captain Watkins wanted the *City of Paris* towed to Queenstown. Roberts, who was the relieving captain for White Star, was very conscious of his duty both to anyone in distress and also to his employers. He offered to do everything possible for the safety of the individuals on the *City of Paris,* but he did not think that he could take the time to tow the Inman and International liner the 200 miles to the Irish port. Since the *City of Chester* (1873; 4,566 tons, 445 feet, 14 knots) had left Liverpool just after the *Adriatic,* Roberts proposed intercepting her since she was of the same steamship line as the *City of Paris.* Shortly afterward in the darkness another steamer was seen approaching the *Adriatic* bound west. Distress rockets were fired to attract her attention, but even though she passed within four miles of the White Star liner and the rockets, no notice was taken, and she soon disappeared from sight toward the west. It was impossible to establish the identity of the ship that ignored the distress signals. Throughout the remaining hours of darkness the *Adriatic, City of Paris,* and lifeboat remained in sight of one another and sent up distress rockets at regular intervals to attract attention.

About 4:00 A.M. Chief Officer Passow came on board the *Adriatic* again to confer with Captain Roberts. They discussed their options, and Roberts said he would go to the aid of the individuals on the *City of Paris* but would not undertake a tow. Passow, for his part, declined to be taken back to his liner and said that he would set out for the Irish coast, hoping to find another vessel or to reach land. Hot food and provisions were passed down to the men in the *City of Paris*'s lifeboat. Farewells were said, and the *Adriatic*'s engines began to turn over as she prepared to make for the stricken *City of Paris.*

Simultaneously a small steamer bound east was sighted. She proved to be the *Aldersgate* of London bound from Galveston, Texas, to Liverpool. Captain Cheshire of the *Aldersgate* brought his freighter around the stern of the *Adriatic* and stopped to offer assistance, whereupon Captain Roberts informed him that it was not the *Adriatic* that needed assistance but the *City of Paris.* He asked if the *Aldersgate* would undertake the tow. The captain of the little freighter promptly said yes. Cheshire believed that a tow at about four knots was possible but said that if the passengers on the Inman liner should be in any danger, he would throw his cargo overboard in order to lighten his vessel enough to accommodate them in safety. This statement was commented upon very favorably by the Admiralty Court at a later date.

Captain Roberts said he would stand by and accompany the

Aldersgate to the *City of Paris* in the event any additional assistance was needed. As soon as they could proceed in safety, the two rescue vessels made for the *City of Paris.* The early dawn revealed the large liner a derelict, wallowing in the slight westerly swell, very far down by the stern. A throng of passengers could be seen crowding the deck forward as the *Adriatic* and the *Aldersgate* steamed up, and a great cheer greeted the arrival of the White Star liner. The *City of Paris* had been drifting dead in the water for sixty hours by that time. Roberts later reported: "We then proceeded in company in case of emergency. On arriving alongside, an officer boarded us presenting Capt. Watkin's request to tow. I said that we had come to save life, that we had boarded the *Aldersgate,* which was bound east, and [she] had agreed to take the people from her [the *City of Paris*]. After waiting a short time, the *City of Paris* hoisted the signal: 'Thanks' 'Go ahead' We then proceeded on our way at 6:24 A.M. leaving the two ships in communication."[10]

The officer who boarded the *Adriatic* from the *City of Paris* exchanged a few words with George Stearns: "'What is your condition?' I asked. 'Pretty bad.' he replied. 'How is your hull?' 'Oh, the hull's all right.' and he boarded his boat to return to his ship."

Captain Roberts brought the *Adriatic* safely to New York on Sunday, April 6, but he sailed into a storm of abuse from some quarters that thought he had abandoned the *City of Paris* without justification. Some passengers on the Inman liner had been incensed when the *Adriatic* steamed away. Roberts was severely affected by the criticism because he believed that he had done everything possible to aid the stricken liner, short of the actual tow, and had not left her until assistance was secured. His defenders said that only ignorance or malice could make such a charge in view of all that the White Star captain had done. It was noted that by not undertaking the tow, Roberts had relinquished the captain's share of a very handsome salvage award that might well have made his fortune for life.

As the tow began, the passengers held a religious service on board the *City of Paris* to give thanks for their deliverance. They also passed a resolution praising Captain Watkins and his crew for their courageous handling of the situation. A subscription of six hundred pounds ($3,000) was raised to be divided between the Liverpool and the New York Mariner's Institute to be used for charitable purposes to aid sailors. Subsequently the American Line's *Ohio,* which had sailed from Liverpool for Philadelphia under the command of Captain Sargeant, encountered the *Aldersgate* towing the *City of Paris* and turned around to escort the tow into safe harbor. The *Ohio* carried word of the rescue to Crookhaven and then steamed back to assist the disabled *City of Paris* into Queenstown. Tugs also were dispatched from the Irish port to assist in getting the big liner to a safe anchorage. The *City of Paris* had been drifting north toward the Irish coast and, save for the tow, would have gone ashore ultimately. The *Aldersgate*'s tow job involved approximately one hundred miles and took something more than twenty-two hours (6:30 A.M., March 28, to 4:00 A.M., March 29). The *City of Paris*'s anxious passengers finally reached port at 4:50 A.M. on March 29, when their liner slowly entered Cork Harbour. By this time the ship was drawing an incredible thirty-five feet astern, and her bow was high out of the water.

Trains had been awaiting the ship's arrival throughout the night. The American mails were manhandled out of the mailroom on the liner onto a waiting tug and got away by 7:00 A.M. Special trains awaited the passengers along with numerous additional personnel to ease the ending of their trip. It was late in the day before the first load of travelers was brought in by lighter from the stricken liner and was on its way. Needless to say, baggage handling without any power proved difficult. The Inman & International Steamship Company, highly conscious of passenger goodwill, paid for the transportation of all those affected to any destination of their choice in the United Kingdom. It is significant of the times that this was regarded as an act of extreme generosity on the part of the steamship line.

James Thomson, the builder of the *City of Paris,* traveled down with Mr. Cummins, the general manager (Liverpool) of the Inman

Line, to meet the ship on her arrival at Queenstown. Plans were undertaken immediately to repair the ship and return her to service. Some comments about the remarkable construction of the liner that had permitted her to survive so devastating an explosion and to bring her passengers and cargo safely to port appeared in newspaper accounts. Her watertight subdivisions had held, and she had remained afloat with two of her largest and most vital compartments completely flooded. At Cork it seemed as though the harder they pumped, the more the ocean flowed into the ship. This should have been no surprise given the damage to the intake valves and pipes lying underneath the wreckage of the engine.

Additional steam pumps were placed on board, and divers did their best to seal the intake pipes so that the Atlantic Ocean would not be recycled. This was accomplished late on March 30, and the *City of Paris* was pumped dry within thirty-six hours.

The condition of the machinery was regarded as sound enough that the decision was made to get up steam in the port engine and to take her to Liverpool under her own power. The majestic flagship of the Inman & International Steamship Company steamed out of Cork Harbour for Liverpool at 9:30 P.M. on April 1, sixty-nine hours after she had been unceremoniously towed in. This must rank as one of the most extraordinary accomplishments of the entire incident even if her coal had been largely unaffected by the disaster and had not become a sodden mess.

Cargo, some passengers' baggage, and apparently a few passengers were unloaded at Liverpool before the *City of Paris* was taken into dry dock at Laird's. In the dry dock the ship could be surveyed, and plans made for the reengining and rebuilding of a vessel that had been launched a brief eighteen months before. It also was possible to review what had happened and to analyze the situation in order to ensure that nothing similar would occur again. As soon as the water was pumped out of the dry dock, it was evident that the starboard shaft had to be broken since the coupling had broken through part of the casing and the screw had slipped aft by at least fifteen inches. The Laird shipyard crew went to work removing the engine room cover so that the surveyors from Lloyd's and other interested parties could view the damage. The crew was prepared to work through the night. About 1:00 A.M., as the ship was vibrating from the efforts to get the steel cover off, the forward end of the starboard shaft broke free from the ship and fell to the floor of the dry dock with a horrendous noise that made everyone seek cover or run for his life. The strain on the bracket was increased by this since it was left supporting the screw without any aid, and it also gave way, dropping the boss and the blades down to the bottom of the dock. The weight of the shaft and the propeller that hit the floor of the Laird dry dock was in excess of forty tons. The propeller broke apart, and one of the manganese blades was bent almost in two by the force of the blow, while the second sliced through the wood of the gridiron on which the liner rested as though it were a piece of cheese, and the third stood upright and uninjured.

The triple-expansion engines of the *City of Paris* were distinct from each other. The high-pressure cylinder had a single piston valve, the intermediate cylinder had two, and the low-pressure cylinder had four. Each cylinder was supported on two A-frames, which were a single steel casting and weighed six tons each. On the cylinders were cast flats, or rubbing faces. The reinforcing of the engines was substantial. Longitudinal tie rods braced the three cylinders together, but not so stiffly that each engine was prevented from taking its own stress. Tie rods also braced the two engines together, and these rods passed through the intermediate bulkhead as additional reinforcement. All the cylinders had coned top covers. The rise of the cover was the same for each cylinder, so that the inclination in the high-pressure cylinder cover was much steeper than the rise in the intermediate, which again was steeper than the rise in the low-pressure cover. The coning was adapted by design to fit the shape of the pistons and was made conical for strength. The attention paid to making the triple-expansion engines of the *City of Paris* the strongest ever constructed for a ship was underlined by the fact that the coning was cast of solid steel. The piston rods of mild steel were twelve inches in diameter. The tail rods were seven inches in diameter. The pistons were secured on the rods by massive bolts. Just behind the bulkhead was the dynamo room, and in this bulkhead was a small watertight door that could be closed at a moment's notice.

At a strategic position on the upper platform was the main stop valve. There were three platforms in the engine rooms of the *City of Paris.* The upper one gave access to the tail rods and their stuffing boxes; the middle one at the level of the link motion; and the third platform at the level of the crankshaft, where all the starting and reversing gears were situated.

Such was the scene in the starboard engine room around five-thirty on the evening of March 25, 1890. As noted earlier, the *City of Paris* was approximately 200 miles from the Irish coast, running at full speed. Her previous day's runs had been March 20, 307 miles; March 21, 440 miles; March 22, 448 miles; March 23, 452 miles; March 24, 446 miles; and March 25, 456 miles. These were excellent runs, but nothing beyond the normal operation of the vessel.

Within each engine room were three men, one on each platform. As the sequence of events was pieced together, the man on the top platform felt the tail rod of the low-pressure engine to check its temperature and began to walk forward. He had not taken five steps when the enormous low-pressure engine broke loose from the deck, rose, disintegrated, and fell in pieces to the floor of the engine room. In a few seconds this great engine, standing about forty-five feet high, was a heap of scrap. The man on the lower platform, who was standing close to the after end of the huge condenser, experienced a miraculous escape, as one of the largest portions of the low-pressure cylinder very nearly fell on him. Shocked out of his wits, he fled for his life past the condenser, and if he had not done so, he would have been drowned in the flood. He had no time to close the Kingston valve emitting water as the engine began to disintegrate and afterward never would have been able to reach it under the tons of debris.

This open valve thus explained the flooding of the starboard engine room. The tail rod of the low-pressure engine was driven through the bulkhead between the two engine rooms, fairly high up, making a hole about a foot in diameter between the two watertight compartments. The bulkhead between the engine rooms was strengthened by a heavy longitudinal shelf piece lying some eight to ten feet above the crank platform. Directly under this reinforcement shelf another piece of flying debris punctured a ragged, extended gash through the watertight bulkhead into the port engine room. Despite the frantic efforts of the engineers on duty in the port engine room, they found it impossible to stem the flood of water that was under considerable pressure from the starboard engine room. They attempted to stuff mattresses into the gash and wedge them into position, but every effort was doomed to failure. The ragged gash, which was the worst of the ruptures to the bulkhead, was almost impossible to get at, let alone to shore up. The screw shaft was ripped out of its bearings from end to end and destroyed the integrity of the after bulkhead on the starboard side so that the dynamo room and the screw alley also filled with water.

Once the debris had settled in the starboard engine room the engineers with great personal courage rushed back into the chamber and screwed down the stop valve so that no more steam could escape and no additional explosions occur. Similar drastic action was necessary in the port engine room, and the *City of Paris* soon drifted to a halt as her engine rooms and the starboard shaft tunnel filled. An observer commented in awe: "Nothing so complete in the way of a breakdown has ever before been seen. The explosion of a great shell might work such havoc in an ironclad. It is difficult in the face of such total destruction to form any theory as to what gave way first."[11]

Once the surveyors from Lloyd's, the builders, and the Board of Trade arrived at Laird's shipyard the serious work began. The devastation in the starboard engine room was awesome. The cylinder cover of the low-pressure cylinder once at the top of the engine was now underneath everything. The six-ton A-frames had ceased to exist in a recognizable form. The connecting rod was still coupled to the crank pin with the large end intact, but the rod, which was about fourteen inches in diameter in the middle, was bent. The piston rod and crosshead were still coupled to the connecting rod and lay folded back. The tail rod was bent like a piece of wire nearly into a semicircle. One side of the condenser had been torn away by the accident, and the tubes were displaced. Some of the condenser tubes were flattened until they were no wider than a kitchen knife as though they had been hammered out on some gigantic anvil. The air pump levers were rolled up like so many bits of metal ribbon. On the side of part of the cylinder was a great crack, but the metal held together in such a manner as to indicate great strength.

An observer noted: "We are puzzled to imagine how it has been possible that material so excellent should have been so completely destroyed. There is not a broken bar or bolt that does not show that it has only given way as the result of the utmost violence. We begin to ask ourselves, if a charge of dynamite had been put in the cylinder and exploded would it have wrought more havoc."[12]

Richardson, Spence and Company was determined to establish the fact that all the safety precautions built into its two great liners had proved worthwhile. They made available to the major engineering and scientific journals of their day copies of photographs taken of the carnage in the starboard engine room of the *City of Paris.* The favorable comments about the openness of the owners to public inspection of their vessel, and the availability of information about the near disaster repaid the firm well. Normally conservative and reserved in its language, *The Engineer* commented:

> It is impossible to see what has taken place in the starboard engine-room of the *City of Paris* and not conclude that she is an enormously strong and safe ship. Nothing so bad ever occurred in an engine-room before. It is impossible, indeed, to imagine that anything worse can ever take place; yet the skins of the ship were uninjured. Not a

single rivet has been started in the hull. Not a life was lost; no one was hurt, save one engineer slightly scalded. The ship has borne a test of absolutely unexampled severity, and she has come through the trial to perfection. The Inman and International Company is to be congratulated on possessing a vessel which has now proved herself not only to be the fastest, but the safest ship afloat. She has beaten the record in the matter of speed long since; she has now beaten the record in the sense of going through perils unscathed.[13]

The engravings of the engine room photographs published in *The Engineer* and in *Scientific American* underlined what the ship had survived and were of enormous contemporary interest. Final expert opinion held that the accident happened when the brass liner on the tail shaft burst through excessive wear, tearing out the lignum vitae strips and permitting the rapidly revolving shaft to come into contact with metal. The tail shaft then ground away the liner in the steam jacket and, when that had been worn away, began to grind away at itself and the bracket. Ultimately the shaft dropped slightly and began to bend back and forth until it snapped just where it came out of the steam tube. The sudden breaking of the shaft released several thousand horsepower, which caused the engines to race and the low-pressure cylinder to blow up.

Among the engineering modifications suggested by the accident was the placing of independently powered pumps somewhere in the liner where they would not be affected by such a disaster and would be available to keep the sea at bay. The pumps on the *City of Paris* were on the same level as the engine room and had been made inoperable by the flooding of that space. The crew was reduced to bailing by hand, which was fruitless in the extreme given the dimensions of the crisis.

Another recommendation was for the installation of improved governors for the engines that would prevent them from racing should anything like this disaster reoccur. Unfortunately governors that automatically adjust the speed of the engines were not totally dependable in

1890. Some were used to protect engines from the results of pitching when a vessel's screws might come out of the water briefly before plunging back under the surface, but they were not universally effective.

The builders, Thomson, and the representatives of the owners in Liverpool, Richardson, Spence, and Company, made every effort to cooperate with the official investigation. In the end the builders and owners were exonerated from any responsibility for the near disaster and were complimented on the remarkable workmanship which had gone into the vessel. That was small consolation to Griscom and the other owners of Inman and International when they realized that the *City of Paris* would be out of service for more than a year as repairs and modifications were made.

Subsequently, on Saturday, June 7, the Admiralty Court in London handed down an award of seventy-five hundred pounds ($37,500) to the *Aldersgate* for the rescue of the *City of Paris.* The American Line's *Ohio* was awarded six hundred pounds ($3000) for her services to the Inman liner. Mr. Justice Butt, who heard the case, said in his decision that if the weather had been inclement after the accident, the *City of Paris* would have either foundered or drifted ashore. It had been a near miss.

Chapter 11

FIRE AT SEA ON THE *CITY OF RICHMOND*

June 1891

The *City of Richmond* (1873; 4,607 tons, 441 feet, 14 knots) was the response of the Inman Line to the new White Star liners of 1871 and 1872. She was an attractive vessel with a slim hull, a clipper bow, two funnels, and three masts. Her passenger accommodations involved berths for 125 in first, 80 in second, and 1,310 in third (steerage). She was not designed to capture the Blue Riband for speed, but with her lines and her tonnage it was intended that she would command respect and earn the patronage of the knowledgeable traveling public.

In the 1860s and 1870s the Liverpool, New York & Philadelphia Steam Ship Company, universally known by its nickname, the Inman Line, was one of the major maritime enterprises on the North Atlantic. It remains one of the most famous and celebrated of all the great nineteenth-century steamship lines carrying on the trade between Europe and America. While the primary route served was from Liverpool to Philadelphia and New York, feeder services from the Continent, such as from the port of Antwerp, resulted in a wider casting of the net for cargoes and passengers.

The economic depression of the mid-1880s resulted in a crisis for

Inman, and the line had its back to the wall financially. Its five remaining ships were an average of more than eleven years old and capable of only nine-day crossings at a time when the Cunard and White Star competition was regularly crossing in a little more than seven days. All three lines shared the responsibility for carrying the Royal Mails. However, the inferior nature of the Inman ships meant that the mails leaving Liverpool on the Tuesday Inman liner often arrived in New York on the same day as the White Star Thursday liner. A stockholders' meeting was called in Liverpool on October 18, 1886, to discuss the courses of action open to the company. Debts and obligations of the line exceeded the value of the fleet by nearly £100,000 ($500,000) and were mounting steadily. Secured creditors were owed no less than £174,500 ($872,500), and unsecured creditors another £91,000 ($455,000). Since the book value of the fleet was less than £168,000, ($840,000) debts exceeded assets by £97,500 ($487,500). Attempts to obtain new funds through a mortgage debenture issue had failed, yet new ships had to be built if the line was to survive.[1]

The critical financial straits of the Inman Steamship Company were common knowledge and became of particular interest to Clement Acton Griscom and the International Navigation Company through Richardson, Spence and Company, their Liverpool business associates. The Griscom shipping interests, which included Peter Wright & Sons of Philadelphia, had purchased some of the debts of the Inman Line and therefore were primary creditors. Since the Inman Line nicely fitted into the expanding operations of the International Navigation Company, Griscom entered negotiations for the purchase of the line. These talks had proceeded quite far and the major stockholders of Inman knew of the American move when the stockholder's meeting was called. On October 18, 1886, it was decided that the company should go into voluntary liquidation and thus pave the way for purchase by certain parties.

A degree of secrecy was evidently necessary as Thomas H. Ismay of the White Star Line was interested in keeping the Inman Line in operation under British management. In later years Ismay "told a story that when the Inman Line was in difficulties he wrote to a well-known gentleman in the same trade, offering to find half the money necessary to keep the line going, if his correspondent would find the other half. The offer was declined. 'And now [1899],' Ismay said, 'we have an American railway company come into the trade, with millions at its back, running under a well-known British flag, and setting us all to work building whether we want to or not. Would not it have been better to have kept the weak Line going?' "[2]

Within two weeks of the stockholders' meeting a new and powerful name appeared among the transatlantic steamship lines' advertisements. The Inman & International Steamship Company Ltd. replaced the name Inman Steamship Company, and the transatlantic passenger lines were confronted with a rejuvenated giant when an imminent demise had been expected.[3] The Inman Line was a subsidized British mail line, and the new American owners saw no need to offend or upset the British government by stressing that American investors had just purchased one of the premier British-flag North Atlantic lines.

The situation vis-á-vis Her Majesty's Government and the new Inman owners was to deteriorate soon enough anyway. The Royal Mail Contract was lost in 1888 when the British Government announced that two sailings each week would be adequate on Wednesday and Saturday, and that Cunard and White Star had won the contracts. Griscom reacted by persuading the U.S. Congress to grant a mail subsidy and then to permit American registration for his two large new ships, the *City of Paris* and the *City of New York,* in 1893.

The services were to commence in March 1893 under the terms of the new Ocean Mail Subsidy Act. This development from a nation that had neglected its merchant marine for thirty years produced considerable unrest in transatlantic shipping circles. The response in Britain was best expressed in the journal *Fair Play,* which stated in May 1892:

> Dismal forebodings cannot be repressed. We remember the days when the Yankees had a practical monopoly of the Atlantic trade and the Stars and

Stripes were found flying from the peaks of the smartest vessels afloat and in every European port. In the days of wooden ships the Americans gave us points in marine architecture. Nobody who knows anything of yachting but is powerfully impressed by the Americans' natural skill in construction and seamanship, wherein they cannot be ranked second even to ourselves. The demand for free ships in America is steadily growing into an articulate cry. . . . When Jonathan returns to reason in shipbuilding and shipowning we shall not have our troubles to seek. Meanwhile, the efforts made in America to meet the case of the American shareholders of the Inman Line and the ambitions of Philadelphia shipbuilders to add thereto are signs of the times which cannot be ignored.[4]

If the future looked bright for Griscom, the day-to-day operation of his steamship lines continued to produce unforeseen strains and challenges. Accidents and losses plagued the Inman & International Company in 1891 and 1892.

The *City of Richmond* sailed from New York on June 3, 1891, for

The City of Richmond *(1873) was an attractive clipper-bowed liner of the Inman Line who established herself as a popular ship on the North Atlantic. She would have an eventful crossing in June 1891 when some cotton bales in her cargo caught fire through spontaneous combustion and threatened to destroy the ship.*

Liverpool under the command of Captain Arthur Redford, a senior officer of the line. The Inman liner at 4,607 tons was a solid and substantial vessel that had served the Line well for nearly twenty years. She was about to have an eventful crossing. The culprit would be a cargo of cotton bales in the hold of the liner which burst into flames through spontaneous combustion. One week out from New York on Tuesday, June 9, around midnight a passenger awoke to find smoke in her cabin, and when she leaped from her bunk, the deck was very hot beneath her feet. Her wild gyrations and screams raised the alarm with considerable vigor, for it was stated that all passengers, including those in steerage, were on deck within three minutes. Most of them hurriedly left their berths and rushed on deck attired in little but their sleeping garments. The scene on the deck after the discovery of the fire was not pleasant. A gale was blowing, and the sea was rough. Many groups of women engaged in prayer, and there was some weeping, although no real hysteria. A passenger reported: "It was a fearful night, the wind screeching through the rigging and the sea washing over the decks. There was little hope of safety in case it should become necessary to take to the boats. The suspense was terrible, but all bore up spendidly, owning to the encouraging words of Captain Redford and his officers. The intermediate and steerage passengers soon were comfortably installed in the saloon, away from the smoke and fumes coming from the burning cotton."[5]

Strenuous efforts promptly were made by the crew of the *City of Richmond* to reach the fire. The hatchway, one removed from that emitting smoke, was opened, and the captain's worst fears were confirmed. There was widespread fire in his cargo of two thousand bales of cotton. Both steam and water were injected into the hold, and the diminishing of the fire was so marked that for a time they hoped it was out. The water appeared to accomplish little, but the new "steam annihilators," which sprayed a heavy mist into the hold, worked wonders by depriving the fire of dry surfaces and quickly reducing the temperature in the hold.

While Captain Redford and the majority of the deck crew were fighting the fire, other crew members rushed provisions on deck and stocked the lifeboats in case they should have to abandon ship. Under the eyes of the anxious but calm passengers the stewards made sure that each lifeboat carried everything necessary for comfort and survival. Many of the male passengers assisted the stewards, and all help was appreciated in the event the fire should break out again and they would have to launch the lifeboats quickly.

The situation was made more difficult by the gale which was blowing and the waves that were causing the ship to roll heavily. As the night wore on, the gusts and seas worsened to the point where leaving the *City of Richmond* was virtually out of the question. By morning Captain Redford thought his ship might survive with luck. It was impossible to discover the full extent of the fire because it was feared that with such a gale blowing if any of the hatches or other apertures were opened, the wind would cause the blaze to turn into a firestorm. In the intervening time the cooks seized the opportunity to cook some two thousand pounds of beef so that every lifeboat would have fresh cooked meat as part of its provisions. Stores near the bulkheads or on the deck above the fire were moved to safer locations to preserve them and to give the fire as little as possible to feed upon should it break through. It was impossible to move one major peril, 140 barrels of oil, stowed close to the burning cotton. The oil remained of great concern.

Captain Redford gave the order for the distress signals to be flown, and around eight o'clock on the morning of Wednesday, June 10, a sail was sighted ahead of the *City of Richmond.* Rockets were fired in hope of drawing attention, but no response was evident for two hours. Then the steamer ahead appeared to slow and go at half speed so that the Inman liner could catch up to her. The vessel was the *Counsellor,* of the Harrison Line, bound from New Orleans to Liverpool under the command of Captain Jones. At ten o'clock, as the two vessels approached, Captain Redford signaled about the fire. Verbal communication in the face of the gale was hopeless. Captain Jones signaled back, agreeing to stand by the Inman liner as long as she was in danger. Everyone on the Inman liner was greatly relieved since if worse came to worst, a rescue vessel was at hand. *The Counsellor* drew alongside the *City of Richmond,* and just as the vessels neared, Captain Jones of the Harrison liner suffered a massive heart attack on his bridge, fell to the deck, and died. His shocked chief officer at once assumed command and continued the navigation of his ship as well as communication with the *City of Richmond.*

The death of Captain Jones became known to the passengers on the Inman liner almost immediately, as some apparently saw him collapse, and the rumor mill on the *City of Richmond* soon churned out a spurious story that he had dropped dead of yellow fever! Needless to say, to already fearful minds that meant the entire crew of the rescue vessel was similarly infected with the deadly disease. Captain Redford did not need more trouble. He rapidly squelched this insidious rumor, but not before it created additional fears and unrest among his frightened and exhausted passengers and crew.

Throughout Wednesday the crew of the Inman vessel continued to pour water and steam on the cotton, which periodically blazed up. In the evening, when conditions moderated a bit, an attempt was made to reach the hold in order to discover the extent of the fire. Four smoldering bales were removed and heaved overboard, but the fire was far more extensive than that, and the influx of air caused the smoke to worsen. It was found imperative to shut up everything and secure the hatch in order to prevent the oxygen-rich air from feeding the flames.

Roughly the same conditions continued the next day, with smoke billowing from beneath the hatch but the fire being contained by periodic soakings of water and steam. A heavy sea continued to run, and the *City of Richmond* rolled substantially as she steamed along at a low speed so that the *Counsellor* could keep up. The *City of Richmond* continued to fly distress signals. The North German Lloyd *Aller* (1886; 4,966 tons, 438 feet, 17 knots) steamed by and exchanged signals with the smoking Inman liner but, seeing the *Counsellor* in attendance, continued her crossing without offering assistance. Toward midnight on Thursday June 11 the Cunard liner *Servia* (1881; 7,392 tons, 515 feet, 16 knots), under the command of Captain Dutton, encountered the two vessels and exchanged signals with the *City of Richmond.* Redford was anxious to get his ship to port as soon as possible before there occurred any possibility of the fire's raging out of control. The *Servia* agreed to accompany the *City of Richmond* to Queenstown, and with grateful thanks to the little *Counsellor,* the two larger vessels steamed away at a much quicker rate for the Irish port. The fire lessened on Friday although it still appeared to be coming from a number of different locations.

The *City of Paris* came over the horizon on Friday afternoon and instantly slowed upon recognizing the *City of Richmond* with the *Servia* in attendance. Lifeboats were launched, and the captains of the three liners met on the *Servia* to discuss the situation. The *City of Paris* was westbound for New York while the *Servia* was eastbound for Queenstown and Liverpool. Since it was possible for the *City of Richmond* to steam fairly fast and not delay the *Servia* appreciably, Captain Dutton graciously urged the *City of Paris* to continue on her voyage in order to maintain her schedule. The *City of Paris* left for New York, and the *City of Richmond* and the *Servia* continued to steam eastward. On Saturday, as the two liners neared Queenstown, it appeared the fire on the *City of Richmond* was extinguished. No flames were seen, the deck was cooling, and little smoke was evident. Everyone was greatly relieved.

Some cabin passengers were able to return to their cabins for the first time in four days. This was most welcome since they had worn the same clothes for that period and had in some cases slept in deck chairs. Part of the passenger list consisted of the Kendal Theatrical Company, whose famous leader was the actor Dacres. All were grateful when Roche's Point was passed and Queenstown finally reached. The *City of Richmond* did not stay long in the Irish port because inspection of her hold indeed did reveal that the fire was out and she was able to sail for Liverpool. It had been a very near miss for all concerned between the fire in the cotton bales, the nearby barrels of oil, and the North Atlantic gale. The *City of Richmond* was well past her prime and was sold to Norwegian interests in 1892 and scrapped in 1896.

Danger from burning cargo was very real. Six months later the *Venetia* (1891; 2,822 tons, 320 feet, 12 knots) of the Hamburg-American Line reported encountering a burning vessel in mid-Atlantic. The steamer, which flew the British flag, was burning fore and aft. There was no sign of anyone on board, and all the lifeboat davits were empty. The foremast and the rigging were gone while the mainmast had a broken masthead. The funnel was black with a red and a white stripe. The *Venetia* steamed around the derelict several times, but no one answered the hails, and no crew or passengers were evident. Subsequently the *Venetia* steamed on while keeping a good lookout for lifeboats or individuals in the water. Fifteen minutes later a lifeboat appeared bobbing in the water. An inspection was made, but the boat was found to be deserted. The *Venetia* took her boat back on board and continued to New York. No further comment about the ill-fated steamer was given, and it remains a mystery of the Atlantic. In the absence of any means for regular communication over substantial distances in the nineteenth century a fire at sea easily could spell catastrophe with no one surviving to write an epitaph. The new sea routes that the major steamship lines adopted in the early 1890s were supposed to enhance safety by placing more vessels on the same general track so that in the event of problems arising, solutions could be at hand.

Chapter 12

THE *CITY OF CHICAGO* AND THE OLD HEAD OF KINSALE

July 1, 1892

William Inman in 1879 made the decision that the Inman Steamship Company Limited needed a record-breaking liner in order to remain competitive with its great rivals, Cunard and White Star. After surveying the British shipbuilding market, the terms offered by the Barrow Shipbuilding Company appeared attractive even if Barrow never had built anything this big before. The contract called for an eight-thousand-ton steel-hulled liner capable of crossing the North Atlantic in under seven days, faster than any other ship. Designing the new record breaker took some months, and when the time for construction neared, there was not enough of the new steel plate available to build her. Barrow's management informed Inman of the situation and told him that either they would have to wait quite some time before they could start on his new steel ship, or else they could build her of iron, which was much more readily available than steel in 1880. Inman pondered the problem and informed Barrow that they could build the new liner of iron, but that he still would hold them to the contract in terms of carrying capacity and speed. Optimistically Barrow agreed, and the new ship soon began to take shape. She was launched as the *City of Rome* (1881; 8,415 tons, 560 feet, 16 knots) on June 14, 1881. Unfortunately William Inman, her principal backer, died three weeks later on July 3, 1881, at the age of fifty-six, and never lived to see her in service.[1]

The Inman Line invested a substantial amount of time and money publicizing their new ship, which was designed to be the largest and fastest vessel in the world. When she took her maiden voyage on October 13, 1881, she was graced by three slender funnels and four towering masts and was one of the most beautiful vessels ever built for the North Atlantic. She also had grave liabilities. First, because of the weight of the iron hull, her cargo capacity was twenty-two hundred tons instead of the thirty-eight hundred tons stipulated in the contract. Second, on her maiden voyage, October 13, 1881, she crossed the Atlantic in a dismal nine days, seventeen hours from Queenstown to New York. This was almost two days, seven hours slower than the record of the Guion Line's *Arizona* (1879; 5,147 tons, 450 feet, 16 knots), which she had been built to beat. Over the next six months the engines of the *City of Rome* virtually were rebuilt, and a new propeller was fitted, but there was no significant improvement in speed. Disgusted, the Inman Line management handed her back to her builders and refused to accept the ship. To put it mildly, she was no record breaker. Some authorities think that had William Inman lived the *City of Rome* would have been accepted on some terms because she still would have represented an asset to the line. The new management, minus Inman, blanched at the thought of the cost of a new vessel that in no way met her contract specifications and opted out.[2] Critics have described the *City of Rome* with her three funnels and four pole masts as "the most stately and well proportioned steamship ever built."[3] Unfortunately, beauty was only skin deep when the Blue Riband was being pursued. In 1882 the *City of Rome* was handed over for employment to the Anchor Line, which had a close business association with the Barrow Shipbuilding Company. She ran for the Anchor Line for eight years and then in various services before an early scrapping in Germany in 1902.

The City of Chicago *(1883) of the Inman Line is shown romping along with some of her sails set in order to take advantage of a stiff breeze. She is westbound from Liverpool to New York since she is flying the American flag at her foremast. On July 1, 1892, in dense fog, she would ram her bow into the rocky promontory known as the Old Head of Kinsale, Ireland, and become a total loss. Miraculously all her passengers and crew members would survive.*

When the Inman Line rejected the *City of Rome,* it became imperative to add a vessel to the fleet as soon as possible. British shipyards were surveyed to see what might be available in terms of new or nearly complete tonnage. Charles Connell & Company of Glasgow, Scotland, was building for the Dominion Line a large five-thousand-ton liner, which had been laid down as the *Vancouver.* After negotiations the ship was bought on the stocks so that when she was launched on May 23, 1883, she went down the ways as the *City of Chicago* (1883; 5,202 tons, 431 feet, 14 knots). There never was any question about the *City of Chicago*'s being a record breaker. Her machinery had not been designed for that. When completed, this liner also would lack something that graced the front of nearly all Inman Line vessels, a clipper bow. The construction of the *City of Chicago* was far enough along at the time of her purchase that no effort was made to change her bow from a straight stem to a clipper. She entered the Inman Line transatlantic service on September 18, 1883, and proved to be a solid performer for the next decade.

The *City of Chicago* was part of the Inman fleet bought by the

American Quaker Clement Acton Griscom in 1886. She became an important unit in the new Inman & International Steamship Company service between Liverpool and New York even if she was half the size and five knots slower than the greyhounds, *City of New York* (1888) and *City of Paris* (1889), which Griscom ordered.

The last major disaster to an Inman & International vessel occurred to the *City of Chicago* on July 1, 1892, and it was spectacular. The liner left New York June 22 under the command of Captain Arthur Redford, who had safely brought the burning *City of Richmond* into Queenstown the year before. She sailed with a good load of passengers, cargo, and the mails. A relatively uneventful crossing of the North Atlantic occurred until the Irish coast was sighted late in the afternoon of July 1. In clear weather at 4:45 P.M. signals were exchanged with Brow Head, which reported the liner's position to Liverpool, indicating that the Atlantic crossing was nearly completed. Steaming along the south coast of Ireland, she reached Fastnet Light on its rocky inlet four miles south of Cape Clear, and Captain Redford changed course for Queenstown. Then a thick fog suddenly set in, and visibility was reduced to nothing. Redford debated the problem. He had some passengers who wanted to be landed at Queenstown. They would be inconvenienced by having to go to Liverpool because they would then have to take a ferry boat back to Ireland. On the other hand, faced with the severe fog blanketing the Irish coast, he was justified in making directly for Liverpool as a matter of safety. The fog lifted slightly over the sea but still obscured the coast even if it looked as though it might be breaking up. Redford decided to make for Queenstown.

As the *City of Chicago* steamed through the fog along the southern Irish coast, one last obstacle lay along her course to Queenstown: the Old Head of Kinsale, a rocky promontory that presented a stern visage to the North Atlantic. For millennia ships had found the Old Head of Kinsale and the surrounding waters a nemesis. Redford caused soundings to be taken, and the line indicated plenty of water under the ship. Unfortunately the soundings were deceptive since the dropoff from the shore was very sheer. The *City of Chicago* was going nearly full speed when she suddenly slammed head-on into a solid wall of rock two hundred feet high. The shock to those on board was extreme with nearly everyone thrown from their feet and sliding along the deck until they hit the housing or the rail. Passengers were terrified, with women shrieking and children crying. Captain Redford and his officers made a quick tour of the deck, calming the mayhem and reassuring individuals that there was no danger of the ship sinking immediately.

Near the outermost point of the Old Head of Kinsale, North Atlantic storms had cut a small fissure into the solid rock, and into that crack the *City of Chicago* had rammed her bow at full speed. She was held fast. The bow was torn off, and her forward compartments rapidly filled with water. Those familiar with the seas and currents in the area said that it was entirely possible for the weather to have created an offshore surge which pushed the *City of Chicago* toward land, causing even her experienced officers to misjudge her position.

When it was found that the steamer could not get off the rocks and was badly damaged, the nine-hundred-horsepower compound engines were kept going ahead in order to keep her secure so that she would not slip off into deep water as the tide rose. The fog was dense, and the scene dismal, with the beetling cliffs soaring high above the *City of Chicago.* There appeared no possibility of the liner refloating, and the passengers were told that they must prepare to abandon ship. Orders were given to launch the boats, none of which were damaged by the collision with the cliff, and distress rockets were fired off to warn the coast guard that a vessel was in distress. The Irish coast guard must have been shocked when a rocket indicating a ship in distress soared into the heavens almost from the base of the lighthouse. Happily they and others onshore responded quickly.

From the top of the towering black cliffs rope ladders were lowered to the gangway of the *City of Chicago,* which was run out over the bow until it touched the face of the rock. By the time the rescue efforts were ready, and the rope ladders secure, a pitch-black night had set in to complement the dense fog. One passenger said: "Some confusion prevailed, but considering the position of the vessel, sunk in the cleft, and the darkness of the night, the safe ascension by the passengers of the perilous cliffs on the swaying ladders was remarkable. The men of the tender *Ireland* state that exactly over where the vessel is lying there is a perpendicular cliff from 200 to 300 feet in height. The bow of the steamer had run into an indentation in the rocks, which formed a nook that was so admirably fitted to receive the bow that it looks as if it had been contrived for the purpose by a most skillful engineer."[4]

The passengers were unanimous in praising the officers and crew of the liner for the care and courage they showed during that bleak and dark night. Crew members climbed the swaying rope ladders again and again, leading passengers to safety. The ordeal for women and children in the pitch-darkness on the swaying ropes was particularly horrifying. Without the encouragement and assistance of the sailors, it was believed many of the women and children would never have ascended the cliff to safety. Probably many of the men as well. The account of the manner in which the Inman & International sailors handled the passengers that night remains a touching example of courage under excruciating stress.

> The sailors laughed and joked with them until they imparted some of their good spirits to the terrified souls, and then would prevail on them to try the climb, telling them that it was as easy as going up stairs. Then when the lady or child would start, a sailor would spring upon the ladder ahead, while another would follow close behind, holding them securely. If the climbers showed the least sign of weakness, the sailors would encourage them with cheering words and helpful hands. Thus the perilous ascent was made until the summit was reached. Here the peasants and coastguardsmen did good service by lifting them from the ladder and caring for them afterwards.[5]

The entire operation passed without injury or loss of life, as fortune smiled. Tragedy was narrowly averted when a six-year-old boy lost his footing and began to fall from a height of over forty feet. Some of the sailors heard the scream and saw the little shape hurtling toward the rocks. Incredibly one sailor was able to catch the boy, knocking the wind out of him but saving his life. The boy was described as "quite badly shaken." The reaction of his parents is not recorded!

Some of the passengers who felt the climb totally beyond their capacity were rowed down the coast until a better landing place was found. All hands reaching the top of the cliff were offered the loan of heavy coats by generous peasants to protect them from the cold and the dampness of the fog. Irish jaunting cars arrived and conveyed the exhausted survivors to the town of Kinsale, about twelve miles through dense fog from the place where the *City of Chicago* was wrecked. The Lloyd's signal station sheltered some sixty individuals until they could be moved to better quarters. All the passengers spoke in the highest manner about the conduct of Captain Redford and his crew.

As soon as the news of the accident reached Queenstown, tenders and tugs were dispatched to take off the mails and the passengers' luggage from the stranded liner. They also would have rescued passengers had they arrived in time, but the fog was so thick they had to crawl through the night in order not to add to the disaster. By the time the tenders felt their way down the coast to the *City of Chicago* all her passengers were safely ashore and en route to town. As soon as the passengers were away, Captain Redford had the derricks rigged and preparations made for hauling the mails and the passengers' luggage out of the hold. When the tenders appeared, the hatches were removed, and the mails and baggage transferred. Redford also thought that if there was any chance of saving the *City of Chicago,* she would have to be lightened. This was accomplished by removing from the holds as much of her cargo as possible and transshipping it into the tenders. While this was under way, the breeze sprang up and the fog lifted, revealing the full extent of the predicament of the ship.

There was little hope of saving her. The stem of the vessel, from the hawser pipes, through which the anchor cables pass, down to the forefoot, was completely gone. The two forward holds had ruptured and filled with water, holding her fast. Beneath the keel the seafloor sheered away very abruptly. In the 430-foot length of the *City of Chicago,* the water went from zero to sixty-six feet. Her bow was ashore, and her screw had eleven fathoms underneath it. The Lloyd's observer guessed that the liner was pivoting at a point just behind the funnel. Quite a swell was moving against the Old Head of Kinsale, and the ship was working and grating against the rocks. The Atlantic was completing the process of ripping the bottom out of the vessel. Any severe working of the hull would break her back, and the next storm would provide the necessary motion. Still, Captain Redford did not give up and remained on board with a picked crew to try to save the ship. Additional pumps were ordered. They were imperative if the depth of the water in the forward holds was to be lessened. In the meantime every effort was made to remove any remaining cargo that could be reached. Fresh beef went to Milford Haven, Wales, on one tug, and another took more than a hundred tons of dry goods to Queenstown.

The weather worsened, and the efforts of four tugs to pull the *City of Chicago* off the rocks on July 5 failed. As the gale increased, the ship swung around with her stern almost parallel to the shore. Two tugs got lines on her and tried to keep the stern in deep water, but the battle was being lost. A full North Atlantic gale pounded the trapped *City of Chicago* during the night of July 6–7. Captain Redford finally gave the order at 10:00 P.M. for the members of his crew to cease their heroic efforts and abandon ship. At about midnight a tremendous crash brought the attention of the watchers on the cliff, who saw the *City of Chicago* broken into two pieces with her stern section also firmly on the rocks. The salvage steamers could do their work no longer. However, even with the liner split into two pieces some still spoke of rigging derricks on the cliff and continuing the removal of whatever cargo might remain.

The cargo successfully salvaged from the *City of Chicago* consisted of: "1,720 boxes of bacon, 595 pails of lard, 431 packages of provisions, 131 packages of leather, 1,100 tons of meat, 1,825 pieces of pipe staves,

110 pieces of lignum vitae, 20 bundles of hides, 31 tierces of tobacco, 588 boxes of cheese, 325 barrels of oil, 32 bundles of rubber, 114 packages of sewing machines, 14 packages of machinery and hardware, 5 bales of furs, 39,965 bushels of wheat, and 308 bags of ore."[6] The salvage list provides an excellent idea of what a liner would be carrying as cargo in the early 1890s between the United States and Britain. It also is a remarkable testimonial to the efforts of Captain Redford and his crew to save the cargo.

As a footnote to the sinking of the *City of Chicago,* three of her passengers were the American Peace Commissioners appointed by the Irish National League for the purpose of bringing about a reconciliation between the warring factions in Ireland. The commissioners were M. D. Gallagher, of New York, O'Neill Ryan, of St. Louis, and George Sweeney, of Cincinnati. The American peace commissioners were to have a rough time of it on land, but nothing to equal the manner of their arrival.

Chapter 13

OCEAN RACING CAN BE HAZARDOUS!

The *St. Paul* and the *Campania* Experience Near Disaster

January 25, 1896

When Clement Acton Griscom, assisted by the Pennsylvania Railroad, succeeded in buying control of the celebrated Inman Line of Liverpool, he immediately sought to rebuild the fortunes of the British-flag line through the ordering of two new ships in Scotland designed to be the largest and fastest in the world. These ships were the *City of New York* (1888) and the *City of Paris* (1889).

Unexpected disaster struck Griscom before the commissioning of the new ships. In 1887 the British government reviewed the arrangements for carrying the mails across the North Atlantic and decided that two sailings a week by Cunard and White Star would be adequate. Both lines were not only British-built and -manned, but also British-owned. Behind the scenes revenge was taken for Griscom's audacity in buying Inman. The third mail each week heretofore carried by Inman was discontinued, and the subsidy paid the line canceled. Unofficially Griscom was informed that the British government saw no reason to subsidize the new American owners of Inman & International even if it remained a British-flag steamship line.[1] This action severely affected the financial solvency of Griscom's American-financed maritime empire. It was questionable whether the two new liners could be operated profitably without some form of guaranteed income through a contract to carry the mails.

In the United States a political movement was under way to reestablish an American mail subsidy designed to encourage the development of the American Merchant Marine. The earliest manifestation of this was the Postal Aid Act of 1891, which created a schedule of subsidies intended to stimulate new American-flag steamship lines. The act did not result in a flood of offers to begin a first-class line of mail steamers on the North Atlantic. In fact not a single offer was forthcoming since a subsidy of only twelve thousand dollars per voyage was far from sufficient inducement to invest millions in a fleet of expensive ocean greyhounds. The offer could look attractive only to an already established line in need of a subsidy, but there was no such commercial endeavor under the American flag.

There was, however, the American-owned and -operated Inman & International Steamship Company, which had been denied the British subsidy and was ready, willing, and able to undertake a transatlantic service under the terms of the U.S. mail contract. Accordingly, this was the moment when Griscom ushered before the Senate Commerce Committee his two new express liners, the *City of New York* and *City of Paris,* both of them Blue Riband liners. He petitioned Congress to allow his two Atlantic champions U.S. registry. In return he offered to build two larger vessels in American yards to complete the quartet of superliners necessary for a regular weekly transatlantic service at a service speed of twenty knots.

Congress did not have to hesitate over the Inman & International offer for several reasons. It did not appear that a transatlantic service would ever be taken up by an American concern. The Inman & International Line nearly filled this qualification since it was wholly owned and operated by American citizens. Furthermore, the establishment of such an important line of ships under the American flag would bolster American pride and interest in the American Merchant Marine. At the same time the action was a slap at the British government, which apparently had tried to ruin the American investors. Finally, the offer to build two consorts for the brand-new and already famous *City of New York* and *City of Paris* in American shipyards promised to provide a great stimulus for the American shipbuilding industry, which could use two such prestigious orders.

On May 10, 1892, Congress therefore approved a measure giving U.S. registry to the *City of New York* and *City of Paris* and thereby paved the way for the return of the American flag to the North Atlantic in a most spectacular manner. The Inman & International Steamship Company changed its name to the American Line.

A key factor in the legislation permitting U.S. registry for the *New York* and the *Paris* was the immediate ordering and construction of two similar units in an American shipyard. When the transfer of the American-owned Inman & International liners to the United States occurred, Griscom took immediate action to convert his promise into reality. Contracts for the construction of two ocean greyhounds were signed with William Cramp & Sons Ship and Engine Building Company of Philadelphia. Griscom was a director of the Cramp shipyard, but little issues like this apparent conflict of interest did not matter in 1892. Cramp had a long and honorable history of solid and dependable ship construction. At the time of the order the shipyard was under the management of Charles H. Cramp, one of the most eloquent and forceful maritime spokesmen of his day. Rarely did he permit an occasion to pass without exhorting his fellow Americans to think about the condition of the American Merchant Marine. In the early 1890s the Cramp shipyard was turning out a substantial number of warships for the United States Navy and was admirably suited to undertake the ambitious project of producing the first American transatlantic greyhounds.

Charles Cramp set to work on the new American Line fliers with a gusto. He was determined to prove that an American shipyard could produce as fine a vessel as any British yard. The plans for the new liners were laid down in the mold lofts by March 1893, and the keel blocks for the first one placed on the stocks about the same time.

It was a source of no little pride to Cramp that the liners would be constructed from the "trunk to the keelson" of American material. He set out to ignore completely the tariff revisions permitting shipbuilders to import necessary construction materials without paying duty.[2] The two new liners were to be as completely American as he could make them. Every order went to American rolling mills, foundries, and forges. The three-quarter-inch steel plates for the ships came from the Wellman Iron and Steel Company, while additional steel was to be supplied by Carnegie, Phipps & Company of Pittsburgh.

The act permitting American registry for the *New York* and the *Paris* stipulated that the new vessels must equal the earlier vessels in size and tonnage. In fact the Delaware ships when commissioned came in at a thousand tons larger than the Clyde pair.

The American Line ships had the following dimensions:

Length overall	554 feet
Length on load waterline	536 feet
Extreme beam	63 feet
Depth of hold	42 feet
Gross registered tons	11,000

In appearance they differed significantly from the *New York* and the *Paris* inasmuch as they had straight stems instead of clipper, two funnels instead of three, and two masts instead of three. The masts, more for ornament than for use, were ordinary pole masts with a fore-and-aft schooner rig. Since this was the first time that quadruple-expansion engines of more than four thousand horsepower were being used in a ship, Cramp was required to show during prolonged trials that the ship could maintain a speed of twenty knots.

The *St. Louis* was launched successfully by the Cramp shipyard on November 12, 1894. The launching of her sister ship, the *St. Paul,* originally was scheduled for March 25, 1895, but the hull stuck, and the actual launching finally took place on April 9, 1895. The *St. Paul* thereby showed her high spirits from her inception, and she was to have an action-filled career. Entering the new American Line service from New York to Southampton in 1895, both new ships quickly became very popular as the fastest, largest, and most luxurious vessels flying the American flag.

Competition was fierce, and some of the most ominous and foreboding maritime headlines that American newspapers ever carried screamed across the top of page one on January 26, 1896: ST. PAUL, SPEEDING IN FOG, GOES AGROUND–IN THE SAND OFF EAST BRANCH, N.J., AFTER A CLOSE RUN WITH HER RIVAL, THE CUNARDER CAMPANIA.

The Cunard liner *Campania* (1893; 12,950 tons, 601 feet, 21 knots) and the new American liner *St. Paul* (1895; 11,629 tons, 554 feet, 20 knots) frequently found themselves competing against each other during the fall and winter of 1895 and 1896. This was not intentional but just occurred by virtue of the luck of scheduling. Both the Cunard Line and the American Line sent one first-class steamer a week in each direction across the North Atlantic, and these two liners were scheduled to sail from Liverpool and Southampton at about the same time. The *Campania* was both larger and more powerful than the *St. Paul.* She was the second-largest passenger liner in the world at 12,950 tons (just 2 tons smaller than her sister ship *Lucania*), while the *St. Paul* was the fourth largest at 11,629 tons (just 1 ton smaller than her sister ship *St. Louis*). The triple-expansion engines of the *Campania* were rated at thirty thousand horsepower, whereas the quadruple-expansion engines of the *St. Paul* were rated at twenty thousand horsepower. The *St. Paul* also was designed to carry substantially more cargo than the *Campania,* while the

The St. Paul *(1895) and her sister ship, the* St. Louis *(1895), at 11,600 tons were the largest passenger liners built in the United States during the nineteenth century. They were built for the American Line by the William Cramp Shipyard, Philadelphia, Pennsylvania. The* St. Paul *nearly met with disaster when she rammed her bow into the shore off East Branch, New Jersey, on January 25, 1896, and remained stuck until February 4.*

Cunarder far exceeded the number of passengers (600, 400, 1000) that the American liner could accommodate (350, 220, 800).[3]

Captain Walker of the *Campania* gave his version of the January 25 "race for New York" afterward:

> "It was about 8:30 o'clock Friday morning," he said, "when we sighted the *St. Paul* about fifteen miles ahead of us off our port bow.
>
> "We watched her smoke for some time without being able to determine who she was, and about the time that we recognized her she must have recognized us, for we both went at it as hard as we could.
>
> "We kept following her, but did not have her abeam until 1 o'clock P.M. We steamed on until 8:30 o'clock P.M., when we ran into the fog, and then ran at a fair speed until 1 o'clock this morning.
>
> "From 1 o'clock until 5:30 o'clock our movement was slow, and we

then anchored. The lead at 5:30 o'clock indicated but ten fathoms of water, and so I backed the ship until I found fifteen fathoms, and then dropped anchor.

"After the anchor was down I knew we were fast to America, and was determined to stick to her. I was satisfied with my position.

"The fog lifted this morning at 9:30 o'clock, we then got underway. I had no idea of where the *St. Paul* was until the lifting of the fog, and I then saw her on the beach."[4]

The historical facts of the near disaster are clear. The *St. Paul* was approximately four hundred miles from New York on the long tract from The Needles to Sandy Hook when the *Campania,* also westbound but from Liverpool/Queenstown to New York, began to overtake her. Captain John Clark Jameson of the *St. Paul,* sighting his archcompetitor in pursuit, asked for and received all possible steam from the engine room. A race for New York began with both big ships producing all the revolutions they could throughout Friday. As a result, the *St. Paul* was able to keep ahead of the *Campania* for the bulk of the day until a fogbank rolled in and obscured the view. Subsequently, the second- and fourth-largest liners in the world continued to slam through the fog, each ignoring everything except her rival. Foghorns thundered at regular intervals, but they appear to have been the only concession to the elements. Passengers on both ships reported constantly hearing the other liner's foghorns as they hurtled through the night. So caught up in the race were the officers on the huge liners that they lost all reckoning of where they were and, even more critical, where their ships should be. Consequently they lost their bearings and went approximately fifteen miles off course. Even though both had slowed appreciably in the early-morning hours, they were still under way at several knots, feeling for the entrance to New York Harbor, when the *St. Paul,* slightly in the lead, suddenly rammed her bow on the sands at East Branch, New Jersey. So gently did she touch that many passengers were not aware of her predicament until they awoke in the morning. The *Campania,* immediately behind her, was warned of the danger by the sudden thunderous blasts of the *St. Paul*'s horns telling of the danger.

The lifesaving crews along the Jersey coast had a busy night. Charles Sexton, a member of Life-Saving Station No. 5, and Joel Woolley, of Crew No. 4, were the first to discover the *St. Paul.* They were on duty patrols shortly after 2:00 A.M. when they saw the approaching lights of the big American liner puncturing the gloom into which they had been staring. They frantically lighted beacons to warn the vessel of her peril, but she had either struck or was just about to strike the sands before the signal could be seen. The two lifesavers hurried to their respective stations, and the crew of No. 4. under Captain Mulligan responded immediately. Captain Wardell of Crew No. 5 said that he thought he would have the huge *Campania* on his hands and did not come at once. By his directions a red light was burned and shortly thereafter answered by the *Campania.* For about a half hour the lights of the Cunarder were seen to pass south of West End, and she was swallowed up by the gloom. Seeing that she was out of danger, Captain Wardell then hurried to the aid of the *St. Paul.* Life-Saving Station No. 3 also had been summoned, so that a team of twenty-four trained lifesavers was on the shore near the grounded liner.

The lifesavers launched three boats through the surf with great difficulty. A breeches buoy was rigged at daybreak, and Captain Mulligan boarded the *St. Paul* to confer with Captain Jameson. When he reached the deck of the American liner, the first question hurled at him by an excited crewman was: "Where is the *Campania?*" Mulligan was a little taken aback by this inquiry because it seemed anyone asking such a question was more interested in the Cunarder than in his own ship. Subsequently he was given the explanation that if the *St. Paul* was ashore, then the *Campania* must have hit the beach also. Fortunately for the Cunarder and the Cunard line this was not the case. There was no immediate danger to the American Line ship although the seas were heavy, dashing against the side of the steamer and sending spray high over the deck. The decision was made by Captain Jameson to keep all passengers on the *St. Paul* and await a tender from New York. The engines stopping and the waves pounding against the side of the ship soon awoke any passengers who were asleep. Those who ventured out on the open deck were not reassured about the safety of their position as they viewed the scene. The long waves rolling in and breaking on the shore did so with a muffled thunder that was not settling to the nerves if your ship was mired in the sand. When the fog thinned, it was seen that the liner had struck the sand bow on and then swung around broadside to the shore. She was firmly stuck and had gone on the bar during a high tide, so none thought she would come off immediately. In fact the comment was made that except for the push of an exceptionally large wave, the *St. Paul* was as stable as in dry dock. This must have been cheerful news to Clement Acton Griscom, managing owner of the American Line, who now was faced with yet another crisis.

Captain Mulligan of the lifesaving station sent word to the American Line agents in New York that they had a big problem ashore. The offices of the International Navigation Company went into high gear immediately. Tugs were dispatched by the Merritt and the Chapman Wrecking Companies, and about 7:00 A.M. the *I. J. Merritt, W. E. Chapman, J. D. Jones, Hustler,* and *Right Arm* were at the side of the stranded vessel. A wreck this size called for the big brass. Captain Thomas Kivlin, wreck master, Arthur M. Smith, secretary, and William M. Chapman, vice-president, all went to the *St. Paul* with the intention of staying with the stranded liner until she was free. Shortly afterward the tugs *Pulver, Millard,* and *Everett* of the New York Towboat Company's fleet also arrived and anchored near the *St. Paul.* However, even eight tugs were not going to budge the heavily laden 11,629-ton hull until she was vastly lightened. Three heavy anchors were soon set offshore as moorings in order to retard or stop the landward drift of the ship. The hawsers running from the anchors to the steam capstans on the *St. Paul* made it possible to produce taut cables and halt her movement. If it was impossible to pull her free, at least it might be possible to ensure that her situation would get no worse.

The American Line marine superintendent, Captain Shackford, hurried down from New York and assumed charge of the work of trying to refloat her. He found the *St. Paul* about one-quarter of a mile north of the Iron Pier, almost beam onto the beach, with her bow pointed to the southwest. News of the stranding soon spread up and down the Jersey coast, and a crowd began to gather. By noon it had swelled to thousands, and the beach for several hundred yards on either side of the stranded liner was full of people braving the elements to see the big ship. To some it was a grand holiday. One young girl clad in bright bloomers and a jaunty cap daringly rode her bicycle up and down the beach. In sharp contrast the scene offshore was impressive as the seas came sweeping in ridges of foam along the *St. Paul*'s sides, the sky had taken on an aspect of sober gray, and over all was heard the panting respirations of eight tugs striving to render aid.

Shortly after noon the paddle-wheel steamer *George Starr* appeared, and the work of transferring passengers and a small amount of hand luggage began. The *St. Paul* had on board 140 cabin passengers and about 120 steerage. They were embarked in lifeboats from gangway ladders lowered from the starboard (leeward) side. The transfer was very tedious with the seas that were running, and it was impossible for the *George Starr* to leave for New York much before 4:00 P.M. Hence the cabin-class passengers did not reach the American Line pier until around 7:30. They were cold, hungry, and irritable. Some first-class passengers were highly incensed that they had to travel on the same paddle steamer as those passengers who had booked second cabin. They were lucky they were not traveling in steerage. Those 120 hearty souls had to withstand a three-hour trip in January up the coast through heavy seas on the open foredeck of the tug *L. Purvel.*

The revenue cutter *Hudson* left New York Harbor with the Deputy Surveyor D. F. Dowling and his staff on board to go to the *St. Paul.* Unfortunately for Dowling and his staff, the *Hudson* returned to quarantine around five because heavy seas and the lines of all the tugboats to the stranded liner created such an obstacle that the vessel could not be boarded. As a special courtesy in order to expedite disembarkation for cabin-class passengers quarantine officials had boarded the *George Starr* so that they could be processed en route to New York. The *St. Paul* also had on board two hundred sacks of transatlantic mail that had to be unloaded with great care to a waiting tug. Only two bags at a time could be handled in safety, so that more than a hundred repetitions had to be attempted before the mails could begin the final leg of their trip to the post office. Besides a substantial general cargo the American liner had over a million dollars consigned to W. H. Crossman & Son in her strongboxes, which had to be guarded.

When Captain Jameson of the *St. Paul* finally was interviewed by the press, he was singularly noncommittal about the circumstances of the accident. One reporter asked him if he thought the stranding was caused by any negligence on the part of the officers or the pilot of the ship, and he absolutely refused to take a position. However, he stated that while he was on the bridge at the time that the *St. Paul* struck the beach, the ship was in the charge of the pilot. If this version of events was accepted, then the accident could not be laid at his door. He also let it be known that the liner had steamed through the fog at about three knots and that soundings had been made throughout the night. The last sounding just before the liner struck revealed seventeen fathoms of water, which was more than adequate. After hitting the shore, Jameson had surveyed the hull of his ship from one end to the other and had seen absolutely no sign of damage or leaking. The hull was as solid as the day she was launched.

Griscom, the president of the American Line, could not stay away from the site where one of his great ships was ashore. Arrangements were made for a special train to carry him from Jersey City to East Branch in order to see the *St. Paul.* One can imagine the delight with which he viewed the scene and the trepidation of those officers on the liner when they saw the "old man" on the shore scowling up at them with his handlebar mustaches twitching. As night fell, the liner was lighted from stem to stern with electric lights, which threw an ethereal cast on the shore. Old-timers along the Jersey coast said that if the liner were refloated within a week, she would be lucky.

That evening at the Cunard pier in New York the officers and crew of the *Campania* were counting their blessings. Some passengers on the big Cunarder claimed, with substantial reason, that she had buried her bow into the sand also, but not as deeply as the *St. Paul,* and had been able to back off into deeper water. On board the *Campania,* now empty of passengers, there was a feeling of heartfelt congratulations from coal passers to captain that it was not their ship that was fast in the East Branch sands. "So intent was every one aboard the *Campania* upon the result of the stern chase that she was giving the *St. Paul,* that the fact that both were out of the regular course was not noticed until one had gone aground and the other received warnings that she fortunately heeded and dropped her anchor."[5]

It was noted in the newspapers that the coastline of the United States in the approaches to New York Harbor hardly represented terra incognita to the two captains since almost every foot of the distance between the southeasterly point of Long Island and Sandy Hook has its depth of water marked on the charts. It should have been possible for the officers of the ships to learn their positions—even with the fog as dense as it was—by judicious use of the lead and close inspection of the log. Few captains in the world had been over this route more than Jameson of the *St. Paul* and Walker of the *Campania.* They were the acknowledged masters of their craft by virtue of having two of the largest ships in the world entrusted to their care.

In hindsight one man on the *Campania* said he had never been carried through the fog at such a rate of speed in his life as he had been the night before. He said he was frightened from the moment the *Campania* entered the fogbank and expected some accident until the welcome order to let go the anchor was given. Chief Officer Pierce of the *Campania* refused to speak of the ship's narrow escape until he was told that she had been saved only because of warnings received from shore. That was too much for Pierce since it flew in the face of the Cunard story, and he then denied that he had seen or heard anything that called his attention to the position of the other ship. The decision simply had been made on the bridge of the *Campania* to stop and drop anchor. A number of passengers vehemently denied that story because even though as passengers it was not their responsibility to be looking and listening for danger, they had seen the lights from the shore and had heard the horns of the *St. Paul* thundering their warning. In response the command obviously had been given on the bridge for the big Cunarder immediately to reverse her propellers in order to try to stop her forward momentum and get her back into deeper water, where she might anchor in safety. A witness on the shore stated that he saw the *Campania* with her bow in the sand struggling to get off and that she only did so after substantial power had been put into going astern. The lifesavers from Station No. 5 were positive that the *Campania* was aground when they were watching her since she took awhile to back away from the shore, and they certainly were the resident experts.

During that time the *Campania*'s whistles were heard sounding regularly from one position in the fog, and she gave no evidence of moving for a prolonged period of time, before the sound of her whistles indicated she was backing off into safe water. The Reuters news report published in the *Times* of London attributed her narrow escape to her hearing the whistles of the *St. Paul* once she had gone ashore.[6] The Cunard management officially denied any grounding, at the same time as they also were denying that their ship was racing the *St. Paul* or that anyone in authority had heard the *St. Paul*'s distress whistles. The proof of the pudding to some was that the *Campania* was anchored only about a mile from the stranded *St. Paul* when the fog lifted the next morning. The conclusion of one contemporary account states: "The Log of the *Campania* corroborates the statement of some of her passengers that her commander did not know the position of his vessel after she entered the fog, for on it is a reference to being abeam of the Fire Island Light, but no time is given, and a pen has been drawn through the entry. The racing vessels were fully fifteen miles out of their course when one ran aground and the other anchored."[7] The American Line and the Cunard Line could protest all they wanted to, but only Providence, and no act of their employees, had spared the North Atlantic what might have been one of its greatest single disasters.

The wrecking tugs working on the *St. Paul* wasted no time trying to get the ship free from the sands of East Branch, New Jersey, before a new winter storm might come howling down the coast and irretrievably compromise the vessel. Through Saturday night and Sunday morning the American Line crew assisted by numerous other personnel succeeded in getting her passengers' baggage and some of the cargo out of the holds and loaded onto the lighter *John Haggerty*, which then took them to the company piers in New York. This lightened the hull by several thousand tons. The gold in the strongbox was left on board until the next to last trip of the *John Haggerty* on January 28, when it went to New York under the guard of three ship's officers. The removal of the cargo continued for four days, through January 29, by which time everything that could be transshipped had been. Meanwhile efforts to try to move the stranded vessel never ceased.

On Sunday, January 26, the liner lay seventy-five to eighty yards from shore, and thousands of people watched the tugs straining to move her into deep water. The bow and forepart of the liner were stuck in about 14 feet of sand and mud. The tugs succeeded in dragging the ship about 150 feet farther north, but since the essential movement was parallel to the shore, rather than into deeper water, the result was not gratifying. Calculations indicated that the *St. Paul* had rammed her bow into the sand at about 2:30 A.M. only one-half hour before high tide on the morning of January 25. High tide on January 26 was only thirteen inches higher than the day before, and that was not enough to free the liner from the sand.

The highest tide of the month was coming on January 29 at 6:28 A.M., and it was intended to use everything possible to free the *St. Paul* at that time. On the morning of January 26 six immense kedge anchors were planted in the sea about a thousand yards from the stranded vessel. Fastened to the kedges were steel hawsers that were connected to the powerful steam capstans of the ship. Six of the big wrecker tugs were secured to the ship by extra-strong hawsers, and another fifty tugs were anchored in the ocean nearby, waiting to help if called upon. Even though it was a Sunday, if a total of fifty-six tugs were occupied off East Branch, virtually nothing else in New York Harbor could have been moving. Finally, everything was ready, and on a given signal the twenty-thousand-horsepower engines of the *St. Paul* were put full astern, the steam capstans of the ship strained at the hawsers made fast to the kedge anchors astern, and the tugs whipped taut their lines and strove mightily to drag the big steamer from her bed of sand. Little by little she moved until a distance of about 170 feet was traveled toward open water, and then she came to a final stop and could not be budged. One of the results was that whereas she had been on a relatively even keel before this attempt, she now had a substantial list and her starboard waterline was about 10 feet in the air. Soundings showed that the stern was touching but just barely, meaning the propellers were still safe. During the afternoon high tide the tug hawsers and capstan lines to the kedge anchors were kept tight so that the hull would not shift further ashore.

Griscom and Charles Cramp, of the shipyard which had built the *St. Paul*, visited the ship and conversed for hours with Captain Jameson and the other officers. A novelty that appeared in the consultation was the first ship-to-shore telephone, although not in the modern sense. In this instance a telephone line was run from the Ocean Avenue offices of the telephone company to the smoking room on the *St. Paul*. The line was kept slack so that movement of ship would not snap it, and it was thereby possible for personnel on the liner to telephone New York.

Visitors to East Branch, New Jersey, that Sunday numbered over ten thousand. They came from New York, the Jersey coast, and inland as far as Philadelphia. Farmers drove into town from as far away as twenty miles to see the stranded ocean greyhound. The scene on Ocean Avenue resembled nothing so much as a country fair. Quickly improvised lunchrooms, cigar stands, traveling speakeasies, and restaurants furnished food and drink to the multitude of hungry and thirsty onlookers. On the front portico of one of the big summer hotels an enterprising individual put up a SEATS TO RENT sign, and he reaped a harvest from the weary. Bicyclists were everywhere, as was the omnipresent amateur photographer taking hundreds of shots of ships, tugs, and people. The customhouse officer Patterson telephoned from the *St. Paul* that a major attempt would be made to get the ship off the shore at five the next morning.

In the meantime her sister ship, the *St. Louis,* which had been sent to Philadelphia for overhaul and the installation of new enlarged smokestacks, was urgently recalled to take the next sailing of the *St. Paul.* The *St. Louis* had just arrived at the Cramp shipyard. The rivets had been driven out preparatory to the removal of both funnels when the news of the disaster to the *St. Paul* was received. Work was held up for a few hours until a second telegram was received detailing the stranding and requesting that the *St. Louis* be made ready for sea immediately. The bolts and rivets were replaced, and the scaffolding was removed so that the *St. Louis* could sail for New York.

When the side-wheeler *George Starr* came alongside the *St. Paul* once again on Monday, January 27, it was for the purpose of transferring crew members. When the *St. Louis* left for ten weeks at the Cramp shipyard in Philadelphia, most of her crew had been let go. Since she suddenly was being placed back in service, replacements were needed, and if there was one thing the *St. Paul* did not need at that moment, it was a full crew. The *George Starr* had been chartered to bring seventy stewards, thirty-two seamen, and seventy stokers from the *St. Paul* to New York for reassignment to her sister ship. As the *St. Louis* came up the New Jersey coast a little after 8:00 P.M. on January 26, she came in close to the shore to salute and exchange signals with her stranded sister. The *St. Louis'* whistle was blown in salute, and the unfortunate *St.*

Paul responded. Then red, white, and blue lights were burned for the American Line, and with a final toot on her whistle the *St. Louis* altered course toward the Sandy Hook and the entrance to New York Harbor. Once there she had to be fully coaled and provisioned for an Atlantic crossing in half the normal time, as well as take on all the cargo and baggage of the *St. Paul.* As the result of heroic labor, the *St. Louis* was able to take her sister's sailing only a few hours late, and the American Line staff could congratulate itself on a difficult job very well done.

Griscom ordered an American Line inquiry held into the stranding of the *St. Paul.* At the hearing on board the liner Captain Jameson and his officers were examined closely about their actions on the evening of the stranding. At its conclusion no one said anything, but Clement A. Griscom, Jr., manager of the American Line, later indicated that he believed Captain Jameson had handled himself well. The efforts to lighten the ship continued. The lifeboats and davits as well as the two topmasts and every detachable piece of deck fixture were removed from the liner and sent to New York. Attempts to move the *St. Paul* on January 29 and 31 and on February 1, 2, and 3 resulted in small gains that eased her toward the open sea but did not refloat her. The Griscoms, father and son, both spent the night of January 29 on the ship, hoping against hope that it would be freed at that time and went away disappointed. Old hands were beginning to say that only a winter storm with higher than normal seas would free the hull. Since the liner was getting low on coal, two hundred tons were brought by barge on January 28, and another hundred tons on January 29.

February 2 was another Sunday, and the notoriety of the stranded liner surpassed every expectation of the numbers of spectators. East Branch, New Jersey, became the center of the world for an American public eager for a midwinter break. It was the greatest day Long Branch and East Branch, New Jersey, had ever seen. The Central Railroad of New Jersey advertised a special train for the accommodation of visitors who wished to see the stranded ship but did not want to catch an early-morning train. Instead of one excursion there was such a crowd at the New York station that four trains were needed to bring sightseers to the scene. The Pennsylvania Railroad also advertised an excursion to accommodate travelers, and the railroad men were flabbergasted by the response. When the hour came for the special to depart from Philadelphia, a mob of nearly twenty thousand was waiting to board. A second train was announced, and before all who wanted to go had been obliged, the Pennsylvania Railroad had sent nine trains of between eight and fifteen cars each to the Jersey shore. This was only one day after a snowstorm, and the weather was both raw and nippy. M. R. Mulford, a conductor on the Jersey Central, contributed to the humor of the occasion when he announced, "Change cars for St. Paul," as his train pulled into Branchport. The tourists knew what he meant, and all jumped from their seats to go see the ship. Once again the enterprising natives of the Jersey shore opened their businesses to care for the hungry and thirsty throng, which may have numbered a hundred thousand. In spite of widespread fines the previous Sunday, liquor was still available for a price. It was reported that every restaurant in East Branch was sold out of all food by 1:00 P.M., and at that point every enterprising butcher, grocer, baker, and delicatessen owner of any kind opened and was soon stripped of his wares. Boys selling pictures of the *St. Paul* coined money, and it was said professional pickpockets and crooks of all descriptions fleeced the unwary.

The fact that the bow of the *St. Paul* was embedded below the sand in the sticky clay was making it difficult to break her loose from the beach. The tugs did move the hull a little at various times, but a good storm was needed to complete the job. The beginnings of a good nor'easter on February 3 rocked the vessel a bit and made it possible for the tugs to shift her 28 feet seaward in the morning and 196 feet that night. The wrecker tugs were pulling in tandem with the *J. D. Jones* and the *I. J. Merritt* on one cable and the *W. E. Chapman* and *North American* on the other. They might have accomplished even more if the waves had not been coming in so high that part of the time their propellers were out of the water as they rode the crest of a wave. The distances the *St. Paul* moved after going ashore on Saturday were: Sunday, 160 feet; Tuesday, 6 feet; Wednesday, 24 feet; Thursday, 6 feet; Friday, 6 feet; Saturday, 15 feet; Sunday, 8 feet; Monday morning, 28 feet; Monday night, 196 feet. Hundreds of people saw the ship move the longest distance yet on Monday, February 3, in spite of driving rain and blustery conditions. Finally, on Tuesday morning, February 4, after having been ashore for ten days, the hull of the stranded liner loosened from the grip of the sand and the clay.

When the wrecker tugs resumed work on Tuesday morning, there were still two hundred feet between the stranded liner and deep water, but the high water brought by the nor'easter and the rocking the hull had taken during the night made them think this was the time. The supreme effort was set for 9:00 A.M., and the *St. Paul* had a full head of steam up for the occasion. Her big propellers went full astern to assist the tugs. There was a long pull, a strong pull, and a pull all together, and the big ship moved from her bed, grating her keel in the sand and bumping and jolting over the bar. When she slipped into deep water, the air was deafened with the shriek of jubilant tug whistles. None of the tugs had wasted any steam in idle exuberance before the *St. Paul* was actually afloat. Long Branchers streamed to the beach to wave farewell to their most famous ship as she bobbed a curtsy in the Atlantic swells.[8]

Almost immediately the tugs cast off, and the *St. Paul* under her own steam turned her prow toward New York. The Queen of the American Merchant Marine had survived an incredible experience, and no one was more relieved than Captain Jameson. The North German Lloyd steamer *Lahn* (1888; 5,099 tons, 449 feet, 18 knots) was rounding Sandy Hook just as the *St. Paul* arrived. The captain of the *Lahn* dipped her colors and blew three blasts on her whistles while her passengers lined the rail and cheered. The *St. Paul* proudly returned the flag and whistle salutes. She cleared quarantine at 12:25 P.M., and Clement Griscom, Jr., came out on the tug *C. E. Evarts* to board her. The two wrecker tugs *W. E. Chapman* and *J. D. Jones* maintained an escort through the harbor and to her berth just in case anything went wrong. If the *St. Paul* attracted little attention as she steamed up the bay, this was not the case as she neared her pier. Her incognito passage was broken by the salute of an observant tug captain on the North River, and soon river craft of all manner were saluting the liner on her safe arrival. On the bridge at the docking were Captain Jameson, pilot William Gormond, Clement A. Griscom, Jr., and Captain Shackford, shore captain of the American Line. An immediate examination of the liner was undertaken by the insurers, who found very little to comment upon. However, they did insist that the ship be dry-docked for a more complete inspection of the hull, and this necessitated a trip to Newport News, Virginia. The insurers were responsible for paying the salvage claims, the cost of lightering the cargo off the ship and into New York, and for the repairs to the vessel.

When Griscom was asked if Captain Jameson would be fired, he replied absolutely not. The American Line had every confidence in him as master of any of its ships. In the subsequent hearings before the Board of Inspectors of Steam Vessels Captain Jameson handled the testimony well. He was fully in command of his facts, and he could prove that he had stopped the *St. Paul* on several occasions to cast the lead in order to try to determine where he was. At the time she went on the beach he was steaming at less than five knots and a recent heaving of the lead had indicated seventeen fathoms of water.[9] In the face of his testimony, which was substantiated by other officers and the ship's records, the Board of Inspectors of Steam Vessels exonerated Captain Jamison of all negligence in the stranding of his ship.[10] The issue of whether or not the *St. Paul* and the *Campania* had been racing does not appear to have been raised by anyone.

The salvage claim of the Merritt Wrecking Company ultimately ended up in court, where the decision of the district court was affirmed by the U.S. Circuit Court of Appeals in April 1898. The award of $131,012.48 was the second largest on record against a ship, and an additional $28,987.52 was affirmed against the cargo. In court the American Line claimed that the evaluation of $2,000,000 for the *St. Paul* was too high, but Merritt produced records that showed that the ship had actually cost $2,650,000 to build just two years before. The wreckers got nearly all that they wanted since the cargo was valued at $2,000,000, over half of which was gold packed in bags and easily handled. Judge Lacombe ruled that there was no reason the gold should not bear a fair share of the cost of the operations and ruled in favor of the Merritt Wrecking Company.[11] The dry docking of the *St. Paul* at Newport News, Virginia, revealed that the hull was virtually undamaged by the grounding of the liner and that all aspects of the machinery were perfect. The *St. Paul* left Virginia on Sunday, February 23, and returned to New York in preparation for taking the Wednesday sailing on February 26. Once again the American Line had four liners to handle the weekly mailings. This was fortunate because all the units of the fleet were in for a rough winter.

Chapter 14

THE LOSS OF HOLLAND AMERICA'S GALLANT *VEENDAM* TO CAUSES BEYOND COMPREHENSION

February 6–8, 1898

The potential danger to Atlantic shipping from flotsam, jetsam, and abandoned wrecks was well known to mariners. In the nineteenth century the ocean was littered with the remains of sailing vessels and steamers as well as natural perils. It was important for every captain to mark the last sighted position of any potential floating obstacle and to keep abreast of any changes. At sea warning of potential danger might appear by virtue of scattered wreckage, but even the most skilled lookout might miss a half-sunken hull drifting with deadly menace just beneath the waves. This is what happened to the Holland America liner *Veendam* and her gallant captain, G. Stenger, in February 1898.

Captain Stenger already had earned the reputation of being one of the most competent master mariners on the North Atlantic. He was both a highly skilled ship handler and very popular with the knowledgeable traveling public. In mid-career Stenger had risen to the command of the premier units of the Nederlandsch-Amerikaansche

Stoomvaart Maatschappij (Holland America) fleet. He sailed from Rotterdam in command of the *Veendam* on Thursday, February 3, 1898, with a typical winter passenger list of 4 saloon, 5 second-cabin, and 118 steerage passengers. The crew of the liner numbered 85, and the general cargo was valued at between three and four hundred thousand dollars.

The *Veendam* originally had a distinguished career as the White Star liner *Baltic* (1871; 3,707 tons, 420 feet, 14 knots). She was purchased by Holland America in 1888, and her original compound engines were replaced with more economical triple-expansion engines in 1890. The Holland America Line (NASM) was founded at Rotterdam in 1873 for the purposes of enhancing the steamship service between the Netherlands and the United States. In the period between 1873 and 1898, Holland America managed to survive economic depressions and to build upon better trading conditions through the judicious purchase

The Veendam *(1888) of the Holland America Line originally had been the* Baltic *(1871) of the White Star Line. She was purchased (1888), reconditioned, and reengined (1890), and served the Dutch line well for a decade until she met with disaster in mid-Atlantic, February 6–8, 1898. The rescue of all her passengers and crew by the American liner* St. Louis *was a tremendous triumph over adversity.*

of secondhand tonnage. Hence, their acquisition of the *Veendam,* which they reengined and refurbished to meet the needs of the Holland America Line. She had a reputation for being a good, solid, steady seaboat under most North Atlantic conditions.[1]

The voyage down the Channel was uneventful, and the *Veendam* turned her bow westward for the run to New York. Weather conditions in February rarely were ideal, and the liner encountered strong northwest gales and high west-northwest seas. As darkness settled on Sunday, February 6, the Dutch liner was five to six hundred miles west of England. Some wreckage was seen bobbing in the waves, and the lookouts were keeping sharp eyes for anything more serious. Suddenly the *Veendam* was lifted by a wave, up and over a large submerged wreck, and then slammed down on top of it. In the engine room Chief Engineer Lichtenbelt was shaken by the blow and the deafening grating sound that followed. The engines were stopped at once, and Lichtenbelt ran aft to the shaft tunnel entrance, where the propeller shaft went into the sea, only to be driven back by inrushing water. The after half of the liner had suffered severe damage. The propeller shaft was broken, and two bulkheads had been shattered by the impact.[2] The *Veendam* had suffered mortal wounds and immediately began to sink. The ship's construction included seven watertight compartments, and three were open to the sea. Frantic efforts reinforced the bulkhead between the fireroom and the No. 3 hold. The steam pumps were set going, but the water flooded in twice as fast as it could be pumped out. Hand pumps were worked, and a bucket brigade began, but nothing could counteract the steadily rising water. The activities of the crew slowed the rate of sinking and did what could be done to ensure that the liner would not make a sudden dive for the ocean floor.

The *Veendam* wallowed without power in the North Atlantic as darkness set in and the stern sank deeper. The inrushing water from the fractured shaft tunnel filled the engine room and fireroom, inexorably pulling the liner stern first under the stormy seas. The watertight bulkheads could not save the ship, but there was a chance they could buy enough time to save the lives of the 212 passengers and crew. All lifeboats were made ready to leave the liner, but no one was willing to go until the last possible moment because the seas were so rough and the wind was so strong. Rockets were fired off at regular intervals in the hope of attracting the attention of a passing vessel. During the next eight hours every able-bodied crew member and male passenger, took many turns at the pumps, desperately trying to keep the ship afloat. Throughout the night Captain Stenger's solid courage and personal heroism sustained all those under his care.[3]

In what is exceedingly rare in maritime lore there are some accounts from steerage passengers of this disaster. Mandel Mandoff and David Devinishke, both from Kovno Gubernia, in Russian Poland, told what happened to them:

> It was after 5 o'clock on Sunday that there came a terrific crash. We did not know what was the matter. The women sprang from their cots, forgetting their seasickness, and began to rush about shrieking in alarm. We asked to be told what the trouble was, but received no information.
>
> The ship stopped, and there began a terrible rushing about overhead. We knew that there must be some terrible trouble, and we began to pray. Suddenly one of the officers appeared in the steerage and ordered all the men on deck. We obeyed and were put to work on the pumps.
>
> Oh, how we worked those pumps. We knew that our lives depended on keeping the water down, but pump as hard as we could it was impossible to lessen the immense quantity that poured in. We were all exhausted. . . .

Chaia Nyitka, who came to this country with her father, Israel, from Sushkovalen, Kalisz Gubernia, Russia, spoke for the women:

> Nearly all of us were sick, and most of the women and children were in their beds when the crash came. But then our sickness was frightened away. I fainted, though, as did some of the other women. But we soon

revived and ran around trying to discover what had happened. When we saw the men saying the "Shema" and the children gathered around us crying, we felt as though the last moment had come.

We followed the men on deck because we were afraid to stay where we could not see. We strained our eyes to see a ship, but nothing was in sight. Then there was a report and great lights shot up. They were firing rockets. When finally we saw the lights of another vessel it seemed too good to be true. The rockets were sent up faster, and the lights on the other vessel grew bigger and brighter. Then we knew they saw us.[4]

At one-thirty the next morning the lights of a large steamer were seen east by south of the *Veendam,* and every possible effort was made to attract her attention. To the infinite relief of those on the Dutch ship the steamer was observed to turn slowly and make for them. As the liner drew near, her searchlights swept the turbulent sea, and those on board the *Veendam* were overjoyed to see that the vessel coming to their rescue was one of the newest, largest, and best-equipped liners on the North Atlantic, the *St. Louis* of the American Line.[5]

Not a moment was lost because the *Veendam* situation was critical. The *St. Louis* was sighted at one-thirty, and by one forty-three Captain Stenger was making arrangements to transfer his passengers and crew to the American liner. Captain William C. Randle of the *St. Louis* took one look at the sinking Dutch ship and wondered if there would be enough time for any rescue. He had sailed from Southampton on February 5 with 221 cabin and 183 steerage passengers, most of whom slept through the night. Randle took the *St. Louis* to within a quarter mile of the *Veendam* but feared to approach any closer because both liners were laboring hard in the high seas. The chief officer of the *St. Louis,* Thomas C. Segrave, made a name for himself that night as the leader of the rescue mission. Segrave called for volunteers from the crew, and eight husky seamen answered his call. Four got into a lifeboat, which was lowered away while they tried to keep it from slamming against the side of the liner. The other four seamen slid down the ropes to the bobbing boat, which nearly swamped even though everyone was as quick as possible. One sea nearly upended the lifeboat and slammed it against the steel side of the ship, but frantic rowing prevented disaster. Segrave said it had been a very close escape, followed by a hard pull to the side of the *Veendam,* but the crack American crew was alongside the sinking liner in seven minutes. Happily the earlier darkness of the night was broken by a bright moon that greatly enhanced visibility. Once the rescuers were alongside the Dutch liner they faced new challenges since the ship had no power and was rolling uncontrollably. Captain Stenger was at the rail, overseeing this critical stage of the operation. After some effort a line thrown from the *Veendam* was seized by those in the lifeboat.

Segrave remained impressed for the rest of his life by the total command of the situation that the Dutch captain showed and by how his own exhausted crew obeyed him and followed his leadership without question. Since there was no such thing as wireless communication yet, Segrave brought a message from Randle that if more boats were needed, the *Veendam* was to make more fire, so that more smoke would come out the funnel, and this was done immediately. Segrave made ready to receive passengers in the lifeboat, and as he reported, "Captain Stenger sent down the children first, and first of all was a wee babe of six months. Life slings were used, and the Captain personally examined the line to see that it was properly tied before any one was let down. The babe was placed in the stern."[6] Segrave got twenty children and five women in his lifeboat, all he thought he could take in safety given the precious nature of his cargo.

The seas were running so heavy that those on the *St. Louis* saw the returning lifeboat only occasionally. Every time it dropped from view in the trough of a wave there were gasps on the Promenade Deck of the American liner as it looked as though the lifeboat had been lost. Furthermore, on occasion it looked as if Segrave had lost sight of the *St. Louis* and had to alter course while at the top of a huge swell as his men strained with all their might to row back to their ship. Two additional lifeboats from the *St. Louis* passed Segrave as his lifeboat struggled to get back to the big American liner.

As the first lifeboat neared the *St. Louis,* an amusing incident occurred. Looking down at the approaching boat, Captain Randle could hardly believe his eyes. It looked as though there was no one in it except the American sailors. From the deck of the *St. Louis* he bellowed at Segrave, "Why don't you bring back the people?" Segrave, somewhat outraged, hollered back, "People! Why, I've got twenty-five babies aboard," and so he did! A boatswain's chair was used to get the women and children on deck while the men in later lifeboats were hoisted aboard by ropes under their arms. In spite of all possible care every one of the lifeboats suffered some damage. The process of boarding the *St. Louis* was slow, but as one observer commented, haste was out of the question in that sea. As soon as the babies and children reached the deck, American Line stewards grabbed them and whisked them inside to the kitchens and dining rooms where they could be warmed as quickly as possible. Rescued passengers were taken to the appropriate class where all could be provided with accommodations, perhaps even superior to that which they had left on the *Veendam.*[7]

Archer Brown, a *St. Louis* passenger, told reporters in New York about the events following the rescue. "The women, having partially recovered, began to demand their children, and if it had not been so tragic, it would have been ludicrous to see the way they ran about seeking their children. And how they cried with joy when they found their little ones. I tell you there were many sniveliers among us, too. The galley was astir, and hot coffee was being brewed in a jiffy. This, and good, fresh rolls were distributed, and lots of warm milk for the children. How they ate! I never saw such a sight."[8]

Launching the additional boats was not easy. George Beckwith, the second officer of the *St. Louis,* had one lifeboat stove in against the side of the ship and had to pull it up and try with a second before he made it to the *Veendam* to rescue an additional eighteen women from steerage. It may have been the intention to take the first-class and cabin passengers off in the second boat, but the uproar from the terrified women, some of whom had seen their children go ahead of them, altered this. "Beckwith said that the steerage passengers were clamoring to be taken off first, and the cabin passengers, who displayed splendid control of themselves, drew back and said: 'We will wait.'" Nothing adds more to the tale of this rescue than the humanity of this gesture. Rescue may have been at hand, but death was also imminent.[9]

The third American Line boat, under the command of Second Extra Officer Campbell, took off eighteen more women. Before that lifeboat got back to the *St. Louis,* Segrave was again alongside the *Veendam,* rescuing another twenty. In all, Segrave's boat saved ninety lives in four trips, and Beckwith's and Campbell's boats each rescued thirty-six in two trips. The crew of the *Veendam,* although exhausted from their struggle to keep the ship afloat, also participated. Two of the Dutch liner's lifeboats were smashed against her side during launching and were lost. A third finally reached the sea successfully and, manned by Dutch sailors, succeeded in transferring an additional fifty people, mostly crew, to the *St. Louis.*

Captain Stenger was the last to leave his ship. "Before he left he went into the main saloon, and piling up everything inflammable, including a lot of furniture, he poured oil over it and touched it off with a match. This was to insure the craft sinking, that she might not float about as a derelict, dangerous to navigation."[10] He did not want anyone else to experience the hell he had just gone through. Since the *Veendam* had seventeen feet of water in her hold, Stenger did not think she could last for more than another six or seven hours. The burning ship lighted the sea with a huge column of fire. Aemilius Jarvis of Toronto, Canada, a delegate from the North American Racing Union to the British Yacht Racing Association, was a passenger on the *St. Louis.* He commented: "It was an impressive sight, and I watched it until the hull of the *Veendam* had fallen below the horizon. Even then its reflection shone in the sky."[11]

The rescue effort was concluded at 4:53 A.M., a little more than three hours after starting. Every single passenger and every crew member on the *Veendam* were safe. The passengers of the *St. Louis* were so proud of their brave crew that they had a meeting and raised a purse of seven hundred dollars, four hundred of which was for the three boat crews and three hundred for the steerage passengers, who had lost everything they possessed. A testimonial also was prepared, honoring the officers in direct charge of the rescue. The *St. Louis* reached the bar at 2:38 A.M. on February 12, but she was held up by fog and did not reach her berth until midafternoon. The news that she brought the passengers and crew of the *Veendam* was sent to the city from quarantine. The information was garbled, and some thought that the *St. Louis* had experienced trouble. The cheers that greeted the docking of the big American liner at Fulton Street belied that.

Captain Stenger was generous in his praise of the efforts of the American Line officers and crew. Interesting in itself was the fact that the passengers from the Dutch ship reached New York three days ahead of schedule on the much-faster *St. Louis.* August William H. Vandentoorn, the New York agent of Holland America, held the *Spaarndam,* which was preparing to sail, at the company pier for one day so that she could take the officers and crew of the *Veendam* back to the Netherlands. They sailed for Rotterdam the morning after their arrival in New York. Captain Stenger released a letter to the press:

> Before leaving New York I wish to make public acknowledgment for myself and for the passengers, officers and crew of the steamship *Veendam,* of our deep gratitude to Captain Randle, Chief Office Segrave, Senior Second Officer Beckwith, and Extra Second Officer Campbell, also to the other officers with the crew and passengers of the American Line steamship *St. Louis.*
>
> Their assistance was promptly, cheerfully, and most judiciously given, when my vessel was sinking. The hearty welcome on board the *St. Louis,* and the constant kindness received during the rest of the voyage, from the ship's company and her passengers, are far above our praise

and shall never be forgotten. God Bless the good steamer *St. Louis,* her gallant commander, and brave officers and crew.[12]

Stenger was no stranger to rescue operations. He and the *Veendam* had stood by the stricken American schooner *Mary Wells* in January 1894, and he had been presented a gold watch by President Grover Cleveland. A critical comment found its way into the press that the *Veendam* had not been equipped with sufficient lifeboats. This was vehemently denied by Holland America, which pointed out that the Dutch liner had complied with all requirements for lifesaving equipment and that although she was carrying 212 persons, her lifeboats had accommodations for 328, 34 percent more than necessary. Holland America faced a substantial problem with the immigrants, who were now destitute. By American immigration law immigrants having no resources were subject to deportation at the expense of the steamship line that had brought them. Agent Vandentoorn made appropriate arrangements with the Immigration Bureau so that almost all the immigrants could be released. After all, it was cheaper than shipping them back to Europe, and their efforts in manning the pumps had been instrumental in buying time to keep the *Veendam* afloat. One young man from Italy, Michael di Jorio, had to be deported because he had a criminal record. He had been found guilty of poaching on a nobleman's estate near his home in Italy. He protested that all he had been guilty of was taking some kindling lying on the ground, but the American immigration authorities were firm that the law refused admittance to the United States to anyone who had been convicted of any crime. They were sorry, but di Jorio would have to go back to Italy at the expense of the Holland America Line. The freighter *Tottenham* was chartered to take the eastbound cargo of the lost *Veendam,* and passengers were transferred to other Holland America ships or provided with tickets with other lines.

Subsequently Captain William Randle and the officers and crew of the *St. Louis* were recipients of handsome testimonials in recognition of their bravery in rescuing the captain, crew, and passengers of the *Veendam.* The presentations were made on board the *St. Louis* at her dock on March 17, 1898. Holland America's representative, Vandentoorn, made a brief address and then presented Captain Randle with a suitably engraved large silver cup. Segrave, Beckwith, and Campbell each received a similar cup, and every member of the crew engaged in the rescue operation was given a sum of money in a sealed envelope. The Life Saving Benevolent Association presented gold medals to Captain Randle and to the three officers and money to the crew members. Clement Acton Griscom also was very proud of the officers and crew of the *St. Louis,* and the International Navigation Company awarded two hundred dollars to Randle, one hundred to the three other officers, and twenty-five to thirty dollars to each seaman, depending upon his term of service. The efficiency displayed in the successful rescue of the passengers and crew of the *Veendam* reflected very favorably on the American Line. Captain Randle in returning thanks for himself and his men remarked: "Events are transpiring now in this country which may lead us into war, and we may be called upon to sacrifice life in defense of our country. But the satisfaction will not be as great as the saving of life, which is more gratifying than the taking of it."[13] Later Captain Randle was honored by Queen Wilhelmina of the Netherlands with a Dutch knighthood in recognition of the gratitude of the Dutch people.

Chapter 15

A SINKING TANKER IN HEAVY WEATHER CAN BE A TRICKY THING

The *Vindobala*

December 1898

The goodwill between the United States and Great Britain was enhanced during the 1898 Christmas season, when the *Paris* went to the rescue of twenty-three seamen on a sinking British tanker. The *Vindobala* of 1,865 tons was bound from Rouen, France, to Philadelphia in ballast. The tanker had been built on the Tyne in 1880 and was owned by J. A. Salton & Company of London, where she was insured by Lloyd's. She sailed on December 15 from the French port and on December 23 in the midst of a violent North Atlantic storm sprang a leak. Chief Engineer Wood went to the bridge and informed Chief Officer Alfred Backmann that water was coming into the tanker's bunkers and engine room. Wood thought that the ship must have ruptured some rivets during the storm of the previous day, but he could not find the leak and knew only that water was entering the vessel amidships. Immediately upon being informed, Captain Michael J. Clarke ordered the bilge pumps, and later the water ballast pumps, to be set going. The effort to clear the engine room of water proved unsuccessful because so much coal dust was mixed in with the water that the pumps became clogged and useless. The crew struggled to slow the rising waters without success, and the tanker began to settle by the bow.

Realizing that the situation was rapidly deteriorating, Captain Clarke ordered the flag flown upside down during the day. When night fell, flares were burned, and rockets occasionally sent up. As she lost headway, it was impossible to keep the bow of the *Vindobala* pointed into the seas, and the empty tanker rolled heavily. The expedient of putting out a sea anchor was tried. This was made of spars lashed to form a triangle over which canvas was laced. Grate bars were then lashed to two of the points to make it float with the third point upward. This was run out with about seven hundred feet of hawser. As soon as the sea anchor took hold, the steamer swung around and was able to keep her bow to the sea.[1]

On December 24 all fires on the *Vindobala* were extinguished by the rising seawater, and the tanker wallowed helplessly on the North Atlantic as the weather worsened once more. Around 7:30 A.M. on Christmas Day everyone's hopes soared when the lookout sighted a large four-masted steamer coming over the horizon heading northwest. Captain Clarke's words:

> It was known that the tanker was doomed. A few hours it was believed must settle her fate, and probably the fate of her crew. There was therefore great rejoicing at the present, seemingly, of life itself, that Christmas had brought. The gray of early morning spread over the ocean. The wind blew in terrific squalls, and the waves flung themselves so high that they filled the air with spray and flecks of spume. They thickened the atmosphere with a mist that rose high, like that from the foot of Niagara, and it was only at times that the steamer, growing bigger on the horizon, could be made out. The men on the wreck knew that they, too, could be made out with difficulty, if at all. But flares were burned and rockets sent up. The dawn was just light enough to obscure

the distress signals and they were not seen. Then the stranger grew smaller again and was lost to view.[2]

The seamen on the *Vindobala* became downhearted. Captain Clarke remarked that it was the saddest time of his life. The men kept at work, however, and obeyed orders. Incredibly the tanker survived another night, although morning brought additional bad news that seawater had got into the freshwater tanks, and all that was left for the twenty-three men were three beakers carried in the lifeboats. No water could be spared for cooking, and the men had only biscuits. Miraculously, the *Vindobala* made it through yet another night in the mountainous seas.

The storm was still raging fiercely, and many on the British tanker had given up all hope when around 8:00 A.M. the lookout spotted yet another ship on the horizon bearing north and about eight miles distant. The men all gathered at the rail and strained their eyes. The British merchant flag was flying upside down at the truck of the tanker's mizzenmast. The *Vindobala*'s crew members could not believe their eyes as the three tall black funnels marked with white bands of the American Line, familiar to all North Atlantic sailors, were seen slowly blending into one when the liner altered course for the stricken ship.

The *Paris* bore down on the helpless tanker and signaled "What assistance do you need?" Captain Clarke promptly flew the signal flags N and D of the international code, signifying, "I must abandon the vessel." The *Paris* responded that she would send a boat. The waves were running so high and the wind was driving so hard that those on the *Vindobala* regularly saw the liner taking water over her bow that was thrown up and over the funnels as she righted herself or that cascaded over the deck before rolling back into the sea.

It took a brave person to cross the Atlantic in midwinter even on the *Paris.* You knew that the weather would be wretched and that the North Atlantic would have a mean bag of tricks. James Davison, a New York businessman who lived in East Orange, New Jersey, wrote an account of the crossing. The *Paris* had left Southampton promptly at noon on Saturday, December 24, and passed The Needles at 1:34 P.M. Davison wrote:

> The weather along the coast was fair and clear until the Lizard was abeam when old Neptune asserted his sway, and many of the passengers retired to their berths to reflect upon the frailty of man and to contemplate his weakness, and the wonderful mechanism of his inner organism.
>
> On Christmas Day a heavy beam sea caused many of the passengers to continue their meditations in the seclusion of their berths, away from the spray and the seas that were constantly washing the decks. On entering the main saloon on the morning of Christmas Day a very pleasing decoration of United States and British flags was arranged in festoons at the head of the saloon. Between the flags was suspended a large bunch of mistletoe, and underneath the whole another flag bearing the name *Paris.* A rough and confused sea prevailed all day Sunday and Monday, constantly increasing in power, deluging the decks with spray, so that the passengers for their own comfort and safety were compelled to remain below. Tuesday morning the gale increased in severity, producing very high and dangerous seas.
>
> A little before 8 o'clock a steamer was sighted, showing signals of distress; the course of the *Paris* was altered and in half an hour we got sufficiently near to read distinctly the signals, which, being interpreted, read that she would have to be abandoned. The distressed vessel lay in the trough of the sea, perfectly helpless. The vessel proved to be the English tank steamer *Vindobala* of London, Captain Michael J. Clarke, in ballast from Rouen, France, to Philadelphia for a cargo of oil.
>
> The *Paris* swung around on the lee of the *Vindobala* and immediately began preparations for rescue. A volunteer crew comprising the First Officer, John Bradshaw, Fourth Officer R. H. Webb, and a crew of eight noble seamen manned a lifeboat, each man wearing a life belt and taking off all superfluous clothing, even their shoes, so that in case of being thrown into the sea, they would be better able to swim and cope

with the waves. In such a terrific sea it was no easy matter to launch the boat, though somewhat protected by the lee side of the ship, but in about five minutes it was successfully done, amid the plaudits and cheers of the passengers and crew. The passengers for the time being seeming to forget their sickness in the desire to witness the thrilling scene of a rescue at sea amid conditions so hazardous and adverse.

The boat when it took to the water was struck by several heavy waves drenching its occupants to the skin. The crew pulled away from the ship, and although but a third of a mile from the tanker, it took over an hour against such terrific seas to get near enough to speak to her, the seas and wind being contrary. It soon became evident that the rescuing boat could not run alongside the *Vindobala* without eminent peril to its own crew, and that the distressed seamen themselves would have to develop heroic measures.[3]

On the *Vindobala* Captain Clarke already had cut away the sea anchor so that the tanker would offer a more sheltered lee for the rescue boat, but this proved inadequate since the very worst of the storm was blowing. Once the *Paris'* lifeboat got within twelve feet of the side of the rolling tanker before having to pull back for fear of being crushed against the hull. So close had the lifeboat come that Captain Clarke had thrown his log and papers into her. An attempt was made to float a line to the rescue boat, but this proved impossible. Then a new scheme was attempted. The strongest swimmer among the sailors on the *Vindobala,* P. Fitzgerald, an able seaman, was lowered overboard with a line tied around him, and he struck out bravely into the tumultuous waters, trying to reach the boat. Time and time again he was flung back and narrowly escaped being dashed and mangled against the steamer's side. Exhausted, he was hauled back on board.

The *Vindobala* was outfitted with four lifeboats, but it was impossible to launch any vessel from the weather side of the ship in such a storm. Of the two lifeboats on the lee side one had been damaged. Captain Clarke ordered the launching of the only remaining usable lifeboat. Eight of the tanker's crew made the daring attempt and barely succeeded. They moved as quickly as possible to launch and then whipped their oars into the sea in order to pull away from the hull. As the tanker's lifeboat neared, First Officer Bradshaw shouted for it to make for the liner.[4]

Back on the *Vindobala* the fifteen remaining sailors had no alternative left but somehow to reach the rescue vessel bobbing just beyond their reach. Captain Clarke tried another strategy. He threw overboard a life buoy attached to a line and succeeded this time in floating it out to the *Paris*'s lifeboat. It was picked up and the boat's painter was tied to it. Then it was hauled back to the tanker, the painter dragging after it. Thus was formed a trolley that could be pulled back and forth. Just as the line was got out, the carpenter of the *Vindobala,* A. Oesterrvick, grabbed the end and jumped overboard, apparently expecting to be picked up by one of the two lifeboats. He had on a cork vest and bobbed in the water. The American sailors watched in horror as a large wave swept the struggling figure aft under the raised counter stern of the tanker, which crashed down on top of him. The man breached the turbulent seas, and the boat from the *Paris* succeeded in getting to within a couple feet of him when he was flung around toward them. Bradshaw hollered: "Cheer up, old man." But there was no response. His face was white, and it was seen that he was dead, probably of a fractured skull. There was a cry from the remaining crew members on the tanker, "Save the living," and the boat was rowed back into position for the next attempt. The lifeboat was kept between forty and one hundred feet of the plunging and rolling tanker as one after the other of the remaining fourteen crew members donned cork life jackets, took hold of the life buoy, dropped overboard, and was hauled to the lifeboat. There was no life jacket left for Captain Clarke, who saw all his crew safely away and then leaped into the sea to be quickly pulled to the lifeboat. As fast as possible the American sailors rowed to the waiting *Paris,* where ropes were hanging down the sides of the ship to aid in bringing the exhausted rescuers and rescued on board. As each man put his foot on the deck of the *Paris,* cheer after cheer went up. The doctor stood by and ladled out liberal quantities of hot whiskey to the frozen men, followed by food and hot baths. The sailors also received quantities of clothes from the passengers. In James Davison's words:

> Too great praise cannot be awarded to the gallant crew who made the rescue at the peril of their own lives. As they left the ship on their errand of mercy many a silent prayer was said. During the rescue the *Vindobala* was frequently lost to sight, except the topmasts and a portion of the funnel, the waves being so high. The small lifeboats disappeared again and again, only to rise on the crest of a huge wave. The rescue took about three and a half hours, and was a time of intense excitement on the *Paris,* as well as to the rescuing crew and the distressed seamen. About noon the *Paris* proceeded on her voyage, leaving the *Vindobala* in Latitude 49 degrees 29 minutes, Longitude 31 degrees 29 minutes, with hatches uncovered, sea anchor cast loose, and sixteen feet of water in her hold. It was believed that she must soon founder.[5]

The officers and crew of the *Vindobala* were well cared for on the *Paris.* Hot baths and solid meals did wonders for their recovery, and they were loud in their praise of the officers and crew of the American liner. The cabin passengers traveling on the *Paris* expressed their pride and appreciation for the officers and crew who had participated in the rescue by raising a purse of three hundred dollars, from which twenty-five dollars were awarded to each of the eight seamen and a suitable watch was to be purchased for each of the two officers. In a formal ceremony on the last evening out, as each man entered the main saloon, they saluted Captain Watkins and received an ovation from the assembled passengers. Subsequently the officers and crew of the *Vindobala* joined the group and also were cheered. Captain Clarke offered sincere thanks on behalf of his crew and him to their rescuers and to the many passengers who had provided clothing to the destitute seamen.

As the celebration was nearing its end, a call came for the very popular fourth officer of the *Paris,* Richard Webb, to speak. Webb had been one of the volunteers who had manned the American lifeboat. Normally he would have been in command of No. 6 Lifeboat, but when the call came for volunteers, he had been first. When his offer was declined in favor of Bradshaw, who was senior, Webb had offered to go in the place of a seaman, and this was permitted. He may have been a bashful young man of twenty-one, but his courage was unquestioned. His response was: "Ladies and gentlemen, I thank you for your kindness. We only did for these men what I am sure they would have done for us under like conditions."[6]

The *Paris* reached New York on New Year's Day—one day late—after a crossing in which the high seas and gale-force winds on the North Atlantic never let up once. The Committee of Lloyd's later bestowed silver medals for heroism upon Captain Watkins, First Officer John Bradshaw, and Fourth Officer R. H. Webb of the *Paris* for saving twenty-two of the twenty-three members of the crew of the *Vindobala*.[7]

Chapter 16

THE WIRELESS BRINGS AID FOR THE FIRST TIME

The *Republic* and the *Florida* in Collision

January 23, 1909

The *New York Tribune* reported on January 24, 1909, the remarkable news that "the White Star liner *Republic,* outward bound for Naples, was rammed and sunk yesterday, about forty-five miles south of Nantucket. Through the agency of wireless telegraphy assistance was sent to her through an almost opaque fog blanket, and not a single soul of the 781 on board was lost."[1] The vessel that rammed the *Republic* (1903; 15,378 tons, 570 feet, 16 knots) was the inward-bound *Florida* (1905; 5,018 tons, 381 feet, 14 knots) of the Lloyd Italiano Line from the Mediterranean. The statement about loss of life was not entirely true since five individuals on the two ships did die as a result of the accident. However, none who survived the collision subsequently lost their lives owing to a remarkable rescue effort made possible by the earliest use of wireless telegraphy to avert a catastrophe.

The *Republic* was a medium-size liner originally ordered from Harland & Wolff, Belfast, Ireland, by the Dominion Line and launched as the *Columbus.* She was 570 feet long and 68 feet wide with twin screws driven by two sets of quadruple-expansion steam engines. When the Dominion Line in 1902 was included in the purchases that ultimately created the International Mercantile Marine, the line lost most of its new tonnage to other units of the combine.[2] Among the vessels that went to other lines was the *Columbus,* which made only two voyages for the Dominion Line in the Liverpool–Boston service (MV, October 1, 1903) before becoming the *Republic* of White Star (FV, December 17, 1903). Dominion's loss was White Star's gain, for the *Republic* proved to be a very useful intermediate liner, maintaining an additional Liverpool–Boston service in the summer high season and then a profitable Boston–Mediterranean service in the fall and winter. Between 1904 and 1909 she engaged in a New York–Mediterranean service that saw her in

The White Star liner Republic *(1903) was an intermediate liner with a solid appearance graced by four masts and a towering single funnel. She was a popular unit on the winter route from New York to the Mediterranean, and in the summer trade from Boston to Liverpool. On January 23, 1909, in dense fog off Nantucket, she was rammed by the Italian liner* Florida *(1905) and was the first ship to call for assistance with her new Marconi wireless, marking a revolution in maritime communication.*

Naples and Genoa on a regular basis in competition with the Italian lines. The *Republic* was large enough to provide a suitable level of luxury for approximately 520 cabin-class passengers while also having commodious accommodations for around 1,000 in steerage on her lower decks. On February 18, 1907, entering the Bay of Naples, the *Republic* had run into the Italian steamer *Centro America* (1899; 3,474 tons, 358 feet, 14 knots) with minimal damage to all concerned.

On Friday, January 22, 1909, she sailed from New York under the command of Captain William Inman Sealby with 461 passengers (250 first and 211 steerage), mostly tourists, leaving the harsh New York winter behind and heading for the warmer weather of the Mediterranean.[3] Besides her passengers the *Republic* was carrying a large amount of supplies for the United States Navy's Great White Fleet, which was returning from its celebrated around-the-world cruise. The supplies reportedly amounted to 650 tons worth some sixty-one thousand dollars. Recently the U.S. fleet had used a great deal of its remaining stores to aid the victims of the great Messina earthquake of December 28, 1905, which in southern Italy and Sicily had cost over eighty thousand lives. The White Star liner also carried the earliest shipments of relief supplies for survivors of the Messina disaster, many of them now seeking to flee their ravaged land.

The westbound *Florida* had been the premier vessel of the Lloyd Italiano Line when commissioned in 1905. The Lloyd Italiano Societa de Navigazione was the brainchild of Erasmo Piaggio, scion of a famous Genoese family of shipowners, who had served as general manager of the Navigazione Generale Italiana and wanted to branch out on his own. The original idea involved a service to South America and the *Florida*'s maiden voyage (September 18, 1905) was from Genoa, Italy, via Naples, to Buenos Aires, Argentina, in the Rio Plate trade. She had accommodations for 25 in first class and a substantial 1,600 in steerage. The names of the original quartet of liners appear to indicate other trading interests since besides the *Florida,* there was the *Indiana* (1906; 4,996 tons, 394 feet, 14 knots), *Lusiana* (1906; 4,983 tons, 394 feet, 14 knots), and *Virginia*

(1906; 5,181 tons, 382 feet, 14 knots). Each of the original quartet was built by Societa Esercizio Bacini, Riva Trigoso, Italy, in which the Piaggio family had an interest. In November 1905 the *Florida* was shifted to the North Atlantic in a new Genoa–Naples–Palermo–New York service, and other vessels were acquired for the Rio Plate service. If the immigrant trade to America in 1908 saw a discouraging 6,126 bookings because of the American recession, it surged in 1909 to 17,564 and more than justified the decision of Lloyd Italiano to concentrate its operations on the United States.[4]

On the evening of January 23, 1909, the little *Florida* under the command of Captain Angelo Ruspini was inward bound to New York in dense fog. She had on board 14 in first class and approximately 824 Italian refugee-immigrants en route to a new life in the United States, as well as a crew of 130. As she neared the Massachusetts coast, the dense fog did not dissipate, and Captain Ruspini searched first for the Nantucket Lightship, which could not be found, and then for the thirty-fathom line, which, with its muddy bottom west of the lightship, told a navigator that he was in a good position to make for the entrance to New York Harbor. Unfortunately any attempt to feel for the thirty-fathom line also ran a good chance of placing a westbound ship in the principal eastbound shipping lane. Around 5:00 A.M. on January 23, this was exactly the situation in which Captain Ruspini found himself. About the same time he began to hear sonorous blasts from the foghorn of a nearby ship, which heralded a potentially deadly situation. The only thing that was sure was that no one on either ship could see anything as the vessels crept through the fog in the dead of the night.

The *Republic* was a comfortable ship with a low-key down-home atmosphere. She was under the command of Captain Sealby, an accomplished White Star captain who had been with the line for more than twenty-five years. The sailing from New York had not been uneventful because as the White Star liner backed out of her pier, she sideswiped the Furness Bermuda liner *Bermudian* with some damage to the other ship. The *Republic*'s damage was minimal, and she was permitted to continue on her way. Unfortunately, as soon as she cleared the Narrows, she found herself enveloped in a thick fog.

Among Sealby's staff on the *Republic* was John ("Jack") Robinson Binns, the lone radio officer, who had worked through the sailing day receiving and sending the normal run of bon voyage messages. Well after midnight, exhausted from the day's labors, he turned off his equipment and retired to his bunk. There was no one to take over for him. The *Republic,* because of her moderate size and the relatively small number of cabin-class passengers, carried only one radio officer. History was to speak very favorably of him.

Suddenly Captain Ruspini on the bridge of the *Florida* heard a whistle blast to starboard and then saw a huge wall appear in front of his ship. In spite of frantic maneuvers to starboard to avoid a collision, the *Florida* sank her bow into the side of the other ship just aft of the single tall funnel. On the *Republic* Captain Sealby heard a whistle at about 5:42 A.M. that appeared very close off the port bow. His reaction was to order full speed astern, and then, when the lights of the oncoming steamer revealed she was on a collision course to hit his ship, he rang full speed ahead in an effort to outrun disaster. The result was that the *Florida* rammed the *Republic* at her most vulnerable place, the main engine room, which soon filled with water.

About 5:40 A.M. Binns's sleep was broken by a sudden increase in the foghorn blasts from the *Republic.* The liner's engines ceased their regular rhythm as the engineers frantically sought to reverse the forward momentum. Then a thunderous crash occurred, and Binns jumped from his bunk and ran to the nearby radio shack. The name was appropriate in the early days of radio communication since most ships carried no formal room for the wireless operator and his workplace literally was a shack bolted to the deck. Wreckage was all over the deck. When Binns got to the radio shack, aft on the top deck, he saw with horror that the port wall was missing and the roof was suspended uneasily over his head. Happily, he soon discovered that his equipment was intact and capable of operating.[5] The set was still attached to an antenna, and a rescue signal could be sent as long as there was electric power. However, almost immediately the power on the *Republic* failed as the engine room filled with water and the electricity went with it. Within the White Star liner stewards passed out candles to illuminate the darkness, but a candle was not going to be of much help to Jack Binns.

Binns switched over to the storage batteries that provided critical power but limited the range of his radio signal to fifty to sixty miles. The freezing January temperatures off the North American coast severely affected Binns since the destruction of one wall of the radio shack had left it open to the elements. The nearest land station was old "SC," Siasconset, Massachusetts, which on this bitterly cold evening was manned by Jack Irwin, a senior wireless operator. The telephone line to the bridge had been severed, and Binns broke precedent by sending out the first CQD—all ships danger—himself. The nearness of the *Republic* to the shore meant that Binns's signal blasted through Irwin's headset. Contact was made, and Binns told Irwin that he would get the details of the ship's position as soon as possible. Shortly thereafter Captain Sealby sent a messenger to Binns to ask if he and his equipment were okay. Binns said yes and told the captain that he already had been in contact with the shore. Captain Sealby sent Binns the official message, which said: REPUBLIC RAMMED BY UNKNOWN STEAMSHIP, 26 MILES SOUTHWEST OF NANTUCKET. BADLY IN NEED OF ASSISTANCE. The call letters of the *Republic* were K W C.

The race against time to get critical assistance for the stricken *Republic* began. At the Siasconset Marconi Station Irwin received the signal and rebroadcast it at full power in a three-hundred-mile arc across the North Atlantic. For the first time the letters *C Q D* were sent out with the message "*Republic* in distress and sinking. Latitude 40:17, Longitude 70." Irwin enhanced the message with his own plea: DO UTMOST TO REACH HER! Marveling at the reach of the new technology, the *New York Tribune* reported: "Station after station took it up, and it reached ship after ship. Ship after ship took it up, and crowded on full steam ahead and forged into the fog wall. The cry of the *Republic* sounded within a radius of from sixty to one hundred and fifty miles of the spot where she was to go down. Highland Light got it, 120 miles away, and passed it on. Newport got it, 108 miles away, and flashed the warning out. New Bedford, 105 miles away, caught it, and the United States ship *Seneca,* in the harbor there, started to the rescue."[6]

From the moment Binns managed to reach Siasconset he left most of the general broadcasting to Irwin because his own set had limited range and the power remaining in his batteries was uncertain, particularly because of the freezing conditions. Fortunately for the *Republic* the ramming happened at one of the great oceanic crossroads, and major units of other steamship lines were nearby. They included *La Touraine* (1891; 8,893 tons, 520 feet, 19 knots) of the French Line, seventy-five miles to the east; the *Lucania* (1893; 12,952 tons, 601 feet, 21 knots) of Cunard, a hundred miles to the east; and the *New York* (1888; 10,499 tons, 528 feet, 20 knots) of the American Line, slightly farther out in the Atlantic. Captain Tournier of the French liner ordered the covers taken off all sixteen lifeboats, and they were made ready to lower with fresh provisions, water, and life preservers in place. He also informed all his passengers that their arrival in New York might be delayed because of the rescue effort. His wireless operators, Monrouzeau and Bour, continuously monitored the situation and never left their stations for the next seventy-two hours. Captain Tournier also made sure that the *Lucania,* some twenty to thirty miles farther out in the Atlantic, knew of the plight of the *Republic* so that the Cunarder would be prepared to assist.

However, nearest and potentially most helpful was the giant *Baltic* (1904; 23,876 tons, 709 feet, 17 knots) of the White Star Line, one of the *Republic*'s "big sisters," which was westward bound nearing New York and less than fifty miles away. A revenue cutter, the *Gresham,* also was dispatched to the aid of the White Star liner from Woods Hole, Massachusetts, and was soon joined by three of her sisters. The problem would be to find the stricken ship in the prevailing dense fog. Again the reporter for the *New York Tribune* was particularly graphic in his description of the situation: "Then began one of the strangest and weirdest scenes recorded in the annals of modern seafaring life. Bound for the same spot, unable to get their bearings, almost feeling their way, unseen, unheard, yet constantly talking to one another as though side by side, were three huge greyhounds of the Atlantic and four United States revenue cutters, the *Seneca,* the *Mohawk,* the *Acushnet,* and the *Gresham.* Collision threatened them, and the fate that had overtaken the *Republic* lurked for them in the fog. They kept on. 'Have you found her?' 'Are you talking with her?' they asked one another."[7] Binns listened in and kept Captain Sealby informed as assistance slowly began to make its way toward them over the next seven hours.

The news that help was headed toward them certainly cheered up the passengers a great deal, but the situation on the liner still was perilous since she clearly was settling in the water. With the coming of daylight White Star stewards brought hot coffee, sandwiches, fruit, and whiskey to the passengers on deck, many of whom had left their staterooms with few clothes. "The possibility of the *Republic* foundering was forgotten, or at least pushed back into the subconscious, at the sight of an elderly, bewiskered gentleman trying desperately to maintain some of his dignity and appear unconcerned with his wife's petticoat around him."[8] By this time the penetrating cold had teeth chattering in more than one individual. A few passengers, with perhaps more courage than common sense, quickly returned to their cabins to dress properly against the cold and to get their valuables.

The *Florida* had no wireless on board and no means of communicating with any other ship except by the human voice. Furthermore, Captain Ruspini also found that he had a personal crisis on his hands when some of his 824 immigrant passengers became convinced that their ship was sinking and nearly rioted. It took awhile for the officers and crew on the *Florida* to convince traumatized earthquake survivors that they were not about to meet another fate particularly when they saw the totally stove-in and crumpled bow of the their ship.

With regard to the threat of violence the reporter for the *New York Tribune* commented: "Little trouble was had with the steerage passengers—Portuguese and Italians. The master of a boat carrying that class lines up the men as soon as they are clear of port and confiscates all the knives and revolvers found on board. The steerage passengers then have little opportunity of getting the upper hand in emergencies."[9] True as this may have been, Captain Ruspini was determined to render whatever aid he could to the passengers and crew of the liner he had rammed. As the *Republic* drifted without power through the fog, the *Florida* inched back toward her, and the two ships made contact again. The *Florida* had lost nearly thirty feet of her bow, which had been buckled back like an accordion against the forward bulkhead by the force of the collision. A huge piece of canvas had been draped over the bow to mask the damage and provide small protection. The good news on the Lloyd Italiano vessel was that her watertight bulkhead was holding and her engines were still working. She was therefore in incomparably better condition than the *Republic,* whose fate was still uncertain.

Communicating by megaphone, the captains made the decision to transfer the passengers from the stricken *Republic* to the *Florida.* Many of the passengers on the Italian liner constantly had to be reassured that their ship was not the one sinking. Since they had survived the disaster of the recent Messina earthquake, their mental state was fragile at best. Captain Sealby informed everyone that the transfer to the *Florida* was a precautionary measure and asked for the cooperation of all passengers. Women and children were to go first, then cabin passengers, followed by steerage and lastly the crew. Sealby appeared remarkably cool-headed, forceful, and confident. The White Star passengers were lowered in the lifeboats and rowed to the *Florida,* which they found quite humble compared with their stately vessel. The *Florida,* nearing the end of a long transatlantic crossing, had little to offer in the way of food, and her public rooms were totally inadequate to handling an additional four hundred passengers. However, she was at least a safe refuge, even if you did have to spend time on the open deck in the freezing weather. Captain Ruspini, his crew members, and the passengers did everything they could to provide for the new arrivals as lifeboat after lifeboat came alongside the Lloyd Italiano liner. Upon discovering that many of the rescued passengers were American, some of the Italian refugee-immigrants from Messina gave up their cabins to accommodate them. They had experienced the generosity of the U.S. Navy during their recent disaster and wished to reciprocate as best they could.

Captain Sealby and a crew of forty-five stayed with the *Republic* after the passengers were safely on the *Florida.* Clearly Sealby did not want to let pass any chance to save his command if there was any possibility of salvation. Hands would be needed to secure and work the ropes if any attempt was made to tow the liner to safety. He also must have had the threat of salvage before him if anyone got a rope on the drifting *Republic* before the Merritt Wrecking Company vessels, hired by White Star in New York, reached his ship. Needless to say, Jack Binns remained at his post throughout the day although he was almost frozen. "Thus each step in the hide-and-seek game in the fog, every measure of succor that was being taken and the assurance of the safety of the passengers were flashed by wireless from station to station, from ship to ship, and, transmitted by Morse code and instruments, told all the waiting, anxious world of the fate of the steamer and her human freight."[10]

When the big White Star liner *Baltic* under the command of Captain Joseph P. Ransom learned of the ramming of the *Republic,* she was about sixty-four miles away off Long Island. Captain Ransom immediately turned his ship around and headed back toward the *Republic.* The fog was thick and during the next twelve hours the large White Star liner steamed over two hundred miles through it, searching for the stricken vessel. The search resembled the children's game blindman's bluff in which whoever is "it" tries to make contact with the other players by sound. By noon the strength of the signal from the *Baltic* was so strong that Binns knew she was less than ten miles away, although with the dense fog she might as well be in Liverpool. The short January day began to vanish, and still, there was no sight of the *Baltic.* "She felt her way through the thickest fog blanket that has encumbered the Atlantic Coast in many years, and although Captain Ransom was sure of getting to the *Republic* he approached the sinking vessel slowly and cautiously. He sent out wireless reports up to 3 P.M. that he had not found her, but expected to get alongside soon."[11]

During the afternoon the *Florida* with about two thousand on board had drifted away, and the *Republic* was all alone once more. On one occasion the senior radio operator on the *Baltic*, Henry J. Tattersall, tried to keep Binns's spirits up by wirelessing that they had built up speed to twenty-two knots. Since the *Baltic* was such a large ship, she warranted two radio operators, and the junior man was G. W. Balfour. This meant that Tattersall and Balfour could relieve each other and trade off the responsibility of maintaining contact with the lone Binns on the *Republic*. The statement that the *Baltic* was making twenty-two knots was preposterous since she was a seventeen-knot ship. Presumably Binns, who knew the ships of the White Star Line, could find some humor in the stately *Baltic* doing twenty-two knots. In actuality, Captain Ransom had been forced to slow his ship and creep through the fog lest he sink one of the other rescue vessels or the *Republic* herself.

When the radio operator on *La Touraine* asked Binns how he was, the young man replied: "I'm on the job, ship sinking, but will stick to the end."[12] Unintentionally, but assuredly, a hero was born. The conditions in the open radio shack were so frigid that Binns began to fear freezing to death or becoming incapacitated. On one occasion he carried a message to the bridge, and his teeth were chattering so badly that Captain Sealby thought the young radio officer was terrified. Warming just a bit, he told the captain that it was not fear but cold that had caused his teeth to chatter. Some people must have felt a bit sheepish about this, and an immediate effort was made to make their radio officer a little more comfortable in his exposed work station. Blankets were brought and wrapped around him in an attempt to conserve some warmth, and sandwiches and hot coffee were also provided.

By 6:00 P.M. no one on either the *Republic* or the *Baltic* had heard any of the bombs or rockets that had been set off by both ships. A bomb in this case was an explosive device capable of making a great deal of noise, not an instrument of destruction. One bomb remained on each ship swathed in the dense fog. The *Republic* had no power and no lights, and darkness was at hand. The last bomb was exploded on the *Republic,* but the *Baltic* radioed back that she had heard nothing. The officers on the two ships coordinated their last chance. The explosion of the bomb on the *Baltic* was scheduled for a precise time, agreed upon in advance. On the *Republic* officers and crew lined the bridge, man to man, facing out, straining to hear. The bomb was exploded on the *Baltic,* and Binns thought he heard it faintly on one quarter, which another officer confirmed. The compass direction was marked, and Binns radioed it to Tattersall on the *Baltic.* A few minutes later Binns heard the mighty foghorn on the *Baltic* in the distance and could radio that she was coming in the right direction. Shortly thereafter those White Star Line officers and crew remaining on the *Republic* heard a huge cheer and knew that it had to have come from the *Baltic.* As night darkened, the most beautiful sight in the world to Binns and his compatriots was the huge shape of the *Baltic* creeping out of the fog with all her lights driving away the gloom. Binns commented: "I looked out the cabin door, and there was the *Baltic,* alongside of us. She was a magnificent and inspiring sight; ablaze with light from every port; all the passengers lining the rail and cheering. They had been on the look-out for us all day."[13]

Captain Ransom and Captain Sealby quickly discussed the situation and decided that the first priority was to get the White Star passengers back from the *Florida* with her meager accommodations and crumpled bow. Accordingly the *Baltic* went in search of the *Florida* and came as close alongside her as conditions would permit so that the 400 exhausted passengers could be transferred from the Lloyd Italiano liner to the tender loving care and luxury of the much-larger ship. This transfer was done between late Saturday night and Sunday morning with many of the White Star passengers finally reaching the warmth and safety of the *Baltic* around 1:00 A.M. In addition, the decision was made to transfer all the passengers of the *Florida* to the safety of the *Baltic.* Therefore, approximately 1,650 individuals were rowed from the *Florida to the Baltic,* and this took a very long time. The *New York* of the American Line stood by the *Baltic* and the *Florida* with some of her lifeboats provisioned and in the water throughout the night as the passenger transfer occurred. By that time the passengers and crew of the *Republic* had been awake for twenty hours, had known the peril of a darkened liner in danger of sinking, and had been transferred at sea twice: once from the *Republic* to the *Florida* and then from the *Florida* to the *Baltic.* They were delighted to arrive on the big White Star liner, but they certainly were exhausted by their ordeal. If the weather was bitterly cold, at least the seas were relatively calm, undoubtedly aiding the proceedings.

At about 3:00 P.M. on Sunday the Standard Oil Company whaleback *City of Everitt* offered to take the *Republic* under tow. Captain Sealby faced a difficult decision. His ship was settling ever lower in the water, and her time was limited. On the other hand, the White Star Line offices in New York had notified him that the Merritt and Chapman Wrecking fleet, including tugs, was coming to his aid; Captain Thomas Fenlon of the *City of Everitt* told him his ship was completely outfitted as a salvage vessel and was capable of towing the *Republic* in toward shore, where she could be beached and repaired. Sealby evaluated the situation and declined Captain Fenlon's offer since rescue supposedly was at hand. By his so doing the last chance to save the *Republic* was lost. Around 10:00 A.M. on January 24 the *Baltic* and the *Florida* left for New York with their passengers. The revenue cutter *Gresham* under the command of Captain Perry arrived and placed two lines on the *Republic*'s bow in order to begin towing her. Jack Binns had remained faithfully at his telegraph key for thirty-six hours when he finally climbed on board the *Gresham.*

By this time the *Republic* had a severe list to port and was down by the stern. Everyone except Captain Sealby and one volunteer, Second Officer Richard J. Williams, an unmarried officer, left her. Sealby had wanted no one with him, but Williams insisted that he was a bachelor and should be allowed to stay. Sealby reminded him that he had parents, and Williams responded that he had banked some money for them and that they would not want him to leave. Finally, Sealby let the young second officer stay with him.

The tow was successful for about six miles. Then, by 8:30 P.M., the end was near as the *Republic* began to go down by the stern. Captain Sealby recounted:

> Williams and I were on the bridge when it was close to the time for us to leave her. The stern began to go down, and she began to rumble and crack.
>
> "Well, what do you think about it?" I asked Williams.
>
> "I don't think it will be a long race," he said.
>
> "Let's make a sprint of it. When you're ready let her go."
>
> "Burn the blue light [signal to be picked up]," I said, and fired five shots from my revolver. That was the signal to the *Gresham* to let go. We ran from the bridge to the saloon deck, burning blue lights and carrying lanterns. As we ran the stern of the ship was sinking rapidly, and the deck was so steep we slipped back. The last I saw Williams he had caught the port rail and was hanging on. I went up the mast as far as the masthead light, about a hundred feet up, and tried to set off a blue light, but it was wet. Then I fired the last shot from my revolver.
>
> Then the water caught me. It got under my great coat and supported me by the air inside, while the weight of my revolver, binoculars and cartridges supported me as a sort of life belt. By this time there was a roaring mass of water all around me. I was churned down in it, but came up and tried to pull off my coat. I did not succeed. There was a lot of wreckage all around, and I finally reached a hatch. On this I lay spreadeagle fashion.[14]

The *Republic* had gone down in about thirty fathoms of water. Captain Sealby, floating on the hatch, grew colder as the searchlights of the *Gresham* played all over the sea where the liner had sunk without shining on him. In desperation he fumbled with his revolver and was able to reload it and fire some shots in an effort to get attention. At the same time a lifeboat from the *Gresham* manned by four U.S. Navy sailors and four crewmen from the *Republic* had been launched. After some time they succeeded in finding Second Officer Williams, who had supported himself between two hatch covers. Williams had a general idea where Captain Sealby might be found, and the sound of the revolver provided impetus. When the lifeboat reached Sealby, he was far gone from hypothermia but was quickly pulled into the boat. In the darkness he could not see the men's faces, but after a few moments he recognized Williams's voice and grabbed him around the neck in his delight at learning he also had been pulled from the sea. "'Williams,' he said, 'game to the last.'"[15]

The *Republic* lasted as long as she did because she was very solidly built, even if her aft watertight bulkheads ultimately gave way under the pressure of the inflowing water. "Had the positions of the vessels been reversed, the *Republic,* it is believed, would have cut the *Florida* in two. The *Republic* kept afloat for about fifteen hours, but the pressure of the sea in the rent made by the *Florida* was too great for her to withstand, and one by one water-tight compartments gave way to the sea."[16] The *Baltic* and the *Florida* stayed together in convoy at about eight knots until they finally reached New York two days later. The *Baltic* received a tumultuous welcome. The *Florida* was repaired and back in service within a month.

Captain William Sealby and a small number of his crew were brought to the White Star pier in New York on January 26 by the revenue cutter *Seneca.* The scene was one of unbridled jubilation.

> Captain Sealby and the others got a reception when they came up the harbor that showed plainly what others thought of the work they had done. Whistles blew and men cheered, and there was a demonstration that lacked nothing in real and spontaneous enthusiasm. It seemed [as] if all the enthusiasm had been kept for the men from the *Republic,* for

The shorn-off and crumpled-back bow of the Lloyd-Italiano liner Florida *(1905) provides vivid evidence of the violence of her meeting with the White Star liner* Republic *(1903) during the night of January 23, 1909. The* Republic *sank the next day but only after all those who had survived the collision had been rescued as the result of the first use of the Marconi wireless to call for assistance.*

there were no whistles and no cheers on Monday when Ruspini triumphantly brought his crippled and almost wrecked vessel into port. To some this seemed a bit unfair, but there was plenty of appreciation of the Italian's work by the passengers he saved.

There was a great crowd on the White Star pier when the little party that had come from the *Republic* on the *Seneca* was landed, and Captain Sealby was lifted on the shoulders of a dozen men and carried to the street. There he escaping from the cheering throng, made his way to the offices of the line, where he and Williams were mobbed by another throng before they could get inside. Some one had found a bugler, and he headed the procession from the pier, blowing triumphant blasts all the way.[17]

Few captains of ships that have been sunk ever have received such acclaim. Sealby in fact was rather shy, and this was all a bit overwhelming.

The memorial of thanks from the board of directors of the International Mercantile Marine, which met in New York on Tuesday, January 28, was a glowing testimonial composed with due regard for its public relations value. Under the chairmanship of Clement Acton Griscom, the Philadelphia Quaker shipping magnate who had created the shipping trust, the board expressed its "admiration for the valiant service rendered and undaunted spirit shown by the officers and crews of the *Republic* and *Baltic* in the face of extreme peril. Such strict adherence to discipline, and readiness to forget all personal safety when the lives of passengers are in jeopardy can but inspire those who 'go down to the sea in ships' with a deeper respect for the seafaring man and a new confidence in the value of that sense of personal responsibility which the trained seaman never fails to show."[18] P. A. S. Franklin, vice-chairman of the IMM board, issued the official IMM statement.

The reality of how White Star treated the "heroes" of the *Republic* was quite different. The surviving crew members of the *Republic* who had lost all their kit when the liner sank found themselves consigned to a dark freight hold on the liner *Baltic* to await shipment home. They discovered that their rights under the British Board of Trade regulations were distinctly limited. The approximately two hundred merchant seamen were addressed by E. W. P. Thurston, British vice-consul. He met with them in the hold of the *Baltic* at her pier in New York, where they had been put on their arrival. There he told them that under British law their pay had stopped the instant the *Republic* sank since she had provided their wages–not the White Star Line. Furthermore, he told them that they need not expect any of their money until they reached Liverpool, or any employment before that time. A small amount might be advanced to each man against the wages he had earned if he was destitute, as they all were. They were informed that out of its own generosity the line would see that any man suffering from a lack of clothes would be provided with "such articles as were positively necessary."[19] Some of the men were partially naked since they had lost everything when their ship sank, and it was January 1909, the dead of the winter. The generosity of the White Star Line appears absolutely minimal, and one wonders what the seamen's benevolent organizations were doing. These men had risked their lives to save every single passenger who had survived the actual collision and had been hailed like heroes shortly before only to be given Spartan accommodations in a freight hold of the *Baltic*.

The one truly pathetic issue the men brought up at the meeting with Thurston was that the hold of the *Baltic* had no beds, and it was very difficult to sleep under those conditions, let alone rest with any comfort. They all were exhausted and needed rest as much as anything. They asked if they could not be allowed to go ashore and be put up at some place that had beds and washrooms, since they also were filthy, until the *Baltic* sailed in several days. Vice-Consul Thurston said he would see about this. Ultimately the White Star crew members were permitted access to the some of the bunks and washrooms in steerage on the *Baltic*!

The White Star Line and Lloyd Italiano Line soon were engaged in a legal and publicity war over who was at fault for the loss of the *Republic*. Each claimed that the captain of its respective vessel had been acting with total propriety. Passengers who had lost everything when the *Republic* sank organized and were encouraged by White Star to file claims against Lloyd Italiano. In some instances these claims were substantial. Mr. and Mrs. George A. Kimball of St. Paul, Minnesota, returned to the Gotham Hotel with virtually nothing but the clothes on their backs. Three days earlier they had left that hotel for the *Republic* with twenty-five steamer trunks. Furthermore, Mrs. Kimball required the services of a physician since the reason for their trip had been her poor health. The White Star Line told the passengers who had survived the sinking that it would transport them to Europe by any other ship that they wanted to cross on, including those of other lines. This news was received very warmly, and the White Star Line earned a great deal of goodwill. However, some passengers decided not to test their luck a second time but to stay home and forgo a European tour in 1909.

The newspaper coverage was worldwide, and Signor Marconi's invention was hailed as one of the greatest boons to humanity. "Such was its success that there was an instant and universal demand that all large ships should be fitted with wireless."[20]

The wealthy passengers on the *Baltic* elected to pay for commemorative watches to be presented to all the officers and crew members of the *Baltic, Republic,* and *Florida,* with four golds ones for the captains and Jack Binns. The watches were inscribed: "From the passengers of the R.M.S. *Baltic* and R.M.S. *Republic* to the officers and crews of the R.M.S. *Republic, Baltic* and S.S. *Florida,* for gallantry, commemorating the rescue of more than 1,700 souls, 24th January, 1909."[21] On the reverse was an engraving of the *Republic,* the letters *C.Q.D.,* and the name *Republic.* The Marconi company also presented Jack Binns with a watch and a testimonial in recognition of his heroism at the key. The shy Binns was mobbed by friendly girls who planted kisses on the young hero and caused him to comment: "Give me a cigarette. This is the worst yet."[22] He received offers to go on lecture tours but wanted nothing so much in 1909 as to return to the relative obscurity of a life at sea. "None of this cheap notoriety for me. All I want is a cigarette, a long sleep and a chance to get back to work."[23] His humility was natural, and it embellished even more his heroism in standing by the wireless on the sinking *Republic* until his captain ordered him off the ship. Binns remained a radio operator for another three years, working on such great White Star liners as the *Adriatic* and the *Olympic,* where he came to know Captain Edward Smith. Finally, he decided to come ashore and begin a new career as a newspaper reporter. Jack Binns arrived at his desk at the *New York American* in April 1912 just as the news hit the wireless of the sinking of another great White Star liner, the *Titanic.*

Chapter 17

THE ULTIMATE CATASTROPHE

The Largest Ship in the World, the SS *Titanic*, Strikes an Iceberg in the Middle of the North Atlantic

April 14–15, 1912

Along the eastern coast of Newfoundland a great oceanic river known as the Arctic Current flows southward across the Arctic Sea until it reaches the North Atlantic. There off eastern Canada it mixes with an even greater oceanic river called the Gulf Stream and is swept east and north again toward Europe. The waters of the Arctic Current emerging from under the polar ice cap are frigid and therefore preserve both the pack ice from the Arctic as well as the great blocks and chunks of ice that annually break off from the Greenland glaciers to be carried south. The 1911–1912 winter had been slightly milder than usual. Many more icebergs than normal reached the North Atlantic, and an estimated seventy-five bergs of over a million tons each had slowly but menacingly drifted into the transatlantic steamer lanes by April 1912.[1]

The North Atlantic was divided into steamship tracks by international agreement. The northern lane followed the great circle route most closely and therefore was a bit shorter, offering slightly better time for passenger liners crossing between Europe and America. The northern lane normally was regarded as safe in the winter and spring, less so in the summer, when icebergs were more prevalent. The warmer weather of the 1911–1912 winter notwithstanding, some of the transatlantic express liners in April 1912 were still using the northern lane because it was fractionally shorter, and they could reach America in slightly less time. The possible peril of doing so was well known. As recently as 1908 the North German Lloyd greyhound *Kronprinz Wilhelm* (1901; 14,908 tons, 637 feet, 22 knots) had rammed a small iceberg at sixteen knots in dense fog off the Grand Banks. To put it mildly, anyone standing on the ship who was not holding on to something was knocked flat, but the strongly built German liner backed away from the iceberg. Her damage bow area was inspected, and since the forward bulkhead was holding, she proceeded on to New York at a reduced speed and in need of a new bow.[2] It was possible to hit an iceberg and survive, but it had to be done right without exposing too much of the vessel to damage. It also did not hurt to be lucky. Ice, then as now, represented an omnipresent hazard of the North Atlantic that everyone knew about and every experienced navigator respected.

The most important shipping event in North Atlantic history was the creation of the International Mercantile Marine in 1902. The giant shipping trust was the brainchild of the Philadelphia Quaker shipping magnate Clement Acton Griscom (1841–1912) and was made possible by the financial backing of the New York banker J. P. Morgan.[3] Among the many American, Belgian, British, Dutch, and German lines involved in the IMM certainly the most famous British-flag steamship concern was the Oceanic Steam Navigation Company, or White Star Line. Griscom was sixty-one when the IMM negotiations were completed. He became the president of the new concern and was a benevolent authoritarian figure. Decisions traditionally were referred to him on matters big and little, and his word was law. The strain of running the shipping trust with dozens of lines and well over a hundred ships representing in excess of a million tons of shipping was enormous. Within eighteen months (October 1903) his health was undermined, and he was feeling the pressure of running so vast an enterprise. Complaints began to be voiced in the White Star organization about the management of the IMM. Dissatisfaction with Griscom's rule even reached the press and the ears of J. P. Morgan.

If Morgan possessed a maritime prejudice, it was that he loved the White Star ships and the way the White Star Line was run by Thomas Ismay and, after 1899, by Bruce Ismay, his son. To Morgan this meant the English method, a quiet, elegant professionalism that brought him back to the White Star liners year after year when he wanted to book his pilgrimages to Europe.[4] In January 1904 Bruce Ismay, Managing Director of White Star, accompanied by Henry Wilding, British vice-president of the IMM, and Lord Pirrie, IMM board member and president of the Harland & Wolff Shipyard, crossed to New York for a series of meetings with Morgan and Griscom. It was said that Ismay brought demands for total control of White Star. The younger Ismay did not particularly like Griscom and chafed under the leadership of the Philadelphia Quaker who had created the American Line, one of White Star's greatest rivals. Frank and vigorous discussions occurred between all parties, and Griscom denied the rumor that he was going to resign. However, Morgan apparently was disturbed enough by the downward drift in IMM stocks and bonds and by the transatlantic management disagreements to take note of Griscom's ill health and, on that less humiliating basis, to encourage him to give up direct control. On February 23, 1904, Griscom surrendered the office of president of the International Mercantile Marine to Bruce Ismay of White Star and agreed to accept the ceremonial office of chairman of the board, which he would hold until his death in November 1912.

Symbolic of the shift of power from Griscom to Ismay was the transfer of the head offices of the IMM from Philadelphia to New York. It also was reported that Ismay was going to move his home from

Liverpool to New York, but this never occurred, and for the duration of his nine-year leadership (1904–1913) he continued to live in Britain with occasional visits to New York. Later Ismay was to explain his position to the British press as having "managerial power" while actual control lay with the voting trust. Managerial power was more than adequate for White Star purposes. The White Star Line gave evidence of its independence by being the only IMM concern not to run the name of the parent organization in its advertising or on its bills of lading.

The election of Ismay to the presidency of the International Mercantile Marine by the board of directors was not unanimous by any means. Apparently various factions favored others for the number one position. After Ismay's selection Bernard Baker of the Atlantic Transport Line caustically remarked: "The English shipping men have their own property again, plus the cash contributed by the syndicate, plus the property of the American lines."[5] At the time of Ismay's accession to power his strongest card was that White Star was the only IMM concern making a profit, in some instances more than five million dollars a year. That was mainly because the IMM had paid such a high price for the steamship lines it acquired that any hope of a profit, short of a government subsidy, was impossible.

When the announcement was made in 1903 that the British government would support the independence of the Cunard Line with a loan to build two large new express liners and a mail contract adequate to repay the loan over twenty years, the White Star situation became critical.[6] When the *Lusitania* and *Mauretania* entered service in 1907, new first-class tonnage for White Star became imperative. Ismay, with the backing of Lord Pirrie, sought to capitalize on his new position by persuading the IMM board to back the construction of three huge liners. There was no question of building the new ships for any line except White Star. With Griscom gone the American Line was out of the running even if the IMM stock certificates proudly showed a huge four-funnel American liner backing out of her New York pier. That ship would never be built as long as Bruce Ismay was in charge. Equally, there was no question about building the new ships anywhere but at the Harland & Wolff Shipyard in Belfast, Ireland. Lord Pirrie's support of the younger Ismay had earned Harland & Wolff the right to continue as the principal builder for the Oceanic Steam Navigation Company by virtue of his invaluable services as one of the godfathers of the International Mercantile Marine. In 1908 the contracts for a trio of superliners designed to be larger and more luxurious than any other ships in the world were placed with Harland & Wolff.[7]

Insofar as Ismay was concerned, there was no need to chase the Cunard speed queens because the machinery to propel such a vessel would consume the profits from the ship. Instead he elected to build upon the formula for success that had served White Star so well since 1899 and the commissioning of the *Oceanic* (II). In 1907 at a dinner party given by Lord Pirrie at his London mansion, Ismay asked him to create plans for three ships 25 percent larger than the Cunarders, but with power plants capable of delivering their passengers to New York in a comfortable six days, not the five days of the Cunarders. Their speed would still make it possible to maintain a first-class service with three ships instead of four. By virtue of their size, over forty-five thousand tons, they would be able to carry sufficient passengers and, by virtue of engines capable of producing twenty-one to twenty-three knots, sufficient speed to maintain a six-day service. Some of the money saved by building ships only slightly slower than the Cunarders would be lavished on making them the most luxurious vessels of the Gilded Age. These would be ships on which even millionaires would feel as comfortable as in their own mansions or private clubs. The names assigned to the White Star trio were calculated to evoke a new sense of grandeur: *Olympic, Titanic,* and probably *Gigantic.*[8]

The *Olympic* (1911; 45,324 tons, 883 feet, 21 knots) was the name ship of the class and garnered unto herself all the journalistic glory. She was launched on October 20, 1910. Her maiden voyage from Southampton to New York began on June 14, 1911, with fabulous accommodations for 735 passengers in first class, 674 in second, and

1,026 in third. She was a sumptuously outfitted quality product of Harland & Wolff, justifying every possible expectation of her owners and builders. With her four towering funnels, she was hailed not only as the largest but also the most beautiful liner afloat. When she survived a collision with the British cruiser HMS *Hawke* in The Solent on September 20, 1911, her reputation as a solid, durable vessel was enhanced. Her sisters were scheduled to follow her at approximately yearly intervals, and in fact the *Titanic* was launched the same day the *Olympic* was turned over to the White Star Line, May 31, 1911. More than one hundred thousand people crowded into the huge Harland & Wolff yard and lined the riverbanks to see the second of the White Star trio enter her element. The keel of the third unit was laid down on November 2, 1911, on the slipway from which the *Olympic* had been launched.

The *Titanic* (1912; 46,328 tons, 883 feet, 21 knots) was the second of the great White Star trio. Her sea trials were the essence of brevity, one day, and at her commissioning on April 1, 1912, she was the largest ship in the world by about 1,005 tons over the *Olympic.* Designed and built by Harland & Wolff, the *Titanic* was the last word in naval architecture from the famous Irish yard. Fifteen transverse bulkheads divided her into sixteen watertight compartments with the watertight doors controlled electrically. The *Titanic* had been described as "practically unsinkable" by the *Shipbuilder*'s souvenir issue so confident was everyone of her construction.[9] Her master was Captain Edward John Smith, the commodore of the White Star Line, with thirty-eight years of service and at age sixty-two nearing retirement when he assumed command of the *Titanic.* Earlier in 1911 he had been the first master after God of the *Olympic* and therefore was thoroughly familiar with the huge, unwieldy, but elegantly beautiful sisters. Shortly after the commissioning of the *Olympic* it was realized that her only shortcoming as a floating hotel was that she did not have enough luxurious suites to meet the demands of her wealthy clientele. This deficiency had been rectified in the *Titanic* by enclosing a portion of the promenade deck in order to meet the demand for the utmost luxury and privacy in accommodations. The *Titanic* cost a reported $7.5 million, which was a phenomenal sum for anything in 1912 but which represented the very finest of materials and workmanship assembled to the highest possible standards by Harland & Wolff.[10]

One deficiency of the *Olympic*-class ships was that their rudders were inadequate to turn the huge ships within any reasonable distance. The *Olympic*-class ships might have been given large balanced rudders, like Cunard's *Lusitania* and *Mauritania,* but the decision to mount three shafts on them precluded this. The position of the center propeller reduced the space available for a balance overhang. In addition, the contrariness on the part of the rudder was enhanced by the positioning of the center propeller immediately forward of the rudder so that a powerful disruptive flow of water constantly occurred against the rudder and reduced efficiency. If the rudder was put over hard, the result was that the *Olympic*-class ships went into a prolonged skid across the ocean for some distance before showing any noticeable effect. They were not terribly maneuverable, but that was why there were tugs, to get you in and out of tight spaces like piers and harbors. Nothing was supposed to require sudden maneuvering on the open ocean.

So delighted was Bruce Ismay with the second of his three ships that he elected to sail on her Maiden Voyage, Wednesday, April 10, 1912, from Southampton to New York.[11] For Ismay to be on the fabulous *Titanic* must have been a heady personal ego trip. She was magnificent, and he knew it. The *Titanic* was over twice as large as any ship his father had built, and the luxury of her accommodations surpassed anything ever commissioned. The plaudits of the people who mattered most to him, the cream of transatlantic society, were available in abundance. The New York piers of White Star already were decorated with flags and bunting in preparation for the *Titanic*'s maiden arrival. Who knew what public recognition from a grateful sovereign and nation might be his in the future?

The maiden sailing of the *Titanic* began on a cool, crisp spring day.

Gracious and majestic from almost every angle, the new White Star superliner Titanic *(1912) leaves the Harland & Wolff Shipyard, Belfast, for a single day of trials in the Irish Sea. The date is April 1, 1912. Exactly two weeks later the "Largest Ship in the World" would rest on the bottom of the North Atlantic after sideswiping a one-million-ton iceberg. The* Titanic *took with her to their deaths 1,503 individuals for the largest peacetime death toll ever.*

A coal strike was under way, and the bunkers of the big White Star queen were filled by robbing other ships of their fuel. Out of a total of 2,566 berths, only 1,316 had been sold, but this still was a good early-spring passenger load. Captain Smith boarded the ship at 7:30 A.M., and the entire crew was mustered on deck at 8:00 A.M., followed by a brief lifeboat drill using two starboard boats.

The *Titanic* was outfitted with sixteen lifeboats capable of carrying 1,178 individuals. This was a generous margin over the Board of Trade regulations, which were based on the size of the ship and had not been seriously revised since 1894, when the largest ship in the world was a little over ten thousand tons. Eighteen years later the *Titanic* was 460 percent larger, but the same regulations applied. The *Titanic* was equipped with a unique double-action lifeboat davit designed by the Welin Davit and Engineering Company Ltd. It had the ability to swing a lifeboat outboard for lowering over the side and then to be swung back inboard in order to serve a second row of lifeboats that were never installed. Ismay wanted more open deck space and vetoed the second row of lifeboats.[12] Hence the *Olympic* and the *Titanic* went to sea each with sixteen wooden lifeboats and four smaller collapsible lifeboats, which, when folded, were stored on the roofs of some of the superstructure aft of the bridge. They gave the White Star superships a lifeboat capacity of 1,178 people. As Joseph Conrad, the famous novelist of the sea, later sarcastically commented, "she had every 'banal hotel luxury,' a French restaurant, Turkish and electric baths, swimming pool, veranda café, palm court, squash racket court, and numerous other luxuries, but boat accommodations for only 53 percent of the number of people she had on board."[13] Even with a reduced passenger load on the April 10 sailing she still would have at least 2,208 on board, 800 more than her lifeboats could accommodate. If anything happened, those 800 would be consigned to the cold ocean waters with nothing but their life belts. The idea also was prevalent in some minds, after the sinking of the *Republic* (1909) without loss of life, that wireless telegraphy always would bring abundant aid. This idea ignored the factors of sea conditions, time, and distance.

Between 9:30 and 11:00 the third-class and second-class boat trains arrived from London, and their passengers boarded the leviathan of the seas. From the Southampton docks the *Titanic* appeared simply enormous to those boarding her. At 11:30 A.M. the splendid first-class boat train arrived, and the cream of society from two continents swept on board and were escorted by attentive stewards to their cabins. Others had elected to motor down to Southampton in order to visit friends in the countryside or to travel at their leisure. First-class passenger William Carter was taking his automobile with him. Those stevedores loading the liner would stow 11,524 pieces in her holds weighing 559 tons. The White Star Line made money out of carrying freight as well as passengers.[14]

The passenger list included Colonel and Mrs. John Jacob Astor—he was reportedly the richest man in America and she was expecting their first child; Benjamin Guggenheim, whose wealth in mineral holdings was staggering; Mr. and Mrs. John B. Thayer, a senior-vice president of the Pennsylvania Railroad, and their teenage son, Jack; Mr. and Mrs. Isidor Straus, the founder of Macy's department store; Major Archibald ("Archy") Butt, President William Howard Taft's military attaché; and Mrs. Molly Brown, a wealthy, rugged individualist from Denver, Colorado, who was to gain fame as the "unsinkable Molly Brown" before the trip was over. On board as well were Bruce Ismay, president of the IMM, and Thomas Andrews, managing director of Harland & Wolff, who also was Lord Pirrie's nephew and one of the principal individuals responsible for the building of the liner. Andrews had wanted additional lifeboats installed, but Ismay had overruled him in favor of open, uncluttered deck space.

The *Olympic* had accommodations for 735 in first, but the *Titanic*'s first-class staterooms could care for 1,034, an enormous increase over her sister. Where first-class accommodations were concerned, she was indeed alone, with a third more berths than any other ship in service and nearly twice as many as her Cunard rivals. Some of the additional first-class staterooms were upgraded from, or interchangeable with, second class since the *Olympic* could carry 674 in second, and the *Titanic* 510. First-class stewards on a premier White Star ship frequently earned far more in salary and tips than officers. The level of service on White Star ships was legendary.

The thunderous blasts of the *Titanic*'s foghorns signified that the liner was about to sail, and promptly at twelve-thirty the queen of the British merchant marine was nudged away from her pier and began to move toward The Solent. Her departure from Southampton nearly was cut short when the enormous suction of her hull passing through the water caused the mooring lines of the American Line's *New York* to snap and brought her swinging out in a deadly arc toward the stern of the new ship. Only the quick action of the tug *Vulcan* prevented the

New York from taking a deadly revenge on the White Star liner that had usurped the position of the next generation of American Line ships. The *Titanic* escaped the near miss and by 1:00 P.M. was proceeding on schedule for Cherbourg, France, to pick up her Continental passengers. At about this time Chief Officer William Murdoch was informed that somehow the binoculars for the lookouts had been left in England. Their absence was regarded as an irritant but by no means a major cause for alarm.

Cherbourg, the French port on the tip of Normandy, was convenient by rail to Paris, while its proximity to Southampton made it convenient for a liner desiring to board those passengers traveling to New York from European destinations. The efficient French railroad system made it possible for passengers to collect from all over Europe in Paris, where they could enjoy the incomparable delights of the French capital, and then go on to board the *Titanic* at Cherbourg. The *Titanic* was slightly delayed in reaching Cherbourg, and her additional 274 passengers, housed in the drafty maritime terminal, did not leave by tender until early evening. Their compensation was to see awaiting them the largest ship in the world, crowned by four towering funnels, with all her decks ablaze with lights, a breathtaking sight. By 8:00 P.M. all were safely on board, and while the *Titanic* turned her bow west for Queenstown, Ireland, they forgot earlier inconveniences as they enjoyed a rich gourmet feast before retiring to their brand-new staterooms.

During the next day, April 11, en route to Queenstown Captain Smith took the opportunity to test some maneuvers with the new ship to see how well she would respond to the helm. Apparently he found nothing at variance from the *Olympic* to bother him. At the very least he may have discussed some impressions with Thomas Andrews, her builder, to get his expert opinion. The Cobh Lighthouse appeared off the starboard side as Captain Smith swung the *Titanic* into his favored anchorage off the southern Irish port. The Royal Mails (1,385 bags) had arrived in Queenstown shortly before and were ferried out to the White Star liner while 7 cabin-class passengers came out to the ship and 113 third-class (steerage) were brought out on a separate ferry so that the classes would never be required to mix. Ireland was still a major source of emigration to the United States, and as long as berths were available, tickets were sold until the last moment. This was one of the primary reasons why the total number of passengers being carried on a passenger liner calling at an Irish or Continental port never was sorted out until shortly before the actual arrival in an American port, when the figures had to be exact for U.S. customs and immigration. In addition, there were a few individuals bound for vacations or business in Ireland who had taken the opportunity to make the trip on a major liner instead of a ferryboat and left the ship at Queenstown. Finally, often there were stowaways, who by their very presence were an illegal nuisance but who affected the total number on board. These factors account for the discrepancies among various sources about the final passenger list of the *Titanic* as she sailed from Queenstown.

The *Titanic*'s bow was turned west toward America, and her engines built up almost to full speed as the green hills of Ireland fell away. In first class the orchestra played, the chefs worked their culinary magic in the great kitchens, and there was little to do in one's luxurious cabin except change clothes several times a day in order to have the correct appearance according to the hour. Some wealthy passengers even took more than one cabin in order to have additional closet space for colossal steamer trunks and wardrobes. Hundreds of trunks "Not Wanted on Voyage" were consigned to the baggage rooms in the holds. An upper-grade first-class cabin on the *Titanic* could cost over $600 in 1912, and a suite of rooms several times that.[15] Those were enormous amounts of money in a day when an American laborer earned $20 to $35 a month and a schoolteacher's salary might be $200 to $250 a year. On the other hand, one could cross in third class, or steerage, on the *Titanic* for around $26.50, which saw someone traveling on the same ship as the wealthy even if the accommodations were far more spartan and the food was best described as "filling" or "wholesome." Third class on the *Titanic* was significantly better than the old White Star steerage dormitories in that every immigrant had an assigned bunk in a cabin.

Friday, April 12, saw the *Titanic* steam 386 miles; on Saturday, April 13, 519 miles; and on Sunday, April 14, a similar distance, as the days were among the finest and smoothest that experienced travelers ever had seen on the North Atlantic. The ocean had its best behavior on show and was like a millpond most of the time. Reports of ice came in by wireless, but it was not within the view of the *Titanic*'s lookouts as she steamed at nearly full speed for New York through a placid North Atlantic. The shortage of coal had resulted in the decision to conserve fuel by not lighting all the furnaces, and a few boilers were not making steam. Hence the *Titanic* was incapable of "racing" even if she still could be making very good time in calm seas. There was not even a trace of fog to blur the horizon. Everything simply was perfect during the maiden voyage of the largest ship in the world. Everyone praised the stability of the ship and the lack of vibration, to the enormous delight of Bruce Ismay and the personal satisfaction of Thomas Andrews and Captain Smith. They had a blue-blood winner at their command.

In fact the problems Andrews dealt with genuinely ranged to the trivial. There were not enough coat hooks in the cabins, and the galley hot press was acting up and might need replacing before a later voyage. Captain Smith certainly had received a number of reports of ice from other steamers, but it was not yet upon him. The weather was clear, and the lookouts were seasoned veterans of the North Atlantic. As the dark April evening settled in, Smith saw no need to take any additional precautions, and the *Titanic* knifed through the North Atlantic at 22.5 knots. Captain Smith may have thought to break the maiden crossing time of the *Olympic* even if there never was any possibility of catching the twenty-five-knot Cunard Blue Riband liners.

In the wireless room on the *Titanic* the two operators, John George Phillips, chief, and Harold Bride, junior, were kept continuously busy with the flow of outward and inward messages largely meant for the first-class passengers. On Sunday, April 14, Phillips's workload had been increased enormously when the Marconi set broke down, and he "had spent over six hours repairing a burned out and grounded transformer secondary."[16] Many early radio operators were highly skilled electricians, as well as telegraphers, who knew their equipment very well, but Phillips appears to have been exceptionally gifted. The time spent fixing the set meant that there was a substantial buildup of messages to send and significant pressure on the radio operators. Wireless reports of ice and icebergs had come in throughout the day. At 9:00 A.M. the Cunard liner *Caronia* reported a huge ice field at 42° north, stretching across from 49′ to 51′ west. The *Noordam, Baltic, Amerika, Californian,* and *Mesaba* all sent out radio messages warning of ice around them in the western reaches of the North Atlantic, where the Arctic Current brings its deadly cargo of ice southward into the steamer lanes. At 1:42 P.M. the ice was 250 miles ahead of the onrushing *Titanic* when the *Baltic* sent her message, but six hours later at 7:30, when the *Californian* (1902; 6,223 tons, 448 feet, 12 knots) wirelessed that she was stopped by pack ice and that there were three gigantic bergs near her, the *Titanic* was only fifty miles away. Still, there was no ice where she was, and until it was unmistakably present, no action to slow the liner would be taken. "At the British Inquiry, a number of veteran North Atlantic shipmasters, all ice experienced, unanimously swore that it had been their invariable and universal practice to maintain course and speed as long as the visibility was good. Schedules must be maintained, and passengers are always in a hurry to reach land. One cannot go slow, or change course, merely because there is ice somewhere ahead."[17]

On the evening of April 14 Captain Smith felt secure enough to accept an invitation to a dinner party in his honor given by the Wideners of Philadelphia, but he left the table to return to the bridge at 8:55 P.M.[18] The captain and Second Officer Charles Lightoller, who had the six to ten watch, discussed icebergs and the difficulties of seeing them at night. No order was given to reduce speed, although Captain Smith ordered that he be called at the slightest change in sea conditions. As his watch neared its end, Lightoller sent a message to the lookouts to watch carefully for icebergs. At 10:00 P.M. Lightoller was relieved by First Officer William Murdoch, who had the ten to two watch. A message from the *Mesaba* at 9:40 P.M. indicated a huge ice field. Because of the pressure of passenger messages, the warning did not reach the bridge. If they had been plotted, the six warnings that the *Titanic* received on Sunday, April 14, would have told her officers about a huge ice field at least seventy-eight miles long and twelve miles wide extending from north to south across the steamer lane. On the route she was traveling there was no way she could avoid having to navigate through, or around, the ice obstacle. Furthermore, the *Titanic*'s officers knew that the sea temperature was falling steadily, a good indication of the presence of ice.

Once again Evans, the lone wireless operator on the *Californian*, who was twenty years old, tried around 11:00 P.M. to warn all vessels that she was stopped by ice which was all around her. His signal was so strong that he nearly blasted the headset off Phillips, the operator on the *Titanic*, who was trying to catch up on all the messages that had been delayed when the equipment broke down. Phillips reacted by telling Evans to shut up because he was so near that he was knocking out the *Titanic*'s attempts to reach Cape Race.[19] Evans listened in until about eleven-thirty and then, at the end of a sixteen-hour day, turned off his wireless set and went to bed. He was the only radio officer on the *Californian*. At 11:30 P.M. the Leyland liner lay in the center of the ice field between ten and twenty miles away from the *Titanic*.

At about the same time the *Titanic*'s lookouts, Frederick Fleet and Reginald Lee, suddenly saw the dim outline of a fifty- to sixty-foot iceberg looming out of what they now realized was a foggy haze, not the horizon. The giant berg was around fifteen hundred feet in front of the *Titanic*. The lookouts screamed a warning to First Officer Murdoch on the bridge that there was an "iceberg right ahead." Murdoch reacted instinctively and sought to avoid the danger by ordering the helmsman to put the wheel over hard a starboard, while ordering the engine room to stop all engines and then to go full astern. Fearing a collision, Murdoch also activated the lever to close all the watertight doors on the *Titanic.* Thirty-seven seconds later, as the liner began to answer the helm slightly, the *Titanic* side swiped the iceberg and rumbled over the undersea ledge extending from the berg.[20] The iceberg slipped down the starboard side of the ship and disappeared from sight as the *Titanic* slowly drifted to a stop with twelve thousand feet of the North Atlantic beneath her hull. She was opened for a third of her length, compromising the watertight integrity of her first five compartments. She had been designed to remain afloat with any three adjacent compartments full of water. Captain Smith raced to the bridge, and Thomas Andrews soon followed. Smith asked Andrews to inspect the ship and report back. Andrews went below to check the damage and returned to tell Smith that the fate of his ship was sealed. The collision with the iceberg happened at approximately 11:40 P.M. The *Titanic,* which had been dubbed "unsinkable," had less than three hours to live.

No person should ever describe any ship as unsinkable, but by contemporary standards the *Titanic* came close. She was constructed with a double bottom running the entire length and width of the vessel to save her from sinking if she ran over anything. In addition, her hull was divided by fifteen transverse watertight bulkheads into compartments that were supposed to make her immune from sinking because of any damage that might occur through human folly.[21] She could float with any three watertight compartments ruptured. This meant that if she was in an accident and was rammed by another vessel at her most vulnerable point, where two watertight compartments came together, she would remain afloat. In fact the imaginary ramming steamer could hit her again and take out another compartment, and she still would remain afloat. She seemed immune from any damage through human error. Unfortunately no one had ever thought the huge liner might sideswipe an iceberg and dent the plates on her side sufficient to let the North Atlantic pour into five compartments, two more than the maximum that she could have full of water and stay afloat. Her magnificent state-of-the-art pumping system could not keep up with the situation. Relentlessly the inrushing North Atlantic was going to pull under the largest ship in the world.

In the radio room a thoughtful Bride arrived early, at midnight, instead of 2:00 A.M. to relieve Phillips, who had spent an exhausting day fixing the installation and sending an endless stream of messages. In his bunk Bride had not even felt the collision with the iceberg so slight had the scrape been. Later he thought he might have awakened when the throb of the engines ceased. Bride took over and Phillips was preparing to leave when Captain Smith rushed in and told the two young radio operators: "We have struck an iceberg and I am having an inspection made to tell what it has done to us. You'd better get ready to send out a call for assistance, but don't send it until I tell you."

The two were dumbfounded. Their ship was unsinkable. Ten minutes later Smith was back and looked grave. "Send out the call for assistance!" he ordered.

"Which call, Captain?" Phillips asked.

"The regular international call for help," was his reply.[22]

Thus at about twelve-five, twenty minutes after the collision, Captain Smith ordered the CQD distress call sent out with the position of the *Titanic* at 41°, 46′ north, 50°, 14′ west. The signal that Cape Race actually received was: "Have struck an iceberg. We are badly damaged. Titanic, latitude 41:46 N., longitude 50:14 W."[23]

Smith also ordered the boilers to be shut down and the remaining steam blown off. Numerous ships on the North Atlantic that April evening answered the distress call of the queen of the world's merchant marine, but time and distance factors were going to prove challenging. The *Frankfurt* of North German Lloyd was 153 miles away, *Mount Temple* of Canadian Pacific 50 miles to the west, and on the other side of the ice, the *Virginian of* the Allan Line was 170 miles to the north, *Birma* of the Russian-American Line 70 miles south, and even the *Olympic,* the *Titanic*'s sister, some 500 miles away to the east, and the *Baltic* even farther. All responded, but all were too far away ever to have a chance of reaching her in time.[24] Only the Cunard liner *Carpathia* (1903; 13,555 tons, 540 feet, 14 knots) was anywhere within steaming range to the south. Her radio officer, Harold T. Cottam, did not hear the SOS and responded to Phillips by asking him if he knew there were messages for the *Titanic* at Cape Cod. Phillips responded to Cottam immediately with: "Come quick, we have struck a berg! It's CQD, old man!" Cottam also was a lone Marconi operator and normally should have turned in for the night. Luck and his interest in the British Coal Strike had kept him up to receive the SOS from the *Titanic.* Captain Arthur Rostron had turned in but was not asleep when Cottam pounded on his cabin door and entered. Rostron was a strict master, and no one would have disturbed him in that way without serious need. The radio operator told him that the *Titanic* was sinking and needed help. Rostron was so amazed that he grabbed Cottam's sleeve and demanded confirmation of the incredible news. When Cottam confirmed the distress call, Rostron said to him: "All right, tell him we are coming along as fast as we can."[25] The *Carpathia* was approximately fifty-eight miles away and would need about four hours to reach the sinking liner. Captain Rostron's message was received on the *Titanic* around 12:33 A.M. The *Titanic* had much less time than that to stay afloat.

Rostron immediately gave his helmsmen the famous order "North fifty-two west" and turned to preparing his command to receive an avalanche of survivors. His ship was off on her historic race against time. The *Carpathia* was en route to the Mediterranean when she began the race north through a dark Atlantic Ocean strewn with ice floes and icebergs. The engineers on the *Carpathia,* informed of the distress signal and the time factor, increased the pressure on her boilers until the old liner's speed crept upward from a maximum of fourteen knots to well over seventeen knots, probably as fast as she ever had gone and to the point that with the increased boiler pressure they began to fear for their safety. As Captain Rostron later said, if he had foreseen how much ice lay between his ship and the *Titanic* he never would have pushed her as hard as he did. The risks he faced were enormous, but hundreds of lives lay in the balance. The preparations which the *Carpathia* crew made at Rostron's command were remarkably thorough. "Every officer and man was roused out and assigned to duty; stokers off watch tumbled out and, without dressing, rushed to the fire rooms to augment the black gang on watch. Preparations for the most remote contingency were made, not the smallest detail was overlooked. Boats were swung out and made ready to lower, lights and ladders were rigged, life lines rove along the side, blankets, life-rings, hot coffee, restoratives, beds, doctors—all were ready. Bosun chairs were rigged for children and the incapacitated."[26]

At Captain Smith's order the *Titanic* began to lower away her lifeboats. Several early lifeboats swung down her towering sides half empty because passengers refused to heed the warnings of officers and take seats in a little lifeboat on the cold Atlantic when the huge, warm *Titanic* still seemed so much less vulnerable a refuge. In fact the first lifeboat to be lowered, No. 7, had only twenty-seven people in a boat with a capacity of sixty-five; No. 1 went next with only twelve passengers, including Sir Cosmo and Lady Duff Gordon, and her personal secretary, Miss Francatelli. Later lifeboats would hold only women and children. On the *Titanic* even young pages and elevator boys, far younger than eighteen, held back because they bore the responsibility of being crew and perished. Those lifeboats that left the White Star liner with many fewer passengers than they should have later refused to return for others out of fear of the ship's suction, or of being overwhelmed by humanity when she sank. Fear was omnipresent and undermined humanitarian instincts. Others on the *Titanic* refused to leave because they felt sure another vessel would reach them in time, particularly if they thought they saw the dim lights of another vessel on the horizon. Rockets arched from the decks of the *Titanic* three hundred feet into the night sky frantically signaling for aid, and Morse code was flashed across the sea by powerful lamps in a vain attempt to get assistance that never came.[27]

By 1:28 A.M. on April 15 Phillips had radioed the *Carpathia* that the engine room on the *Titanic* was flooded and to come as quickly as possible. At one point he looked up and saw Bride working with his lightweight clothes on. Phillips took a moment to tell his young assistant to go dress warmly. They did not know what they might be in for that morning. The noise from the boilers blowing off steam deadened the ears of the radio officers because of the proximity of the radio room to the funnels. Captain Smith, learning of this, tried to get the sound reduced a little so that Phillips and Bride could hear a little better, and the engineers did their best to comply. Bride carried the messages to the Bridge, where Captain Smith remained remarkably calm even when he told the junior radio officer that the ship probably had only thirty minutes. Phillips stepped out from the Radio Shack just once and noted that the situation looked bad. Well he might. When he made that observation around 2:00 A.M., the bow had already slipped under the sea. The *Titanic* was down to only a few lifeboats, and there was a sudden upsurge in a demand for the few remaining spaces as the deck took an ominous slope toward the bow. Slowly but surely the largest liner in the world was being pulled under as her forward compartments filled with seawater and her stern steadily rose farther out of the sea. "Finally, at 2:05 A.M., the last lifeboat, a collapsible, pulled away from the liner, leaving more than 1,500 people behind."[28] Those safe in the little flotilla of lifeboats that had pulled away from the liner saw her three immense propellers, blade after blade, rise from the sea as the water lapped over the bow and reached the bridge at the opposite end of the eight-hundred-foot liner. In between on the fully lighted open decks was a mass of humanity numbering slightly over fifteen hundred souls with little hope of salvation. The drama was heightened when the first funnel collapsed, and the screams of terror grew more pronounced with the increase in the angle of the ship.

Captain Smith made one last trip to the radio room and told Phillips and Bride: "Men, you have done your full duty; you can do no more. Abandon your post. Now it is every man for himself."[29] Phillips kept on for another few minutes until around 2:00 A.M., when he asked

Bride to look outside and see if all the boats had gone. When he saw that all the boats were away and that the water was lapping over the forward end of the boat deck, Bride returned to Phillips and shouted, "Let's clear out." They had prepared candles in order to work after the power failed, but the electricity stayed with them until the end. There indeed was nothing more that they could do. Bride helped get the last collapsible lifeboat off the roof of the Radio Shack. It landed in the ocean upside down only a short fall from the deck. Bride followed it into the cold Atlantic and later was among the small group that clung to the upturned collapsible to await the end. Phillips went down with the ship. In the end Bride was rescued by the *Carpathia* with his feet frostbitten and very painful. On the Cunard liner, when he learned that Cottam was close to fainting after working three days solid, Bride had himself carried to the *Carpathia*'s radio room, where he relieved his exhausted colleague and sent messages from a propped-up position. When the Cunard liner arrived at her New York pier, Bride did not even notice since he still had a pile of more than a hundred messages in front of him. The Marconi people found him in the radio shack and told him his work was done and that an ambulance was at the dock to take him to a hospital. At that point Bride quit sending. He even managed a smile for reporters when he was carried off the *Carpathia* on her arrival in New York. Among many heroic individuals Phillips and Bride stand out.

The waters of the North Atlantic continued to rush in, and the bow of the *Titanic* slowly was pulled beneath the surface of the ocean as her huge counter stern soared into the starlit night until her propellers and rudder were totally clear of their element. Thirty-five members of the engineering staff remained in the bowels of the liner, laboring to keep her pumps going and her lights on for as long as possible. None survived. Finally, around 2:16 A.M., as water poured in through the top of the second funnel, giant boilers, triple-expansion engines, and dynamos broke loose from the huge bolts designed to secure them in upright positions, and the lights went out. For a few seconds the ship hung, perpendicular, as if suspended in space, and then the hull broke into two pieces with a shower of sparks and the forward section with an ever-increasing pace began its dive for the bottom of the Atlantic more than two miles beneath her. The remaining section of the hull rapidly filled with water and also soared into the air almost vertically before quietly following the bow section to the ocean floor. The time was 2:20 A.M.; the date April 15, 1912.

As the ship sank, fittings broke loose everywhere. The wires holding the forward funnel in place had given way earlier under the strain, and the smokestack fell overboard into a mass of swimmers. Some were crushed to death instantly. Others, such as Colonel John Jacob Astor, were sucked inside the funnel, where the vortex of water swept them around and around like a washing machine, knocking the victims senseless, obliterating facial features, and quickly drowning those not already dead. In the water the screams and pleas of the dying ceased in about twelve minutes as the twenty-eight-degree temperature brought on hypothermia, a sense of euphoria, and then the cessation of all bodily functions through excessive cold, death. As Walter Lord, the preeminent historian of the *Titanic,* wrote, "it was the sea itself that broke a man's resistance. The temperature of the water was 28 degrees F.—well below freezing. To Second Officer Lightoller it felt like 'a thousand knives' driven into his body. In water like this, lifebelts did no good."[30] Those in the safety of the lifeboats waited in terror for some of the sounds to die down before any returned to the sight of the disaster lest they be swamped by too many frantic souls. The screams of the dying were to live with them forever. Finally Fifth Officer Harold Godfrey Lowe managed to transfer all nonessential individuals from Lifeboat No. 14 to Lifeboats Nos. 10, 12, and 4 and Lifeboat D. Almost an hour after the *Titanic* went down, Lowe rowed Lifeboat No. 14 back to the scene of the sinking and managed to pull into the boat four people, one of whom died shortly after being rescued. Too much time had passed, and the difficulties of finding weakened voices in the dark defeated Lowe's best intentions.[31]

Among the survivors was Bruce Ismay, president of the International Mercantile Marine, who, at the urging of a sailor, had gotten into a lifeboat that was being lowered with one unoccupied seat. He saved his life and lost his reputation as 1,503 of those to whom his firm had sold tickets for a safe passage to the New World died in the sinking of the White Star Line flagship.

About an hour later, around 3:35 A.M., the Cunard liner *Carpathia* came over the horizon, steaming as fast as conditions would permit. Those on her saw a green light and thought the *Titanic* still afloat, but as they got closer, they realized that it was a light carried by one of her lifeboats. The *Carpathia* reached the scene of the disaster around 4:00 A.M. and drifted to a halt as close to the lifeboats as she could approach in safety. At 4:10 the Cunard liner took the first survivors on board, and it was confirmed that the *Titanic* had gone down 110 minutes before. They were too late by a small but fatal margin. Ultimately 711 out of 2,201 who had sailed from Queenstown on the *Titanic* were rescued.[32] That there was room for a minimum of another 473 persons in the surviving lifeboats of the *Titanic* compounded the tragedy more than any other single fact. At least that many died totally unnecessarily and without acceptable moral reason. Only 13 people were pulled alive from the ocean into the lifeboats.

Dawn came at four-thirty, and Captain Rostron viewed with horror the huge ice barrier to the north and the incredible number of icebergs the *Carpathia* had managed to miss in reaching the *Titanic*'s position. At seven-thirty the last lifeboat was pulled on board. Rostron prudently retained a number of lifeboats from the *Titanic* since he now had so many additional lives in his care. After reviewing all possible courses of action and consulting with Ismay, Captain Rostron turned the *Carpathia* around and retraced her route to New York. The *Olympic* had offered to rendezvous with the *Carpathia* in order to have the survivors transferred to her, but Ismay and all concerned shuddered at the thought of another mid-ocean lifeboat drill, especially to the *Olympic*.

The death toll per class remains a vivid testimonial to class consciousness at the beginning of the twentieth century. Of the 144 first-class women passengers, only 4 died, and 3 of them because they would not leave their husbands. Out of 93 second-class female passengers, 13 died, but 76 of 165 third-class women passengers perished. Among children 1 out of 29 in first and second class perished, while 52 out of 79 in steerage died. Among the male passengers on the *Titanic,* 57 out of 175 in first class died; 154 out of 168 in second class; and 387 out of 462 in third. Of the crew of 885 men and women, 673 died and 212 were saved.[33] The salaries or wages of all White Star personnel serving on the liner ceased the moment the *Titanic* went under. Under British law, the "ship," not the steamship line, was paying them, meaning that her sinking terminated their incomes. As if their agony had not been enough, the White Star Line accountants, in recognition that the liner had sunk in mid-Atlantic, deducted an appropriate sum from the wages payable to crew members or their survivors. The final death toll certified by the parliamentary inquiry was 1,503.

Personal wealth represented the universal standard of individual worth when the *Titanic* sailed. The ancient Anglo-Saxon wergeld, meaning "the worth of a man," had been fundamental to Western society and, under various other terms, to other world social orders, for two millennia. In 1912 this was only beginning to change, and in part it was responsible for the heavy death toll in third class.

When the *Titanic*'s first distress call went out, in the distance, perhaps twenty miles away, was the Leyland liner *Californian* (1902; 6,223 tons, 540 feet, 14 knots) under the command of Captain Stanley Lord. Lord was a martinet whose officers and crew feared him. He was awakened by his officers, who told him of a vessel firing off rockets, but the conclusion was that she simply was trying to see her way through the ice and not in distress. It also was thought that there was more than one vessel in the immediate area and that another ship—a medium to small-sized tramp steamer that earlier in the evening did not answer the Morse and continued on her way—lay between the *Californian* and the *Titanic.*[34] The single wireless operator on the *Californian,* Cyril Furnstone Evans, had been told by the *Titanic* to shut up and quit bothering them shortly before the White Star liner hit the iceberg. Evans had been on duty from 7:00 A.M. until after 11:00 P.M., a long shift for a salary of $20 a month. He had done what he had every right to do: He had turned off his wireless and gone to bed. Hence minutes later there was no one on the *Californian* to receive the *Titanic*'s distress call. "No reproach whatsoever attaches to him, but the tragedy, with its appalling loss of life, exposed to the public the wretched penuriousness of some steamship companies, so justly and forcibly condemned by Senator Smith, Lord Mersey, Marconi, the newspapers, and many others."[35]

Captain Lord was vilified in the subsequent hearings and reports for failing to go to the aid of the *Titanic.* Today this judgment has been questioned. The original evidence seemed indisputable in that the *Californian* saw a vessel pass her, took note of eight rockets being shot off, and then noted the disappearance of the ship in question around 2:20 A.M. All this fitted the *Titanic,* and she may have been the ship. At the same time rational later judgment indicates that the *Californian* may not have been within visible distance of the disaster and that Captain Lord, in the absence of any wireless communication to the contrary, may not have had any reason to assume that the other vessel had a problem. At the British inquiry in mid-May Captain Lord, Second Officer Herbert Strong, and Apprentice Gibson, who had been on the bridge of the *Californian* when rockets were seen, all claimed that the vessel was not large enough to have been the *Titanic.* Furthermore, they testified that the vessel concerned was showing only one masthead light, not two like the *Titanic*'s.[36] Captain Lord's principal accuser was a second donkey engine man on the *Californian,* Ernest Gill.[37] Gill later sold his accusatory story for a sum equal to a full year's salary to a newspaper and left never to be heard from again.[38] In fairness to Captain Lord the unsubstantiated word of an opportunistic individual may be questioned. On the other hand, Third Officer Charles Groves of the *Californian* offered testimony against Captain Lord that, on first reading, seems damning because he asserted that the steamer to the south was a passenger liner, not a tramp steamer. The 1912 investigation totally missed the point that Groves described a ship that he said had all her deck lights off when in fact the *Titanic* had everything ablaze until the moment she went under. Hence the testimony of Groves, who was no friend of Captain Lord, also needs to be placed into perspective.[39]

The distinguished American maritime historian Edwin L. Dunbaugh has written: "It is hard to believe that the thousands of people who have devoted years of their lives to studying every iota of evidence about the *Titanic* tragedy have all concluded that the lights these people saw were those of the *Californian* when the evidence indicates that they were probably the lights of a different vessel."[40] The possibility exists that a Norwegian sealing vessel, the *Samson,* was somewhere in the vicinity, and the testimony of her highly respected first officer, Henrik Naess, documents this important fact.[41] The *Samson* fled the scene because she thought a Canadian government revenue vessel might be pursuing her for catching seals illegally. Years later Naess, who during a long career received a number of medals in honor of significant maritime services to sailors of several nations, said he believed that the *Samson* had been the ship near the *Titanic.* Therefore the *Samson,* which did not have a wireless, may have been the vessel which the officers on the *Californian* saw.[42] A doctor on the Canadian Pacific liner *Mount Temple* (1903; 8,790 tons, 485 feet, 13 knots) also contended that he had seen the *Titanic* from the western side of the huge floe of pack ice that represented an impenetrable barrier just five miles to the west of the White Star liner. He provided a sworn testimonial to the *Titanic* inquiry of the U.S. Senate, but that group was too horrified at the thought that rescue might have been at hand and ignored the letter.[43] Furthermore, from the position of the *Mount Temple,* if the *Titanic* had swerved and managed to avoid the iceberg, she would have had great difficulty in avoiding a collision with the enormous field of pack ice within another few miles. Presumably such a collision would have been far less disastrous.

The circumstances with regard to the *Californian* were simply that while she lay within a reasonable distance of the sinking *Titanic,* her wireless was turned off, and therefore no call for aid ever reached her within the time necessary to be of assistance. Captain Lord was awakened, told about a ship firing off rockets, and did nothing to ascertain the reason.[44] Nothing absolves Lord from this. In the race to find a scapegoat Captain Lord, with his stern arrogance, became an unwitting target and paid for it dearly. The aid the *Californian* offered the next morning, when he learned of the sinking, changed course, and picked his way through the ice to the scene of the disaster, was too little too late. If the other vessel nearby had been the Norwegian sealer *Samson,* she was long since gone on her way to Iceland, where her officers and crew some days later learned of the loss of a huge liner near where they might have been. A final historical judgment on the role of the *Californian* never is likely, but the subject always should be approached with great care and evaluated without prejudice.

All over the world newspaper headlines carried the news to a stunned public. In New York the Stock Exchange virtually ceased trading and had an extremely low day. In London the business worst hit after the IMM itself was Lloyd's, which had insured the *Titanic* on some of the best terms ever because she seemed unsinkable and therefore an excellent risk. Government and public buildings everywhere lowered their flags to half-mast in respect to those who had lost their lives. "The sinking aroused an epidemic of sensational rumors, wild charges, and acrimonious controversy. It was made the subject of two thorough inquiries, the first by the United States Senate and the other by the British Board of Trade, under the presidency of Lord Mersey, noted Wreck Commissioner."[45]

In the hearings on both sides of the Atlantic Ocean the knowledge learned was sobering. The basic facts were that the *Titanic* had suffered a glancing blow from an iceberg. The liner had remained afloat for nearly three hours under virtually ideal conditions in which to get 2,002 souls safely into lifeboats to await the arrival of a rescue vessel which it was known was coming. Yet more than 1,500 individuals had lost their lives in the largest peacetime death toll on the North Atlantic. The experienced Captain E. J. Smith, commodore of the White Star Line, and 77 percent of the crew had gone down with the ship.[46]

The fact that Bruce Ismay, President of the International Mercantile Marine and Managing Director of the White Star Line, survived the sinking when 1,503 of his passengers did not produced a great deal of caustic criticism in the press. When it looked as if Ismay were determined to leave the United States on the first White Star liner, the *Cedric,* to sail after the *Carpathia* arrived, this also did not sit well. Since the *Titanic* was a British-flag vessel that had sunk in international waters after hitting an iceberg, the investigation should have been exclusively a British matter. However, the heavy loss of American lives meant that some in Congress wanted to be involved. Senator William Alden Smith (R., Michigan) of the U.S. Senate Committee on Commerce engineered the creation of a subcommittee to investigate the situation under his personal chairmanship. He rushed to New York and boarded the *Carpathia* before anyone even disembarked in order to ensure Ismay's cooperation.[47] He then firmly requested Ismay remain in the United States, and during the subsequent hearings, which began on April 19 at the Waldorf-Astoria Hotel, the White Star president was subjected to a rigorous cross-examination. The British government and public became substantially irritated at the American hearings. Although everyone shook hands at the conclusion of the American hearings, the final analysis seemed to be that Bruce Ismay as President of the IMM was responsible for the *Titanic* and everything that happened to her and everyone who sailed on her. He was vilified in the American press, which was in no mood to be generous.

The British inquiry opened on May 2 in a huge building, London's Scottish Drill Hall, under the direction of Lord Mersey, an experienced jurist in commercial law, but not a nautical authority—yet. He conducted a thorough review of the disaster over thirty-six days that particularly explored the technical side of the loss. What was documented in the hearings was that the *Titanic* had not been carrying anywhere near sufficient lifeboats for all those on board even if her builders and owners had exceeded the minimum requirements of the law. In response White Star immediately ordered sufficient lifeboats for all its vessels, but not before they tried to send the *Olympic* to sea on her next crossing (April 24) with an inadequate number of lifeboats and were stopped only when the crew refused to sail with her.[48] The number of lifeboats on the *Olympic* was increased from twenty to forty-eight, much closer to the number Harland & Wolff had originally wanted.[49]

Any reliance on wireless to bring assistance at any time was foolhardy. In the future additional wireless operators would be required on passenger ships to provide an around-the-clock service. The inquiries also underlined the fact that a double bottom in ship construction must run well up the side of the vessel in order to be effective in every instance. In the *Titanic* the bulkheads had run up to E Deck, which was only eleven feet above the waterline. If they had been taken up to D Deck, the ship would have remained afloat somewhat longer. Moreover, if the ship had had coal bunkers running across the vessel, she also might have survived. As a result of the loss of the *Titanic,* the White Star Line spent over six million dollars practically rebuilding the *Olympic* with an enhanced double bottom that in effect resulted in a double hull in order to restore public confidence in the ship and the line.

In terms of international precautions the International Ice Patrol was established (1913) in the North Atlantic to keep track of the movement of ice as it drifted south into the steamer lanes. Shipping lines immediately would announce their intentions to have their captains take nothing except the extreme southern route in order to avoid the possibility of encountering ice. One other international modification was a significant tightening of the rules involving the use of rockets. Before the loss of the *Titanic* rockets could be used for a variety of purposes: to salute another ship at night, as a courtesy signal, to find one's way at night, to recall fishermen, and for other nonemergency needs.[50]

It was not exceptional or unusual for rocket signals at sea to be ignored, and the tragic result was that a vessel in distress might not attract the attention it desperately needed.

In the inquiries it was stressed that the *Titanic* had remained afloat long enough for all her passengers and crew to leave the ship *if there had been enough lifeboats and life rafts.* The "if" was damning. "Certified to carry 3547 persons she had boats for only 1178, and even this meager figure was nearly double that required by the antiquated Board of Trade law of 1894, which had not been revised in 18 years. Therein lay the ironic tragedy of the *Titanic.* Perfect weather and ample time for launching boats, such as few sinking ships have ever been fortunate enough to have—but there were not enough boats."[51] As the noted American naval authority Admiral Alfred Thayer Mahan "so aptly stated, 'Corporate responsibility is notoriously fugacious and elusive.'"[52]

In Britain the regulations of the Board of Trade speedily were revised. "The destruction of the *Titanic* by a spur of ice shattered popular faith in the supremacy of technology, progress and privilege. The age of self-confident belief in the inexorable progress of society through the application of science was over. In retrospect the utter failure of this microcosmic machine, and all that it represented, symbolized the end of the nineteenth century. The twentieth century had begun."[53] When everything is taken into consideration, the 1,503 persons who died with the *Titanic* did not die in vain, even if they never should have perished. At the time that was small consolation to their loved ones and does nothing to relieve the horror of the sinking even today.

On seeing the *Carpathia,* Colonel Archibald Gracie commented: "In the midst of our thankfulness for deliverance, one name mentioned with deepest feeling of gratitude was that of Marconi. I wish that he had been there to hear the chorus of gratitude that went out to him for the wonderful invention that spared us many hours, and perhaps days of wandering about the sea in hunger and storm and cold."[54] Incredibly Marconi was waiting in New York for the arrival of the *Titanic,* on whose first eastbound crossing (April 20) he had been scheduled to sail. The great inventor was stunned and said that the loss of the ship seemed almost impossible. Mayor William Gaynor of New York started a fund to aid the *Titanic* victims, and within three weeks more than $111,460 had been received from all over the United States.[55]

Ultimately the British inquiry exonerated Ismay of any wrongdoing and for saving his own life when he took the last vacant seat in a lifeboat since no one else was around at that moment. After the dust had settled a bit in 1913, Ismay resigned as president of the IMM.[56] According to the official IMM release, he had decided to retire from the shipping trust in February 1912, months before the *Titanic* disaster. He was succeeded by Harold A. Sanderson on June 30, 1913. His departure was unlamented by many. In Britain he was a bit of a social pariah, and he retired to live in the country, where he died in relative obscurity in 1937.

As a postscript, one week after the disaster, on April 20, 1912, the North German Lloyd liner *Bremen* (1897; 10,525 tons, 525 feet, 15 knots) was in the vicinity of the *Titanic* sinking when icebergs were sighted. Passengers were informed and rushed to the open deck in spite of the bitterly cold weather. It was late in the afternoon of a bright, sunny day when suddenly the passengers saw not only a large iceberg but a number of dead bodies floating in the icy water. The *Bremen* steamed by a dead woman who had a baby clasped to her chest, and another woman was holding tightly to a large dog that looked like a St. Bernard. Some men were floating in a group around a deck chair. The scene was horrifying in the extreme to those on the *Bremen*.[57] One is led to wonder what the *Bremen* was doing in those waters if all the North German Lloyd steamers had been ordered to follow the extreme southern route in order to stay well clear of any ice. The news of the "floating dead" stimulated immediate action.

The Canadian cable steamer *Mackay-Bennett*, chartered by the White Star Line, sailed from Halifax one week later on a morbid mission to find and identify as many of the dead as possible. The reason for this voyage was the news that a substantial "raft" of bodies had been identified floating in the Atlantic Ocean north of the Gulf

Stream. In addition, the stories of the passengers on the *Bremen* shocked many. The orders given to Captain Lardner of the *Mackay-Bennett* were to retrieve every body that he could find. This proved impossible because when the Canadian vessel reached the scene, there were too many dead bodies and the ship's embalming supplies were inadequate to the challenge. In a matter of several days the crew succeeded in recovering the bodies of 190 *Titanic* victims and of burying at sea another 116, mostly dead crew members or those seriously mutilated. Refuse from the sunken liner dotted the North Atlantic in all directions. The *Mackay-Bennett* was assisted by another cable steamer, the *Minia,* which found 14 corpses. The *Mackay-Bennett* returned to Halifax on the morning of April 30. "While the city's church bells tolled and British flags fluttered down to half mast, the *Mackay-Bennett* steamed slowly into the harbor. She reached her dock in the navy yard shortly after 9:30 o'clock. Her own flag at half-mast, the death ship docked slowly. The crew manned the rails with bared heads, and on the aft deck were stacked the coffins with the dead."[58] Of the 190 bodies she brought in, 130 were identified, including the remains of Colonel John Jacob Astor, Isidor Straus, and Frank D. Millet, the artist. Colonel Astor's body was recovered with his money belt containing the twenty-five hundred dollars in cash he normally carried. Some 60 bodies remained in the simple morgue awaiting identification, which never came. Ultimately they were buried in a Halifax cemetery at the expense of the White Star Line.

The rediscovery of the remains of the *Titanic* on September 1, 1985, by a joint Franco-American expedition under the leadership of Dr. Robert Ballard made newspaper headlines almost as large as when the liner sank.[59] Since then a wealth of information about the ship and the disaster has been obtained. Artists, such as Stephen J. Card and Kenneth Marschall, have been inspired, and a major movie by James Cameron bearing the ship's name has captured the public imagination.[60]

Chapter 18

FOG IN THE ST. LAWRENCE CAN BE DEADLY

The Loss of the *Empress of Ireland*

May 29, 1914

Among the greatest transportation enterprises ever created in North America was the Canadian Pacific Railway Company, whose origins date to 1873 but whose formal incorporation under the presidency of George Stephen did not occur until February 16, 1881. The Canadian Pacific Railway sought to provide Canada with an overland route from the Atlantic to the Pacific independent of any similar American enterprise. The main line of the Canadian Pacific Railway spanning the continent from Montreal to the Pacific Ocean, one of the greatest construction and engineering achievements of the nineteenth century, was completed in 1886.

However, much more was required than just the railroad if the imperial mails were to be delivered with the speed desired. Two steamship routes also had to be created, first, from Liverpool, England, to Quebec, Canada, and, second, from Vancouver, British Columbia, to Yokohama, Japan. In the future Canadian Pacific was to play a major role in the development of transatlantic steam navigation. In particular the St. Lawrence route was to be heralded as ensuring travel a day less on the North Atlantic than any other track. After a ship left Montreal and Quebec City, one day's steaming lay within the relatively sheltered waters of the St. Lawrence, the majestic North American fjord. Any vessel steaming north, down the St. Lawrence River and through the Gulf of St. Lawrence toward the Atlantic Ocean, could expect to experience fog that could be challenging.

The Pacific route received a mail subsidy in 1889 of approximately three hundred thousand dollars a year on the condition that three liners of eighteen knots be built for the service. These ships, *Empress of India, Empress of Japan,* and *Empress of China,* each 5,905 tons, entered the service in 1891. They soon proved exceptionally popular. On the Atlantic side the Government Post Office (GPO) agreement required vessels capable of crossing from England to St. John or Halifax, Nova Scotia, in five days, but the implementation of the service did not move forward until 1903. The creation in 1902 of the International Mercantile Marine (IMM), the American-inspired shipping trust, undoubtedly had an influence here since Canadian Pacific always was wary of such maritime combinations. The means of quickly achieving a regular passenger service involved the Canadian Pacific purchase of the Elder Dempster Line, which had a fleet of fourteen twin-screw passenger and cargo steamers named for various lakes or words beginning with the letter *M.* On April 6, 1903, the formal transfer of the ships occurred with the hoisting of the red-and-white-checked flag of the Canadian Pacific over the *Lake Champlain* (1900; 7,392 tons, 346 feet, 13 knots), which had been built by Barclay, Curle & Company, Glasgow, Scotland, and initially had accommodations for 100 first-, 80 second-, and 500 third-class accommodations; later third class was revised upward to 1,000 to 2,000. The *Lake Champlain* usually is credited with having been the first steamship in the world fitted with wireless, on May 21, 1901, and with taking the first Canadian Pacific sailing when she left Liverpool on April 14, 1903, with 57 first-, 52 second-, and 1,017 third-class passengers.

"Canadian Pacific derived many advantages from entering the North Atlantic trade, one of the most important being that they obtained control of all three sections—Atlantic, rail and Pacific—of an 'All Red' overland route from Europe to Japan and China. A few years later they acquired an interest in the Canadian-Australasian Line between Vancouver, New Zealand and Australia. In this way, they became 'the world's greatest transportation system' and their services 'bridged two oceans and linked four continents.'"[1]

The regal Empress of Ireland *(1906), with her sister ship, the* Empress of Britain *(1906), were the flagships of the Canadian Pacific service from Canada to Great Britain. Between 1906 and 1914 the* Empress of Ireland *completed ninety-five round-trip voyages on the North Atlantic before disaster struck. On May 29, 1914, she was rammed and sunk by the Norwegian coaler* Storstad *with the loss of 1,014 lives—the heaviest Canadian death toll in a maritime disaster and one that occured in the St.Lawrence, within sight of land.*

Canadian Pacific immediately sought to upgrade the St. Lawrence service, and it was appropriate that the new Atlantic steamers receive the same "imperial" designation as the Pacific steamers. The new vessels therefore were christened *Empress of Britain* (1906; 14,189 tons, 549 feet, 18 knots) and *Empress of Ireland* (1906; 14,191 tons, 549 feet, 18 knots). Both new liners far outclassed previous tonnage and all rivals. They were built by the Fairfield Shipbuilding and Engineering Company Ltd., Glasgow, and had accommodations for 310 in first class, 470 in second, and 750 in third. Two sets of quadruple-expansion engines provided the service speed of eighteen knots. The *Empress of Britain* entered service on May 5, 1906, and the *Empress of Ireland* on June 29, 1906. It is accurate to say that they proved very popular vessels and that Canadian Pacific was very proud of them.

The *Empress of Ireland* between June 1906 and May 1914 completed ninety-five successful round-trip voyages on the North Atlantic. At 4:30 P.M. on Thursday, May 28, 1914, the *Empress of Ireland,* under the command of an experienced officer, Captain Henry George Kendall, RNR, backed away from her quay at Quebec City and, leaving the majestic Château Frontenac Hotel behind, headed downstream. Captain Kendall had been a master with Canadian Pacific for six years, but this was his first voyage in command of the *Empress of Ireland.* Quebec City was her second Canadian port of call outward bound since she had left Montreal earlier in the day and made her way downstream with the assistance of a river pilot to Quebec City. Additional passengers watched her slowly come around the bend near the Plains of Abraham and dock at Quebec City, where they then boarded. Sailing days always were scenes of confusion as a large number of new passengers found their way around a strange ship and baggage handling strained the resources of the crew. On this crossing the liner had a good load of 1,057 passengers in all classes. Her officers and crew numbered 420.[2]

Certainly the biggest single group of passengers was a delegation from the Canadian Salvation Army, which was traveling to England to take part in the International Congress in London. More than a thousand people had gathered in the Salvation Army Hall in Toronto the day before the ship sailed to listen to speakers and to wish the delegation of nearly one hundred safe journey. Among the delegation was a band of musicians famous in Canada for their spirited playing. Appropriately the ship's band on the *Empress of Ireland* played a stirring hymn as the big liner moved out into midstream and there were many tearful good-byes. Smaller vessels from ferryboats to lumber vessels and every imaginable form of general traffic dotted the river and paused to watch the departure of the majestic *Empress.* Within minutes she was well out into the St. Lawrence River bound north for the Gulf of St. Lawrence and the Atlantic Ocean.

The first meal on board the *Empress of Ireland* was consumed by her hungry passengers with relish because the liner was still well within the protection of the New Brunswick shoreline, which made the waters so smooth. This was part of the delight of an *Empress* crossing for the first twenty-four hours. Passengers had the opportunity to get their sea legs, real or imaginary, before experiencing the wave action on the North Atlantic.

Fog was expected, and in late spring it was reasonable to expect that it would be thick. Captain Kendall knew this well, and he also was well aware that there was a small margin built into the schedule for just such an eventuality. Accordingly he slowed the *Empress of Ireland* as she proceeded northward. Early in the evening it was still clear when the Allan Line's large new passenger liner *Alsatian* (1913; 18,481 tons, 571 feet, 18 knots) steamed into view inward (southward) bound. The two liners passed close enough that their passengers could have the thrill of seeing each other.[3] Both were very beautiful units of their respective fleets.

At Rimouski, Quebec, Captain Kendall brought the *Empress of Ireland* in close to the entrance of the port so that the last bags of the Canadian Royal Mails could be transferred to the ship for delivery in Liverpool five days later. Rimouski lies about 180 miles downstream from Quebec, and the mail was brought by ferry and train to the port for transshipment to the Canadian Pacific liners. At this point the St.

Lawrence River is approximately 30 miles wide, and if there is any fog at all, it cannot be seen across. In the river the channel, which runs about 20 miles from the Quebec shore and about 10 miles from the New Brunswick coast, is deep, and there are few obstacles to navigation. That night the combination of the flow of the river and the tide made for a rather substantial current. As midnight neared, the thermometer dipped, and the air possessed a distinct sting to it even if the breeze was very slight. Most of the passengers retired to their berths exhausted by the activities of sailing day. A dedicated few had written quick letters to loved ones, which left the ship at Rimouski.

The *Empress of Ireland,* all her lights ablaze, slowed around 1:30 A.M. at Father Point to drop the pilot, M. Bernier, and then picked up full speed as she headed north. Shortly thereafter after passing the Cock Point buoy, Captain Kendall on the bridge took note of two things. In the St. Lawrence River bound toward him was a small Norwegian coaler, the *Storstad,* and coming out from the New Brunswick shore was a fog-bank that soon would lie between him and the approaching vessel. Captain Kendall estimated that the other vessel was about two miles away at that time. The *Storstad* was en route from Sydney, Nova Scotia, to Montreal with coal.

Kendall obviously did not like the way things were developing because he took the following actions: He rang full speed astern on the engines in order to stop the *Empress of Ireland,* and he ordered three blasts on the whistle to indicate "I am going full speed astern."[4] Subsequently he thought he heard one long blast from the *Storstad,* and he went out on the wing of the bridge to confirm that his command had stopped dead in the water. Captain Kendall ordered two blasts on the whistle to indicate to the other ship that he was totally stopped in the water, and again he thought he was answered by a single blast. Shortly thereafter, however, to his horror he saw the red and green lights of the steamer, indicating that she was approaching bow on to the *Empress of Ireland.* With his megaphone Captain Kendall screamed at the *Storstad* to reverse her engines, while ordering the

Empress to go full speed ahead with the helm hard aport in an attempt to lessen the blow. The heavy steel bow of the *Storstad* sliced into the engine room of the *Empress of Ireland* on the starboard side at a point almost between the funnels. According to Captain Kendall, he shouted at the *Storstad* to keep full speed ahead in order to fill the hole she had made, but she pulled away almost immediately, separating the two ships.[5] Kendall now rang down to the engine room for full speed ahead in an effort to reach the shore and beach the *Empress,* but the St. Lawrence River was rushing into the huge hole in a torrent and almost immediately flooded the engines, making this impossible. It is estimated that the hole in the side of the *Empress of Ireland* was in excess of 350 square feet and that water poured in at a rate of 260 tons a second. Her two largest compartments were opened to the sea with a length of 175 feet, well over a third of her length (548 feet). The watertight doors on the Canadian Pacific liner had to be closed by hand, and there simply was no time. All lights went out on the *Empress of Ireland,* and almost at once she took an enormous list to starboard and began to settle in the water.

Sleeping passengers in their staterooms suddenly were thrown from their bunks in a pitch-black ship that was utterly strange to them. Disoriented in a world that was turning topsy-turvy, they sought the open deck, often to be frustrated by the stairway design on the liner that saw side stairs rising to a central set of stairs that became impossible to scale as the liner's list worsened. Those who could find anything to cling to and who jumped into the St. Lawrence soon found themselves perishing of cold as hypothermia took its relentless toll.

On the bridge of the *Storstad* there was great confusion also. Chief Mate Toftenes was in command, assisted by Third Mate Saxe and with a quartermaster at the wheel. Toftenes later swore under oath that he had seen the lights of the *Empress of Ireland* appear in line just before the fog obscured everything. If that was true, he had had reason to assume that she had elected to pass port to port. He had judged the distance to be around two miles and reduced speed. Fearing that the two ships were too close for comfort, Toftenes had then ordered the helm to port in a maneuver he hoped would take his ship away from the approaching passenger liner. The currents were such, or the steering so stiff, that the *Storstad* would not answer her wheel, and Third Mate Saxe took the helm from the quartermaster to force the issue. He turned the helm hard aport. At about this time First Mate Toftenes had felt unsure enough to call Captain Andersen, who arrived on the bridge just in time to see his ship ram the side of the *Empress of Ireland.*[6] At the conclusion of the hearing Toftenes was criticized for not having summoned Captain Andersen much earlier than he did.

Ronald Ferguson, the senior wireless operator on the *Empress,* who had just gone to bed, heard the whistle of the *Storstad,* thought it was too near for comfort, and got up to look out the cabin port, which was on the port side of the liner. At that moment he saw nothing. There was only a short distance from their cabin to the radio room, and in five seconds Ferguson reached it. Edward Bamford, the junior officer, had the watch. He felt the slight jar and stepped outside just in time to see the lights of the *Storstad* slide by. As he did so, Ferguson rushed in. He also saw the lights of the Norwegian ship pass down the starboard side of the *Empress.* He did not wait for authorization from the bridge but started to work the telegraph key immediately and hollered at Bamford to bring him some warm clothes. Ferguson sent out a distress signal: "CQ, CQ HERE MPL. HAVE STRUCK SOMETHING AND MAY NEED ASSISTANCE, EMPRESS OF IRELAND. I sent it slowly as I knew that only juniors would be on watch at that time of the night. My idea was to pave the way for an SOS and have seniors on watch to deal with it. Crawford Leslie, nineteen years old, junior on duty at Father Point, answered me immediately with 'Here we are!' I told him, 'Get your senior!' "[7] When Bamford brought him some clothes, Ferguson sent him to the bridge for orders. "There had been no word or warning of any kind; no orders; nevertheless, in less than the space of three minutes, or less, the air had been cleared, the radio was ready and a shore station, tense and alert, was standing by."[8] Fighting his way along the sloping deck, Bamford looked back to see Chief Officer Steede talking with Ferguson and assumed that he was getting his orders, so he returned to the radio room. Quickly Ferguson sent W. J. Whiteside, the Father Point senior operator, the message "SOS, LISTING TERRIBLY, STAND BY."[9] Whiteside phoned the captain of the Canadian government boat *Lady Evelyn* at Rimouski, who dashed for her. Meanwhile his assistant, Leslie, ran to the home of the local shipping agent, J. McWilliams, and hammered SOS on his door. When McWilliams opened his door, Leslie told him of the desperate situation of the *Empress of Ireland:* that she had been rammed and was sinking. McWilliams saw the mail boat *Eureka* coming into the dock. He dialed the phone at the Father Point's pier and screamed at Captain Belanger: "The *Empress of Ireland* is sinking. Go to her assistance. Rush!"[10] Captain Belanger still had steam up since he had just gotten back from taking the mails to the *Empress of Ireland.* He dropped the phone, ran to the *Eureka,* and told his crew to cut the lines so that they could get under way almost immediately. Ferguson on the sinking *Empress of Ireland* suddenly realized that he had not given Whiteside at the Father Point Marconi Station a position. He sent a cryptic message that the *Empress* was twenty miles past Rimouski, which Whiteside repeated back to him for confirmation. As Ferguson started to reply with "yes," the power failed, and all he could do was hold his key down so that Whiteside could hear the end. At Father Point Whiteside knew what that awful dying power sound meant. That was the last he ever would hear from the majestic *Empress of Ireland.* Whiteside thought Ferguson might still be able to receive, so he told him that help was coming. Then Ferguson turned his attention to any other possible source of help on the St. Lawrence and for five hundred miles in every direction. Many would hear the SOS of the *Empress of Ireland* and alter course to try to reach her. No one would because the big ship had taken such a mortal wound that she went down in fourteen minutes.

Ferguson on the *Empress of Ireland* felt his radio room rolling farther and farther over. He dropped to the wall, which was now the floor, and slid out the door to let Chief Officer Steede know that help was on the way but not for an hour. Steede told Ferguson that the *Empress* had less than five minutes and to get away. Ferguson pulled himself back to the radio room to try to reach the *Lady Evelyn.* Seconds later the port side lifeboats ripped loose from the deck and crashed across to the starboard side, crushing and killing many of those in their path. Ferguson's life was spared by his devotion to duty. Finally he crawled out of the radio room for the last time, grabbed a chair, and, stepped into the river as the *Empress of Ireland* went under behind him.

Captain Kendall reported that he ran along the deck, freeing as many lifeboats as he could, and then returned to the bridge, where he gave the order "Get the boats out as quick as possible."[11] The huge liner staggered, listed, and then plunged beneath the cold waters of the St. Lawrence. "In the brief space of time between the shock of the collision and the sinking of the liner there was little chance for systematic marshalling of passengers. Indeed, everything indicates that hundreds of those on the steamer probably never reached the decks."[12] When the stewards gave the warning, if anyone waited to dress, he was lost. Lifeboats were filled, lowered away, and rowed away from the sinking liner as fast as possible. In a practice lifeboat drill under ideal conditions in port it is believed that five minutes is a very good time. The officers and crew of the *Empress of Ireland* heroically managed to get nine boats away in twelve minutes in the face of horrendous conditions. "That was remarkable discipline. That these nine boats were lowered successfully in the few minutes remaining before the ship took her final plunge is something that will be remembered forever."[13] The rapid increase in the list soon made it impossible to launch any of the remaining boats, the bow of the *Empress* rose higher into the air, as the stern sank lower, and the end came very quickly. The *Empress of Ireland* sank in 150 feet of river water less than three miles from shore.[14] Flotsam and jetsam was everywhere, some pieces large enough to support life, but most of the passengers and crew on the liner died with her.

Captain Andersen examined the *Storstad* and found that the fore-hold was not taking on water, as he had feared. His vessel, minus her bow, was fairly secure. He turned his attention to the vessel that his ship had rammed. Slowly the *Storstad* groped her way back through the fog toward the scene of the accident. Certainly she was the closest potential rescue vessel even though she had heard nothing alarming from the other vessel. As Andersen neared the collision site, he heard the screams and hollers of people dying in the water. He stopped the *Storstad* instantly so as not to plow under any of the survivors and launched his four lifeboats, which were dispatched to the scene to do whatever they could. Second Mate Reinertz rescued fifty swimmers against the backdrop of the sinking *Empress.* He rowed back and got those individuals safely on board the Norwegian coaler and then returned to the scene as the Canadian Pacific liner rolled over and sank before his eyes. As the Norwegians searched for more survivors, morning dawned and the fog began to lift, but there was no one else alive in the cold waters of the St. Lawrence River.

The Canadian government boat *Lady Evelyn* reached the scene as quickly as possible, but her efforts saved only a few, although she did take on board nearly fifty bodies. Shortly thereafter two other Canadian government boats arrived, the *Lady Grey* and the *Strathcona,* but by that time there was little to be accomplished except a thorough search of the wreckage.

The *Lady Evelyn* came alongside the *Storstad* and someone hollered, "Marconi!" Ferguson the radio operator from the *Empress of Ireland,* had just reached safety on the Norwegian coaler and turned at hearing the shout. The *Lady Evelyn* had a wireless but no operator. Ferguson was given a coat and hurried on board the *Lady Evelyn,* where he found the radio room locked. He broke the window in order to get in and then had another frantic search through the engine room for the switch to turn on the power. Once he had power, Ferguson told the throng of passengers clamoring around him that if they would write out brief messages, he would send them. When all the scraps of paper on the *Lady Evelyn* were used, Ferguson directed those who had not had

Not much is left of the bow of the Storstad *as she docks following her collision on May 29, 1914, with the ill-fated* Empress of Ireland *(1906). The tragedy in the St. Lawrence occurred only a few miles from shore and cost 1,014 persons their lives.*

a chance to write out their messages to use the starched white shirt-front of an obliging purser. As Ferguson sent the last message written on the purser's shirt, Bamford, his colleague, found him on the *Lady Evelyn,* and they had a joyous reunion.[15]

Captain Kendall was swept off the bridge as the *Empress of Ireland* rolled over onto her starboard side with her two funnels in the water and sank stern first. Lifeboat No. 3 managed to reach him and pull him from the water. The lifeboat already held about thirty, but Kendall had the crew pull another twenty into it, while yet another ten were roped to the sides. The captain then ordered the badly overloaded lifeboat to pull for the nearby *Storstad,* and the passengers were transferred as quickly as possible. Kendall and a crew of six pulled back to the site of the sinking as quickly as possible. They found no one alive and, after an extensive search, returned to the *Storstad.*

Captain Thomas Andersen of the *Storstad* had a different view of what had happened from that of Captain Kendall. He asserted that when she was first sighted, the *Empress of Ireland* was off the port bow of the *Storstad,* and should have given the Norwegian coaler the right-of-way. When the Canadian Pacific liner was seen through the fog, Captain Andersen thought that she still was making considerable headway and that she had placed herself in the compromising position. He stated that he tried to stop the *Storstad* by reversing her engines and that she had very little headway on when she rammed the *Empress.* He said that it was the forward momentum of the Canadian Pacific liner that broke loose the *Storstad*'s bow while he was trying to keep it in the hole in order to stabilize the situation.

Andersen also asserted that he and his crew of 27 had done everything possible to save lives when the *Empress of Ireland* sank and that the majority of the 250 saved had been rescued by the *Storstad.* He deeply regretted the loss of life and vehemently repeated that he and his crew had done all that was possible to aid those in need as a result of the disaster.

Those who had been rescued were taken by the government steamers to Rimouski, where doctors could see to their needs. Many were given shelter in private homes. The temperature had dropped to freezing during the night, and the cold had severely affected many, soaked and without suitable clothing. The trauma they had been through was so great that another twenty-two died after being pulled from the river.[16] A special train with survivors was sent from Rimouski to Lévis, opposite Quebec, where a small convoy of ambulances had crossed on the ferries and waited for them. A number of the badly injured were rushed from the train to Quebec hospitals for major medical care.[17] Once he reached shore Captain Kendall was quick to blame the *Storstad* for the loss of his ship and all those who had drowned with her.

Sir Thomas Shaughnessy, president of Canadian Pacific, immediately released a statement to the public.

> The accident occurred at a time when the passengers were in bed and the interval before the steamship went down was not sufficient to enable the officers to rouse the passengers and get them to the boats, of which there were sufficient to accommodate a very much larger number of people than those on board, including passengers and crew. That such

an accident should be possible in the river St. Lawrence to a vessel of the class of the *Empress of Ireland* and with every possible precaution taken by the owners to insure the safety of the passengers and the vessel is deplorable.

The saddest feature of the disaster is, of course, the great loss of life, and the heartfelt sympathy of everybody connected with the company goes out to the relatives and friends of all those who met death on the ill-fated steamship.[18]

The Canadian premier, Sir Robert Borden, expressed the condolences of the Canadian government to all those families who had suffered loss. The opposition leader, Sir Wilfrid Laurier, issued a similar statement but also expressed indignation that such a disaster could happen in the St. Lawrence River and so close to shore. He noted "that in proportion of loss of life this exceeds even the *Titanic*."[19] Some sources thought it necessary to point out "that wireless is in the nature of a remedy rather than a preventive. After the accident has occurred it is invaluable. To prevent a specific accident it is almost useless, although by its means warnings of obstructions to navigation or the vicinity of other ships may be had."[20]

The subsequent hearings were presided over by Lord Mersey, who had found himself in a familiar position after the *Titanic* sinking. Lord Mersey was a dry, if not acerbic, individual. He was not known for his good humor, and he was known for rarely praising anyone. During the hearings on the loss of the *Empress of Ireland*, when the role of the two wireless operators, Ronald Ferguson and Edward Bamford, was discussed, Lord Mersey made the comment "You two young gentlemen did great credit to the service you are in."[21] This was high praise indeed from the crusty old judge.

The Mersey hearings were held at Quebec and lasted eleven days with fifty-nine witnesses. On the Canadian side the behavior of Captain Kendall in stopping his vessel received critical comment: "Had she proceeded slowly ahead, when, as Kendall claimed, he heard the other ship six points, and therefore safely on his starboard side, the collision would have been averted. As it was, the Canadian Pacific liner continued to lie still in the water, blind and unwitting, dead in the collier's path. She had some thirty miles of sea room northward with not another ship in sight, when the fog closed in."[22] Deputy Minister of Justice Newcombe stated that "excess of caution" by Captain Kendall was part of the cause of the collision. Furthermore, when cross-examined by Lord Mersey, Newcombe replied: "But certainly the accident could not have happened if the *Empress of Ireland* had not taken this extraordinary course of reversing and stopping almost in the track of the approaching *Storstad*."[23]

This evidence notwithstanding, Lord Mersey was not to be deterred from his intention to uphold the Canadian Pacific and the actions of Captain Kendall of the *Empress of Ireland*. In the end, Mersey handed down a verdict that First Mate Toftenes was guilty of wrongfully changing course and negligent in not summoning Captain Andersen earlier, that the coaler *Storstad* therefore was totally at fault in the ramming and loss of the Canadian Pacific liner *Empress of Ireland* on May 29, 1914, in the St. Lawrence River. The Norwegian official inquiry into the disaster, on the other hand, exonerated the *Storstad* and blamed the *Empress of Ireland*.[24] There was more than enough controversy, fault, and ill will to go around.

The death toll on the *Empress of Ireland* reached 1,014, the vast majority of whom were passengers (840 out of 1,057), although 174 out of her 420 crew members also perished.[25] The details of the death toll remain horrendous. "Particularly tragic was the fate of the children. Out of four in the first class, one was saved; two out of 32 second class children were rescued, and only one child survived out of the 102 in third class. A veritable slaughter of the innocents! Four saved out of 138! Two hundred and forty-eight out of the 420 crew survived their ship; 41 women out of 310 were rescued, while 172 men out of a total of 609 were saved. All the officers except the captain, first officer, and the two very lucky radiomen—perished."[26] One of the largest losses of life was recorded among the Salvation Army delegates, many of whom did not have the time to find the deck from their second-class cabins or who, if they reached the deck, bravely gave way to others in filling the lifeboats. The hundred-member Canadian delegation of the Salvation Army to the International Congress virtually was wiped out, including Commander and Mrs. David M. Rees, two daughters, and a son. The loss of life on the *Empress of Ireland* remains the largest Canadian death toll on a merchant vessel and third only to the *Titanic* (1,503) and *Lusitania* (1,198) in the history of steam navigation on the North Atlantic.

Chapter 19

THE *LUSITANIA* MEETS AN UNTIMELY FATE

May 7, 1915

In 1907 the British press universally hailed the commissioning of the largest and fastest liner in the world, the magnificent transatlantic greyhound *Lusitania* (31,550 tons, 790 feet, 25 knots) of the Cunard Line. She was 20 percent larger than her biggest competitor with a revolutionary steam turbine power plant capable of driving her at well over 25 knots. Superlatives were everywhere, and she was shown leaning against the Great Pyramid of Gizeh, where her 790-foot hull towered over the largest stone building in the world, whose height was given as 500 feet. She was celebrated as "the greatest vessel which has ever floated on the waters of the planet."[1] In October 1907 on her second voyage she crossed the North Atlantic from Daunt's Rock to Sandy Hook in four days, nineteen hours, fifty-two minutes at an average speed of 23.99 knots and regained the Blue Riband of the Atlantic for Britain.[2] It was the first time that the vast reaches of the North Atlantic had been crossed in less than five days.[3] In the long run her sister ship, *Mauretania* (1907; 31,938 tons, 790 feet, 25 knots), proved slightly faster and held the Blue Riband for twenty-two years, from

1907 to 1929, but for the elegance of her public rooms the *Lusitania* was exceptional. She soon proved an extraordinarily popular vessel.

The position of the Cunard Steamship Company Ltd. in 1900 was that of the senior British-flag North Atlantic Line. Since its founding in 1840 Cunard had carried the Royal Mails and been a remarkably successful, if conservative, transportation enterprise. At the turn of the century major changes in the organization of the transatlantic steamship trade were about to occur. As early as 1900 John Burns, first Lord Inverclyde, Managing Director of the Cunard Line, had been approached by a number of individuals interested in buying the company.[4] Within the next year the creation of the International Mercantile Marine by the American shipping magnate Clement Acton Griscom, assisted by his banker, J. P. Morgan, placed enormous pressure on the Cunard Line to join the shipping trust as well. A substantial offer from the IMM for the shares of the Cunard Line, similar in nature to the White Star Line offer, would have to receive serious consideration from the Cunard directors. In simple terms, they could not turn down a good offer from the IMM without running the risk of being sued by their own stockholders. Complicating matters, Lord Inverclyde died unexpectedly in 1901, and a substantial number of Cunard shares suddenly were available from his estate. On March 18, 1902, Messrs. Watson and Smith, a firm of Glasgow stockbrokers, approached the trustees of Lord Inverclyde's estate with an offer to buy an unlimited quantity of Cunard shares at the highest price they had commanded over the previous ten years (£20 sterling) ($100).[5] George Burns, second Lord Inverclyde succeeded his father as managing director of the Cunard Line and found that the challenges of his first year might well involve absorption or annihilation.

At the same time Lord Inverclyde had the normal challenge of trying to maintain the first-class North Atlantic service with an aging fleet in the face of strong German and now American competition. The last major Cunard liner commissioned for the first-class service was the *Lucania* (1893; 12,952 tons, 601 feet, 21 knots), placed in service nearly a decade before. After 1897 the German greyhounds of North German Lloyd and Hapag held the Blue Riband for speed. After 1899 White Star, Cunard's great British-flag competitor, was commissioning vessels almost twice the size of existing Cunarders, even if they were of moderate speed. With all the new capital available to the new shipping trust there appeared no limit to what White Star might decide to order.

Lord Inverclyde's well-planned move was to solicit the advice of His Majesty's Government. On March 8, 1902, as soon as he learned of the February agreement signed by Griscom, Morgan, and his rivals in New York, Lord Inverclyde informed Lord Selborne, First Lord of the Admiralty, that they had a major problem on their hands. There was the very real possibility that the Cunard shareholders would accept an IMM-backed offer if it involved a comfortable premium. Lord Selborne's reaction on March 17 was to suggest that Cunard unilaterally add a clause to its Admiralty contract forbidding the transfer of ships to foreign ownership for the duration of the agreement. Inverclyde told Selborne he could not possibly make such a large concession on the part of his stockholders without suitable adjustments in the agreement. Lord Inverclyde did offer to reserve thirteen of Cunard's best ships for Admiralty purposes if the subvention could be increased. Selborne declined, and the next six months involved protracted negotiations between Cunard, the Admiralty, and the British Government.

The Cunard management explained to the government that it wished to remain totally British in management and ownership but could not guarantee maintenance of the existing situation because of American economic pressures. If the government believed it desirable for Cunard and its ships to remain totally British and available at all times for naval service, then a way would have to be found for Cunard to receive assistance not only in operating but also in replenishing its first-class fleet. Inverclyde, armed with a sheaf of pages showing the relative subsidies of various non-British steamship lines, sought to persuade the government to be generous. The terms of the American subsidy to the International Navigation Company were described as superior to that of the British Government to Cunard. Furthermore, the generous increases before Congress in the new Frye bill to enhance American shipping were calculated totally to imbalance the situation. Cunard required a much more secure position.

Late April 1902 finally brought an offer from Griscom through Henry Wilding for Cunard to join the IMM. The offer was at a rate of £18 ($90) per share for up to 55 percent of the shares. Lord Inverclyde might have considered £20 ($100) per share for the entire company, but an offer aimed at just a controlling interest was unacceptable. Much later he wrote to Bruce Ismay explaining his position: "I stated that neither the basis on which the offer had been made, nor the price indicated commended themselves to me. Further, that unless the offer was for the Cunard Company as a whole, I must be satisfied before placing it before the shareholders, that the proposed combination would have as much interest in keeping up the Cunard Company as in developing any other section of the syndicate."[6] It seems incredible that in view of what the creators of the IMM already had swallowed, they would draw back from the investment necessary to secure 100 percent control of Cunard. The IMM management blinked, and Cunard remained uncommitted. The explanation apparently was that the Cunard fleet simply was regarded as so aged and so decrepit that the line was not worth owning. The potential threat to the IMM from a rejuvenated competitor was ignored.

In May 1902 the British government asked Cunard to make a new proposal. When Lord Inverclyde did, he thought expansively in terms of a twenty-year agreement involving £5.2 million ($26 million) at 5 percent for a new fleet of nine fast liners capable of serving the Admiralty as armed merchant cruisers. In one fell swoop Cunard's aging fleet would be replaced at the expense of the British Treasury, but the cabinet balked at this expense.

Sir Christopher Furness, another British shipping magnate, entered the picture with an offer to buy enough Cunard shares to take over the company, and Lord Inverclyde used this opportunity to turn the heat up a few more degrees on the government. On May 31 he sent a letter to all Cunard stockholders in which he let them know that negotiations on the future of the company were under way. That was vague enough to mean anything, and it served to confuse everyone, as he intended. There was even talk of a rival British shipping combine led by Sir Alfred Jones that might involve Cunard, Elder Dempster, and Allan.[7] Rumors of that were calculated to upset the digestion of Lord Pirrie, at the Harland & Wolff Shipyard, in Belfast, Ireland, who might be afraid part of his market was evaporating.

Lord Selborne at the Admiralty took the opportunity on May 10 to write Lord Inverclyde that the government strongly objected to Cunard's joining the IMM "and will do all we can to assist you to justify yourself to your shareholders for not doing so."[8] Selborne stopped short of making a firm commitment, and Inverclyde was irritated. "I think the time has come when you should say what you intend to do with regard to the Cunard Company and not continue on the present indefinite course."[9] The government encouraged negotiations toward an all-British consortium in June, but the plans came to naught when the participants could not agree. By July 1902 Lord Inverclyde was blaming the British government for most of Cunard's problems. He had kept Cunard out of the IMM at the request of the First Lord of the Admiralty and now had to explain to his stockholders that he had gained nothing by obliging the British government. If the government did nothing, Lord Inverclyde believed Cunard faced catastrophe. Accordingly he submitted a new plan for immediate action. The Cabinet met and agreed to consider the new plan on August 7. The urgency of the problem was accepted, and with what constituted minor revisions, Lord Inverclyde's proposals were accepted. The one point on which the Cabinet refused to be budged was his request for an immediate increase in the subsidy.[10] An exchange of letters between Ernest Balfour and Lord Inverclyde resulted in Cunard's being permitted to dispose of aging tonnage, and the agreement was certified.[11] Inverclyde was extremely relieved and wrote a friend: "At last my labor has had some result, but, in the end everything has been carried through with such rapidity that I hardly realize that it is all done with."[12]

Absolute secrecy was required until the government decided how and when to announce the agreement, but Inverclyde could hardly restrain his enthusiasm. "Personally I am satisfied and the more I think of it the more do I consider that it is one of the biggest and the most important arrangements which has ever been made between a private Company and the government of this Country."[13] He also stated: "I am sure that, in this country, at any rate, there will be great satisfaction that the Cunard Company will still be the great British Line on the Atlantic, and once again, I hope, lead the procession."[14] Brown, Cunard's New York agent, responded to Inverclyde in a private letter dispatched "Per UMBRIA": "I shall be very greatly disappointed if the rank and file do not heartily endorse the Government's action in putting its oldest and most prominent line in a position to enable it to stand firm against any and all efforts of the powerful new ship combine to drive it out of business or force its Directors to sell out and transfer its allegiance to a foreign flag."[15] The Cunard stockholders officially were informed of the agreement in a circular on September 30, 1902, when the details were made public.[16]

Cunard's management received appropriate assurances that made it possible for them to rebuff the shipping trust. Specifically, the line was lent the money to build two new ships, *Lusitania* and *Mauretania* (£2.4 million [$12 million] at 2.5 percent), and provided with an annual subsidy of £150,000 ($750,000) once the two liners were commissioned.[17] Under the terms of the agreement between the Cunard Steam Ship Company Ltd. and the British government the management of the Cunard Line, its stockholders, and the ownership of its ships were to remain British forever.[18] Lord Inverclyde told the Cunard stockholders that, "the cardinal principle upon which the Government is treating with us, and to which we desire to adhere [was] namely–that the Company is to be, and is to remain British."[19] By this stroke, the goal of the creators of the IMM was denied them. They never would be able to control all the major steamship lines between Great Britain and the United States, let alone on the North Atlantic, and competitive rate wars continued to rage throughout the first decade and a half of the twentieth century.

The maritime and naval architect Leonard Peskett was given the responsibility in the summer of 1903 for designing two new superliners that would serve the needs of the Cunard Line while meeting the requirements of the Admiralty, which wanted two ships that could make twenty-five knots, carry twelve six-inch guns, and have machinery sufficiently low in the hull to meet the protection standards for Royal Navy cruisers. "So Peskett was faced with the challenge of creating what amounted to a floating hotel, capable of holding 2,300 passengers and 900 crew, that could double as a warship if needed."[20]

The machinery of the *Lusitania* and *Mauretania* would be revolutionary since the decision was made to use the new Parsons steam turbines. The four sets of turbines would produce 68,000 shaft horsepower but would require the services of 176 furnaces firing 25 boilers in four boiler rooms. At full speed the *Lusitania* would consume six hundred tons of coal a day and over three thousand tons per crossing, all of which had to be shoveled by hand into her furnaces. Coal bunkers were arranged on each side of the four boiler rooms for additional protection. An auxiliary coal bunker forward of the first boiler room was designed to serve as a powder and shell magazine in the event of naval deployment. The hull was divided by ten bulkheads into 11 major watertight compartments and further subdivided for a total of 175 watertight compartments throughout the ship. In addition, there was a double bottom running the length of the hull and extending around the curve of the bilge. The rudder was especially designed to operate below the waterline in order to provide additional protection against hostile gunfire.

The *Lusitania* was built by John Brown's Shipyard in Clydebank, Scotland, and the *Mauretania* by Swan, Hunter and Wigham Richardson in Wallsend-on-Tyne, England. Construction of the *Lusitania* proceeded at a fairly fast pace, and she was launched on June 7, 1906. Lady Inverclyde served as her sponsor, and it was both a joyous and a sad day since Lord Inverclyde had died suddenly the year before at the age of forty-four and was not present to view the great liner his negotiations had made possible.[21] The *Mauretania* was christened by the Dowager Duchess of Roxburgh and launched on September 20, 1906, in the rain at Tyneside.

The first-class dining salon of the *Lusitania* was done in the style of Louis XIV and finished in a white and gold dome that soared nearly three decks high. In the first-class lounge James Millar, John Brown's Scottish architect and interior designer, had chosen a Georgian design, again graced by a domed ceiling resplendent with a skylight of stained and painted glass. The effect was one of great expansiveness and elegance.[22] The first-class smoking room was paneled in Italian walnut with pear wood carvings and featured a fireplace as its centerpiece. The library and writing room on the liner was done in the Adams style with the walls hung in gray silk. Besides the customary mahogany writing desks there were a number of Sheraton-style settees and armchairs for the comfort of passengers. Second class was not ignored and on the *Lusitania* involved a generous use of mahogany paneling in the second class lounge, which was done in the Georgian style. The theme was carried through the second-class dining salon, painted in a soft eggshell white, and the second-class smoking room. The second-class music room was done in the style of Louis XVI in order to provide some variety. The broad sweep of the promenade deck on the *Lusitania* was so expansive that a passenger starting to stroll along it from one end hardly could see the other as it curved along the nearly eight-hundred-foot length of the ship.

At her trials on the Firth of Clyde, the *Lusitania* easily worked up to 25.4 knots and even slammed along at 26.5 knots for a brief time, to the delight of her builders and owners. More than two hundred thousand people came to see the new Cunarder off at Liverpool on September 7, 1907. Her departure was delayed briefly by the *Lucania,*

The personification of "Majesty at Sea," the four-funnel Cunard speed queen Lusitania *(1907) slams along at a speed in excess of twenty-five knots. She would capture the Blue Riband as the fastest ship and maintain the premier North Atlantic service of Cunard from 1907 to 1914 with her sister ship, the* Mauretania *(1907). On May 7, 1915, the* Lusitania *was torpedoed by* U-20 *off the Old Head of Kinsale, Ireland, and went under eighteen minutes later with a death toll of 1,198—the second-highest loss of life on the North Atlantic.*

which was scheduled to sail that afternoon and did not get away until 5:00 P.M. The result was a spectacular treat as the huge vessel lighted the Liverpool Landing Stage and the night sky while her passengers boarded. "Finally, around 9 P.M., she cast off to the strains of Rule Britannia and a thunderous ovation from the assembled multitude. Heading down the Mersey, the *Lucy* (as she was already known) was accompanied by whistle and horn salutes from nearby ships and tugs. One correspondent reported that 'no vessel in the British mercantile service ever inaugurated her career more splendidly.'"[23]

A maiden call at Queenstown to collect the mails and the remainder of her 2,165 passengers, and Captain J. B. Watt turned the *Lusitania*'s massive bow westward for the three-thousand-mile run to

New York. She was manned by 850 crew, nearly 350 of whom were needed in the engine department. Fog on the North Atlantic restricted her speed to twenty-three knots on her maiden crossing, and she failed to break the record of the *Hapag Deutschland* (1900; 16,502 tons, 661 feet, 22 knots) by a substantial margin. When she reached New York on September 13, 1907, she was the first major ship to use the new Ambrose Ship Channel inward bound. A huge flotilla of harbor craft steamed out to meet her and to escort her up the bay to her pier. If it was not a triumphal salute, it was a splendid reception for the new Cunarder, which was the largest ship in the world at that moment.

The *Lusitania* captured the fabled Blue Riband of the North Atlantic on her second voyage and in fact did the "double" by achieving the fastest times both westbound and eastbound. The British public was ecstatic that the *Lusitania* was not only the largest liner in the world but also the fastest. On November 16, 1907, she was joined by the *Mauretania* in the first-class service of the Cunard Line from Liverpool to New York. Since *Mauretania* was the second ship of the new class, only fifty thousand people came to see her off. New propellers in 1908–1909 resulted in a series of brilliant crossings in the spring of 1909, when the *Lusitania* crossed at an average speed of 25.65 knots and knocked nearly three hours off her record of July 1908.[24] The two Cunarders proved so popular and successful that arrangements were made in December 1910 with John Brown's to build a third ship for the service. This would be the *Aquitania* (1914; 45,647 tons, 902 feet, 23 knots), a full deck and ten thousand tons larger, but two knots slower since she did not need to have the same speed as her consorts. Cunard already "owned" the Blue Riband. The *Aquitania*'s maiden voyage began on May 30, 1914, but the celebration was somewhat subdued as a result of the news of the sinking of the *Empress of Ireland* in the St. Lawrence River the day before. Many of the crew members manning the Canadian Pacific liner were from Liverpool, and their fate was unknown. For a brief period of two months the Cunard Line had the ultimate three-ship service with three giant liners in the first-class service from Liverpool to New York. The dream did not last.

World War I intervened with the outbreak of hostilities in August 1914. The *Lusitania* made the first wartime departure from New York on August 4, with her portholes blackened and a paltry, but courageous, two hundred passengers on board. She sailed at 1:00 A.M., and a radio blackout was observed as she worked up to full speed for the dash through Atlantic fog to Liverpool. The absence of regular reports bred concern, but early on the morning of August 14 the giant Cunarder was sighted in the Irish Sea with smoke billowing from all four funnels as she raced for the Liverpool bar and safety. During the remainder of the summer of 1914 the *Lusitania* and the *Mauretania* were employed bringing stranded Americans home from Europe. Americans had booked European tours for the summer of 1914 as though nothing were wrong. No one had ever thought there would be a war over the assassination of the Archduke Franz Ferdinand of the Austro-Hungarian Empire on June 28, and in fact hostilities had not broken out for a month. The *Aquitania* was taken over immediately by the Admiralty in August 1914 for wartime duties as an armed merchant cruiser, but it was soon realized that she simply was too big and valuable to be utilized in this manner. Accordingly, she was laid up pending reconsideration of future service and shortly was joined by the *Mauretania*.

The *Lusitania* was now the only first-class Cunard liner remaining on the premier New York–Liverpool service. She maintained the service with lesser vessels for nearly a year. The Cunard crimson was gone from her funnels, which were painted solid black. "She sailed with watertight doors closed and the boats swung out. Her only defense was her great speed and even this was hampered by the decision to shut down six boilers in the name of economy."[25] Her engines still were capable of driving her at twenty-one knots, nearly twice the speed of a German Navy U-boat, but not fast enough to evade the fastest German raiders.

In May 1915 the *Lusitania* represented the only way to cross for many celebrated individuals. Regardless of the state of war between Great Britain and Germany, the big, fast Cunard liner was the ultimate vessel for a North Atlantic crossing. Accordingly the first-class passenger list boasted such names as Alfred Gwynne Vanderbilt, American financier and horseman; Charles Frohman, the celebrated American theatrical producer; Alexander Campbell, general manager of John Dewar and Sons of London; Elbert and Alice Hubbard, he being one of the most famous American authors and lecturers of his time; and Margaret Mackworth, Lady Rhondda, a famous British suffragist, with her tolerant father, D. A. Thomas, a member of Parliament representing a Welsh district.[26] Only the last two of these celebrities survived.

As the *Lusitania* was preparing to depart New York on May 1, 1915, an advertisement appeared in some of the New York newspapers warning passengers that there was a state of war existing between Germany and Great Britain. Vessels entering the war zone ran the risk of being torpedoed. Unrestricted submarine warfare represented a new aspect of naval activities. The World War I submarine, a relatively slow and terribly vulnerable undersea offensive weapon, had to be able to strike from hiding and utilize surprise. As a result, Imperial Germany had to scrap all previously honored guidelines for naval warfare. The U-boat absolutely could not take the time to order a victim to stop and then wait until all passengers and crew had taken to the boats before sinking its prey. First, the victim probably could escape by outrunning the U-boat; secondly, the victim would call for aid on its radio, notifying everyone of the presence of the U-boat; and thirdly, the elapsed time necessary to permit everyone to abandon ship was intolerable for the long-range survival of the U-boat. Unrestricted submarine warfare during World War I, of necessity, violated the existing code of ethics in naval warfare.

Insofar as Great Britain was concerned, the regular crossings of the *Lusitania* simply were too valuable a means of transporting critically needed military supplies to be suspended. British authorities in the United States on a regular basis assigned top-secret shipments of military equipment and supplies to the *Lusitania*.[27] This certainly was the case on the May 1, 1915, sailing, when significant quantities of .303 rifle cartridges (4,927 boxes of a thousand each), 1,248 boxes of three-inch filled shrapnel shells (weighing fifty-two tons), and other contraband of war were loaded onto the Cunard liner.[28] It also is true that American authorities elected to turn a blind eye on the proceedings, thereby aiding and abetting the shipment of contraband on the *Lusitania* which irretrievably violated and compromised any claim of innocence. Only the unknowing passengers booking passage on the liner were innocent. A German agent informed Secretary of State William Jennings Bryan of the contents of the *Lusitania*'s cargo, and he reported the information to President Woodrow Wilson, who made no effort to stop the Cunarder from sailing.

The *Lusitania* left the United States for Great Britain on May 1, 1915. She had 1,959 passengers on board. "Only four months earlier, on February 5, the *Lusitania* managed to evade two submarines in the Irish Sea by flying the American flag at her stern. Captain Dow reasoned that this was perfectly legitimate since he had aboard several hundred neutral Americans. As it developed, she steamed full speed in to Liverpool, not even stopping to pick up a pilot, where Dow's tactic met with mixed reaction."[29] The British were not so sure of the ethics of this tactic, but it remains incredible that any German U-boat would confuse the huge four-funnel Cunard liner for any other ship sailing the seven seas.

The eastbound transatlantic crossing of the *Lusitania* was noteworthy for its uneventful character. Captain William Thomas Turner was a highly competent and knowledgeable master mariner. He did everything by the book. When he received an Admiralty message that there was submarine activity a hundred miles behind him, but that did not warn him about anything in his course, Captain Turner thought it safe to steam in a straight line along the southern coast of Ireland, past the 256-foot-high promontory of the Old Head of Kinsale. This permitted him to ascertain his exact position before entering the Irish Sea on the final run to Liverpool. He was more concerned about being torpedoed waiting off the Mersey bar than off Queenstown, Ireland. The *Lusitania* thus began to steam a straight course which took her immediately across the path of the submarine *U-20,* with one torpedo left in her arsenal.

The *U-20,* under the command of Kapitänleutnant Walther Schweiger, had left the U-boat base at Emden just a week before. After crossing the North Sea, Schweiger had taken the *U-20* to the north of Scotland and down the Irish coast to the Atlantic approaches, where he had experienced very good hunting. The Admiralty, having broken the German code, tracked the *U-20* the whole way and knew her position almost as well as the German naval authorities at Wilhelmshaven.[30] The British naval intelligence team knew during the previous two days that the *U-20* had attacked and sunk without warning two Harrison Line steamers and may have known she had shelled and sank a sailing vessel. The morning of May 7 found the submarine off the Old Head of Kinsale, about twenty-five miles west of Queenstown, in an excellent position to intercept shipping. As the fog burned off, Kapitänleutnant Schweiger observed the horizon until he saw the telltale sign of an approaching steamer. Quickly he took the *U-20* beneath the waves in order to escape detection. "2:05 P.M. Submerged to 11 meters and travelled with high speed on course converging toward steamer, hoping she would change course to starboard along Irish Coast."[31] Unwittingly Captain Turner obliged, and the *Lusitania* became a U-boat captain's dream target as she passed by at a right angle to her bow.

Schweiger carefully watched his target and then ordered a torpedo to be fired. It sped away from the submarine on a seven-hundred-meter course to intercept the liner.[32] On the starboard side of the *Lusitania*'s forecastle Seaman Leslie Morton suddenly saw the streak made by the approaching torpedo. He hollered through a megaphone toward the bridge that there were torpedoes approaching on the starboard side. Captain Turner and others on the Cunarder's bridge heard the warning, but it was too late to take any action as the torpedo slammed into the side of the liner just behind where they were standing. The time was 2:10 P.M. Almost immediately an enormous secondary explosion occurred from inside the hull that virtually blew the bottom out of the ship in front of the bridge. Many thought this was a second torpedo, but the *U-20* had fired only one torpedo, and it already had fulfilled its destiny.

The *Lusitania* had been mortally wounded. Her quadruple screws continued to turn, driving her forward with only a slight reduction in speed. To his horror Captain Turner felt his ship begin to list to starboard and rapidly go down by the bow. No one realized that the *Lusitania* was gulping in thousands of gallons of water with every foot of forward motion, and she never was destined to stop. Seawater had swept into the hull so quickly that the generators had been flooded and the fires had been extinguished within minutes. Therefore, there was no steam power available to reverse the turbines. Efforts to launch the lifeboats were fruitless because the big Cunarder was still moving, and anything reaching the water was either ripped away or smashed to smithereens against the steel hull of the onrushing liner. Some of those in the water ended their lives quickly as they were fed into the quadruple screws. Only when her bow was down so far that her slowly turning screws came out of the water did her forward momentum lessen substantially, and by then it was too late.

The Marconi Company had radio operators on board. Senior Radio Officer Robert Leith tore out of the second-class dining room, through the passageways, and up the ladder to the radio shack. He shoved his junior assistant aside and, without authorization, rapidly began to send out an SOS with the *Lusitania*'s call letters *MSU*: "COME AT ONCE, BIG LIST, 10 MILES SOUTH OLD HEAD OF KINSALE."[33] The main power failed in four minutes at 2:14 P.M., and the radio room transferred to emergency power. Passengers rushing to get life belts from their cabins were impeded by the list of the ship, which soon made movement difficult to impossible. The *Lusitania* had fourteen minutes to live.

Thirty-five miles to the southeast of the *Lusitania* was the Anglo-American Oil Company tanker *Narragansett* (9,196 tons; 11 knots). Talbot Smith, her young radio officer, raced to the bridge with the SOS, and Captain Charles L. Harwood immediately turned the tanker around and headed for the sinking liner's position as fast as she could go. Her engineers soon had the *Narragansett*'s speed up to a remarkable fourteen knots. The Leyland liner *Etonian*, under Captain

W. F. Wood, and the Ellerman Line's *City of Exeter,* under Captain G. R. Rae, also were nearby and turned around to head for the *Lusitania.*

Ashore the SOS from the *Lusitania* was heard in a variety of locations and places. Nearby the signal station at the top of the Old Head of Kinsale heard and passed the message to Queenstown, where there were Royal Navy facilities. Rear Admiral Sir Charles Coke, commanding officer at Queenstown, was notified, and his duty officer ordered the tugs *Julia, Flying Fish, Warrior,* and *Stormcock* to sail as quickly as humanly possible. They soon were steaming out of the great natural harbor. Another officer notified was Rear Admiral H. L. A. Hood, who had just arrived on the aged cruiser HMS *Juno* to take command of the Irish coast patrol and who immediately ordered his squadron, consisting of HMS *Juno, Isis, Sutlej,* and *Venus,* to sea. A small fleet of fishing boats and other vessels also headed to sea as soon as they got the word that the *Lusitania* was in dire trouble.

On the *Lusitania* the dread of all knowledgeable individuals was that the liner might capsize, so horrible was her list. Radio Officer Leith shortened his message to say: "SEND HELP QUICKLY, AM LISTING BADLY!" as he held on to the desk and fought the list. The time was 2:25 P.M., and the end was near. Captain Turner noted it was 2:28 as the bow went under and the water reached the bridge and roared by him. He hoped that there was no one else left on the ship, but this was a faint hope. As the *Lusitania* went under, her captain was swept away and found himself afloat in the Atlantic. The stern of the ship soared into the heavens as the bow plunged under the surface and headed for the ocean floor. Then unbelievably the *Lusitania* seemed to hang there in the sky for a couple of brief moments. The explanation was simple: Her bow already had plowed into the muddy bottom of the North Atlantic some 290 feet down, and the rest of her 800-foot length still soared out of the sea. Seconds later her momentum plowed a deep furrow in the floor of the ocean. The rest of the liner went under to break in two between the third and fourth funnels and to rest on her starboard side. The *Lucy* was no more, 11 miles from shore, almost due south of the

Old Head of Kinsale, and approximately 270 miles from Liverpool. She had gone down in the incredibly brief time of eighteen minutes. Of the 1,959 passengers who had left New York on the *Lusitania,* 1,198 were dead including 124 Americans.

When the *Narragansett* was about eleven miles from the *Lusitania*'s position, suddenly a torpedo was seen streaking toward her. Remarkably it passed just slightly astern of the tanker, and she was spared. The opinion on the bridge of the *Narragansett* was that the radio message had been a hoax to lure the tanker to disaster. Captain Harwood ordered a diversionary course and zigzagged away from the scene of the *Lusitania*'s torpedoing. As the *Etonian* and the *City of Exeter* neared the scene, they were close to each other and used signal flags to check if the other had seen anything. Suddenly a periscope appeared between them and then quickly disappeared. The two vessels instantly made turns to the west and left the rescue effort to the Royal Navy. Their captains were gratified by how much more power the engine rooms could produce under the threat of submarine attack. Both ships had been seen by survivors floating in the Atlantic. The rescue work that was done was largely completed by the flotilla of fishing boats and tugboats from Queenstown. The squadron of aged vessels under Sir H. A. L. Hood returned to port after rescuing a few swimmers. It was thought that HMS *Juno* and her escorts represented targets that were too tempting. Few British destroyers were available for convoy or patrol duty because of the demands of the Dardanelles campaign in the eastern Mediterranean. The Admiralty had not yet recognized the critical need for escort vessels in the approaches to British ports.[34]

The British and American publics were horrified at the loss of innocent lives, and the German public was jubilant that in some way the British blockade of Imperial Germany was being avenged. International relations between Washington and Berlin became more strained, although another two years passed before America became involved in the war.

Individuals in the British Admiralty, as part of their bureaucratic efforts at damage control tried to pin the blame on Captain William Turner, the crusty but competent master of the *Lusitania.* He had survived the sinking of his ship and been cheered when he reached shore. In particular, Captain Richard Webb, director of the Admiralty's Trade Division, responsible for the movement of all British merchant shipping and therefore of the *Lusitania,* sought to cover his trail. It was Captain Webb who had sealed the fate of the big Cunarder when he approved sending a message to Captain Turner informing him that there was U-boat activity a hundred miles behind him, off Fastnet, but not where he was. Turner had therefore felt secure in confirming his position by steaming near the Old Head of Kinsale. By so doing he had perfectly positioned the *Lusitania* for the torpedo of the *U-20.* For its part the Admiralty knew other ships had just been torpedoed in those waters. Captain Turner did not.

The system for classifying messages, which divided them into "Admiralty Instructions," which had to be obeyed, and "Admiralty Advises," which could be ignored, produced enormous opportunity for confusion. The Admiralty's attempt to blur further any distinctions after the tragedy was both disreputable and unethical. How close the Admiralty case came to succeeding is made vividly clear in the process by which its heavily doctored report was prepared and presented to the subsequent hearings. Full credit must go to Charles Bigham, Lord Mersey, who presided over the Board of Trade inquiry and detected the cover-up. In the end Captain Turner missed becoming a scapegoat by a hair.

One critical issue always has been whether or not the British government willfully ordered the shipment of contraband and explosives on the *Lusitania.* There is little reason to question that this was the case. Rules of fair play often are suspended in war. As a result, any claim of the Cunard passenger liner to immunity from submarine attack was compromised. There is no question that the large cargo of shells and other military paraphernalia the *Lusitania* carried when she left New York violated U.S. neutrality laws. Only her passengers were innocent. The German submarine *U-20* had every right to torpedo the *Lusitania* when she did so, regardless of the consequences to the civilians on board. This is a harsh fact of the disaster.

The torpedoing and sinking of the *Lusitania* were but one step toward the American involvement in World War I. The disaster provided the first great outrage by Imperial Germany of American sensitivities. However, when Woodrow Wilson finally asked Congress for a declaration of war two years later on April 5, 1917, he did not even mention the loss of the *Lusitania.* Her sinking paled in comparison to other German transgressions, such as the Zimmermann Telegram, which offered Mexico a German alliance against the United States and promises of American territory if she would distract the U.S. Army by declaring war.[35]

The deaths of 1,198 passengers and crew in the sinking of the *Lusitania* resulted in the second-largest loss of life on an Atlantic liner. An American court of inquiry ruled that the Cunard liner had indeed been an innocent merchant ship, and Berlin protested.

In July 1993 Dr. Robert Ballard, oceanographer, led a *National Geographic* expedition to southern Ireland to explore, photograph, and study the wreck of the *Lusitania.* Included among the expedition staff were Eric Sauder, historian, and Kenneth Marschall, marine artist. The expedition utilized the research vessel *Northern Horizon,* which had on board the remote operating vehicles *Jason* and *Homer* and the two-man submarine *Delta.* The principal goal was to map photographically the entire sunken liner, which, besides being sunk, had suffered from depth charging during World War II and in the 1950s. The results contributed to a *National Geographic Special* and resulted in two additional books about famous shipwrecks by Dr. Ballard, *Exploring the Lusitania* (1995) and *Lost Liners* (1997). Other authors who recently have revisited specifically the subject of the *Lusitania* include David Ramsay, who has written *Lusitania: Saga and Myth* (2001).

Chapter 20

FIRE AT SEA, A DEAD CAPTAIN, AND A SOCIOPATHIC KILLER

The *Morro Castle* Disaster

September 8, 1934

The Spanish-American War awakened American interests in the island of Cuba as never before. Save for some indiscreet commitments by President William McKinley, Cuba probably would have joined Puerto Rico and the Philippines under the Stars and Stripes at the conclusion of hostilities. As it was, Cuba was to exist in a form of international limbo for several decades, neither wholly free nor a part of the American empire assembled after 1898. Very shortly after the conclusion of the Spanish-American War, American-flag passenger liners, such as the *Paris,* undertook winter cruises to the ports of Cuba (1899), and the development of tourism on a substantial scale began to occur. One of the American-flag operations that took advantage of this situation was the Ward Line.

The firm of James E. Ward & Company since 1856 had operated a fleet of sailing vessels from New York to the Caribbean under the general label of the Ward Line.[1] John Roach, the Philadelphia shipbuilder and maritime entrepreneur, had two ships building in 1877 for a proposed service to Brazil. When international politics involving the British-flag Liverpool, Brazil, and Rio Plate Line jeopardized the Brazilian mail subsidy, Roach sought other employment for the ships. He approached James Ward and convinced him that this was an opportunity that should not be ignored.[2] Therefore, in 1877 the Ward Line commissioned the new steamer *Niagara* (1877; 2,265 tons, 294 feet, 14 knots) built by John Roach & Son, Chester, Pennsylvania, which was a substantial advance on anything Ward previously had owned and began a regular service to Mexico and Cuba.[3] This move also was stimulated by the success of the Alexandre Line, the first American-flag steamship service to Mexico and Cuba. In an effort to expand capital and take advantage of new trading possibilities the Ward Line officially became the New York & Cuba Mail Steamship Company in 1881 and purchased the assets and goodwill of its competitor, the Alexandre Line, in 1888. Ward Line vessels played an active role in the Spanish-American War with most of its ships being taken over by the U.S. government for a variety of purposes. The *Yucatan* (1890; 3,525 tons, 336 feet, 14 knots) had the fame of carrying Colonel Theodore Roosevelt and his Rough Riders to Cuba for the invasion.

The Ward Line maintained a close relationship with the shipyards of the Delaware River, the American Clyde. As a result of the increase in passengers and freight to Cuba after 1898, the line ordered a rather remarkable vessel for the New York–Havana service, the *Morro Castle* I (1900; 6,004 tons, 400 feet, 18 knots). Unfortunately the New York & Cuba Mail Steamship Company overextended itself in the middle of the decade and was caught in the economic depression of 1907. As a result, the firm was purchased by Atlantic, Gulf and West Indies Steamship Company (AGWI) in 1908 and made part of a large consortium of smaller steamship lines, including the New York and Porto Rico Line, Clyde Line, and Mallory Line, all engaged either in the American East Coast trade or to the Caribbean.

As a part of the shipbuilding effort during World War I two major units were built for the Ward Line by the Cramp Shipyard, Philadelphia.

The *Orizaba* (1918; 6,937 tons, 423 feet, 17 knots) and the *Siboney* (1918; 6,938 tons, 423 feet, 17 knots) both had twin screws and were superior to any other tonnage in the fleet. Their initial employment was as American troopships, and after demobilization the owners decided to try a transatlantic service from New York and Cuba to northern Spain. The two sisters sailing from New York–Havana–Corunna–Santander–Bilbao had accommodations for 306 first-, 60 second-, and 64 third-class passengers and made several voyages in 1920–1921 before withdrawing because of inadequate business.

Returning to familiar Ward Line services in the Caribbean in November 1921, the two ships enjoyed remarkably successful careers, particularly because of Prohibition. Suddenly the Ward Line cruises to Havana were one of the quickest and least expensive ways to enjoy alcohol-enriched vacations. Unfortunately other steamship lines decided to compete for the same market with tonnage that in some cases was infinitely superior. The American-owned P&O Line of the Standard Oil industrialist and Florida magnate Henry Morrison Flagler ran similar cruises from Miami to Havana. What was more imposing was the threat from the Cunard Line, which sent the transatlantic Blue Riband liner *Mauretania* (1907; 31,938 tons, 790 feet, 25 knots) to Cuba on a series of winter cruises and followed this up in 1928 with an entire season of cruises on their highly respected *Caronia* (1905; 19,687 tons, 678 feet, 18 knots). Before bringing the *Caronia* across, the Cunard Steam Ship Company Ltd. made a friendly arrangement with the Atlantic, Gulf, & West Indies Steamship Company (AGWI, Ward Line) to divide the Havana trade. Cunard agreed to carry no freight to or from Cuba, and the Ward Line was able to offer a 25 percent discount on its pricing. They had to since their ships were far outclassed by the Cunarders. When American interests protested and the U.S. Shipping Board offered the *President Roosevelt* (1922; 13,869 tons, 535 feet, 18 knots) in competition for one year, Cunard responded the next season by partnering the *Caronia* with her sister, the *Carmania* (1905; 19,566 tons, 678 feet, 18.5 knots) and doubling the stakes. Something had to be done.

Fortunately for the Ward Line the passage by the U.S. Congress of a new merchant marine subsidy act in the spring of 1928 led the way for a renaissance. The Jones-White Act authorized the U.S. Shipping Board to provide a loan for up to 75 percent of the cost of new vessels built in American yards at 3 percent interest repayable over twenty years. The Ward Line moved on this as quickly as possible. The naval architect Theodore F. Ferris was commissioned to design two sister ships larger and finer than anything in the Ward fleet. Events moved ahead so fast that bids were requested on December 21, 1928, from Newport News Shipbuilding and Drydock, Sun Shipbuilding, New York Shipbuilding, Bethlehem Shipbuilding, and Federal Shipbuilding and Drydock. All had been provided information well in advance of the bid request because just two weeks later on January 2, 1929, it was announced that Newport News Shipbuilding and Drydock, Newport News, Virginia, had won the contract to build the two liners with a low bid of $4,350,000 per ship. The delivery terms of Newport News also were very favorable, involving keel layings later in the spring of 1929, simultaneous construction of the two liners, and completion by November 1930.

One week after awarding the contract to Newport News, the Ward Line announced that its two new liners were to be powered by turbo-electric machinery provided by the General Electric Company. If the new liners could steam at twenty knots and reduce the passage time from New York to Havana to around fifty-eight hours, they stood to earn an additional $750,000 in a new mail subsidy. A great deal was riding on their cruising speed.

Newport News Shipbuilding and Drydock moved ahead quickly on the Ward contract. The first ship bore Yard No. 337, and the second 338. On July 27, 1929, it was announced that construction of the second ship had begun, while it was casually mentioned that the keel of the first ship had been laid down some weeks before. The stock market crash of October 1929 did not influence the rate of construction in any way. Satisfied with the progress of its new ships, the Ward Line announced on February 19, 1930, that the vessels would be named *Morro Castle,* for the imposing fortress at the entrance to Havana Harbor, and *Oriente,* for the beautiful garden province of eastern Cuba. Slightly less than nine months after her keel laying the *Morro Castle* was launched on March 5, 1930. The daughter of the Ward Line's president, sixteen-year-old Ruth Mooney, was the sponsor of the *Morro Castle* before an elite assembly of government and industry leaders. Nine weeks later the *Oriente* was launched on May 15, 1930, by Virginia Hoyt, the fifteen-year-old daughter of AGWI Vice-President Richard F. Hoyt, before another group of invited elite quests, including the Cuban ambassador to the United States.

Fitting out proceeded so fast that the Ward Line was able to

The Morro Castle *(1930) was a beautiful addition to the Ward Line fleet when she was delivered by the Newport News Shipyard. The liner ran from New York to Havana, Cuba, in a demanding schedule that strained both crew and ship to the limit. Here she is shown sailing from New York.*

announce on June 15, 1930, the maiden voyage of the *Morro Castle* for August 23, 1930, ten weeks earlier than originally planned. Her first master, Captain Joseph E. Jones, was appointed on July 21. Captain Jones, a veteran of twenty-five years with the Ward Line, had spent the last six years in command of the *Orizaba.* He did not have much time to adjust to his new command because she left the Newport News yard for her trials on August 8, 1930. On board were key figures in the leadership of the shipbuilding yard and the steamship line, as well as her architect, Theodore F. Ferris, who had every right to be proud of his latest creation. The question was: "How would her new turboelectric engines perform?" and the answer was "Superbly." Off the Virginia capes the new engines worked up to 18,162 shaft horsepower, and the *Morro Castle* justified every expectation by slamming along at 21.02 knots over the measured mile.

The new flagship of the Ward Line was handed over to her owners on August 15, 1930, and sailed for her home port of New York. Her berth was Pier 13, North River, not far from the financial district of New York. The *Morro Castle* (1930; 11,520 tons, 482 feet, 21 knots) was a handsome product of American shipbuilding for one of the more noteworthy American-flag steamship lines, but the celebration of her maiden arrival was undermined by the serious economic depression already settling over the country. A free lunch on August 19 brought over two hundred government, industry, and port officials to the ship for speeches and tours. On August 21 the *Morro Castle* was thrown open to the public, and an estimated two thousand New Yorkers trooped around the decks, admiring the cabins and public rooms of the new American liner.

The maiden sailing of the *Morro Castle* from New York with all flags flying occurred on August 23, 1930, but she had only 342 passengers on board in spite of accommodations for 468, 393 first and 75 second. She sailed with the expressed hope of establishing a new American record for the 1,168-mile run from New York to Havana. On the first day (August 24) she covered 330 miles from Scotland Light to Cape

Hatteras with an average speed of 20.5 knots, right on the money. The next day (August 25) she was off Palm Beach, Florida, and fifty-four hours after leaving New York (2:37 A.M. on August 27) she was lying off the great fortress that was her namesake. All that delayed her was that she had to wait for Cuban customs to open before being permitted to dock at 7:45 A.M. When her passengers disembarked, the ladies received complimentary bouquets and the gentlemen boxes of Cuban cigars as souvenirs of the maiden voyage.

All flags were flying again on August 28 in honor of the arrival of President Gerardo Machado of Cuba for a welcoming luncheon with the cream of Havana society. The *Morro Castle* definitely was a very beautifully appointed vessel, and she impressed all who saw her. On the return leg of her maiden cruise she covered the distance from Havana to New York in sixty-five hours, fifty-two minutes, three hours, nine minutes faster than the best northbound time of the *Orizaba.*

The *Oriente* bested the measured mile of her sister with a twenty-one-knot performance (17,935 shaft horsepower), was commissioned on November 21 at Newport News, and reached New York on December 10. The *Oriente* (1930; 11,520 tons, 482 feet, 21 knots) then became the flagship of the Ward Line, and Commodore Jones shifted to her from the *Morro Castle,* where he was succeeded by Captain Robert B. Wilmott. The *Oriente* left New York on December 17, 1930, on her maiden voyage, which was also a "Christmas Sailing" for those returning to Cuba for the holidays. The economic downturn definitely was settling in, for she sailed with only 185 passengers even if more than 1,000 visitors had come to see them off. In the future Ward Line sailings would be from New York on Wednesday and Saturdays and from Havana on Tuesdays and Saturdays.

The Ward Line tried to depict Havana as "The Gayest City in the Western World." The availability of alcohol and the absence of prohibition made it impossible for any American metropolis to offer much competition. The social gulf in Cuba between a small wealthy aristocracy and a huge poverty-stricken peasantry was truly enormous. Social unrest was inevitable, complicated by constantly shifting military alliances that made Cuban politics during the early 1930s unstable. President Machado was overthrown in a coup d'etat during August 1933, and a stricter regime installed. Frequently the Ward liners carried on their manifests boxes of "machinery" or "sporting goods" that clearly were guns or ammunition bound for various factions. The November 11, 1933, sailing of the *Morro Castle* from Havana was not without its humor. As the liner's band played a sprightly rendition of "Happy Days Are Here Again," two Cuban gunboats used the liner as a shield to take potshots at a fort held by an opposing faction. Machine guns let fly with bullets that cut across the path of the liner and bounced off the aft docking bridge, where Second Officer John Freedman dived for cover. During the fracas passengers were advised to remain inside, and no one on the liner was injured.

The Ward liners and their 240-man crews were driven without mercy. The *Morro Castle* was not dry-docked for nearly four years, not until May 6, 1934. "To make matters worse, the *Morro Castle*'s sailing schedule was such that for over two hundred members of the crew the ship was virtually a prison."[4] No crew members could leave the ship without losing their jobs, and this was the height of the Great Depression. The ships were in port only about twenty-five days a year so that crew members became more and more exhausted. Even though it was a job—when a job was hard to come by—fewer and fewer American seamen chose to work on the Ward Line ships. By 1934 over half the crew (134 out of 240) was foreign born, creating a situation in which there could be substantial problems in communication during a crisis.

The *Morro Castle* returned to service after her May 1934 dry docking and completed a successful summer season. On September 1, 1934, she left New York with 318 passengers and 231 crew members on board. The voyage south under Captain Robert Wilmott, her experienced captain, was uneventful. She docked at Havana on September 4, and some of her passengers disembarked for vacations in Cuba, others returned to their homes, and still others had brief visits to Havana before rejoining the ship for the remainder of a cruise back to New York. When the *Morro Castle* steamed out of Havana Harbor at 6:00 P.M. on September 5, she had 316 passengers on board, and it was her 174th return trip to New York. It was not to be a normal voyage.

"Of all fires, a fire at sea is potentially the most hazardous in terms of human life. Yet if it be resolutely tackled by officers and men well trained in fire-fighting technique, a successful conclusion to their efforts is highly likely. If, on the other hand, such training has been neglected, then the fire must always 'start favourite' in the battle to follow."[5] This would be the case with the beautiful *Morro Castle.*

Incredibly, Captain Wilmott died suddenly and unexpectedly in his cabin at 7:45 P.M. on September 7, two days out of Havana, as the *Morro Castle* began her run up the East Coast of the United States. Cause of death initially was thought to be a heart attack, and the news brought an abrupt end to the usual last-night parties. Most passengers retired early. Command of the liner passed to First Officer William Warms, who was shocked by the death of Captain Wilmott and who appears to have been overwhelmed by his situation. A squall was blowing off the New Jersey coast in the early hours of the morning of September 8, and the sea was choppy as the *Morro Castle* steamed through the night.

At 2:51 A.M. potential disaster struck. Smoke was detected by a passenger who told Assistant Beverage Steward Daniel Campbell.[6] It was coming from a locker used for the storage of writing supplies and 150 blankets in the first-class writing room on the promenade deck. As Campbell later testified, "I opened the door and what I once knew as a locker was just a mass of flames from top to bottom and from one side to the other."[7] He sought immediate assistance by telephoning the chief steward and informing the night watchman. After sounding the alarm, Campbell then tried to use a portable fire extinguisher and was unsuccessful since the writing room was completely ablaze. Apparently, when Campbell and others left the scene, the doors to the room had not been closed, providing a draft that greatly enhanced the fire. At approximately the same time the deck watchman reported to the bridge that smoke was coming from a ventilator. Acting Second Officer Clarence Hackney was ordered to investigate the situation. When he found the writing room consumed in flames, he returned to the bridge, and Captain Warms assumed command about this time.

The immediate problem with regard to the *Morro Castle* was that "in common with the then current world practice, the ship was constructed with large quantities of highly combustible linings and furnishings in the passenger and crew accommodations. Plywood partitions and linings were extensively used in the staterooms, dining saloons, lounges, cabins and other public rooms. Luxuriously equipped throughout, the ship had a 'fire load' which was obviously of a high order."[8] Furthermore, while the *Morro Castle* had fire-resistant partitions at the statutory 130-foot intervals, her main staircases were open from deck to deck down through the ship and were lined with the same combustible materials as the public rooms and staterooms. The ship's automatic fire alarm system, which was intended to provide advance warning throughout the passenger accommodations and officer quarters, had never been extended through the public rooms, where a blaze was free to take hold undetected.

The fire spread in minutes through the false ceiling of the first-class public rooms and down the main stairway into the region of the first-class passenger cabins. Hoses were not readily available, and hydrants had been capped so that untrained and ill-prepared sailors were totally unable to cope with the situation. The hoses that were hooked up often could not be used because of low water pressure. Crew members, assisted by passengers, smashed windows in order to spray water on the fire and by so doing created unbelievable drafts to feed the fire. Five minutes after the discovery of the fire Captain Warms sounded a general alarm which brought sleepy passengers from their cabins into the smoke-filled public rooms. Confusion existed everywhere.

"Overall, there was an absence of command and discipline—the simmering personality conflicts and poor crew conditions aboard plus a lack of boat and fire drills for passengers and crew all conspired to make a disastrous tragedy despite many individual acts of seamanship and heroism."[9] The fire raged through the center of the ship, cutting off the officers on the bridge from the bulk of the passengers, who had fled toward the stern. In between lay the lifeboat stations and the lifeboats that might have provided some degree of salvation. Captain Warms failed to realize the seriousness of the situation and kept the *Morro Castle* steaming at eighteen knots into a twenty-knot wind that created a gale that whipped the fire into a conflagration. Not until 3:00 A.M., after an explosion of the gunpowder for the Lyle gun, which unbelievably was stored in the ceiling above the writing room, did Captain Warms change his course toward the New Jersey coast. Time was running out for any effort to save the *Morro Castle.* The main electrical cable burned through at 3:29 A.M., and the ship was plunged into darkness. "Smoke was soon drawn down into the engine-and-boiler rooms from the upper part of the lounge and the boat deck; and about 3:31 A.M., conditions in the engine room became impossible."[10] Chief Engineer Eban S. Abbott ordered power shut off, and the engine room was abandoned. He then went to the bridge to report what he had done to Captain Warms. The overall situation on the liner was not helped by the fact that Captain Warms and Chief Engineer Abbott hated each other with a passion that was unique even on this unfortunate faction-laden vessel. The anchor was dropped, and the *Morro Castle* was dead in the water with all power lost and a stiff breeze still fanning the flames. Subsequently Abbott left the ship on the first lifeboat that got away. Of the thirty-two individuals in that boat, only one was a passenger.[11]

At 3:25 A.M. the first SOS signal finally was sent out from the *Morro Castle.* Second Assistant Radio Officer Charles Maki, who was on duty, had awakened Chief Radio Officer George Rogers and First Assistant George Alagna shortly before 3:00 A.M. and told them of the fire. Chief Radio Officer Rogers had waited by his key for orders from Captain Warms. In the meantime he heard other vessels in the vicinity ask the U.S. Coast Guard station at Tuckerton, New Jersey, if there was any news of a ship on fire off the New Jersey coast.[12] Unlike other radio officers in history, he took no personal initiative and refused to take any action until Captain Warms ordered it. The radio officers wet down towels in order to cover their faces from the growing clouds of smoke. Alagna made his way to the bridge in order to try to get Captain Warms to order an SOS but could not attract his attention. When he returned to the radio room, "he informed Rogers that there was 'a Hell of a fire raging.'"[13] About this time the power failed, and the lights went out. Alagna made yet another valiant trip, his fourth or fifth, to the bridge of the liner and finally got Captain Warms to order an SOS. After stumbling back to the radio room through the smoke and flames, Alagna shouted to Rogers to send an SOS with their position as being twenty miles south of Scotland Light. "Out went the distress call on full power–SOS de KGOV [the *Morro Castle*'s call]."[14] It was 3:23 A.M. and far later than it should have been. The screams of trapped passengers could be heard from their cabins belowdeck, even if, by a series of miracles, most had reached the open deck. The two main stairways were in flames, and only two circuitous routes fore and aft made it possible for those trapped below to reach the open deck and an uncertain fate. At least it finally had been acknowledged that the situation was out of control and an SOS had reached out across the seas.

Rogers already knew that he was likely to be fired from his job and would be leaving the ship as soon as she reached New York.[15] He and Captain Wilmott had had many disagreements, and the chief radio officer was not grieving the captain's passing. The cremation of the dead captain's body in the fiery inferno of the *Morro Castle* conveniently eliminated the possibility that any forensic investigation might have revealed foul play in his death. Over the years the possibility that Captain Wilmott was murdered by poison has been raised.[16] At the very least it appears Rogers had a vengeful nature and was prepared to let matters take their course if it made the Ward Line and the other officers on the ship look bad. It seems too that Rogers, who had a technical school education, possessed a good knowledge of chemistry.[17] The place where the fire started and the speed with which it spread also has raised the issue of arson. "Arson is indicated if a fire reaches great intensity before it is discovered, if it spreads rapidly and in an unusual manner, and if the flames change color when water is applied, indicating the presence of chemicals. In the case of the *Morro Castle* fire all of these elements were in evidence.

"'Never before in the history of the merchant service has a fire started in the locker in a writing room of a ship ended by destroying the ship,' William McFee, the noted marine authority, reported afterwards. 'If I had read it in a fiction story, I would have said a landlubber wrote it.'"[18] The fact is that Chief Radio Officer Rogers a couple of years later, 1938, would be tried, found guilty of attempted murder in another situation, and sentenced to life in prison.[19] In 1953 he was given yet another life sentence for a double murder. This has resulted in many unanswered questions about the disaster to the *Morro Castle.* That Rogers was a vengeful sociopath capable of anything is possible. In his favor he stayed in the radio room working the key with a flashlight while his feet rested on the rungs of his chair because the deck already was too hot for his feet. One of his last messages was: "'Can't hold out much longer–fire under radio room.' It was about 3:35 to 3:37 A.M."[20] Rogers and Alagna then escaped to the bridge and down to the forecastle, where they awaited rescue.

Seven lifeboats with a capacity of 408 were lowered from the burning *Morro Castle.* These lifeboats contained only 85 persons, nearly all of whom were crew members. Captain Warms's orders for the lifeboats to drop back toward the stern in order to save passengers was ignored. The SOS brought the freighter *Andrea S. Luckenbach,* the tanker *City of Savannah,* and the Furness liner *Monarch of Bermuda* (1931; 22,424 tons, 553 feet, 19 knots) as well as U.S. Coast Guard cutter *Tampa.* The liner, flames soaring into the night sky, could be seen from the New Jersey shore, and it also brought fishermen to her aid. The screams of passengers and crew members left on the burning liner could be heard across the stormy sea. Some passengers were trapped in their cabins and hanging out of their portholes.

The rescue fleet launched lifeboats as quickly as it could and pulled from the sea passengers who had either leaped overboard to escape the flames or slid down ropes into the choppy seas. Passing rain showers provided temporary relief for those still on board the *Morro Castle.* At Blodgett's Landing, Point Pleasant, the weather was too rough for fishing, but captains and crews from a number of commercial fishing vessels were sitting around, chewing the fat, and hoping that the winds might die down. That there was a burning vessel a few miles off shore was known but had produced no sense of urgency because the initial radio announcement said that everyone had been rescued. Then twenty-six-year-old Captain James Bogen decided to check on the situation. He called the coast guard to see if he could help and was told; "You sure can. Get out there as fast as you can."[21] Bogen, the youngest captain on the coast, immediately telephoned along the fishing dock to see whom he could get to go with him on a rescue mission into rough seas. Ultimately, his "crew" consisted of six highly competent New Jersey fishing boat captains, his own father, who owned his boat, and his younger brother, who normally was with him. As a result the fishing craft *Paramount* (30 tons; 54 feet 5 inches long), under the command of Captain Jimmy Bogen, was the first vessel on the scene. The broad beam of the *Paramount* made her perfect for handling the choppy seas and for rescuing survivors. Before they ever reached the burning *Morro Castle,* they slowed and began to fish people out of the sea. Bogen said they did not bother with bodies but raced to take on board every live swimmer they could see. Even the broad-beamed fishing vessel was pitching quite a bit, and on one occasion John Bogen, Sr., who was wrestling to get a large woman on board, was pulled overboard, hit his chin, and was knocked out. However, he never lost his hold on the lady. Two other captains, Lovegren and Fuhrman, leaped into the sea to rescue him and found him still clutching the woman. They got Bogen safely back on the *Paramount,* but the substantial lady was such a challenge they finally swung out one of the rope hoists from the mast and landed her that way.[22] Ultimately nine

New Jersey fishermen on the *Paramount* managed to rescue an incredible fifty-five survivors over a wide area of the sea. Perhaps the most incredible "catch of the day" for the Bogens was when they pulled on board two close friends who lived down the street from them and with whom they often had fished. Mr. and Mrs. Paul Lampecht were on their honeymoon, and all the young wife could do was throw her arms around Jimmy Bogen and say, "Thank God."[23] Most of the individuals were grouped together and, in some cases, were even supporting dead bodies. "Children clung to adults. 'It was a strange and pitiful sight,' he related. 'Some of the women were in evening gowns and wore all their jewelry.'"[24]

The dramatic arrival out of the darkness of the *Monarch of Bermuda* gave hope to many as Captain Francis maneuvered his large liner with her quadruple screws so close that she almost fouled the anchor chain of the burning ship. Warms hollered across from the bow of the *Morro Castle* that they were all right there for the time being, please rescue passengers off the stern at the other end of the fire. Francis turned the *Monarch of Bermuda* on a dime and maneuvered to within sixty feet of the stern in order to provide shelter and assist in the rescue. On board the big Furness liner every possible preparation to receive survivors had been made. A sign that passengers could hand donated clothes to the purser on C Deck was even posted. In the end the *Monarch of Bermuda* rescued 71.

Captain Diehl of the tanker *City of Savannah* was near Scotland Light when he received the distress call. He turned his ship around and steamed as fast as he could back to the site, about twenty-two miles away. Diehl arrived at 6:16 A.M. "to find virtually the whole ship aflame and a lurid glow reflected by low hanging clouds, visible for miles."[25] The *City of Savannah* accounted for 65 survivors, while the *Andrea S. Luckenbach* took on board another 26. Remarkably another 150 survivors (55 credited to the *Paramount*) were rescued by U.S. Coast Guard vessels and local fishing boats. A few individuals who had jumped overboard from the burning liner even managed to swim to shore, six to eight miles away. The next morning airplanes flying over the area spotted some additional swimmers and directed rescue vessels to them. One of the pilots was Governor A. Harry Moore of New Jersey, who had flown out to see the disaster and stayed to be of critical assistance as a spotter. This may have been the first time a sea rescue was assisted by aircraft. Certainly the planes provided hope to exhausted swimmers. Hope can be a powerful stimulus to survival.

Captain Warms and the remaining officers and crew finally abandoned the still-burning *Morro Castle* and were taken on board the U.S. Coast Guard cutter *Tampa* at 11:55 A.M. The anchor chain that had secured the *Morro Castle* to the ocean floor had been painstakingly cut with hacksaws, and a twelve-inch line secured to the *Tampa,* which tried to tow the liner to New York. Deteriorating weather conditions with rising winds and heavier seas made this extremely difficult. The tow parted under the strain at 6:30 P.M., and the *Morro Castle,* still burning, drifted ashore at Asbury, New Jersey, near the Convention Hall. She was an instant tourist attraction. Of the 555 passengers and crew who had left Havana for New York looking forward to a pleasure cruise, 133 were dead.

The American inquiry that followed the *Morro Castle* disaster was an acrimonious and difficult experience for all concerned. Sworn testimony was taken at the Steamboat Inspectors Investigation in the New York Custom House in September 1934. In particular Theodore F. Ferris, the liner's architect, was devastated by the complete destruction of one of his masterpieces. She was beautiful but flammable. The judge was Dickerson Hoover, who produced a report from twelve volumes of testimony that was published by the U.S. Department of Commerce in October 1934. Subsequently major legislation rewrote the standards for ship construction in the United States, for crew conditions, and for firefighting and lifesaving capacities. The action, or inaction, of those in command of the *Morro Castle* came in for severe criticism. Acting Captain William Warms and Chief Engineer Eban S. Abbott were castigated for

Still burning, the wreck of the Morro Castle *is shown in September 1934, when she drifted ashore at Asbury Park, New Jersey. Earlier, on September 7, 1934, her captain, Robert Wilmott, had died suddenly, and on the next night while the liner was steaming toward New York along the New Jersey coast, a severe fire broke out that ultimately consumed the ship and cost 133 persons their lives. Both circumstances long have been considered suspicious.*

incompetence that approached the level of criminal behavior. After the hearings both men actually faced criminal charges and were tried on several counts. Captain Warms was found guilty and sentenced to two years in prison. Chief Engineer Abbott, also found guilty, was sentenced to four years in prison. On appeal the U.S. Circuit Court of Appeals in April 1937 set aside both convictions and commended Warms for having remained on the bridge of the *Morro Castle* until it actually burned away beneath him. The management of the Ward Line was not immune from criticism, and Vice-President Henry E. Cabaud faced criminal charges, which his lawyers managed to sidestep. He was fined $5,000 for "wilful" negligence, and the line was fined $10,000, which the judge acknowledged was woefully inadequate but which was the most the statute permitted in 1934.[26] The claims against the Ward Line totaled $1,250,000, and the line offered $890,000, which was accepted. The wreck of the

Morro Castle was towed to Gravesend Bay, New York, where it finally was sold to the Union Shipbuilding Company of Baltimore for $33,605 and towed to Baltimore for scrapping. One other result was that the nearly eighty-year-old name Ward Line ceased to exist because of the adverse publicity from the disaster. As a postscript the cause of the fire that destroyed one of the most beautiful American liners, the *Morro Castle,* never has been discovered.

Chapter 21

IT NEVER SHOULD HAVE HAPPENED

The Collision of the Italian *Andrea Doria* and the Swedish *Stockholm*

July 26, 1956

The launching of a giant new liner always is a festive occasion, but when the launching of a ship represents the resurgence of a nation, then it is truly worthy of celebration. Such was the situation on June 6, 1951, when a new Italian liner was given the name of one of Italy's greatest maritime and naval heroes, Admiral Andrea Doria (ca. 1466–1560). His Eminence Cardinal Siri, archbishop of Genoa, blessed the ship, and Signora Giuseppina Saragat, wife of a former minister of the merchant marine, christened the vessel. Admiral Doria had served his city-state of Genoa well by securing its independence from Spain and assisting in the creation of the Genoese Republic. Having retired to a monastery, he was called back into service in his mid-eighties to lead the Genoese republican forces in a great victory over the French (1547), and he died in his mid-nineties. In many ways Andrea Doria was regarded by northern Italian contemporaries and

Genoese down through the centuries as the father of his country. His name was appropriate for a great ship in any century.

The owners of the *Andrea Doria* were known in the United States as the Italian Line and in Italy as Italia. The origins of Italia lay in the unification of the principal North Atlantic steamship lines ordered by the Italian government during the Great Depression of the 1930s. In 1932 the big three Italian-flag lines—Cosulich, Navigazione Generale Italiana, and Lloyd Sabaudo—were combined into Italia Flotte Riunite Cosulich-Lloyd Sabaudo-NGI.[1] In return the Italian government helped with the construction costs of the two giant greyhounds *Rex* (1932; 51,062 tons, 880 feet, 28 knots) and *Conte di Savoia* (1932; 48,502 tons, 815 feet, 27 knots), which had been launched but had not entered service yet, and provided an annual subsidy for a first-class Italian-flag operation on the high seas. Italia began operations with a capital of 720 million lire and a substantial fleet of twenty-two ships, totaling 400,476 tons, not including the two new superliners, engaged in both North Atlantic and South Atlantic services. This arrangement between the steamship line and the Italian government was maintained for more than forty years, until 1977.

"By the end of 1949, only four years after the war, Italy had a fleet of 22 ships totaling 219,000 grt [gross registered tons] and had re-instituted its main passenger services."[2] This involved six separate services: Genoa-New York; Genoa-Buenos Aires; Adriatic-South America; Genoa-Valparaíso; Italy-Vancouver; Italy-South America. In 1949 ships of the line had completed approximately seventy-five voyages, steamed 1,056,861 miles, carried 105,229 passengers, and 287,218 tons of cargo.[3] The decision was made to do something spectacular. By 1950, when the Italian merchant marine heralded the birth of a new queen designed to be superlative in every way, the horrors of World War II lay five years in the past. The contract was awarded to Ansaldo's Sestri Ponente shipyard, in a suburb of Genoa. The *Andrea Doria* bore yard No. 918, and on February 9, 1950, the keel was laid down on the same slipway that had been graced by the *Rex* twenty years before.

The *Andrea Doria* (1953; 29,082 tons, 700 feet, 23 knots) combined a level of luxurious fittings that provided both privacy for individuals and a sense of grandeur in the great public rooms. The Italian Line liked to boast in its ads that "artists" were creating the ship and that the finished product would be a "work of art" worthy of the admiration of the ages. She was 626 feet long between perpendiculars (700 feet overall), with a beam of 90.2 feet. The new liner was designed with public rooms and cabins for three classes. She had accommodations for 218 first, 320 cabin, and 703 tourist in air-conditioned comfort.[4] Her crew numbered 572 on a normal crossing. The machinery of the liner consisted of two sets of single-reduction geared turbines capable of driving her the four thousand miles from Genoa to New York at a service speed of twenty-three knots.

The ship was completed as a floating palace of Italian art and industry and on November 6 took her initial sea trials, which were not entirely satisfactory. There were some engine problems which it was imperative to resolve. The maiden voyage was shifted from December 14 to January 14 in order to ensure adequate time for modifications. Finally, in a second sea trial between December 3 and 9 the *Andrea Doria* performed very well. At her trials over the Italian measured mile from Portofino–Punta Chiappa the liner delighted everyone when her engines worked up to a speed of 26.667 knots, making her not only the fastest ship in the Italian merchant marine and the fastest ship in the regular Mediterranean service of any line but also one of the fastest ships in the world. "The machinery installation occupied three watertight compartments with the five main diesel generators producing 3,750 kilowatts forward, two donkey boilers and four main Foster-Wheeler water-tube boilers working at 450 deg. F., and 633 psi [pounds per square inch] amidships and aft, two sets of Ansaldo-Parsons turbines double reduction geared to twin screws. Cruising speed was maintained by 35,000 shp [shaft horsepower] and 134 rpm. Both were reliable performers and singularly free of vibration."[5] The *Andrea Doria* had eleven watertight compartments and a full double bottom running the length of the vessel. Her lifesaving equipment included two emergency boats with a capacity of 58 individuals, two motorboats with a capacity of 70 each, and twelve lifeboats each with a capacity of 148, a total of 2,032 individuals.

The *Andrea Doria* returned to Genoa on December 9 and was turned over to Italia on December 19, 1952. She took a short Mediterranean cruise between December 23, 1952, and January 7, 1953, to work out any problems. The Christmas–New Year's cruise saw the *Andrea Doria* visit Casablanca, Las Palmas, Funchal, Lisbon, Cádiz, Palma, and Cannes, earning some incredible publicity in Moroccan, Portuguese, Spanish, French, and Italian newspapers.

The *Andrea Doria* was designed to have something for everyone, including being the first transatlantic liner to boast three outside swimming pools, one for each class. She commenced her maiden voyage on January 14, 1953, from her home port of Genoa to Cannes, France, and then on to Naples before heading out through the Strait of Gibraltar for her first Atlantic crossing to New York. The ports of call plus the southern direction of the eastbound transatlantic crossings meant that the Italian Line often described these 4,350-mile trips to Europe as "Cruises to the Sun." According to the eloquent Peter Kohler, "The Italian genius at making the functional beautiful achieved sublime perfection with *Andrea Doria* and *Cristoforo Columbo.*"[6] The *Andrea Doria* remains one of the most beautiful passenger liners of the past century.

On the bridge of the *Andrea Doria* was her master, Captain Piero Calamai, age fifty-five, scion of a famous Genoese seafaring family. Calamai had been at sea since he was eighteen and had served on twenty-seven different vessels before receiving command of the *Andrea Doria.* His career had been fault-free and remarkably successful. His one shortcoming as the master of a major liner was that he was a somewhat shy teetotaler who really did not enjoy socializing with passengers.[7] He usually had his staff captain take his seat at the captain's table in the first-class dining room, and he preferred to give brief tours of the bridge when it was necessary to deal with the rich and the famous.[8] By July 1956 Captain Calamai knew every aspect of his vessel after having completed fifty voyages on her back and forth from Genoa to New York over the previous three and a half years. In August 1956 he was scheduled to take command of her slightly newer, larger sister, the *Cristoforo Columbo* (1954; 29,191 tons, 627 feet, 23 knots), named for Genoa's other great seafarer. The change of command never occurred.

As the *Andrea Doria* cleared the Strait of Gibraltar on July 20 and turned her bow to the northwest, Captain Calamai noted in his personal logbook that there were "1,134 passengers (190 first class, 267 cabin class, and 677 tourist class), 401 tons of freight, 9 autos, 522 pieces of baggage and 1,754 bags of mail."[9] With 1,134 passengers and 572 crew totaling 1,706 people on board, the seats in the lifeboats totaled 2,032, more than enough for everyone. Celebrities in first class included Mayor and Mrs. Richardson Dilworth of Philadelphia, the actress Ruth Roman, Mr. and Mrs. Ferdinand Thieriot, he being circulation manager of the *San Francisco Examiner,* and Camille Cianfarra (Madrid correspondent of the *New York Times*). Second class held mostly American tourists returning home from European tours, and tourist class was largely populated with Italian immigrants seeking new lives in America.

As the *Andrea Doria* neared New York on July 25, the last night out, Captain Calamai's renowned nose for fog held true when he arrived on the bridge with the first haze. He was famous for being a weather barometer. As patches of fog became evident, he ordered a slight reduction of speed from 23 knots to 21.8 knots–after all, the scheduled arrival at the pier in New York the next morning had to be met–watertight doors were closed, an extra lookout placed at the forecastle, and the engine room informed. The method of reducing speed on the Italian Line ships was to reduce pressure in the boilers since that required less fuel and was cheaper, rather than just cutting down on the number of nozzles spraying steam on the turbines. The downside of this method was that it was impossible to produce additional power instantly because it took time to build pressure in the boilers. As usual the shipping lanes in and out of New York Harbor and along the East Coast of the United States were busy. The two radars on the bridge showed increased traffic as the fog thickened. One of the blips soon to appear on the radar screen of the *Andrea Doria* would be a Swedish-American liner.

The white-hulled yachtlike vessel was the *Stockholm* (1948; 11,700 tons, 525 feet, 19 knots), the first post–World War II vessel of the Swedish-American Line and the fourth vessel owned by the line to bear this proud name. After difficulties having a new liner completed in a foreign yard, the contract for the *Stockholm* had been given to the Gotaverken yard of the southern Swedish port of Gothenburg. She was launched on September 9, 1946, and took her maiden voyage from Gothenburg to New York on February 21, 1948. Given the fact that the *Stockholm* was intended to operate in the northern reaches of the North Atlantic and in the Baltic Sea she was constructed with a reinforced bow for ice conditions. Initial accommodations were for 113 first class and 282 tourist class, but this proved both unsatisfactory and unremunerative so that she was returned to her builders in 1952 for modification which involved reconfigured and enhanced berths for 86 first- and 584 tourist-class passengers. Her tonnage increased from 11,700 to 12,644 as a result of the rebuilding. In 1955 her first-class accommodations were reduced to 20, barely keeping her within the conference regulations for Atlantic passenger liners. In 1953 the commissioning of a much-larger liner for the Swedish-American fleet, the *Kungsholm* III (1953; 22,071 tons, 600 feet, 19 knots), meant that passengers desiring to travel in first class on the Scandinavian run could book on her. The *Kungsholm* had accommodations for 176 first-class and 626 tourist-class passengers. Furthermore, the Swedish-American Line by 1955 had a sister ship on order from the Ansaldo shipyard in Genoa which would be delivered in May 1957 as the *Gripsholm* II (1957; 23,190 tons, 631 feet, 19 knots).[10]

The owner of the *Stockholm* was the Svenska Amerika Linien, always known in the United States as the Swedish American Line. The

Swedish shipping concern, Rederiaktiebolaget Sverige-Nordamerika, was founded on November 30, 1914, shortly after the outbreak of World War I, when it appeared that there would be a market to Scandinavia for a steamship line under a neutral flag. The first challenge facing Dan Brostrom, managing director, was to find acceptable tonnage since no Swedish yard could handle an order for a large enough vessel, all British yards were overwhelmed with government orders, and World War I hostilities prohibited the transfer of German vessels to the Swedish flag. Brostrom solved the problem by persuading the Holland-America Line to sell him their aging *Potsdam* (1900; 12,606 tons, 550 feet, 15 knots), and that liner, renamed the *Stockholm*, took its maiden sailing on the Gothenburg–New York service on December 11, 1915. During the next two years she was highly profitable even while operating only as a single ship. After the armistice the Swedish-American Line moved from strength to strength, branching out into the winter cruise market for its ships in the 1930s.

Among the frustrations the line experienced were the burning and total destruction of a new *Stockholm* II in December 19–20, 1938, while fitting out in Trieste, Italy. A replacement, *Stockholm* III, was ordered and launched on October 3, 1940, only to be taken over by the Italian government during World War II (1942) and sunk at Trieste. Attempts to build overseas were fruitless and frustrating for the Swedish American Line. Hence, the decision to build a smaller, yacht-like passenger liner at home. The fourth *Stockholm*, like other Swedish American liners, was painted white with a blue circle containing three gold crowns on the funnel. This made a striking and unique appearance. It was said during World War II that there were few more dramatic scenes than to see the brilliant white *Gripsholm* (1925; 17,993 tons, 575 feet, 16 knots) fully lighted amid a darkened sea when she was sailing as a repatriation ship. The courage of her officers and crew was constantly tested, for while a submarine might not fire a torpedo at a fully lighted vessel with a white hull, floating mines were far less selective.

The *Stockholm* sailed from Pier 47, North River, at the foot of Fifty-seventh Street, at 11:31 A.M. on July 26, 1956, and turned her bow downriver toward the mouth of New York Harbor. Just minutes before, the passengers on the Swedish liner had been treated to the sound of French nursery rhyme songs floating over the North River as that venerable grand dame of the North Atlantic, the giant *Île de France* (1927; 44,356 tons, 793 feet, 23 knots) of the French Line, blew three blasts on her huge horns and backed out into the river to begin her own voyage to France.[11] The *Stockholm* followed the massive black stern of the quadruple-screw *Île de France* down the river and out into the Atlantic, where the French liner worked up to full speed and rapidly pulled away from the smaller Swedish vessel. There was no fog where the *Stockholm* was as she left the harbor, turned eastward, and began the run along the East Coast of the United States toward the Nantucket Lightship, where she would turn north for Scandinavia. She followed the same eastbound track in or out of New York Harbor and, as a result, when leaving always steamed toward inward-bound traffic. The *Stockholm* was on her 103d crossing of the North Atlantic and had a completely modern bridge outfitted with radar for safe navigation in fog or inclement conditions. Her master, Captain Gunnar Nordenson, had no problems, once clear of the busy harbor, to leave the bridge in the care of his third officer, J. E. Carstens-Johannsen (twenty-six years old), who was on his fourth voyage. Carstens-Johannsen had orders to call Captain Nordenson at the first sign of fog. The Nantucket Lightship notified by radio all ships in the area that fog conditions were beginning to prevail. The outward-bound *Stockholm* still was not in fog, and Carstens-Johannsen was fully occupied with navigating the Swedish liner. On two grounds—that he was busy and that there was no fog around—Third Officer Carstens-Johannsen elected not to notify Captain Nordenson of the warning message from the Nantucket Lightship. The *Stockholm* remained at full speed ahead.

On the bridge of the *Andrea Doria,* which had observed only a token reduction of speed because of the fogbank, Second Officer

Curzio Franchini noticed about 10:45 P.M. a large, fast vessel approaching them about seventeen miles away and four degrees to starboard. By Italian Line standards the approaching vessel was in their inbound lane and should not have been there. However, not all steamship lines observed the lanes (tracks), nor were they required to do so, and this definitely was true of the Swedish American Line ships bound for the northern route to Scandinavia. The *Stockholm* had every right to be where she was on the same track she had sailed on 103 previous occasions. Franchini, on observing the radar, thought the two ships would pass at the distance of about one mile. Actually the liners were on a course that would bring them less than a mile apart, and the distance was closing. The normal rule for two liners approaching each other at sea was that they ought to pass port to port.

Fifteen minutes later the assessment on the bridge of the *Andrea Doria* was that the approaching liner was four miles away and closing fast. Twenty minutes later at 11:05 P.M. Captain Calamai, on evaluating the situation, decided to turn his ship slightly more to starboard, taking her farther away from shore for a starboard to starboard passing. He had been informed that a starboard passing was likely, and he wanted to increase the measure of safety. He also was concerned about going much farther to port, which would have taken him in toward shore, because of the prevalence of fishing boats and trawlers in the waters off North America. The change to starboard on the part of the *Andrea Doria* was so slight as not to be noticed by the oncoming vessel. The maneuver also was too little too late.

On the bridge of the *Stockholm* at 11:05 P.M. Third Officer Carstens-Johannsen thought the opposing liner was twelve miles away when she actually was only about two miles. It appears probable that the Swedish liner's radar was set on the wrong range.[12] Since she was not yet in fog, no foghorn was being sounded, compounding the communication gap. Suddenly, at 11:07 the Swedish lookout sighted the masthead lights of the other ship emerging from the fogbank. He phoned down to the bridge that another ship was in sight. Carstens-Johannsen took the

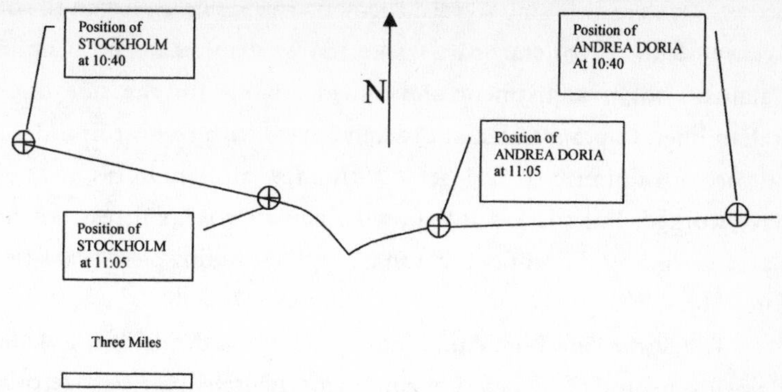

The deadly final maneuvers of the Andrea Doria *and the* Stockholm *are shown in this diagram as the navigating officers on the two ships sought to avoid a collision by changes in course that made it inevitable. Misuse and misinterpretation of radar ultimately caused what should have been preventable.* DIAGRAM BY JOHN SAMARDZA.

call and also took his eyes off the unfolding scene for a moment. Realizing that if the lookout could see the other ship, the vessels were far too close, he ordered a twenty-degree-to-starboard turn in order to try to widen the distance between the two ships. Captain Nordenson's standing orders were to keep any other vessel at sea at least one mile away from his ship. Running out on the flying wing of the *Stockholm*'s bridge, Carstens-Johannsen was horrified to see that his most recent maneuver had placed the reinforced bow of his ship on a direct line to intercept the side of the other vessel. He gave the order for full speed astern, but there was neither enough time nor sufficient distance for the command to be effective.

On the bridge of the *Andrea Doria* at 11:07 the Italian officers had every reason to be nervous. There was another fast ship near them, but no sound had been heard from her foghorn. Where was she? Then out of the mist at a distance of about a mile and 20–25 degrees off the starboard, they saw the reassuring glow of the other ship's lights. The two would pass close but at a safe distance. Comfort had come too soon. Third Officer Eugenio Giannini suddenly noticed that the lights of the other ship were swinging toward them. As the *Stockholm* began to turn twenty degrees to starboard, she more than matched Captain Calamai's slight adjustment and aimed directly for the side of the Italian liner. Captain Calamai ordered a hard turn to port in order to outrace or minimize the impact. "With a few more minutes, it would have worked, but instead it exposed *Andrea Doria*'s entire starboard flank, including the empty fuel tanks, to the speeding *Stockholm*'s reinforced bow."[13]

The *Stockholm*'s bow knifed into the starboard side of the *Andrea Doria* just behind the bridge. For a moment the Italian officers watching the scene unfold thought the Swedish liner's bow was going to destroy the bridge itself, but fortunately for the command structure this did not occur. It was the only fortunate thing for the *Andrea Doria.* The bow of the *Stockholm* remained embedded in the side of the Italian liner for only a few seconds before the enormous pressure of the *Andrea Doria*'s forward momentum wrenched it free from the wound and dragged it down the side of the Italian liner with sparks flying everywhere. As a direct result of the violent separation of the two liners, the bulkhead to an additional forward compartment on the *Andrea Doria* was destroyed, leaving even more of the liner open to the inrushing sea. Deafening everyone, the whistle of the *Andrea Doria*'s was set off by the impact and screamed into the quiet night. In quick succession Captain Calamai ordered the engines stopped, ordered the closing of any watertight doors not already shut, made an announcement in Italian on the public-address system that all passengers should go to their muster stations with their life belts, and instructed the radio officers to send out an SOS. This was absolutely critical since the *Andrea Doria,* which was designed never to list more than fifteen degrees, listed a horrifying eighteen degrees almost immediately. Something was dreadfully wrong.

The ice-reinforced bow of the *Stockholm* cut a huge V-shaped wedge in the side of the Italian liner, stretching through four passenger decks and into the depths of the ship, where her great fuel tanks, now half empty, lay. As designed, the *Andrea Doria* was capable of carrying enough fuel for a complete round-trip voyage. This was both a blessing and a potential liability. The orders were for the fuel tanks to be filled with seawater as they emptied in order to maintain the stability of the vessel. If this was done, the time and expense of emptying them of seawater and scrubbing them out before they could be refilled with fuel were substantial. The decision therefore was to allow the spent fuel bunkers to remain empty. The price paid was that the *Andrea Doria* near the end of a voyage would be tender and her stability compromised if the unthinkable should happen and something should rupture those empty fuel tanks. The unthinkable had just occurred, and the inrushing water almost immediately pulled the liner so far over that she was in dire danger of capsizing. After 1948 the SOLAS (Safety of Life at Sea) regulations were such that no modern passenger liner appropriately ballasted ever should be in danger of capsizing from any disaster. Furthermore, the eighteen-degree list made it possible for the water to flow from one watertight compartment to another and doomed the Italian ship to an early death. The only question before Captain Calamai was could he get his surviving passengers and crew off before that occurred. This was highly uncertain because with an eighteen-degree list it was impossible for the *Andrea Doria* to launch half her lifeboats. Her lifesaving capacity was reduced to 1,016 individuals for a total of 1,706 on board.[14]

Realizing the lifeboat problem, Captain Calamai did not give an abandon ship order because then there would have been a likelihood of panic among the passengers and crew. Since the policy of the Italian Line was to muster passengers in public rooms and then have crew members direct them to lifeboats, the critical nature of the situation was not evident to those waiting in the public rooms. One factor soon evident was that there were very few crew members around. The answer was simple: Many were preparing to leave.

The nearest potential rescue vessel was the *Stockholm* herself, whose anchor chains had rumbled out of the ruptured bow and cascaded through the ocean to the bottom of the continental shelf. The Swedish liner was not going anywhere for the time being, and since her damage was confined to the area of the reinforced bow, she specifically was designed to survive this type of disaster be it iceberg or ship. Captain Nordenson on the bridge of the *Stockholm* radioed Captain Calamai on the *Andrea Doria:* "LOWER YOUR LIFEBOATS, WE CAN PICK YOU UP."

Calamai replied: "WE ARE TOO BENDING IMPOSSIBLE TO PUT BOATS OVER SIDE. PLEASE SEND LIFEBOATS IMMEDIATELY."[15] The Swedish officers could hardly believe what they were hearing but made ready to launch some of their lifeboats. Passengers on the *Stockholm* were reassured that their boats were going to the rescue of the passengers on the other liner and that their ship was not in danger of sinking.

It was possible to launch some of the starboard side lifeboats of the Italian liner. The official policy was that these boats should be lowered to the windows of the enclosed promenade deck, where passengers could step into them and be lowered the rest of the way to the sea. The list of the *Andrea Doria* made this impossible, and the lifeboats had to be lowered to the sea, where passengers and crew had to scramble down rope lines, rope ladders, and the net covering of the tourist-class swimming pool cover, which instantly became enormously useful. Many, particularly those immigrants in tourist class with children, were fearful with the superstructure of the giant liner hanging over them in an ever-increasing list. Some children were dropped to waiting arms in the lifeboats, but at least one child hit the side of a lifeboat and died of injuries. Among those rescued by the starboard lifeboats were 229 passengers and 222 crew members. The first eight boats took 40 percent of the 572-man crew, most of whom never returned to the Italian liner to rescue anyone else.

The SOS from the *Andrea Doria* gave her position as nineteen miles west of the Nantucket Lightship and some sixty miles off the Massachusetts coast. Acknowledgments came into the radio room on the sinking Italian liner: The USS *Pvt. William H. Thomas,* a military transport, was ten miles away with eight boats; a freighter, *Cape Ann,* was nearby with two boats; another freighter, the *Laura Maersk,* radioed she would be there in two hours. All this was appreciated and helpful, but short of what was needed.

On the bridge of the huge *Île de France* Captain Raoul de Beaudéan was on his first voyage as master of the great French liner. By coincidence he had been watching the radar when the *Stockholm* and the *Andrea Doria* hit and later wrote: "'She's going to hit her,' I said, joking casually."[16] About half an hour later at eleven-thirty the radio officer of the *Île de France* hurried to the bridge and announced to Captain Beaudéan that there was an important message, an SOS, and that it involved a collision between the *Andrea Doria* and the *Stockholm.* Calculations were made on the bridge of the *Île de France,* and it was ascertained that the two ships were forty-four miles away. Captain Beaudéan plotted a new course for his ship and radioed the *Andrea Doria:* "ÎLE DE FRANCE, 0330 G.M.T. 40 28′N. 68 56′W. DO YOU NEED ASSISTANCE?"

The reply left no room for doubt. "0340 G.M.T. MASTER ILE DE FRANCE. NEED IMMEDIATE ASSISTANCE."[17]

Not much to go on, but enough that there was no question in Captain Beaudéan's mind. Slowly the *Île de France* swung around in a huge arc and headed back along the course she had just come through the fog. Captain Beaudéan summoned his second-in-command and the security officer and gave directions to prepare the *Île de France* for a major rescue effort. He gave the order to prepare eleven boats for launching but only on his command because he intended to place the giant French liner as close to the *Andrea Doria* as possible. Beaudéan later wrote: "These two officers, asked to improvise a rescue operation in one hour in the middle of the night, with people who are asleep, go off without a single objection. They return ahead of time to announce the solution of the problem laconically; the flotilla is ready to leave."[18] Such was the esprit de corps of the French Line.

The fog was like pea soup, and the massive *Île de France* was slicing through it at top speed, more than twenty-four knots. Fortunately there were not too many vessels answering the SOS, and the radar,

Arguably one of the most beautiful passenger liners ever built, the sleek Andrea Doria *(1953) of the Italian Line represented the renaissance of the Italian Merchant Marine after World War II. Her sinking on July 26, 1956, after being rammed by the Swedish liner* Stockholm *(1948), was watched by millions and represented an international tragedy.*

which initially revealed nothing, soon became active with only a few blips heading toward the disaster position. The radio messages from the *Andrea Doria* were getting weaker, and the freighter *Cape Ann* at 5:05 A.M. relayed a message that the Italian liner needed boats for a thousand passengers and five hundred crew. As she raced through the foggy night, there were many questions on the bridge of the *Île de France.* Why was there not more activity on the part of the lifeboats from the stricken liner? What was going on? Why wasn't the *Andrea Doria* doing more to rescue her own people? Captain Beaudéan prayed for the fog to lift, and when the radar of the *Île de France* indicated she was about six miles from the scene, suddenly the fog began to dissipate. At two and a half miles Beaudéan gave the order to cut the speed to eleven knots, and the nearly eight-hundred-foot-long French liner began to slow in order not to collide with or run over any smaller rescue craft. The ocean was illuminated with the lights of the victim and the assembled rescuers. Suddenly the French officers on the bridge of the *Île de France* realized why the *Andrea Doria* could not help herself. She was almost on her side and well on the way to capsizing. At one mile Captain Beaudéan gave the order to reverse engines as his giant charge slowly drifted into a position calculated to maximize the rescue effort by providing an eight-hundred-foot-long wall to deflect wind and wave action. At the last moment Captain Beaudéan gave the order "Reverse all engines! Light up our name, the funnels, the decks. Light up everything, quickly!"[19] The officers and crew on the *Île de France* had heard the clamor for help drifting over the water from the *Andrea Doria* as they slowly came to a halt near her. With just her nighttime running lights and in the crisis of the moment the arrival of the giant black-hulled *Île de France* had not been noticed by many on the stricken Italian liner. As Captain Beaudéan recounted, "Behind me I hear the sound of scurrying footsteps. Switches click on everywhere. An immense red-and-white reflection glows on the sea and the *Doria.* A petrified silence replaces the sinister clamor. The ship-wrecked people catch sight of us. Fear seems to retreat. We represent salvation, in all its radiant glory. Silent with emotion, the unfortunates watch us, hypnotized by our very closeness."[20]

Out of the dark and foggy night, which had not offered much but despair to the thousand passengers and three hundred crew members remaining on the sinking *Andrea Doria* came an unbelievable vision. The enormous, majestic form of the 44,356-ton, 793-foot-long *Île de France,* one of the largest ships in the world, all her lights ablaze and her name spelled out between her two funnels in huge letters, appeared before them. Salvation was at hand.

Captain Beaudéan gave the order to lower the lifeboats, and the eleven designated hit the water almost simultaneously and in record time. Of the 827 crew members manning the *Île de France,* 160 rowed the lifeboats.[21] With between 1,300 and 1,500 people to rescue it was going to take at least thirty trips on the part of the French lifeboats.

Rescue boats from other vessels began to bring survivors to the *Île de France* because she was so much closer. Comradery abounded, and when a motor on one of the French Line's gigs went dead, a motorized lifeboat from another vessel towed it to the *Île.* Whenever possible, the rowers on the French lifeboats were given breaks by tows from motorized craft. By the end of the night 753 passengers and crew from the *Andrea Doria* were safely on the *Île de France,* and the decision was made to return to New York with such an enormous increase in passengers.

The most remarkable survivor of the crash was a fourteen-year-old girl, Linda Morgan, who went to bed in cabin 52 on the *Andrea Doria* and woke up alive on the bow of the *Stockholm,* where her bed had been scooped up as the Swedish liner ripped loose from the Italian

Not too much is left of the bow of the Swedish liner Stockholm *(1948) after her collision with the Italian liner* Andrea Doria *(1953) off Long Island during the night of July 26, 1956. As a result of the collision, the* Stockholm *limped back to New York while the Italian liner capsized and sank the next day.*

liner. On board the *Stockholm* she looked around, found her surroundings strange, and said: "I was on the *Andrea Doria.* Where am I now?"[22] The momentary response was stunned silence. Her stepfather, Camille Cianfarra, and eight-year-old stepsister, Joan Cianfarra, were killed by the crushing power of the *Stockholm*'s bow. Her mother was seriously injured but rescued by the *Île de France,* and mother and daughter would be reunited in New York several days later.

Captain Beaudéan radioed to Captain Calamai asking permission to leave for New York with those who had been rescued, including about twenty who were critically injured. Captain Calamai confirmed that the USS *Pvt. William H. Thomas* and the U.S. Coast Guard cutters would stay with him and gave his permission for the *Île de France* to leave. Earlier Captain Nordenson of the *Stockholm,* who had 425 survivors on board, had made the request of Captain Beaudéan that the *Île de France* stand by and accompany the damaged Swedish liner back to New York. Captain Beaudéan under the pressure of the moment had sent a quick radio message asking Nordenson to find someone else because his schedule was imperative. What he meant was that he had at least twenty survivors on board who might not live if they did not reach a hospital as soon as possible. Later some regarded his cryptic message as unacceptable. It sounded as though Captain Beaudéan thought more of the French Line schedule than of helping a fellow master with a damaged ship. This was not the case, and Captain Beaudéan later apologized to Captain Nordenson if there had been any misunderstanding about the message.[23]

The *Île de France* carefully circled the stricken *Andrea Doria,* dipped her flag three times, and sounded three blasts on her siren as a salute. Captain Beaudéan radioed the French Line agent in New York about his intentions for a quick turnaround, and the response was he was crazy if he thought he could bring the *Île de France* into New York and leave quickly. His ship and all those who served on her were heroes. The next day, as the *Île de France* approached the entrance to New York Harbor and passed through the Narrows, everything in the harbor began to salute her. Sirens, horns, and whistles were answered by the great French liner in a welcome that rivaled any maiden arrival. Pier 88 was jammed with people greeting the ship, as were nearby streets, and television cameras recorded the scene live for the first time. In the few hours between the safe arrival of the survivors on board the *Île de France* and her docking at New York the superefficient purser's office on the French liner had prepared lists for American immigration and customs authorities. The disembarkation was swift because the survivors had precious little to declare.

"The U.S. Coast Guard's *Hornbeam* arrived just after 9:00 A.M., and embarked Captain Calamai and his officers. From her decks they watched *Andrea Doria*'s final agony. At 9:45 A.M., she was on her beam ends, her entire starboard side submerged to the center of the funnel. For the next 15 minutes she seemingly stayed so, then her bow dipped lower, her funnel submerged, and the waves washed over her port side. Some of the unused port side lifeboats broke free while others remained fast in their davits. Finally, at 10:09 A.M., her port quarter, reading only 'Andrea,' disappeared beneath the sea in a swirl of foam and debris. *Hornbeam* radioed a terse epitaph: "SS ANDREA DORIA SANK IN 225 FEET OF WATER AT 261409Z IN POSITION 40.29.4 NORTH 69.50.5 WEST."[24]

The damaged *Stockholm,* minus a bow and with her forward compartment flooded, slowly made her way into New York. She would be repaired and sail again for a very long career under several flags.

The legal maneuverings through the official inquest which began in New York on September 19, 1956, and the trial that followed were a bitter experience. Captain Piero Calamai in particular was vilified by some of the press and emerged from the proceedings a broken man. There was more than enough blame to go around, making the legal deliberations even more difficult. On the part of the Italian Line there were major concessions. It was acknowledged that the *Andrea Doria* was speeding in fog, that she was improperly ballasted, that she had compromised fundamental navigation rules by turning to port, away from approaching danger, before the collision instead of turning to starboard, toward danger, in order to minimize impact. The broad side of the *Andrea Doria* had been exposed to the cold steel of the *Stockholm*'s bow. In addition it was "unfortunate" that her logbook had not been saved to provide supporting documentation.

As for the *Stockholm,* the Swedish liner had been twenty miles north of the recommended eastbound track, and her officers should have been exercising extreme caution. The captain was not on the bridge in an area of heavy traffic. Even if there had been no surrounding fog at the moment, the *Stockholm*'s officers had been warned that a fogbank was immediately ahead of them, and they were still maintaining her top speed of eighteen knots. At the time of the collision there was fog all around, she was at full speed, and her master was not on the bridge. Fog warnings were noteworthy by their absence when at the very least it would have been judicious to sound the foghorn as a safety measure. Finally, without adequate consideration maneuvers were made that turned the *Stockholm* "directly into the *Andrea Doria.*"[25] Seamanship on both sides left something to be desired.

The Italian Line attorneys made an offer to the Swedish American attorneys to settle on a fifty-fifty basis before the trial began. The Swedish American Line attorneys refused on the apparent strength of their position. In the end the two sides did settle out of court, but the terms were such that the Swedish American Line footed the bill for the repairs to the *Stockholm,* approximately one million dollars, and the Italian Line absorbed the loss of their thirty-million-dollar liner. The settlement was on the basis of thirty to one instead of fifty-fifty.

The efficiency and heroism among the members of the rescue fleet that came to the aid of the stricken *Andrea Doria* were outstanding and remain the brightest aspect of this deplorable disaster, which cost fifty-one individuals their lives. The *Stockholm* lost five crew members, and the *Andrea Doria* forty-six passengers.

The *Île de France* brought in 753, the navy transport USS *Pvt.*

William H. Thomas rescued 158, the United Fruit Company's *Cape Ann* collected 129, the destroyer USS *Allen* had 77, including Captain Calamai, and the Tidewater tanker *Hopkins* rescued one lucky sailor. All the modern equipment in the world can be built into a ship, but it will never eliminate human carelessness or error.

Chapter 22

A FINAL VOYAGE CAN HAVE MORE THAN ONE ENDING

The SS *Seabreeze I*

December 18, 2000

A positioning voyage without passengers and with a limited number of crew can present challenges. The *Seabreeze* I (1958; 21,010 tons, 606 feet, 22 knots) owned by International Shipping Partners Inc. and operated from 1997 to 2000 by Premier Cruises had experienced a long and varied career. Originally she had been built for the Costa Cruise Line as the *Federico C* (1958; 20,416 tons, 606 feet, 22 knots) and was employed in the Italy–South America trade until jet airplanes made such runs unprofitable.[1] Her original accommodations were for 264 first-, 202 cabin-, and 672 tourist-class passengers. In 1971 she became a one-class cruise ship, and after approximately a decade of Caribbean cruising, she was sold to Premier Cruises in 1983 and renamed *Starship Royale* with a bright red hull.

The Premier Cruise Line was founded in 1983 with the goal of providing family cruises within the Caribbean. Initially the company was the official line for Walt Disney World and operated its ships under the banner of the "Big Red Boats," with the hulls of their ships painted bright

In December 2000 the graceful Seabreeze I *(1958) of Premier Cruises was on a positioning voyage from Halifax, Nova Scotia, to Charleston, South Carolina, when severe engine problems rendered her helpless about 220 miles off North Carolina. All thirty-four of her officers and crew were rescued by United States Coast Guard helicopters in the face of fifty-foot seas and seventy-knot winds just before she sank.*

red. In 1988 Dolphin Cruises bought the liner from Premier, extensively rebuilt and renovated the ship, and renamed her *Seabreeze.* Dolphin Cruises painted her hull a deep blue and utilized her on a number of Caribbean cruise routes. *Seabreeze* returned to the Premier Cruise fleet in 1997, when Premier Cruises, the Dolphin Cruise Line, and Seawind Cruises consolidated under a single management in an effort to maximize advertising and reduce overhead costs. In the 1990s Premier lost the Disney contract as Disney started its own cruise line with far superior vessels. At the same time the short-cruise trade in the Caribbean became very competitive. Rising fuel costs, the expense of operating older vessels, and a series of equipment failures in 2000 brought the end of Premier Cruises. When it looked as though other creditors were about to move, the principal creditor holding mortgages on the ships foreclosed, and Premier was out of business on September 14, 2000. *Seabreeze* I operating an Atlantic cruise was ordered into Halifax, Nova Scotia, where her unhappy passengers disembarked. She lay there for three months before being ordered to sail to Charleston, South Carolina, for basic repairs prior to making the long final voyage to India for scrapping. In one of the bankruptcy deals *Seabreeze* was sold to one of the Premier Cruises' creditors, who in turn had sold the forty-two-year-old liner for scrapping.

The *Seabreeze* I was en route from Halifax to Charleston for repairs when she found herself buffeted by heavy seas and high winds about two hundred miles off the Virginia coast. The sequence of events on board the liner remains unclear, but she was manned by a skeleton crew of only thirty-four. While she was working her way south, one engine quit, and the other was laboring hard to keep the old liner on course. Within the engine room something broke loose, and the *Seabreeze* I began to take on water rapidly and develop a substantial list. Heavy seas were sweeping over the bow, and there was little hope for improvement in the weather along the coast.

The engineers could not deal with the growing list of mechanical problems and informed Captain Simon Papadopoulos that there was little hope for the ship. Accordingly the captain ordered an SOS to be sent out. It was heard by the U.S. Coast Guard receivers along the east coast. Two HH-60 helicopters and two HC-130H airplanes took off from Elizabeth City, North Carolina, and headed for the scene 220 miles offshore. When the USCG helicopters reached the *Seabreeze* I, the weather conditions had further deteriorated with fifty-foot waves and seventy-knot winds. The liner was listing badly and, with the pummeling of the waves, threatening to capsize.

Following USCG procedure, a rescue swimmer was lowered to the deck of the listing liner with the specific responsibility of calming the crew and expediting the rescue effort. The USCG expert placed the crew two at a time in a swaying rescue basket, which raised them to the waiting helicopter hovering overhead. In the high winds this thrilling procedure was reenacted thirteen times. Technically the HH-60 helicopter should not carry that many individuals, but there was no thought of stopping until the helicopter cabin was crammed full with twenty-six sailors from the *Seabreeze* I and the USCG rescue swimmer had been retrieved by his crew. The second helicopter then moved in and snatched another eight persons, including Captain Papadopoulos, who was the last to leave the deck of the sinking liner. The two USCG rescue helicopters now headed for the Oceana Naval Air Station at Virginia Beach,

Virginia, where hospital facilities were available for some of the crew members who had minor injuries or were suffering from hypothermia. Later that day the *Seabreeze* I rolled over and sank about 220 miles off the Virginia coast. The USCG rescue mission to the *Seabreeze* I was a spectacular 100 percent success story and was viewed by millions of Americans on the news. The perils which can be experienced on the North Atlantic, as on any large body of water, are truly myriad even in the present day.

NOTES

Chapter 1.

1. *Illustrated London News* (May 25, 1850), 368.

Chapter 2.

1. Howard Robinson, *Carrying British Mails Overseas* (London, 1964), 115. The *Roscius* was the first ship to exceed a thousand tons in the mail service and one of the largest transatlantic ships of her day.
2. John H. Gould, "Ocean Passenger Travel," in F. E. Chadwick, USN, et al., *Ocean Steamships* (London, 1892), 121–22.
3. N. R. P. Bonsor, *North Atlantic Seaway,* 2d ed. (Newton Abbot, 1978), in 5 volumes, I, 201.
4. Bonsor, *North Atlantic Seaway,* I, 203.
5. David Budlong Tyler, *Steam Conquers the Atlantic* (New York, 1939), 201–2.
6. Tyler, *Steam Conquers the Atlantic,* 212.
7. Alexander Crosby Brown, *Women and Children Last* (New York, 1961), 26.
8. Brown, *Women and Children Last,* 49.
9. Arthur J. Maginnis, *The Atlantic Ferry: Its Ships, Men and Working* (London, 1900), 231–38. Captain Luce's letter to Collins certainly represents one of the most dramatic and poignant reports of a disaster ever penned.
10. Bonsor, *North Atlantic Seaway,* I, 207.
11. Tyler, *Steam Conquers the Atlantic,* 220.
12. Lieutenant Matthew Fontaine Maury, "Ocean Steamer Lanes," *Nautical Magazine* (June 1855), New York.

Chapter 3.

1. Bonsor, *North Atlantic Seaway* (Jersey, Channel Islands, 1978), II, 733, 755–56.
2. Roy Anderson, *White Star* (Prescot, U.K., 1964), 53. Anderson's work remains one of the finest maritime histories of the twentieth century. He was a protégé of N. R. P. Bonsor's.
3. Keith A. Hatchard, *The Two Atlantics: The Shipwreck of the SS Atlantic at Prospect, NS April 1, 1873* (Halifax, N.S., 1981), 25–26. Hatchard states that Williams's accident on the *Republic* occurred in 1871, but the liner was commissioned only in 1872 and took her maiden voyage on February 1, 1872, so the events must have happened less than a year earlier. Given nineteenth-century orthopedic medicine and the severity of his leg fracture (a triple fracture), there is no reason to question that Williams would have experienced severe pain upon occasion.
4. The *New York Times,* April 2, 1873, states that the distance at midnight on March 31 was thought to be thirty-nine miles from the *Atlantic* to Sambro Light, according to Second Officer C. L. Brady, while other sources state forty-eight miles (Anderson, *White Star,* 53).
5. Anderson, *White Star,* 53.
6. *New York Times,* April 4, 1873.
7. Anderson, *White Star,* 54.
8. John P. Eaton and Charles A. Haas, *Falling Star: Misadventures of White Star Line Ships* (New York, 1989), 26.
9. *New York Times,* April 3, 1873.
10. *New York Times,* April 5, 1873.
11. Hatchard, *Two Atlantics,* 94.
12. *New York Times,* April 4, 1873.
13. Hatchard, *Two Atlantics,* 95–96.
14. Anderson, *White Star,* 56–57.
15. *New York Times,* April 4, 1873.
16. *New York Times,* April 14, 1873.
17. *New York Times,* April 3, 1873.
18. "Report of Investigation into the Cause of the Wreck of the Steamship *Atlantic,* Halifax, N.S., April 18, 1873," 37

Victoria, Sessional Papers (No.4), A.1873 (Appendix No. 38). Also Hatchard, *Two Atlantics,* 118–26.

19. Hatchard, *Two Atlantics,* 114. Captain Williams remained a respected White Star officer, and when his suspension was over, he received the command of another White Star ship.
20. *New York times,* April 19, 1873; Hatchard, *Two Atlantics,* 119; Eaton and Haas, *Falling Star,* 29, state 565; Bonsor, *North Atlantic Seaway,* vol. 2, 756, states 585 dead; Anderson, *White Star,* gives a figure of 585. Whether or not the 14 stowaways were ever counted remains a mystery. Also the exact number of passengers who joined at Queenstown is uncertain, as is usually the case. Immigration at New York rectified these figures when a ship finally arrived—if it ever did.
21. Anderson, *White Star,* 58.

Chapter 4.

1. Bonsor, *North Atlantic Seaway,* I, 190–92. The founding firm was Herout & de Handel, Paris and Le Havre. The line received an annual subsidy of four hundred thousand francs but realized losses of two million francs in one year and suspended operations (February 1848).
2. Bonsor, *North Atlantic Seaway,* I, 341–45. The management was Gauthier Frères & Compagnie (Paris and Lyons) and ambitiously sought to establish services to both North and South America. Revenues were disappointing, and the line ceased operations in March 1857.
3. Bonsor, *North Atlantic Seaway,* I, 204. The exact death toll from the loss of the *Arctic* is never likely to be known. She was carrying 233 passengers and a crew 150. Of the total of 383, between 285 and 351 lost their lives.
4. John H. Shaum, Jr., and William H. Flayhart III, *Majesty at Sea: The Four Stackers* (New York, 1981), 143.
5. "Shipbuilder and Marine Engine-Builder," *The French Line, Compagnie Générale Transatlantique, Quadruple-screw Turbo-electric, North Atlantic Steamship,* Normandie, *The World's Largest Liner,* Souvenir Number (London, June 1935), 6.
6. Ronald W. Warwick and William H. Flayhart III, *QE2* (New York, 1985), 16.

7. Bonsor, *North Atlantic Seaway,* II, 626, 652. Bonsor states that the tonnage of the *Ville du Havre* was increased from 3,376 to 3,950 tons by the lengthening process. The *New York Times* report differs.
8. William Henry Flayhart III, *The American Line, 1871–1902* (New York, 2000), 22. Both the Inman Line's *City of Montreal* at 433 feet and the White Star's *Atlantic* at 435 feet were longer than the *Ville du Havre,* but in both cases their hulls were narrower, at 44 feet and 41 feet, than the French liner's 49 feet, giving her the larger tonnage.
9. *New York Times,* December 2, 1873.
10. *New York Times,* December 2, 1873; Mr. Mackenzie, CGT agent, stated that the last position was latitude 47°, longitude 38°. Therefore, there is a discrepancy.
11. *New York Times,* December 2, 1873, states that the *Trimountain,* built in Medford, Massachusetts, in 1850 and owned by J. H. Winchester & Company of South Street, New York, was carrying a general cargo of 200,000 pounds of oil cake, 1,475 gallons of fish oil, 36 hogsheads of tobacco, 47,890 bushels of wheat, and 700 barrels of flour.
12. *New York Times,* December 2, 1873.

Chapter 5.

1. Flayhart, *American Line,* 18–19.
2. Inman Line, Red Star Line, and American Line, *Inman and International Steamship Company Limited* (New York: nd [ca.1888], 49. This early publication of the Inman and International Line gives a detailed history of the backgrounds of the three steamship lines.
3. American Steamship Company (ASC), "Minutes," August 9, 1871, *Minute Book I, 1871–1876,* 29–31. The formal contract was dated August 30, 1871.
4. American Steamship Company, 29–31. Cramp may have had a few reservations about the final contract because the American Line board required the builders to provide a mortgage on the vessels, an assignment of all the insurance policies that might be taken out on the vessels, and "per-

sonal security to the amount of $100,000 on each vessel; the parties to be satisfactory to the Steam Ship Co."

5. The completion dates proved optimistic. The premier unit, *Pennsylvania,* was to be ready by September 1, 1872; the *Ohio* by November 1, 1872; the *Indiana* by December 1, 1872; and the *Illinois* by January 1, 1873. None of these deadlines would be achieved.
6. *New York Times,* March 11, 1874, 4.
7. *New York Times,* March 12, 1874, 6. "Captain Lewis T. Bradburn, commander of the *Pennsylvania,* was about forty-two years of age, and had been engaged in the trade between New York and Liverpool for the past twenty-five years. For six years previous to his engagement with the American Line he acted as mate to Captain Sumner on several packet steamers, and when Sumner took command of the *Pennsylvania,* Capt. Bradburn was selected First Officer. Upon retirement of the first-named gentlemen, he took command of the vessel on August 21, 1873, and has proved himself a man well-fitted for the position. Capt. Bradburn was a native of Maryland. The deceased leaves a wife, who is at present residing at Glasgow, Scotland. This was his last voyage, as he had been appointed Port Captain at Liverpool. Mr. Sweetman, First Officer, had but recently been promoted to that position, and was pronounced a thoroughly competent man; and Mr. Ross, Second Officer, also bears a high reputation for efficiency. These with two seamen, one James Daltron, American, and the other unknown, comprise the lost."
8. *New York Times,* March 12, 1874, 6. Description of saloon passenger C. H. Walton of New York about the near disaster to the ship.
9. *Brady v. American Steamship Company,* "Amendment to Libel," 4. Cadwalader Papers, Historical Society of Pennsylvania.
10. "Michael Murphy, Q.M. (Excerpt from Deposition)," *Brady v. American Steamship Company,* Cadwalader Papers, Historical Society of Pennsylvania.
11. *Brady v. American Steamship Company,* "Deposition," mss; Cadwalader Papers, Historical Society of Pennsylvania.

12. "Joseph Pullius, Q.M., Afterwards 2nd Offr. (Excerpt from Deposition)," *Brady v. American Steamship Company,* Cadwalader Papers, Historical Society of Pennsylvania.
13. "Edwin Coleman, Seafaring Man since 1862 (Excerpt from Deposition)," *Brady v. American Steamship Company,* Cadwalader Papers, Historical Society of Pennsylvania.
14. "Peter McCarroll, Q.M. (Excerpt from Deposition)," *Brady v. American Steamship Company,* Cadwalader Papers, Historical Society of Pennsylvania.
15. "Frank Reedstone, Seaman (Excerpt from Deposition)," *Brady v. American Steamship Company,* Cadwalader Papers, Historical Society of Pennsylvania.
16. "George Keabea, Sailor for 20 Years (Excerpt from Deposition)," *Brady v. American Steamship Company,* Cadwalader Papers, Historical Society of Pennsylvania.

Chapter 6.

1. *New York Times,* January 4, 1895.
2. N. R. P. Bonsor, *North Atlantic Seaway,* II, 829-61 (International Navigation Company, Red Star Line); III, 920–48 (American Steamship Company, American Line).
3. *Philadelphia North American & United States Gazette,* February 18, 1873.
4. Bonsor, *North Atlantic Seaway,* III, 923.
5. N. R. P., Bonsor *North Atlantic Seaway,* II, 833.
6. Flayhart, *American Line,* 96, 100.
7. *New York Times,* March 20, 1877.
8. *New York Times,* March 20, 1877.
9. *New York Times,* March 20, 1877.
10. *New York Times,* March 20, 1877.
11. *New York Times,* March 20, 1877.
12. *New York Times,* March 19, 1877.

Chapter 7.

1. Maginnis, *Atlantic Ferry,* 205.
2. Bonsor, *North Atlantic Seaway,* I, 218.
3. Bonsor, *North Atlantic Seaway,* V, 1866.
4. *New York Times,* January 9, 1883.

5. *New York Times,* January 9, 1883.
6. *New York Times,* January 9, 1883.
7. *Times of London,* January 9, 1883.
8. *New York Times,* January 9, 1883.

Chapter 8.

1. *New York Times,* March 15, 1886.
2. *New York Times,* March 16, 1886.
3. *New York Times,* March 15, 1886.
4. *New York Times,* March 16, 1886.
5. *New York Times,* March 15, 1886.
6. *New York Times,* March 16, 1886.
7. *New York Times,* March 15, 1886.
8. *New York Times,* March 16, 1886.
9. *New York Times,* March 16, 1886.
10. *New York Times,* March 16, 1886.
11. *New York Times,* March 15, 1886.
12. *New York Times,* March 16, 1886.
13. *New York Times,* March 16, 1886.
14. *New York Times,* March 15, 1886.
15. *New York Times,* March 15, 1886.
16. Bradley Sheard, *Lost Voyages: Two Centuries of Shipwrecks in the Approaches to New York* (Locust Valley, N.Y., 1998), 49–57. This is a beautifully done work on marine archaeology.

Chapter 9.

1. *Harper's Weekly* (May 28, 1887), 393.
2. Eaton and Haas, *Falling Star,* 40; states 176 cabin and 300 steerage. Variable statistics are common in these instances.
3. Anderson, *White Star,* 63. Quoted from the White Star Line's *Official Guide.*
4. *Harper's Weekly* (May 28, 1887), 393; Eaton and Haas, *Falling Star,* 41, claim *Celtic* was going 13.5 knots at the time of the collision.
5. *New York Herald,* May 20, 1887; Eaton and Haas, *Falling Star,* 41.
6. *Harper's Weekly* (May 28, 1887), 393.
7. *Harper's Weekly* (May 28, 1887), 393.
8. *Harper's Weekly* (May 28, 1887), 393; Bonsor, *North Atlantic*

Seaway, II, 756–57, does not list any fatalities; Anderson, *White Star,* 199, states a death toll of three. Eaton and Haas, *Falling Star,* 40, record four dead and nine severely wounded in steerage. Little note often was taken of the deaths of passengers or crew after they reached shore.

Chapter 10.

1. Flayhart, *American Line,* 113–23.
2. Inman Line, Red Star Line, and American Line, *Inman and International Steamship Company Limited,* 7.
3. Inman and International Steam Company, *The Inman Line* (1888), 8.
4. Inman and International, *Inman Line,* 9.
5. Inman and International, *Inman Line,* 10.
6. *New York Times,* March 29, 1890.
7. *New York Times,* March 29, 1890.
8. *New York Times,* March 31, 1890.
9. Flayhart, *American Line,* 129.
10. *New York Times,* April 7, 1890.
11. *Engineer* (April 18, 1890), 315.
12. *Engineer* (April 18, 1890), 315.
13. *Engineer* (April 18, 1890), 316.

Chapter 11.

1. Maginnis, *Atlantic Ferry,* 68.
2. Anderson, *White Star,* 87.
3. Flayhart, *American Line,* 124.
4. *New York Times,* May 21, 1892, quote from *Fairplay* (May 20, 1892).
5. *New York Times,* June 15, 1891.

Chapter 12.

1. Bonsor, *North Atlantic Seaway,* I, 233–34.
2. Bonsor, *North Atlantic Seaway,* I, 233–34.
3. Bonsor, *North Atlantic Seaway,* I, 233.
4. *New York Times,* July 3, 1892.
5. *New York Times,* July 3, 1892.
6. *New York Times,* July 8, 1892.

Chapter 13.

1. Bonsor, *North Atlantic Seaway* (Prescot, U.K., 1955; First Edition, supplement added 1960), 67.
2. Charles H. Cramp, *Commercial Supremacy and Other Papers* (Philadelphia, 1894), 43. This was a privately published collection of some of Cramp's many essays and papers.
3. Bonsor, *North Atlantic Seaway,* I, 154 (statistics for *Campania*); III, 944 (statistics for *St. Paul*).
4. *New York Times,* January 26, 1896.
5. *New York Times,* January 26, 1896.
6. *Times* of London, January 27, 1896. Article based on Reuters' telegrams from New York. The *Times* also reported the contents of a "Dalziel telegram" from Long Branch that quoted Captain Jameson, the commander of the *St. Paul*: "We lost our reckoning in the dense fog and were only going about five miles an hour and feeling our way. The man who was heaving the lead reported 17 fathoms two minutes before she struck, but this was evidently a mistake. I was on the bridge when she grounded. The Cunard liner *Campania* was in sight for two days, but there is no truth in the report that we were racing." Owing to Captain Jameson's taciturn nature it is questionable that he gave this interview to anyone. No one got to the ship to interview him for days. The story has the air of a prefabrication about it.
7. *New York Times,* January 26, 1896.
8. *New York Times,* February 5, 1896.
9. *New York Times,* February 7, 1896.
10. *New York Times,* February 20, 1896.
11. *New York Times,* April 17, 1898.

Chapter 14.

1. H. A. Dalkmann and A. J. Schoonderbeck, *One Hundred and Twenty-five Years of Holland America Line* (Edinburgh, 1998), 102–3.
2. "Mishaps at Sea," *Marine Engineering* (March 1898), 27–28. The British maritime journal contended that it was unlikely that the *Veendam* had hit a sunken hull. Instead it suggested that the tail shaft had broken and that the outboard end,

weighed down by the propeller, had been flung around, breaking the stern tube and the aft frame. Ultimately three of the seven compartments of the liner were flooded, dooming her. However, the British commentator was not present at the disaster and the Dutch officers were.

3. Flayhart, *American Line,* 247–49.
4. *New York Times,* February 13, 1898.
5. Flayhart, *American Line,* 249.
6. *New York Times,* February 13, 1898.
7. Flayhart, *American Line,* 251.
8. *New York Times,* February 13, 1898.
9. Flayhart, *American Line,* 252.
10. *New York Times,* February 13, 1898.
11. *New York Times,* February 15, 1898.
12. *New York Times,* February 15, 1898.
13. *New York Times,* March 18, 1898.

Chapter 15.

1. Flayhart, *American Line,* 282.
2. *New York Times,* January 1, 1899.
3. *New York Times,* January 2, 1899.
4. Flayhart, *American Line,* 285.
5. *New York Times,* January 2, 1899.
6. *New York Times,* January 2, 1899.
7. Flayhart, *American Line,* 287.

Chapter 16.

1. *New York Herald,* January 24, 1909.
2. *New York Herald,* January 24, 1909.
3. Anderson, *White Star,* 104.
4. Bonsor, *North Atlantic Seaway,* III, 1342–44.
5. Karl Baarslag, *SOS to the Rescue* (New York, 1941), 18–19.
6. *New York Tribune,* January 24, 1909.
7. *New York Tribune,* January 24, 1909. In her haste to reach the *Republic,* the revenue cutter *Mohawk* ran aground on Palmer's Island, New Bedford, Massachusetts, and missed all the action. She was pulled undamaged into deep water by

the U.S. navy tug *Pontiac* the next day. *New York Tribune,* January 25, 1909.

8. Baarslag, *SOS to the Rescue,* 23.
9. *New York Tribune,* January 25, 1909.
10. *New York Tribune,* January 24, 1909.
11. *New York Tribune,* January 24, 1909.
12. Baarslag, *SOS to the Rescue,* 26.
13. Baarslag, *SOS to the Rescue,* 28.
14. *New York Tribune,* January 27, 1909.
15. Anderson, *White Star,* 105. *New York Tribune,* January 27, 1909. Some of the details of this story may involve "journalistic license," but it has the ring of truth about it, and I am inclined to accept it at face value.
16. *New York Tribune,* January 24, 1909.
17. *New York Tribune,* January 27, 1909.
18. *New York Tribune,* January 29, 1909.
19. *New York Tribune,* January 27, 1909. "Generosity" was relative, but matters would be no different when the *Titanic* sank three years later.
20. Anderson, *White Star,* 105.
21. Anderson, *White Star,* 105.
22. *New York Tribune,* January 27, 1909.
23. *New York Tribune,* January 27, 1909.

Chapter 17.

1. Walter Lord, *The Night Lives On* (New York, 1986), 262, reiterates the philosophical comment that he first made in his celebrated work on the *Titanic, A Night to Remember* (1955): "[I]t is a rash man indeed who would set himself up as a final arbiter on everything that happened the incredible night the *Titanic* went down." I could not agree more. Unfortunately where great tragedies are concerned fanatical followers often abound. The following is one person's view without fear or favor.
2. Shaum and Flayhart, *Majesty at Sea,* 20.
3. Flayhart, *American Line,* 315–36.
4. *Fairplay* (January 21, 1904), 78.

5. *Philadelphia Press,* March 20, 1904.
6. Flayhart, *American Line,* 348–49.
7. Michael McCaughan, *The Birth of the Titanic* (Montreal: 1999), 43. A superb selection of Harland & Wolff photographs by the distinguished Belfast photographer R. J. Welch (1859–1936) from the Ulster Folk and Transport Museum enhanced by a solid text.
8. Anderson, *White Star,* 106. The debate over the name of the third White Star liner will go on forever. Anderson believed that *Gigantic* represented a logical procession, and I concur. That she ultimately was named *Britannic* following the *Titanic* disaster represented an equally logical adjustment to circumstances. N. R. P. Bonsor, author of *North Atlantic Seaway* and arguably the twentieth century's most distinguished maritime historian, who knew some of the principals in the White Star Line, provided this viewpoint in a conversation with the author.
9. John Maxtone-Graham, *The Only Way to Cross* (New York, 1972), 62.
10. John P. Eaton and Charles A. Haas, *Titanic: Triumph and Tragedy* (New York, 1986), 21. This is one of the finest works published on the *Titanic.*
11. Donald Hyslop, Alastair Forsyth, and Sheila Jemima, *Titanic Voices: Memories from the Fateful Voyage* (New York, 1997), 13–35, provide an excellent illustrated overview of the transfer of the White Star Line transatlantic terminus from Liverpool to Southampton.
12. Wyn Craig Wade, *The Titanic: End of a Dream* (New York, 1986), 41.
13. Baarslag, *SOS to the Rescue,* 44.
14. Eaton and Haas, *Titanic,* 64.
15. The purchasing power of six hundred dollars nearly a century later defies analysis, but a factor of twenty (twelve thousand dollars) probably is not far off. The highest-priced luxury suites on the *Titanic* at three thousand dollars in 1912 might well cost between fifty and sixty thousand now. The highest-priced suites on the Cunard liner *Queen Elizabeth 2* in 2001 were advertised at around twelve thou-

sand for a one-way crossing, but advertised specials often reduced this by half.

16. Baarslag, *SOS to the Rescue,* 45.
17. Baarslag, *SOS to the Rescue,* 46–47.
18. Patrick Stenson, *The Odyssey of C. H. Lightoller* (New York, 1984), 154–55.
19. Baarslag, *SOS to the Rescue,* 48–49.
20. Baarslag, *SOS to the Rescue,* 50.
21. *Report on the Loss of the "Titanic" (S.S.),* Report of the Court, 30th day of July, 1912, Mersey, wreck commissioner (London, 1912), 8.
22. Baarslag, *SOS to the Rescue,* 52–53.
23. Baarslag, *SOS to the Rescue,* 53.
24. Baarslag, *SOS to the Rescue,* 56. J. Durrant, wireless officer on the *Mount Temple* realized the urgency of the situation and also the need not to trouble Phillips on the *Titanic* with any unnecessary messages. On receiving Durrant's news, the captain of the *Mount Temple* turned his ship around and began to retrace his way eastward at twelve knots. Ultimately she had reached a position about twelve miles from the *Titanic* when she became trapped by ice and could go no farther. Eaton and Haas, *Titanic,* 169–75, provide an excellent illustrated coverage of the vessels involved with the *Titanic.*
25. Baarslag, *SOS to the Rescue,* 54. Sir Arthur Rostron recorded this exchange in his biography *Home from the Sea* (London).
26. Baarslag, *SOS to the Rescue,* 55. Captain Rostron was praised at the American Inquiry for the thoroughness of the preparations made on the *Carpathia* to receive the survivors of the *Titanic.* He later received a knighthood from King George V.
27. Lt. Cmdr. Craig McClean, NOAA, and David L. Eno, "The Case of Captain Lord," *Naval History,* vol. 6, no. 1 (Spring 1992), 26.
28. Shaum and Flayhart, *Majesty at Sea,* 125.
29. Baarslag, *SOS to the Rescue,* 62.
30. Walter Lord, *A Night to Remember* (New York, 1995), 115.
31. Walter Lord, *A Night to Remember, Illustrated Edition* (Toronto, 1978), 143.
32. *Report on the Loss of the "Titanic" (S.S.),* 42.

33. *Report on the Loss of the "Titanic" (S.S.)*, 42.
34. Baarslag, *SOS to the Rescue,* 67.
35. Baarslag, *SOS to the Rescue,* 43.
36. *New York Tribune,* May 15, 1912.
37. *New York Tribune,* May 15, 1912. Reporting on the British inquiry held in London.
38. McClean and Eno, "The Case of Captain Lord," 26–27. Lord, *The Night Lives On,* 176–79.
39. Lord, *The Night Lives On,* 167–69.
40. Edwin L. Dunbaugh, "Titanic—from a Different Angle," *Steamboat Bill, Journal of the Steamship Historical Society of America,* vol. 61, no. 1 (Spring 2001), 6. Dunbaugh is a maritime historian of some sixty years' standing who was honored by the Samuel Ward Stanton Lifetime Achievement Award of the SSHSA in 1996.
41. McClean and Eno, "The Case of Captain Lord," 29.
42. McClean and Eno, "The Case of Captain Lord," 26–27. I think McClean and Eno's research commands respect and is well founded.
43. Dunbaugh, "Titanic—from a Different Angle," 6.
44. Maxtone-Graham, *Only Way to Cross,* 68–69.
45. Baarslag, *SOS to the Rescue,* 40–41.
46. Baarslag, *SOS to the Rescue,* 40.
47. Lord, *Night Lives On,* 193–95.
48. Robert D. Ballard and Rick Archbold, paintings by Ken Marschall, *Lost Liners* (New York, 1997), 100–101.
49. Shaum and Flayhart, *Majesty at Sea,* 126–27.
50. McClean and Eno, "The Case of Captain Lord," 28.
51. Baarslag, *SOS to the Rescue,* 41–42.
52. Baarslag, *SOS to the Rescue,* 43.
53. McCaughan, *Birth of the Titanic,* 2–3.
54. Baarslag, *SOS to the Rescue,* 70.
55. *New York Tribune,* May 1, 1912.
56. *New York Tribune,* January 1, 1913.
57. Hyslop, Forsyth, and Jemima, *Titanic Voices,* 165–66.
58. *New York Tribune,* May 1, 1912.
59. Ballard and Archbold, *Lost Liners.*
60. Rick Archbold, *Ken Marschall's Art of Titanic* (Toronto, 1998).

Chapter 18.

1. Bonsor, *North Atlantic Seaway,* III, 1284.
2. Baarslag, *SOS to the Rescue,* 80.
3. Logan Marshall, *The Tragic Story of the Empress of Ireland* (London, 1972), 15. This volume, edited by W. H. Tantum IV, was originally published in 1914 and represents a contemporary account of the sinking and the subsequent hearings.
4. Marshall, *The Tragic Story of the Empress of Ireland,* 18, 29.
5. Marshall, *The Tragic Story of the Empress of Ireland,* 30.
6. Baarslag, *SOS to the Rescue,* 84.
7. Baarslag, *SOS to the Rescue,* 88. In the many accounts of the disaster there exists a great deal of confusion and numerous inaccuracies. Baarslag's text was based on actual interviews with Ferguson and Bamford and commands respect.
8. Baarslag, *SOS to the Rescue,* 88.
9. Baarslag, *SOS to the Rescue,* 89.
10. Baarslag, *SOS to the Rescue,* 89, from an interview of Baarslag with Senior Wireless Operator Ferguson who by that time (late 1930s) was the joint general manager of the British Marconi Company. Baarslag also personally interviewed Edward Bamford, who rose to be executive member of the British Association of Wireless and Cable Telegraphists. Marshall, *Tragic Story of the Empress of Ireland,* 38. This contemporary source said: "For God's sake, get down stream at once. The *Empress of Ireland* has gone under."
11. Marshall, *Tragic Story of the Empress of Ireland,* 31.
12. Marshall, *Tragic Story of the Empress of Ireland,* 23.
13. Marshall, *Tragic Story of the Empress of Ireland,* 26.
14. Baarslag, *SOS to the Rescue,* 79.
15. Baarslag, *SOS to the Rescue,* 94–95.
16. *New York Tribune,* May 30, 1914.
17. *New York Tribune,* May 30, 1914.
18. Marshall, *Tragic Story of the Empress of Ireland,* 28.
19. *New York Tribune,* May 30, 1914.
20. *New York Tribune,* May 30, 1914.
21. Baarslag, *SOS to the Rescue,* 80.
22. Baarslag, *SOS to the Rescue,* 85.

23. Baarslag, *SOS to the Rescue,* 85.
24. Baarslag, *SOS to the Rescue,* 97. Records that the *Storstad* was seized at Montreal and later sold to satisfy a judgment. Rumor had it that her previous owners used an agent to buy her back. Certainly Edward Bamford said that he saw her in a French port a couple of years later and that Captain Andersen was in command with First Mate Toftenes to assist him. During World War I the *Storstad,* carrying Belgian relief supplies, was sunk in the North Sea.
25. Robert G. Albion, *Five Centuries of Famous Ships* (New York, 1978), 340–41.
26. Baarslag, *SOS to the Rescue,* 95–96. The figure normally given for the death toll on the *Empress of Ireland* is 1,014.

Chapter 19.

1. *Sphere* (August 3, 1907), 96.
2. David Ramsay, *Lusitania: Saga and Myth* (New York, 2002), 29.
3. Shaum and Flayhart, *Majesty at Sea,* 78–79.
4. Lord Inverclyde to Mr. Jardine, May 3, 1902, Cunard Papers (D42/Ca40), University Archives, University of Liverpool. George Burns, second Lord Inverclyde succeeded his father on the latter's death in 1901 and in this letter reviewed the actions of the Cunard Board of March 27, 1900.
5. Francis Hyde, *Cunard and the North Atlantic 1840–1973* (London, 1975), 139.
6. Hyde, *Cunard and the North Atlantic 1840–1973,* 141.
7. Hyde, *Cunard and the North Atlantic 1840–1973,* 143.
8. Hyde, *Cunard and the North Atlantic 1840–1973,* 144. Lord Selborne to Lord Inverclyde, May 10, 1902.
9. Hyde, *Cunard and the North Atlantic,* 144.
10. Lord Inverclyde to Mr. Watson (member Cunard board), August 8, 1902, Cunard Papers (D42/Ca39), University Archives, University of Liverpool. "Of course the least satisfactory part of it is that the Cunard Company gain on immediate benefit. That is comparatively small matter to the great future I consider is before it, closely bound as it will be to the Government of this Country. And, of course, the sooner we get the new ships built the better it will be for us."

11. Lord Inverclyde to Mr. Gerald Balfour, August 8, 1902, Cunard Papers (D42/Ca39), University Archives, University of Liverpool. This is accompanied by the "Memorandum of interview between Mr. Gerald Balfour and Lord Inverclyde" relative to the agreement between Cunard and the British government and signed by both men.
12. Lord Inverclyde to Mr. Watson (member Cunard board), August 8, 1902, Cunard Papers (D42/Ca39), University Archives, University of Liverpool.
13. Lord Inverclyde to Mr. Watson (member Cunard board), August 8, 1902, Cunard Papers (D42/Ca39), University Archives, University of Liverpool.
14. Lord Inverclyde to Mr. Vernon Brown, August 8, 1902, Cunard Papers (D42/Ca39), University Archives, University of Liverpool.
15. Vernon H. Brown to Lord Inverclyde, August 22, 1902, Cunard Papers (D42/Ca39), University Archives, University of Liverpool. Brown also recommended that no position on the Cunard board be reserved for any government representative since that would only create future problems.
16. Cunard Steam Ship Company Ltd., "The Statement Made by the Chairman at the Shareholders' Meeting, 29th July, 1903," University Archives, University of Liverpool, Cunard Papers (D42/Ca42), 9.
17. Cunard Steam Ship Company Ltd., "The Statement Made by the Chairman," 29th July, 1903, 10.
18. Cunard Steam Ship Company Ltd., "The Statement Made by the Chairman," 12.
19. Cunard Steam Ship Company Ltd., "The Statement Made by the Chairman," 12.
20. Daniel Allen Butler, *The Lusitania: The Life, Loss, and Legacy of an Ocean Legend* (Mechanicsburg, Pa., 2000), 7.
21. Shaum and Flayhart, *Majesty at Sea,* 64–66.
21. Ballard and Archbold, *Lost Liners,* 43–44.
23. Shaum and Flayhart, *Majesty at Sea,* 70.
24. Shaum and Flayhart, *Majesty at Sea,* 80.
25. Shaum and Flayhart, *Majesty at Sea,* 90.
26. A. A. Hoehling and Mary Hoehling, *The Last Voyage of the*

Lusitania (New York [1956], 1991), 33–47; Butler, *Lusitania,* 124–27; David Ramsay, *Lusitania,* 58–62, also covers passengers.

27. Shaum and Flayhart, *Majesty at Sea,* 91–92.
28. Butler, *Lusitania,* 123.
29. Shaum and Flayhart, *Majesty at Sea,* 90.
30. Butler, *Lusitania,* 120.
31. Hoehling and Hoehling, *Last Voyage of the Lusitania,* 17.
32. Ramsay, *Lusitania,* 80–82.
33. Hoehling and Hoehling, *Last Voyage of the Lusitania,* 106.
34. Ramsay, *Lusitania,* 244–45.
35. Ramsay, *Lusitania,* 258–63.

Chapter 20.

1. Peter C. Kohler, "Triumph and Tragedy T.E.L. *Morro Castle* and *Oriente,*" *Steamboat Bill, Journal of the Steamship Historical Society of America,* vol. 46, no. 2 (Summer 1989), 107–27, provides interesting background and a well-founded overview of the two sister ships by one of the best contemporary American maritime historians.
2. Leonard Alexander Swann, Jr., *John Roach, Maritime Entrepreneur: The Years as Naval Contractor, 1862–1886* (Annapolis, 1965), 96–99. A second Roach ship, *Saratoga,* also was purchased by Ward but never ran for them because they had a chance to sell it at a substantial profit to the Russian government in 1878.
3. Swann, *John Roach, Maritime Entrepreneur,* 99. Ultimately Roach succeeded in founding the United States and Brazil Mail Steamship Company (1877) but only after agreeing to build ships that were more than a thousand tons larger than the *Niagara,* which remained under the Ward Line flag.
4. Thomas Gallagher, *Fire at Sea: The Story of the Morro Castle* (New York, 1959), 13.
5. Frank Rushbrook, *Fire Aboard: The Problems of Prevention and Control in Ships and Port Installation* (New York, 1961), 51.
6. Rushbrook, *Fire Aboard,* 52.
7. Baarslag, *SOS to the Rescue,* 179.
8. Rushbrook, *Fire Aboard,* 51.

9. Kohler, "Triumph and Tragedy T.E.L. *Morro Castle* and *Oriente,*" 117.
10. Rushbrook, *Fire Aboard,* 53.
11. Rushbrook, *Fire Aboard,* 54.
12. Baarslag, *SOS to the Rescue,* 182.
13. Baarslag, *SOS to the Rescue,* 181.
14. Baarslag, *SOS to the Rescue,* 185.
15. Gallagher, *Fire at Sea,* 14–15.
16. Gallagher, *Fire at Sea,* 26–27.
17. Gallagher, *Fire at Sea,* 55–56.
18. Gallagher, *Fire at Sea,* 53.
19. Gallagher, *Fire at Sea,* 251. Rogers was working for the Bayonne, New Jersey, Police Department, and attempted to murder his superior, Lieutenant Vincent Doyle, with a bomb. Later during World War II he was released for military service. After the war (1953) he swindled money out of an elderly man and his daughter living near him and then brutally beat them to death. He was caught, tried and convicted of the double murder, and sentenced to life imprisonment again, 253–56.
20. Baarslag, *SOS to the Rescue,* 187.
21. Gallagher, *Fire at Sea,* 178.
22. Gallagher, *Fire at Sea,* 181–82.
23. Gallagher, *Fire at Sea,* 182.
24. Baarslag, *SOS to the Rescue,* 191–92.
25. Baarslag, *SOS to the Rescue,* 192.
26. Gallagher, *Fire at Sea,* 233–35.

Chapter 21.

1. Bonsor, *North Atlantic Seaway,* III, 1605. The amalgamation of NGI and Lloyd Sabaudo into Italia at Genoa occurred, while Cosulich retained some independence and a separate management at Trieste. This represented the old competition between western and eastern Italian ports.
2. Peter C. Kohler, *The Lido Fleet: Italian Line Passenger Ships & Services* (Alexandria, Va., 1998), 175.
3. Kohler, *Lido Fleet,* 175.
4. Bonsor, *North Atlantic Seaway,* III, 1611, 1619.

5. Kohler, *Lido Fleet,* 189.
6. Kohler, *Lido Fleet,* 189.
7. Kohler, *Lido Fleet,* 188.
8. Alvin Moscow, *Collision Course: The Andrea Doria and the Stockholm* (New York, 1959), 14.
9. Moscow, *Collision Course,* 24.
10. Bonsor, *North Atlantic Seaway,* IV, 1453–62.
11. Bonsor, *North Atlantic Seaway,* II, 663–64.
12. Kohler, *Lido Fleet,* 197.
13. Kohler, *Lido Fleet,* 197.
14. This is the author's figure on the basis of 50 percent of the lifeboats not being operational. Kohler, *Lido Fleet,* 199, states that the remaining eight boats could accommodate 1,004.
15. William Hoffer, *Saved!: The Story of the Andrea Doria—the Greatest Sea Rescue in History* (New York, 1979), 131.
16. Raoul de Beaudéan, *Captain of the Île,* trans. Salvator Attanasio (New York, 1960), 194.
17. Beaudéan, *Captain of the Île,* 195.
18. Beaudéan, *Captain of the Île,* 197.
19. Beaudéan, *Captain of the Île,* 199.
20. Beaudéan, *Captain of the Île,* 200.
21. Hoffer, *Saved!,* 133.
22. Moscow, *Collision Course,* 151.
23. Beaudéan, *Captain of the Île,* 202–03.
24. Kohler, *Lido Fleet,* 201.
25. Kohler, *Lido Fleet,* 201.

Chapter 22.

1. N. R. P. Bonsor, *South Atlantic Seaway* (Jersey, Channel Islands, 1983), 476–81 (Costa Line).

BIBLIOGRAPHY

General Bibliographies

Broeze, Frank, ed., *Maritime History at the Crossroads: A Critical Review of Recent Historiography,* Research in Maritime History No. 9, International Maritime Economic History Association, St. John's, Newfoundland, 1995.

Hattendorf, John B., ed., *Ubi Sumus? The State of Naval and Maritime History,* Naval War College Historical Monography Series, No. 11, Newport, R.I., 1994.

Manuscript Sources

Bonsor, N. R. P. "Sailing Schedules of the American Steamship Company, 1873–1884." Ms. in the author's collection.

——. "Sailing Schedule of the Société Anonyme de Navigation Belge-Américaine (International Navigation Company–Red Star Line), 1879–1893." Ms. in the author's collection.

——, "Sailing Schedule of the American Line (1893), 1893–1895." Ms. in the author's collection.

Brady, Cornelius L., "Deposition (July 11, 1874," *Brady v. American Steamship Company,* "Amendment to Libel," Papers of John Cadwalader, judge of the District Court of the United States in and for the Eastern District of Pennsylvania, Historical Society of Pennsylvania, Philadelphia. Deposition materials from other crew members are included in Judge Cadwalader's Papers.

Cunard Steam Ship Company Limited Papers, University Archives, University of Liverpool, U.K.

Hermans, Lt. François, January 16, 1966, forwarded by Mr. Paul E. R. Scarceriaux, chairman of the Belgian Nautical Research Association, dealing with the early history of the Société Anonyme de Navigation Belge-Américaine (Red Star Line).

Herrick, Walter, R., Jr., "The American Naval Revolution 1890–1898," Winter Park, Fla., 1965. Unpublished doctoral dissertation in the archives of the University of Virginia, Charlottesville, Va.

Pennsylvania Railroad Company, "Minutes of the Board of Directors of the Pennsylvania Railroad Company," Minute Book No. 5 (November 1865–November 1871), Pennsylvania Railroad Collection, Hagley Museum and Library (Soda House), Wilmington, Del.

——, "Statement of the Financial Committee of the American Steamship Company," December 8, 1874, Pennsylvania Railroad Company, Secretary's Papers, M-85, Board File No. 95, Pennsylvania Railroad Collection, Hagley Museum and Library (Soda House), Wilmington, Del.

——, "Subcommittee of the Finance Committee," Board of Directors, PRR, January 24, 1877, Pennsylvania Railroad Company, Secretary's Papers, M-85, Board File No. 95, Pennsylvania Railroad Collection, Hagley Museum and Library (Soda House), Wilmington, Del. Discusses resolution of ASC debt to PRR.

Smith, Robert W., secretary, PRR, ALS., to Samuel Rea, assistant to the president, PRR, January 13, 1897, M-87, BF-156, Pennsylvania Railroad Collection, Hagley Museum and Library (Soda House), Wilmington, Del. Discusses the history of the PRR involvement in the bonds of the American Steamship Company.

Welsh, Henry D., president, American Steamship Company, ALS.

to the president and board of directors of the Pennsylvania Railroad Company, January 25, 1876, minutes of the PRR Board, M85, Board No. 95, Pennsylvania Railroad Collection, Hagley Museum and Library (Soda House), Wilmington, Del. Detailed ALS discussing the need for additional ships.

Williams, Lt. Osgood, July 23, 1965, from the past director of the Peabody Museum, Salem, Mass., Osgood Williams, relating information on the American Line available at the museum as well as his personal reminiscences of a crossing on the *New York* in June 1914, among other things. In the author's collection.

Newspapers and Magazines

Daily Mail, 1900–1905.

Engineer, 1890–1910.

Fairplay, 1900–1905.

Glasgow Herald, 1873–1874.

Harper's Weekly, 1850–1902.

International Journal of Maritime History, 1989–1998.

Journal of Commerce and Commercial Bulletin (New York), 1900–1905.

Liverpool Courier, 1900–1905.

Liverpool Mercury, 1900–1905.

Liverpool Daily Post, 1900–1905.

Liverpool Journal of Commerce, June 23, 1873.

Marine Engineering, 1880–1905.

Mariner's Mirror, 1914–1998.

Mitchell's Maritime Register, August 30, 1872.

New York Commercial and Shipping List, 1900.

New York Herald, 1865–1905.

New York Times, 1865–1905.

New York Tribune, 1890–1905.

Philadelphia Commercial List and Price Current, December 1870–July 1882.

Philadelphia Evening Bulletin, 1873–1905.

Philadelphia North American United States Gazette, January 13, 1873.

Scientific American, 1886–1905.

Sphere, 1907.

Times of London, 1865–1905.
United States Investor, 1902.
Wall Street Journal, 1890–1905.

Published Documents

Annual Report of the Commissioner of Navigation, London, 1901.

Buell, Augustus C., *The Memoirs of Charles H. Cramp,* Philadelphia, 1906. Highly edited documents and accounts written by Charles H. Cramp and compiled by Augustus C. Buell.

Cramp, Charles H., *Commercial Supremacy and Other Papers,* Philadelphia: nd, [ca. 1894].

[Cramp] *The William Cramp & Son Ship and Engine Building Company,* Philadelphia, nd [ca. 1894]. Philadelphia Public Library.

Griscom, Clement Acton (misindexed "Grisco"), Testimony before the Senate Subcommittee on "Revival of the Merchant Marine," Senate Miscellaneous Documents, No. 149, 56th Congress, 1st Session, 100–109.

Inman Line, Red Star Line, and American Line, *The Inman and International Steamship Company,* New York: nd [ca. 1888]. Privately published description of the ships and services of the three lines preceded by a brief history of the lines. New York Public Library.

International Navigation Company, *American Line,* New York, 1898. Collection of documents and accounts concerning the transfer of the Inman Line to the United States and the formation of the American Line (1893), which introduces a documentary account of the employment of the American Line vessels during the Spanish-American War (1898) and is followed by a detailed description of the liners. Mariners Museum, Newport News, Va.

Messrs. Peter Wright & Sons, *The Red Star Line, Belgian Royal and U.S. Mail Steamships, Facts for Travelers,* New York, nd [1883?]. Independence Maritime Museum Collection, Philadelphia.

Postmaster-General (U.K.) to William Inman (Post 51/46), "Contract of 9th March 1869. United States Mails. Liverpool via Queenstown to New York," GPO Historical Records Office, St. Martins-le-Grand, London.

Postmaster General (U.S.), *Report of the Postmaster General* (43d Congress, 2d Session), vol. 1638, 13–14.

Postmaster General (U.S.), "Report of the Postmaster General," in *The Abridgment. Message from the President of the United States to the Two Houses of Congress at the Beginning of the First Session of the Fifty-second Congress, with the Reports of the Heads of Departments and Selections from Accompanying Documents,* ed. W. H. Michael, Washington, D.C. 1892.

"Report of Investigation into the Causes of the Wreck of the Steamship *Atlantic,* Halifax, N.S., April 18, 1873," 37 Victoria, Sessional Papers (No. 4), A. 1873.

Report of the Merchant Marine Commission, 58th Congress, 3d Session, Senate Report No. 2755, 1905.

Report on the Loss of the "Titanic" (S.S.), Report of the Court, Mersey, wreck commissioner, London, 1912.

U.S. Congress, *Report 201,* 57th Congress, 1st Session, part 2, 1902.

Books and Published Sources

Abbot, Willis J., *The Story of Our Merchant Marine,* New York, 1919.

Albion, Robert Greenhalgh, *Five Centuries of Famous Ships,* New York, 1978.

——, *The Rise of the Port of New York,* New York, 1939.

Anderson, Roy, *White Star,* Prescot, U.K., 1964.

Anthony, Irvin, *Down to the Sea in Ships,* Philadelphia, 1924.

Appleton, Thomas E., *Ravenscrag–The Allan Royal Mail Line,* Toronto, 1974.

Archbold, Rick, *Ken Marschall's Art of Titanic,* Toronto, 1998.

Armstrong, Warren, *Atlantic Highway,* New York, 1962.

Baarslag, Karl, *SOS to the Rescue,* New York, 1941.

Baker, W. A., and Try Trychare, *The Engine Powered Vessel,* New York, 1965.

Ballard, Robert D., *Exploring the Lusitania,* New York, 1995.

——, and Rick Archbold, with paintings by Ken Marschall, *Lost Liners,* New York, 1997.

Barbance, Marthe, *Histoire de la Compagnie Générale Transatlantique,* Paris, 1955.

Barrow, Clayton, ed., *America Spreads Her Sails: A Century of Sea Power, 1873–1973,* Annapolis, 1973.
Bauer, K. Jack, *A Maritime History of the United States: The Role of America's Seas and Waterways,* Columbia, S.C., 1988.
Beaudéan, Raoul de, *Captain of the Île,* New York, 1960.
Bessell, George, *Norddeutscher Lloyd 1857–1957,* Bremen, 1957.
Blake, G., *BI Centenary 1856–1956,* London, 1956.
Bonsor, N. R. P., *North Atlantic Seaway,* Prescot, U.K., 1955 (supplement 1960).
——, *North Atlantic Seaway,* Jersey, Channel Islands, 1975–1980, 2d ed. in 5 vols.
——, *South Atlantic Seaway,* Jersey, Channel Islands, 1983.
Bowen, Frank C., *A Century of Atlantic Travel,* New York, 1930.
Boyce, Gordon H., *Information, Mediation and Institutional Development: The Rise of Large-scale Enterprise in British Shipping, 1870–1919,* Manchester, 1995.
Braynard, Frank O., *Famous American Ships,* New York, 1956.
——, *SS Savannah—The Elegant Steam Ship,* Athens, Ga., 1963.
Broeze, Frank, "Albert Ballin, The Hamburg-Bremen Rivalry and the Dynamics of the Conference System," *International Journal of Maritime History,* vol. 3 (June 1991), 1–32.
——, "Shipping Policy and Social-Darwinism: Albert Ballin and the *Weltpolitik* of the Hamburg-America Line 1886–1914," *Mariner's Mirror,* vol. 79, no. 4 (November 1993).
Brown, Alexander Crosby, *Women and Children Last,* New York, 1961.
Bundy, C. Lynn, *The Maritime Association of the Port of New York, Historical Review of the Past Fifty Years,* New York, 1923.
Burgess, George H., and Miles C. Kennedy, *Centennial History of the Pennsylvania Railroad Company 1846–1946,* Philadelphia, 1949.
Bushell, T. A., *Royal Mail: A Centenary History 1839–1939,* London, 1939.
Butler, Daniel Allen, *The Lusitania: The Life, Loss, and Legacy of an Ocean Legend,* Mechanicsburg, Pa., 2000.
Cable, Boyd, *A Hundred Year History of the P.&O.,* London, 1937.
Carosso, Vincent P., *The Morgans,* Cambridge, Mass., 1987.
Carter, Craig J. M., *Ships of the Mersey,* London, 1966.

Cecil, Lamar, *Albert Ballin: Business and Politics in Imperial Germany 1888–1918,* Princeton, 1967.

Chadwick, F. E., et al., *Ocean Steamships,* London, 1892.

Chandler, Alfred D., Jr., *Scale and Scope: The Dynamics of Industrial Capitalism,* Cambridge, Mass., 1990.

——, *Strategy and Structure: Chapters in the History of American Industrial Enterprise,* Cambridge, Mass., 1962.

——, *The Visible Hand: The Management Revolution in American Business,* Cambridge, Mass., 1977.

Chandler, George, *Liverpool Shipping: A Short History,* London, 1960.

Clark, Alexander, *Summer Rambles in Europe,* New York, 1879.

Corson, F. Reid, *The Atlantic Ferry in the Twentieth Century,* London, 1929.

Dalkman, H. A., and A. J. Schoonderbeck, *One Hundred and Twenty-five Years of Holland America Line,* Edinburgh, 1998.

Dudden, Arthur Power, *The American Pacific,* New York, 1992.

Duff, Peter, *British Ships and Shipping,* London, 1949.

Dugan, James, *The Great Iron Ship,* London, 1953.

Dunbaugh, Edwin L., "Titanic–from a Different Angle," *Steamboat Bill, Journal of the Steamship Historical Society of America,* vol. 61, no. 1 (Spring 2001), 6.

Dunmore, Walter J., *Ship Subsidies: An Economic Study of the Policy of Subsidizing Merchant Marines,* Boston, 1907.

Dunn, Laurence, *Passenger Liners,* Southampton, U.K., 1961.

——, *Famous Liners of the Past–Belfast Built,* London, 1964.

Dunnet, Alistair, *The Donaldson Line: A Century of Shipping, 1854–1954,* Glasgow, 1960.

Eaton, John P., and Charles A. Haas, *Titanic, Triumph and Tragedy,* New York, 1986.

——, *Falling Star: Misadventures of White Star Line Ships,* New York, 1989.

Emmons, Frederick, *The Atlantic Liners 1925–1970,* Newton Abbot, U.K., 1972.

Fairfield Shipbuilding and Engineering Company Ltd., *Fairfield 1860–1960,* Glasgow, 1960.

Farr, Grahame, *The Steamship Great Britain,* Bristol, U.K., 1965.

——, *The Steamship Great Western,* Bristol, U.K., 1963.

Fatout, Paul, ed., *Mark Twain Speaking,* Iowa City, 1976.
Flayhart, William Henry, III, "Four Fighting Ladies," in *America Spreads Her Sails: A Century of Sea Power, 1873–1973,* ed. Clayton Barrow, Annapolis, 1973.
——, *The American Line, 1871–1902,* New York, 2000.
Fry, Henry, *The History of North Atlantic Steam Navigation,* London, 1896.
Gallagher, Thomas, *Fire at Sea: The Story of the Morro Castle,* New York, 1959.
Gibbs, Commander C. R. Vernon, *Passenger Liners of the Western Ocean,* rev. ed., London, 1957.
Gould, John H., "Ocean Passenger Travel," in F. E. Chadwick, USN, et al., *Ocean Steamships,* London, 1892.
Griffiths, Denis, *Power of the Great Liners,* Sparkford, U.K., 1990.
Griscom, Lloyd C., *Diplomatically Speaking,* New York, 1940.
Hatchard, Keith A., *The Two Atlantics: The Shipwreck of the SS Atlantic at Prospect, NS., April 1, 1873,* Halifax, N.S., 1981.
Haws, Duncan, *Merchant Fleets in Profile 2,* Cambridge, U.K., 1979.
Headley, J. T., *The Travels of General Grant,* Philadelphia, 1881.
Heinrich, Thomas R., *Ships for the Seven Seas: Philadelphia Shipbuilding in the Age of Industrial Capitalism,* Baltimore, 1997.
Heyl, Erik, *Early American Steamers,* 3 vols., Buffalo, 1953-1956.
Hoehling, A. A., and Mary Hoehling, *The Last Voyage of the Lusitania,* New York, 1991.
Hoffer, William, *Saved!: The Story of the Andrea Doria—the Greatest Sea Rescue in History,* New York, 1979.
Holbrook, Stewart H., *The Age of the Moguls,* Garden City, N.Y., 1955.
Holman, H., *A Handy Book for Shipowners & Masters,* 7th ed., London, 1911.
Holmes, Sir George C. V., *Ancient and Modern Ships, Part II, The Era of Steam, Iron & Steel,* London, 1906.
Hovey, Carl, *The Life Story of J. Pierpont Morgan,* New York, 1911.
Howarth, David, and Stephen Howarth, *The Story of P&O,* London, 1986.
Hyde, Francis E., *Cunard and the North Atlantic 1840–1973,* London, 1975.
Hyslop, Donald, Alastair Forsyth, and Sheila Jemima, *Titanic*

Voices: Memories from the Fateful Voyage, New York, 1997.
"Inman, William 1825–1881," *Dictionary of National Biography,* vol. X.
Isherwood, J. H., *Steamers of the Past,* Liverpool, 1966.
Johnson, Emory R., *Principles of Ocean Transportation,* New York, 1919.
——, T. W. Van Metre, G. G. Huebner, and D. S. Hanchett, *History of Domestic and Foreign Commerce of the United States,* 2 vols., New York, 1915.
Keiler, Hans, *American Shipping: Its History and Economic Conditions,* Problems der Waltwirtschaft, Schriften des Instituts für Desverkehr und Waltwirtschaft an der Universität Kiel, June 1913.
Kirkaldy, Adam W., *British Shipping, Its History, Organization and Importance,* London, 1919.
Kludas, Arnold, *Great Passenger Ships of the World,* 5 vols., Cambridge, U.K., 1975.
——, and Herbert Bischoff, *Die Schiffe der Hamburg-Amerika Linie,* 3 vols., Herford, Germany, 1979.
Knap, Ger, H., *A Century of Shipping,* Amsterdam, 1956.
Kohler, Peter C., *The Lido Fleet: Italian Line Passenger Ships & Services,* Alexandria, Va., 1998.
——, "Triumph and Tragedy T.E.L. *Morro Castle* and *Oriente,*" *Steamboat Bill,* Journal of the Steamsboat Historical Society of America, vol. 46, no. 2 (Summer 1989).
Labaree, Benjamin W., ed., *The Atlantic World of Robert G. Albion,* Middletown, Conn., 1975.
Lee, Charles E., *The Blue Riband,* London, 1930.
LeFleming, H. M., *Ships of the Holland America Line,* London, 1965.
Lindsay, W. S., *History of Merchant Shipping and Commerce,* 4 vols., London, 1883.
Logan, Marshall, *The Tragic Story of the Empress of Ireland,* London, 1972.
Lord, Walter, *The Night Lives On,* New York, 1986.
——, *A Night to Remember, Illustrated Edition,* Toronto, 1978.
Lott, Arnold S., *A Long Line of Ships,* Annapolis, 1954.
Maber, John, *North Star to Southern Cross,* Prescot, U.K., 1967.
McCabe, James D., *A Tour around the World by General Grant,* Philadelphia, 1879.

McCaughan, Michael, *The Birth of the Titanic,* Montreal, 1999.
McClean, Lt. Comdr. Craig, and David L. Eno, "The Case of Captain Lord," *Naval History,* vol. 6, no. 1 (Spring 1992).
McCluskie, Tom, *Ships from the Archives of Harland & Wolff, the Builders of the Titanic,* Edison, N.J., 1998.
McLellan, R. S., *Anchor Lines (1856–1956),* Glasgow, 1956.
Maginnis, Arthur J., *The Atlantic Ferry: Its Ships, Men and Working,* London, 1900.
Marshall, Logan, *The Tragic Story of the Empress of Ireland,* London, 1972.
Marvin, Winthrop I., *The American Merchant Marine,* New York, 1902.
Maury, Lieutenant Matthew Fontaine, "Steam-Lanes across the Atlantic," *Nautical Magazine* (June 1855).
Maxtone-Graham, John, *The Only Way to Cross,* New York, 1972.
Meeker, Royal, *History of Shipping Subsidies,* New York, 1905.
Morris, James M., *Our Maritime Heritage,* Washington, D.C., 1979.
Moscow Alvin, *Collision Course: The Andrea Doria and the Stockholm,* New York, 1959.
Musk, George, *The Canadian Pacific Afloat 1883–1968,* London, 1968.
Nicholson, John, *Liners of the Clyde,* Glasgow, 1994.
Noble, Dennis L., *That Others Might Live: The U.S. Life-Saving Service, 1878–1915,* Annapolis, 1994.
Oldham, Wilton J., *The Ismay Line,* Liverpool, 1961.
Oost, Tony, et al., *Henri Cassiers 1858–1944,* Antwerp, 1994.
Paine, Lincoln, "The Loss of Arctic, 1854," *Professional Mariner,* no. 59 (October–November 2001).
Parker, Captain Walter H., *Leaves from an Unwritten Log-Book,* London, n.d. (ca. 1930).
Phelps, Edith M., ed., *Selected Articles on the American Merchant Marine,* 2d ed. Debaters' Handbook Series, New York, 1920.
Ramsay, David, *Lusitania: Saga and Myth,* New York, 2002.
Rentell, Philip, *Historic Cunard Liners,* Truro, U.K., 1986.
——, *Historic White Star Liners,* Truro, U.K., 1987.
Ridgely-Nevitt, Cedric, *American Steamships on the Atlantic,* Newark, Del., 1981.
Robinson, Howard, *Carrying British Mails Overseas,* London, 1964.

Rowe, William Hutchinson, *The Maritime History of Maine,* New York, 1948.

Rushbrook, Frank, *Fire Aboard: The Problems of Prevention and Control in Ships and Port Installations,* New York, 1961.

Russell, W. H., *The Atlantic Telegraph,* rev. ed., London, 1972.

Satterlee, Herbert L., *J. Pierpont Morgan: An Intimate Portrait 1837–1913,* New York, 1939.

Schotter, H. W., *The Growth and Development of the Pennsylvania Railroad Company: A Review of the Charter and Annual Reports of the Pennsylvania Railroad Company 1846–1926, Inclusive,* Philadelphia, 1927.

Sears, Marian V., *International Mercantile Marine Company,* Harvard Business School Case Study, Cambridge, Mass., 1953.

Shaum, John H., Jr., and William Henry Flayhart III, *Majesty At Sea: The Four Stackers,* New York, 1981.

Shaw, David W., *The Sea Shall Embrace Them: The Tragic Story of the Steamship Arctic,* New York, 2002.

"Shipbuilder and Marine Engine-Builder," *The French Line, Compagnie Générale Transatlantique, Quadruple-screw Turbo-electric, North Atlantic Steamship,* Normandie, *The World's Largest Liner,* Souvenir Number, London, June 1935.

Smith, Eugene W., *Passenger Ships of the World Past and Present,* Boston, 1963.

Smith, Philip Chadwick Foster, *Philadelphia on the River,* Philadelphia, 1986.

Society of Naval Architects and Marine Engineers, *Historical Transactions 1893–1943,* New York, 1945.

Spears, John R., *The Story of the American Merchant Marine,* New York, 1910.

Staff, Frank, *The Trans-Atlantic Mail,* London, 1956.

Swann, Leonard Alexander, Jr., *John Roach, Maritime Entrepreneur: The Years as Naval Contractor, 1862–1886,* Annapolis, 1965.

Taylor, James, *Ellermans—A Wealth of Shipping,* London, 1976.

Tute, Warren, *Atlantic Conquest,* Boston, 1962.

Tyler, David Budlong, *Steam Conquers the Atlantic,* New York, 1939.

Vale, Vivian, *The American Peril,* Manchester, U.K., 1984.

Wade, Wyn Craig, *The Titanic: The End of a Dream,* New York, 1986.
Warwick, Ronald W., and William H. Flayhart III, *QE2,* New York, 1985.
Weigley, Russell F., ed., *Philadelphia, A 300-Year History,* New York, 1982.
Whitehurst, Clinton H., Jr., *The U.S. Shipbuilding Industry,* Annapolis, 1986.
Winther, Oscar Osborn, *The Transportation Frontier,* New York, 1964.
Wright, Edward N., "The Story of Peter Wright & Sons, Philadelphia Quaker Shipping Firm, 1818–1911," *Quaker History,* vol. 56 (1967).

INDEX